PILGRIMS OF LOVE

To Dick

PNINA WERBNER

Pilgrims of Love

The Anthropology of a Global Sufi Cult

INDIANA University Press

Bloomington & Indianapolis

First published in North America in 2003

Indiana University Press
601 North Morton Street
Bloomington, Indiana 47404-3797, USA

http://iupress.indiana.edu

Telephone orders 800-842-6796
Fax orders 812-855-7931
Orders by e-mail iuporder@indiana.edu

Printed in India

Library of Congress Cataloging-in-Publication Data
Werbner, Pnina
Pilgrims of love: the anthropology of a global Sufi cult / Pnina
Werbner.
p. cm.
Includes bibliographical references and index.
ISBN 0-253-34098-5 (cloth: alk. paper)—ISBN 0-253-
21528-5 (pbk.: alk. paper)
1. Muslim saints—Cult. 2. Sufism—Customs and practices.
3. Sufism—Doctrines. 4. Naqshabandåiyah. 5. Islamic
sects. I. Title.
BP189.585.W47 2003
297.4'8—dc22
                          2003014791

1 2 3 4 5 08 07 06 05 04 03

ACKNOWLEDGEMENTS

In the end this book almost wrote itself. The research on which it is based was supported by the Economic and Social Research Council (ESRC), UK, during the years 1989–90, by a Leverhulme fellowship in 1990–1, and by a Leverhulme award in 1999–2000. I am grateful to both the Leverhulme Trust and the ESRC for their generous support. A sabbatical year granted me by Keele University during 2000–1 enabled me to complete the writing. I thank Muhammad Talib for his meticulous corrections to the Urdu glossary.

Many people made this study possible. Zindapir Sahib allowed me to share in his divine grace. His family and especially his son Badshah Sahib welcomed me at the lodge and trusted me as a friend and sister. Hajji Bashir Muhammad guided me along the path and was a creative force throughout the research. Chapter 9 in particular could not have been written without him. Dr Allah Ditta was generous with his time and ideas. Nyla Ahmed and Munir Choudri were immensely helpful both as friends and as research assistants. I am particularly grateful to them for their translation of the texts presented here. Shaheen and Majid Khan were, as usual, friends in need who gave selflessly of their time, insight and knowledge. Sonia, and Shaheen's family in Rawalpindi, the Khans, provided me with a home away from home. Their marvellous warmth and generosity, support and sheer capacity for fun made the research enjoyable as well as fruitful. I am eternally grateful to them for their unstinting generosity and warmth.

The disciples of Zindapir and his *khulafa* were generous well beyond the call of duty. Pakistanis are the most generous of hosts and I am indebted for all the delicious meals, the care and hospitality I received from numerous people.

My colleagues Helene Basu, Jürgen Frembgen, Sam Landell Mills, Charles Lindholm, Jamal Malik, Barbara Metcalf, Hafeez ur-Rahman, Muhammad Waseem and Lukas Werth gave me enormous intellectual support, shared their ideas with me and criticised my work. I deeply value their friendship. The Pakistan Workshop which meets annually at Satterthwaite in the Lake District was a testing ground for most of the chapters of this book. It would be impossible to thank all the participants at the workshop but Peter Parkes, Anjum Werth, Michael Fischer and Wenonah Lyon have, over the years, deepened my insight into Pakistan society, as have Sylvia Vatuk, Peter van der Veer, Hastings Donnan, David Gilmartin and Karen Leonard.

My family, as is usual in anthropological research, bore it all with stoicism. The research would never have happened if it had not been for my husband Dick, who inspired my interest in ritual in general and regional cults in particular. Travelling around north-east Botswana with him in the late 1970s as he studied the Mwali cult, I never imagined that I would encounter similar types of social organisations thousands of miles removed from South-Central Africa. My intellectual debt to him is evident in this book.

Several chapters draw on parts of published articles: the introduction on Werbner and Basu (1998b), chapter 3 on Werbner (1996c), chapters 4 and 5 on Werbner (1995), chapter 6 on Werbner (1998), and chapter 7 on Werbner (2001). All Urdu notations and spellings follow John D. Platt's *Dictionary of Urdu, Classical Hindi and English*, Oxford, Clarenden Press, 1984.

In order to protect identities, most of the names presented here are pseudonyms. Given, however, that the study has some historical significance, the names of the saint, his family and close *khulafa* in Pakistan have not been changed. I have also preserved the names of all the places in Pakistan and of the larger cities in Britain, again, in the light of the potential historical significance of the research, but smaller places in Britain are in some cases given pseudonyms in order to protect people's identities.

Keele, June 2003   P. W.

CONTENTS

Contents

PHOTOGRAPHS

FIGURES

THE SPIRITUAL GENEALOGY OF
THE NAQSHBANDI SUFI ORDER OF
GHAMKOL SHARIF, KOHAT, PAKISTAN

Oh Allah!
   Bless me, for the sake of Your Greatness,
   For the sake of Your Chosen Prophet.

   Give me most perfect truth and sincerity
   For the sake of Hazrat Abu Bakr,
   The Truthful and Righteous, Commander of the Faithful

   Give me divine love
   For the sake of the sincerity of Hazrat Salman Farsi,
   Companion of the Prophet.

   Give me steadfastness
   For the sake of Imam Qasim, grandson of Abu Bakr Saddique
   And Imam Jaafar, the Truthful and Most Pure.

   For the sake of the Guides,
   The Great Helper, the Axis of the world,
   The most elevated of Sufi Masters, Bayazid.

   Make my heart beat with God's remembrance
   For the sake of the modesty
   Of Abu'l Hasan of Kharqan.

   Free me from sin
   For the sake of Khajah Abu Qasim of Gargan,
   Who is filled with light

   Grant me good deeds
   For the sake of Khaja Hazrat 'Bu-Ali of Farmid,
   Saint of the World.

   Make my selfish soul surrender
   For the sake of the Leader,
   Khaja Abu Yusuf of Hamadan.

   Grant me perfection
   For the sake of the most wonderous saint, the Leader,
   Khaja Abdul Khaliq of Ghadjdawani.

For my faith,
Let the holiness of Hazrat Hoja Muhammed Arif of Rewagar
Prevail upon me.

Teach me the lesson of mercy
For the sake of the limitless pearl, the man of truth,
Hazrat Mahmood Al-Khair of Faghna.

May Your Name be dear
For the sake of the most honest
Hazrat Khaja Azizah Ali of Ramatin.

Fill my heart with love
For the sake of that lover,
Baba Samasee, Lover of God.

Grant me perfect righteousness
For the sake of the Pious Sayyid
Hazrat Shah Kalal Mir, who is filled with generosity.

Imprint Thy Name on my heart
For the sake of the Saint of Saints, the exalted self,
The King, Baha Udin Naqshband.

Perfume my heart
For the sake of the joyous face of
Hazrat Khaja Ala-Udin of Atar.

Turn me from idleness and neglectfulness
For the sake of Memu Maha,
And of Hazrat Yaqoob Charkhi,
helper of the destitute.

Make me Your absolute lover
For the sake of Khaja Ubaidullah,
The Noble, the Free, the Beloved.

Grant me abstinence too
For the sake of the wonderous ascetic,
Hazrat Khaja Muhammed Zahid.

Make me special before the saintly ascetics
For the sake of the saintly ascetic, Man of Cloak,
Khaja Darwesh Muhammed.

Make me a fellow disciple
For the sake of the manifestation of God's secrets,
Man of God, Khaja Muhammed Mazhar.

Make me Thy confidant
For the sake of the Confidant of God,
King of Saints, Khaja Muhammad Baqi Billah.

Grant me greatness in this world and the hereafter
For the sake of the incomparable Guide of the Truth,
Hazrat Mujaddid-i-Alif Thani.

Give me divine guidance to worship You
And turn me away from evil
For the sake of Muhammed Shah Husain, God's Trusted.

Grant me Your Love, and the love of Mustafa (Peace Be Upon Him),
For the sake of Sayyid Abdul Basit,
Of the auspicious face.

Oh Sustainer!
At my death may I die a believer
For the sake of Muhammed Abdul Qadr,
The Leader, may God have mercy on him.

Protect me from the enemies of religion and the world
For the sake of Sayyid Mahmood,
One of the Blessers.

Make my hidden being
Accord with my appearance
For the sake of Khaja Abdullah, leader of God's Friends.

Fill me with light from head to toe
For the sake of Shah Inayatullah,
The Sincere.

Shelter me, Oh God, for I am destitute,
For the sake of Hafiz Ahmed,
The Gracious.

I am no ascetic, no worshipper, only a man of God,
For the sake of Abdul Sabur sahib,
The Faithful.

I am never separate from you, Oh God,
For the sake of Raja Gul Muhammad,
He who is filled with light.

Cast an eye on my miseries, Oh God,
For the sake of Hazrat Abdul Majid sahib,
One of the Sufis.

All the Naqshbandi shaikhs give me their love
For the sake of Muhammad Shah Maluk
One of God's people.

My sins exceed all limits, Have mercy,
For the sake of Abdul Aziz.
To my relatives too, for the sake of Mustafa (Peace Be Upon Him)
For the sake of Shah Nizam Udin, God's Beloved.

Accept the intercession of these saints in my favour:
Hazrat Muhammad Qasim Morvi,
The Great Helper of the World,
The most noble of Saints,
The Beloved of God.

Have mercy on me, Give me blessings
For the sake of Khaja Hazrat Shah of Ghamkol,
God's Beloved, God's Great Helper,
The King of Sufis.

And our Perfect Saint, Hazur Qibla Zindapir,
The Great Helper of the Times, of Ghamkol Sharif.
Whose value is beyond all the Friends of God.

[In Birmingham it is added:]

Give me burning love to overcome my selfish self
For the sake of Khaja Sufi Muhammad Abdullah,
Slave of Mustafa (Peace Be Upon Him).

1

INTRODUCTION

SUFISM AS A TRANSNATIONAL RELIGIOUS MOVEMENT

RELIGIOUS GLOBALISATION AND THE TRANSNATIONAL SPREAD OF SUFI CULTS[1]

The revival of new religious movements, spreading their message to ever more remote corners of the globe, has raised new questions for research. This book is about one such globalising movement. It focuses on a Sufi Naqshbandi order founded by a living saint, Zindapir, whose enchanting central lodge nestles in a small valley in the North West Frontier Province of Pakistan. During the saint's lifetime, his cult extended globally: to Britain and Europe, the Middle East and Southern Africa.

1. The valley of Ghamkol Sharif

[1] By globalisation here is meant the global diffusion of ideas, images and consumer goods; transnationalism refers to the organisational crossing of national boundaries. It differs from internationalism which denotes relations between states in the international arena.

1

Map 1.1. The regional cult of Zindapir in Pakistan

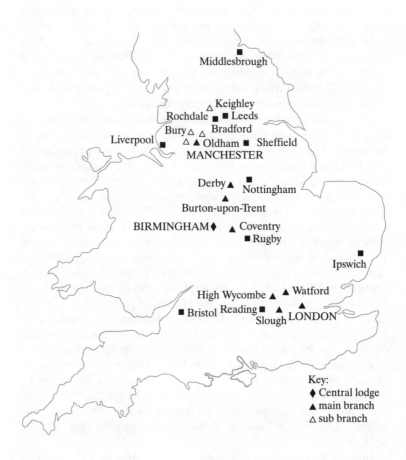

Map 1.2. The regional cult of Zindapir in Britain

The book considers Zindapir's order, established in the dying days of Empire, as a late capitalist, postcolonial, global religious movement. But it is important to recognise that the global spread of Sufism is not a new phenomenon. Almost from its inception as a mystical religious strand within Islam more than a millennium ago, Sufis have followed the trade routes and paths of imperial conquest into the remotest corners of the globe, from the Near East to North Africa, Iran, Central and South Asia, Indonesia, and East, West and Southern Africa. *Hijra*, the migration of the Prophet to Medina, has traditionally been repeated in the extensive travels of illustrious Sufis, *saliks*, or travellers, seeking the path to true knowledge, as many saintly hagiographies document.[2]

In South Asia, after the initial Arab conquests of Sindh and Multan in the eighth century, Islam was spread primarily through holy men. Indeed, Annemarie Schimmel has argued that despite the occasional appearance of Sufi-soldiers in the frontier provinces of India, 'the Islamisation of the country was achieved largely by the preaching of dervishes, not by the sword' (Schimmel 1975: 346). Hallaj, one of the great mystics of the Near East, travelled to Sindh in 905 (ibid.: 345). Following the second wave of Muslim conquests, around the year 1000, came mystics like Hujwiri, popularly known as Data Ganj Baksh, whose treatise on Sufism, *Kashf Almahjub* soon became a classic, and whose shrine in Lahore still attracts thousands of daily pilgrims. In the late twelfth and early thirteenth centuries, Mu'inuddin Chishti founded the Chishtiyya order, which is distinctive to the Indian subcontinent. His tomb in Ajmer is still revered today, as are the shrines of key disciples at Pakpattan and Delhi (ibid.: 344–51). The circulation of Muslim mystics between the subcontinent, the Near East, Persia and Central Asia continued throughout the Mughal period during which further Sufi orders were established in India, among them the Suhawardiyya, Qadiriyya and Naqshbandiyya, the last being introduced into India from Central Asia by Khwaja Baqi Billah and developed by his disciple, Ahmed Faruqi Sirhindi (1564–1624), who played a major role in Indian religious, and to some extent political, life (ibid.: 367).

Since the nineteenth century, but even earlier, mystical Islam has also been transplanted into Dutch and British colonies[3] by South Asian traders

---

[2] E.g. Saheb 1998, Lings 1971; see also the contributions to Eickelman and Piscatori 1990.

[3] There are still active 250-year-old Sufi shrines on the Cape peninsula, known as *kramat*, venerated by the Malay community whose ancestors were brought to the Cape as slaves from Indonesia in the 17th century by the Dutch East Africa Company.

and indentured labourers, and in the post-Second World War era, by refugees and economic labour migrants, moving in search of work from
their rural villages to the expanding cities of the developing world, or to
the West and the Gulf states. These mass counter-movements have created new diasporas and have forged, along with them, new connections
to Sufi sacred centres in the migrants' homelands, across regional, national
and international boundaries.

Thus in South Asia the transnational movement of Sufi saints has historically been a key to the spread of Islam.[4] So too the Sufi regional cult
at the centre of this study has expanded through movement: of army regiments; of retired soldiers returning to civilian life in their villages or
towns; of labour migrants to the Gulf or to Britain; of pilgrims meeting
on Hajj; and of disciples meeting at the central lodge of Zindapir weekly,
monthly, or annually, during the *'urs*, the three-day festival commemorating the mystical 'marriage' of a deceased saint with God.

The present study describes these various forms of transnational movement through which space is deterritorialised and reterritorialised.[5] In
belonging to a Sufi regional cult, labour migrants transplanted to foreign
lands renew a unitary, cross-national, religious identity and subjectivity.
In gathering together disciples normally widely scattered internationally,
occasions such as the *'urs* or the pilgrimage to Mecca are critical events
of joint transnational ritual celebration.

Sufism has never respected national boundaries. Its counter-move-
ment into the West today can be grasped as quite distinct from the global
spread of political Islam.[6] But even if it is rarely militant or revolutionary,
Sufism is not simply apolitical. As I argue in this book, the attitudes of
Sufis to temporal power and authority are highly ambivalent, a mixture of
moral superiority and pragmatic accommodation, but they are never outside of politics.

A broad debate among sociologists of religion concerns the reasons
for the global revival of new forms of religiosity in the face of modernity

[4] This is documented in depth in the works of Richard Eaton 1978a, 1993; Susan Bayly
1989; Sara Ansari 1992; and David Gilmartin 1988.

[5] My use of these terms deviates from the original contrast drawn by Deleuze and
Guattari 1984, who speak of the deterritorialisation of capitalism leading to schizo-flows
and to reterritorialization, often by repressive fascist regimes (ibid.: 244–5 and *passim*). By
deterritorialisation I refer to the dismantling of territorial boundaries through the transnational flow of labour, followed by reterritorialisation as migrants renew a unitary, cross-
regional and national subjectivity.

[6] This movement is addressed in relation to Islam more generally in a large number of
studies. See, for example, the volume edited by Barbara Daly Metcalf 1996.

and the secular state. Whereas the rise of capitalism and liberalism led initially to a rationalisation and reform of the great religions, often with a stress on unmediated individual prayer and the separation of religion and state, the late twentieth century witnessed a rise of communalist, 'fundamentalist' or 'magical' religious movements. One dominant view is that the rise of these new religious movements, including the spread of Christian Pentecostalism, Hindu nationalism and political Islam, is a response to a 'failed' modernity or postmodernity.[7] If Weber posited that modernity would lead to the 'disenchantment' of the world, the end of magic, then the failure of modernity has reversed that trend towards secularisation.

There is, of course, some truth in this thesis in so far as postcolonial developing countries are concerned. Underdevelopment, the perceived autocracy or inefficiency of regimes and their dependence on the West, and the moral uncertainties of disorganised (post) modern life, lead people to seek legitimate grounds for dissent and to look to utopian or millenarian futures, based (in the case of Islam) on the perfect community of Muslims at the time of the Prophet. For some, including Pakistani migrant-settlers to Britain, millenarian forms of religion may indeed afford 'magical' solutions to their predicament and sense of malaise.

But a more persuasive thesis for the global rise of the new religious movements, both in the West and the developing world, is that these provide certain modern 'solutions' and platforms for geographically and socially mobile subjects. This is an argument put forward in relation to the spread of Christian charismatic churches in Latin America by Bernice Martin (1998), against the failed postmodernity hypothesis suggested by Zygmunt Bauman in the same volume (1998). It is an argument which may equally be used to counter the failed modernity thesis in relation to the rise of political Islam.[8]

In any case, Sufism is not an oppositional movement in any simple sense. Rather than rejecting modernity, a case can be made for the continued vitality of Sufism as a positive response to modernity. Sufi fraternities and saintly blessing legitimise and support worldly achievements, as

[7] On Hindu nationalism see Blom Hansen 1999 and Jaffrelot 1996. Modernity refers here to the rise of industrial capitalism, of scientific inquiry and of rational bureaucratic systems of governance, whereas postmodernity is usually taken to refer to the fragmentation of control, the stress on personal identity and consumption and the loss of certainty and faith in earlier, modernist grand narratives of progress.

[8] There is a vast literature on political Islam as a response to failed modernity. See, for example, Kepel 1994.

argued in chapter 7. They provide mutual support in work contexts, the experience of moral amity in the face of urban anonymity, an intellectual challenge to disciples lacking formal educational qualifications, and a platform for the leadership aspirations of those beyond the official public sphere (on the last, see P. Werbner 2002).

This is not to argue that Sufis are 'moderns', who are simply living out an 'alternative' modernity. Sufism rejects ideas of individual religious agency, autonomy and rationality which are the bedrock of liberal modernity, stressing instead the embodied charisma, perfection and transcendence of the Sufi master, whose spiritual intimacy with God leads to the magical enchantment of the world. Yet despite the valorisation of world renunciation, Sufi followers easily integrate into worldly contexts of work and contemporary politics.

Hallencreutz and Westerlund (1996) make the point that even in the case of the Islamists, it is often not modernity *per se* that is rejected but secular modernity and, above all, the secular state (1996: 6).[9] Sufis, by contrast, tend to thrive on the liberalism and pluralism of the secular state, and to cooperate well with its political representatives, extracting boons for their orders in exchange for promised political support. Yet in South Asia, the movement cannot be conceived as merely quietist. It engages in constant critique of the mendacity and hypocrisy of politicians. Its *'ulama* (clerics) and lay preachers are attune to popular political sentiments, and frequently make fiery political speeches against the West. On the whole, however, such sentiments remain at a rhetorical and symbolic level. Sufism and its world-renouncing saints are almost everywhere committed to peaceful coexistence and tolerance. It is these which allow regional cults to expand and prosper, despite changes of regimes and local political conflicts.

In a sense, then, Sufism, at least in the Pakistani version described in this book, represents a counter-globalising trend to political Islam. It is traditional and sentimental. It stresses personal renewal, group amity, mutual support and tolerance. It is accommodating to worldly politics and encourages thrift and worldly success. A *murid*, a saintly disciple, is a lover who seeks intimacy with his *shaikh* and with God. Sufi regional cults, this book shows, are produced in all their organisational complexity by the forces generated through the love of *murids* for their saint.

---

[9] It has been widely noted, for example, that global religious movements, including Islamist ones, use sophisticated media technology to propagate their message.

THE REFORMIST CRITIQUE AND THE CONTINUED
VITALITY OF SUFISM

The veneration of saints at saintly shrines in South Asia, as elsewhere in the Muslim world, has been castigated by Islamic reformists as idolatrous innovation replete with non-Islamic, 'Hindu' customs, a view often accepted by Western scholars. Against this, it has been argued:

> The error of both reformers and Western ethnographers is to consider only two forms: a rather fundamentalist conception of Islam, on the one hand, and Hindu customs on the other. They ignore an important middle form, namely medieval Sufi piety, which is responsible for most of the devotions to saints and which was imported to India from abroad (Gaborieau 1989: 234).

In other words, Sufi rituals denounced by the reformists as 'Hindu', in fact have their origins outside South Asia, in the medieval world of Europe and the Near East. Nevertheless, the growing Islamic reformist and modernist critiques against saint cult practices[10] led historically to an increasing self-consciousness among Sufi adherents, and to the emergence of reformist Sufi regional cults which stressed Islamic law and *Shari'at* and prohibited some of the more extravagant celebrations at saints' shrines. The regional cult founded by Zindapir falls clearly within this reformist tradition, one which emerged as early as the seventeenth century among Naqshbandi Sufi followers. In line with strict Naqshbandi practice, Zindapir prohibited the playing of instrumental music, radio and television at the lodge, although he did allow the singing of praise poems to the Prophet, and of loud, melodic forms of *zikr* (remembrance of God) which became over time the characteristic feature of the order.

Such self-consciousness, hedonistic restraint and stress upon *Shari'at* are not to be taken, however, as leading to Sufi decline, or to the diminution of faith in the perfection of the *shaikh* and his powers of intercession. Nowhere did I encounter an apologetic double-consciousness in the face of modernity of the kind that Ewing (1997) reports from her fieldwork among Sufi saints and followers. On the contrary, feelings of love and devotion expressed by both ordinary and modern, educated *murids* (disciples) and *khulafa* (vicegerents, deputies, emissaries), for Zindapir were so intense that these *murids* found it inconceivable that anyone who encountered the *shaikh* would not, like them, be totally overwhelmed by his extraordinary spirituality.

---

[10] There are numerous scholarly accounts of this critique. See, for example, Metcalf 1982.

2. The mosque of Ghamkol Sharif

Both the colonial and postcolonial Pakistani governments have acted to regularise the finances or take over the management of many shrines previously controlled by descendants or disciples of famous saints, and to abolish some of the allegedly unIslamic practices and tribute-collecting arrangements at these shrines (Gilmartin 1984, Malik 1998b). Unlike these shrines, Zindapir's lodge has retained its autonomy since the *shaikh* is an originary saint and founder of a new regional and transnational cult. As such he is the owner of the lodge and all that surrounds it, built with voluntary labour and donations freely given by his disciples. He thus exemplifies both the old and new in Sufi Islam, the settlement of the wilderness, on the one hand, and the embeddedness of Sufi cults in the postcolonial state and in processes of globalisation, on the other.

Above all, Zindapir's regional cult proves that despite the modernist challenge, revitalised by the constant rise of 'new' charismatic saints the vigour of Sufism in South Asia remains quite remarkable. Such continued vitality challenges the assumption that Sufi 'folk' or 'magical' beliefs and, even more fundamentally, notions of saintly intercession, are antithetical to the modern state or industrial capitalism.

Proponents of the Sufi and saintly cult 'decline' hypothesis, such as Gellner (1981), draw a rather straightforward analogy between Sufism and Catholicism, and thus equate the rise of Islamic reform movements with the historical emergence of Protestantism in Christianity. This analogy is, however, misleading. There are elements in Sufism, the present book argues, which, like Calvinism and Protestantism more generally, support this-worldly orientations towards individual achievement and autonomy. By contrast, most reformist movements in South Asia, while disapproving of some Sufi practices and rejecting notions of divine intercession in favour of the sacredness of the Qur'an and *Hadith*, replicate Sufi forms of regional and transnational social organisation focused around exemplary charismatic leaders. Moreover, the Islamic reformists still continue to stress communal rather than individual goals and achievements.

There is a possible additional reason why Sufism in South Asia did not suffer the same decline in prestige and pervasive influence which it may have experienced in North Africa and the Near East. In the more religiously plural context of South Asia under British colonial rule, a scholarly movement of *'ulama*—the Barelvi movement—developed, to defend the practices at saints' shrines and the belief in intercession (Metcalf 1982, Malik 1998b). This meant that the confrontation between Sufism and reform Islam was not simply (as elsewhere) one between *'ulama* and saints, but between different types of *'ulama*, espousing different Islamic approaches (see P. Werbner 1996a).

Recognising the elective affinity between Sufism and the achievement of worldly individual success in a modern and postmodern world is, I suggest, a key to understanding Zindapir's popular appeal to members of the armed forces and other top civil servants in Pakistan. It also explains the popularity of the *shaikh* in Britain where the order is led by a *khalifa* based in Birmingham who was Zindapir's companion during his army days. This *khalifa* has built the British order up into a major British regional cult, while continuing to recognise the ultimate authority of Zindapir and the lodge in Pakistan.

SACRED INTIMACY AND THE MYTHOLOGICAL IMAGINATION

Although Sufism in South Asia may not be in terminal decline, the question remains: what is the relation between the 'magical' customs at saints' tombs and Sufism, conceived of as an abstract philosophical system? Zindapir himself, in true Naqshbandi fashion, prohibited extreme expressions of adulation towards his person, or even the distribution of his picture during his lifetime. Shortly after his death, however, as chapter 12 discloses, his shrine was already becoming the focus of customary saintly veneration.

For the secular observer as for the Muslim reformist, the obsequious prostration of supplicants at the tombs of dead saints, or disciples' obeisant kissing of a living saint's hands and the edges of his gown, summon up a world of magic and superstition. It is a world that seems utterly remote from the imaginary universes, ideal symbols and abstract qualities described in the works of famous Sufis. A large number of scholarly studies have analysed these elaborate mystical worlds and spheres of reality, constructed by Sufi thinkers who claim to have retraced their mystical journeys towards sacred intimacy and unity with God through a series of theophanic visions.

To bridge the apparent gap between ritual custom and abstract philosophy we need to bear in mind that the persona of a saint, alive or dead, his very body, is believed by Sufi followers to irradiate divine sanctity. So powerful is this embodiment that merely to touch anything that has come into contact with the saint is to absorb some of his magical potency. In South Asia great saints like Zindapir often stand in danger of being mobbed by crowds of devotees and must be protected from the intense love that their followers feel for them. It is this feature of charismatic embodiment which provides a clue to the integral relationship between Sufi theosophy and the apparently superstitious practices at saints' shrines.

Sufi theosophy is entirely devoted to describing and authenticating the transformation of the persona of the saint through Sufi practice. This ritual passage is postulated to be as much physical as it is spiritual, and occurs as a mystic reaches closer and closer towards sacred intimacy with God. But this intellectual elaboration of the Sufi symbolic universe should not be conflated with the phenomenological experiences of practising mystics.

Adopting a phenomenological approach, Henry Corbin (1969) defines the world of the Sufi 'creative imagination',

> ...a world of Idea-Images, of archetypal figures, of subtile substances, of 'immaterial matter'. This world is real and objective, as consistent and subsistent as the intelligible and sensible worlds; it is an intermediate universe 'where the spiritual takes body and the body becomes spiritual', a world consisting of real matter and real extension, though by comparison to sensible, corruptible matter these are subtile and immaterial. The organ of this universe is the active imagination; it is the place of theophanic visions... (Corbin 1969: 4).

It seems evident, however, that the intricacies of Sufi cosmology are not the direct product of theophanies or epiphanies. Rather, mystical theophanies—which usually consist of lights, colours, or visions of angelic and prophetic figures (ibid.: 153–4, 156, 162–3, 272)—have been transmuted and systematised by Sufi thinkers through rigorous intellectual work. In chapter 9, I suggest that it may be more appropriate, therefore, to speak not of a Sufi creative imagination but of a Sufi mythological imagination. Following Lévi-Strauss (1966) I take mythical thought to be a science of signs, systematically interrelated through a series of homologies and analogies. The producer of myths is likened by Lévi-Strauss to a *bricoleur* who creates logical systems out of the bric-à-brac of daily life.

So too, as shown in chapter 9, Sufi theory posits a perfect structural order of signs based on equations and oppositions between mystical elements. The system follows a predictable recursive logic, and the imagined world thus created is intellectually ordered, quite apart from the visions and theophanies of particular Sufi mystics. Beyond its elaborate structures, the point of Sufi theosophy, regarded as myth, is to show how a frail and finite human being can come to be so suffused with divine light that he is transmuted into an eternally present and active agent.

In the sense that they all believe in this transcendental physical and active survival of the saint after death, there is an affinity, as Corbin too recognises, between simple believers and mystics, although they speak (and act) on different levels (1969: 231). Both start from the assumption that a true Sufi saint, in achieving sacred intimacy with God, is alive from the grave. Similarly, while the Sufi saint becomes a conduit of God's grace in the world, neither practising mystics nor supplicants and disciples confuse the saint with God Himself. It is the saint's intimacy with God which is venerated.

Sufi concepts and Sufi knowledge are common currency among Sufi adepts, whether or not they achieve experiential gnosis. This is highlighted in chapters 8, 9, and 12. Chapter 8 traces the particular approaches to Sufism adopted by different *khulafa*, deputies, of Zindapir. Chapter 9 discusses the intellectual and mythical construction of Naqshbandi Sufi cosmology by a *khalifa* who finds himself, nevertheless, incapable of achieving the kind of experiential gnosis depicted by the perfect mythological system he has envisaged. It goes on to contrast Sufi theory with the technologies of knowledge deployed by the saint, through which he exerts control over his close followers.

Chapter 12 considers the interregnum following Zindapir's death and his transition from a living saint to a saint alive from the grave, reflecting on the apparent verbal silence that seemed to follow the saint's death; an erasure of the delightful presence of the living Zindapir, a man who, during his lifetime, was a trickster figure, an entertaining and witty yarn spinner and mythologiser. In some sense, then, the chapter argues, the saint in his death became for most people a sign or cipher, a prototype of the class of saints rather than a unique individual as he was during this lifetime. Not so, however, for the poet of the lodge who embarked on a project of commemoration; the publication of his praise poetry for the saint and of a written chronicle (in Urdu) of his life and miracles. These texts may well determine whether the saint outlives his physical death in the public imagination. Arguably in South Asia, it is the quality of written texts along with the architectural splendour of shrine complexes which single a saint out after his death as an important historical and religious figure.

In relation to this, the chapter raises the further question whether the mythical narratives I recorded as an anthropologist, told to me by the saint and his followers during his lifetime, will be preserved through the present book, and if so, what inadvertently interventionist role such written anthropological documents might have in preserving the image of the saint for posterity.

PERSON, SPACE AND MOVEMENT

Ideologically Sufi saints are conceived of in South Asia as tamers of the wilderness for human cultivation. Historically they appear to have been instrumental in uniting groups across tribal or caste divisions, a point highlighted in chapter 7. Ansari (1992) has shown that saints contributed to the reorganisation of canal-based agriculture in Sindh towards the end of the nineteenth century, while in Bengal, they were at the vanguard of new rice cultivation (Eaton 1993).

The relation between person, body and space is a key to the charisma of a living saint. Chapter 3 sets out to unravel the significance of the opening ritual act of the *'urs*, the annual festival marking the mystical union of a departed saint with God. The public performance of the *julus* (procession) in British cities, the chapter argues, sacralises and Islamicises the neighbourhoods where Pakistani migrants have settled. In Pakistan, the equivalent to the *julus* is the *qafila*, the convoy of vehicles which carries people hundreds of miles from their towns, factories and villages to attend the annual three-day ritual at the central lodge. In both processions and convoys disciples chant the *zikr* as they traverse through space. In doing so they inscribe the earth with the name of Allah.

More generally, Sufism is characterised by the intersection between several types of journey: the personal journey on the Sufi path discussed more fully in chapter 9; the originary journey of the saint to the lodge in Pakistan, which laid the foundation for his regional cult and is referred to in legends about the saint's life, analysed in chapters 4 and 5; the pilgrimage journeys of disciples to the lodge discussed in chapters 6 and 7; and the counter-colonial journey from the East to the West, in which new British Sufi saints bring Islam to a Christian land by marching through its previously alien spaces. Chapter 11 considers the embeddedness of Zindapir's cult in wider religious cum political movements in Pakistan.

THE LIMITS OF POSTMODERN ANTHROPOLOGY

The book concludes by highlighting some of the dilemmas and paradoxes of postmodern anthropology. It addresses deconstructive critiques levelled against modernist anthropology, according to which ethnographic writing perpetuates Western hegemonic knowledge by suppressing the voices of the subjects studied, and disguising the limitations of ethnographic research and writing. The new critics advocate more dialogical styles of ethnographic writing, ones which involve the anthropologist in joint writing ventures with her or his interlocutors.

Responding to such criticisms, the conclusion considers the possibility of a truly dialogical anthropology in the face of the pitfalls I encountered in writing up my research. Such hurdles are familiar ones, confronted by many anthropological fieldworkers, but they were especially acute in a study of a secret (and secretive) hierarchical society.

Paradoxically, I argue, it is dialogical conflict that is often most culturally revealing of the commitments and passions, taboos, secrets and implicit assumptions of a social group. And yet to sustain trust and goodwill, fieldworkers must assiduously aim to avoid such conflicts. Second, the writing of a study of absolute religious faith from a detached, sceptical perspective cannot possibly satisfy the people studied. Finally, the plurality of voices, often conflictual, within a single group makes collaborative writing a utopian project. Even the very production of a written text aiming to represent the cult of a mediating *shaikh* emerged in the course of my writing as a contradictory project.

This is the bitter lesson which the research on Zindapir's regional cult taught me: cherished cultural ideals may contradict the anthropological project. Even more, to be of lasting value, anthropological research cannot turn a blind eye to the contradictory narratives or micro-political field of conflict into which it is inserted. But to analyse such contradictions and politics in their historical specificity, the anthropologist is forced to distance herself from the people studied, while at the same time attempting to empathise with their motives and to draw generalisations from the evident force of their cultural beliefs, interpersonal rivalries and religious passions.

The following chapter discusses Sufi cults in the light of regional cult analysis which highlights the complex relations between such cults and bounded territorial communities, power structures and political movements.

2

REGIONAL CULT ANALYSIS AND THE POLITICAL DOMAIN[1]

In any locality in South Asia, there is a wide range of Sufi saints or *pirs*, from major shrines of great antiquity, managed by *sajjada nishins*, descendants of the original saintly founder and guardians of his tomb, to minor *pirs* with a highly localised clientele (see Troll 1989, Werbner and Basu 1998a). In any generation, only some outstanding living saints succeed in founding major regional cults which extend widely beyond their immediate locality.

The following chapter examines the spatial expansion of Zindapir's cult as a regional cult. Regional cults are, distinctively,

…cults of the middle range—more far-reaching than any parochial cult of the little community, yet less inclusive in belief and membership than a world religion in its most universal form. Their central places are shrines in towns and villages, by cross-roads or even in the wild, apart from human habitation, where great populations from various communities or their representatives, come to supplicate, sacrifice, or simply make pilgrimage. They are cults which have a topography of their own, conceptually defined by the people themselves and marked apart from other features of cultural landscapes by ritual activities (R. Werbner 1977: ix).

Like other regional cults, Sufi cults interpenetrate rather than generating contiguous, bounded territories. They leapfrog across major political and ethnic boundaries, creating their own sacred topographies and flows of goods and people. These override, rather than remain congruent with, the political boundaries and subdivisions of nations, ethnic groups, or provinces (ibid.).

Anthropologists have repeatedly warned against the dangers of naive holism, according to which, as Werbner puts it, 'essential relations with a wider context get stripped away when a small group, little community or

---

[1] The original ASA volume which set out a comparative analysis of regional cults (R. Werbner 1977) included cases from the Middle East, North Africa, South Central Africa, and South America. Earlier work on pilgrimage by Victor Turner drew on examples from India, Europe and Mexico, and later work on regional cults in Peru (Sallnow 1987).

tribe is studied as an isolated whole' (ibid.). In the present study I show that Sufi lodges and shrine complexes cannot be studied in isolation from the wider regional and transnational cult generated around the sacred centre, or the political contexts in which the cult operates.

But an equally misguided theoretical trap—one often applied to the study of Islamic societies—is a tendency to adopt a 'correspondence' theory, according to which different domains (ritual, political, economic) underwrite each other, so that ritual and belief become mere representations of political divisions or economic interests (ibid.: xviii).[2] In Sufi regional cults, the symbolic order cuts across political divisions and remains in tension with the postcolonial and capitalist economies of modern-day Pakistan, and even more so in post-imperial Britain.

Regional cult analysis aims to disclose hidden structural interdependencies and ruptures between different domains of action: economic, ritual, political. Like other regional cults Sufi regional cults are both linked to centres of political power and in tension with them. Various historical studies have highlighted the pragmatic tendencies of Sufism in South Asia which have enabled Sufi saints to accommodate to a variety of different political regimes and circumstances, over many centuries of imperial and postcolonial rule.[3] The relationship between the political centre and the sacred centre is a changing, historically contingent one, and in this sense, as in others, regional cults are historically evolving social formations.[4]

In a landmark study of sacred peripherality, Victor Turner defined pilgrimage centres as 'centres out there,' beyond the territorial political community, and in doing so opened up a whole new set of questions regarding ritual journeys as transformative movements (Turner 1974: ch. 5).

[2] R. Werbner ibid. Such correspondence theories draw on simplistic Durkheimian or Marxist approaches. Werbner also cites Robertson Smith's theory of sacrifice among the Semites as an example.

[3] See, for example, Gilmartin 1984, 1988; Eaton 1978a, 1984, 1993; Mann 1989; Liebeskind 1998; on North Africa see Eickelman 1976, 1977; Evans-Pritchard 1949.

[4] An example of the complex, historically unstable relations between Sufi regional cults and indigenous political rulers in South Asia is highlighted in Susan Bayly's study of south India during the volatile precolonial period from the 17th to the early 19th centuries (Bayly 1989). Initially following the trade routes into the hinterland, Sufi regional cults drew extensive patronage from a wide variety of Muslim and Hindu petty rulers who struggled to legitimise their rule by claiming spiritual dominion via important Sufi shrines or Hindu temples. The sacred networks of individual shrines extended well beyond a ruler's administrative territory and were thus perceived to be a source of power, so that displays of generosity towards a famous *dargah* became 'important touchstone[s] in the competitive acts of state-building pursued by professing Hindu and Muslim rulers' (ibid.: 221).

Turner conceptualised pilgrimage centres as alternative loci of value within feudal type societies. Like the rites of passage of tribal societies, he argued, the ritual movement in pilgrimage culminated in a liminal (or liminoid) moment of '*communitas*' which was anti-structural and anti-hierarchical, releasing an egalitarian sociality and amity. Pilgrimage centres thus embodied an alternative ethical order, one uncircumscribed by territorially defined relations of power and authority.

In critiquing the series of dichotomous contrasts generated by Turner's theory—inclusive versus exclusive relations, peripherality versus centrality, generic versus particularistic sociality, egalitarian or homogeneous relations versus hierarchical or differentiated ones—regional cult analysis aims to highlight the dialectic resulting from the complex conjuncture of these apparently opposed types of relationships, coexisting in a single cult (R. Werbner 1977: xii *et passim*).

As the history of Sufism in South Asia shows, Sufi regional cults are enmeshed in regional politics. This is because Sufi cults are not simply inclusive. They foster an exclusive membership, and yet the sacred centre and the major festivals around it are open to all. Relations between initiates are said to be (generic) relations of love and amity, stripped of any prior status, idealised as beyond conflict or division, yet the organisation of regional cults is based around the ingathering of elective groups from particular, defined political and administrative communities—villages, towns, city neighbourhoods—while cult relationships are often, as this book highlights, marred by interpersonal rivalries. The egalitarianism between initiates comes alongside internal relations of hierarchy, and all disciples, whatever their rank, are subject to the absolute authority and discipline of the saint or his successors at the cult centre. Indeed, worldly status, class and caste are implicitly recognised at the central lodge, while saintly descendants often vie bitterly for the succession after the decease of the founder.[5] If there is a moment of experienced communitas during the annual ritual at a Sufi regional cult centre, it is the product of complex logistical planning, a highly disciplined division-of-labour, and constant vigilance on the part of the organisers.

In the face of criticisms levelled against Turner's theoretical model (R. Werbner 1977, Sallnow 1987, Eade and Sallnow 1991; and for India see Fuller 1993: 212–13), it seems more accurate to say that sacred pilgrimage creates not 'anti'-structure but 'counter'-structure. Nevertheless,

---

[5] Caste is even more in evidence in the complex regional cult organisation of the Swami-narayans of Gujarat who divide ascetics from lay followers and recognise divisions by caste among the ascetics (Williams 1984).

Turner's key point, that pilgrimage centres and the cults they generate produce sacred geographies where alternative, non-temporal and non-administrative ethical orders are ritually embodied and enacted, still seems valid. In this spirit, regional cult theory aims to conceptualise the dynamics of spatially alternative focal organisations to those centred on bounded, territorially based states or administrative units.

The Sufi cultural concept which best captures the idea of a Sufi region is *wilayat*. *Wilayat*, a master concept in Sufi terminology, denotes a series of interrelated meanings: (secular) sovereignty over a region, the spiritual dominion of a saint, guardianship, a foreign land, friendship, intimacy with God, and union with the Deity. *Wilayat* encapsulates the range of complex ideas defining the charismatic power of a saint—not only over transcendental spaces of mystical knowledge but as sovereign of the terrestrial spaces into which his sacred region extends. The term 'regional cult', a comparative, analytic term used to describe centrally focused, non-contiguous religious organisations which extend across boundaries, seems particularly apt to capture this symbolic complexity.

SUFI ORDERS AND *TA'IFAS*

The adoption of regional cult theory as the basic model for understanding Sufi orders gains further support from Trimingham's analysis of the Sufi orders of Islam (Trimingham 1971). On first reading it might appear that Trimingham traces a three-phase historical development of Sufism from the early *khanaqahs*, small, relatively egalitarian urban hospices and centres of meditation, in the first phase; to the emergence of major, transnational orders, the *tariqa*, in the second phase, in which distinctive Sufi doctrines, litanies of prayer and ritual practices were established; and finally, to the third phase, that of the *ta'ifas*, religious organisations focused upon a sacred centre of a living saint or, more commonly, his shrine.

On closer reading it is clear, however, that in Trimingham's view, the larger orders have never been viable organisations; their expansion took place, and continues to do so, via the *ta'ifas*. This was true of the Suhardiyya order which was never, he says, a unified order but merely a 'line of ascription from which derived hundreds of *ta'ifas*' (Trimingham 1971: 179). He continues:

> Similarly with the Qadiriyya; the descendant of 'Abd al-Qadir in Baghdad is not recognized as their superior by an Arab Qadiri *ta'ifa*. Even the nineteenth-

century Tijaniyya, as it expanded, has tended to lose its centralized authority. The *shaikh* of the central Darqawi *zawiya* has no control over the many off-shoots (ibid.).

Only very small, parochial orders are coherent, he says, maintained by tours undertaken by the *shaikh* and his emissaries (ibid.).

Sufi *ta'ifas* are comparable to other regional cults in their basic central place organisation. The *shaikh*, a living saint or his descendant, heads the *ta'ifa* by virtue of his powers of blessing. Under the *shaikh* are a number of *khulafa* appointed by him directly to take charge of districts or town centres. In a large order each regional *khalifa* may have sectional leaders under him (ibid.: 173–4; 179). The sacred centres and subcentres of the cult, known as *zawiya* in North Africa, and *darbars* or *dargahs* (royal courts) in Pakistan and India, are places of pilgrimage and ritual celebration, with the tomb of the founder being the 'focal point of the organization, a centre of veneration to which visitations (*ziyarat*) are made' (ibid.: 179). The centre is regarded as sacred and protected, *haram*, a place of sanctuary for refugees from vengeance.

Chapter 8 shows the way the exemplary centre has replicated itself throughout Zindapir's regional cult through scores of deliberate and conscious acts of mimesis. In different parts of the Punjab important *khulafa* of the saint reproduce in their manners, dress and minute customs the image of Zindapir, along with the ethics and aesthetics of the cult he founded. Such mimesis, the chapter argues, creates a sense of unity across distance: the same sounds and images, the same ambience, are experienced by the traveller wherever he goes in the cult region. Along with this extraordinary mimetic resemblance, each *khalifa* also fosters his own distinctiveness, his own special way of being a Sufi, and the chapter goes on to consider the individual lifeworks of key Sufi *khulafa* of Zindapir living in Pakistan and in Britain.

In other ways, too, Trimingham's account accords with regional cult theory. He makes the point that *ta'ifas* 'undergo cycles of expansion, stagnation, decay, and even death' (ibid.: 179), but that since there are 'thousands of them, new ones [are] continually being formed' (ibid.: 172).

The fallacy of linear theories of Sufi historical evolution is to mistake a phase in the cycle of a particular regional cult with a general historical trend. Buehler (1998), for example, posits an irreversible trend from 'directing' *shaikh* to 'mediating' *shaikh*. He argues that the intimate relations between Sufi *shaikh* and disciple,[6] in which the *shaikh* instructed

---

[6] Known as *suhbat* (Schimmel 1975: 366).

his followers on practices of self-purification and meditation leading towards intimacy with God, have been displaced in the twentieth century. True, he says, the rural, uneducated peasant masses of the Punjab— drawing on their experiences of bureaucratic patronage in South Asia— have always been content to regard the saint, usually interred in the grave, as a mediator with God (ibid.: 169, 191, 210).

But the radical change in the twentieth century, according to Buehler, was the rise of the media *shaikh* in the context of the Barelvi movement, exemplified by the figure of Jama'at 'Ali, a Qadiri *shaikh* from Sialkot district in the Punjab. This type of mediating *shaikh* used the press, formal *anjumans* (voluntary associations), large conferences and various types of media technology to propagate a message of love for the *shaikh*, represented as mediating the love for the Prophet—in effect a double mediation with God which, Buehler proposes, absolved followers from the need to attempt to reach God directly via Sufi practice. This new type of mediating *shaikh* was remote from followers, who could only gaze at him from a distance rather than know him intimately (ibid.: 191 *et passim*, 195).

Such a theory of historical phases—from the living, directing *shaikh* to the mediating, dead *shaikh* or peripatetic, media-cum-mediating *shaikh*, ignores the organisational cycles typically undergone by Sufi orders and regional cults, characterised by periodic rise and fall, waxing and waning (Trimingham 1971, R. Werbner 1977). At any historical moment, only rare individuals rise to be new living saints and directing-shaikhs of real distinction. The cults they found seldom retain the same charismatic aura of the original founders under their successors.

Zindapir was, during his lifetime (he died in 1999), a classic directing *shaikh*: much beloved by his disciples, he never left his lodge but spent most hours of the day and night meeting supplicants, and a good deal of time with his closest *khulafa*. But the case of Zindapir also shows that living *shaikhs* are perceived and experienced differently by individual disciples, who make varying demands on them. Some followers approach a saint in the hope of obtaining intimacy with God through his guidance or very presence; others regard him as the subject of love who mediates their mundane life desires with God. The very same saint can thus be both mediating and directing, depending on the situation, or on a disciple's expectations. In this sense it is the disciples who define and determine the nature of the connection between saint and follower, as much as the saint himself does.

It seems clear that to understand processes of Sufi regional cult formation, the need is to look at the way cults are founded and expand during
the lifetime of an originary, living saint. This is the challenge of the present study. Linked to this is the need to disclose what endows some men
with extraordinary charismatic authority and hence the power to found
new Sufi regional cults and expand their organisational ambit.

The word *ta'ifa* was not used by members of the regional cult at the
centre of this study. They spoke of the cult as a *tariqa*, but to distinguish it
from the wider Naqshbandi order to which it was affiliated, it was known
as 'Tariqa Naqshbandiyya Ghamkolia'. By appending the name of the
cult centre, Ghamkol, to their regional cult, they marked its distinctiveness as an autonomous organisation. Zindapir, as the head of order, was
by the time of my study the head of a vast, transnational regional cult,
stretching throughout Pakistan to the Gulf, Britain, Afghanistan and
Southern Africa. He had founded the cult centre in 1948.

CHARISMA AND MODERNITY

At the centre of a Sufi cult, alive or interred in a shrine complex, is a
charismatic saint. He is believed to be a unique, exemplary individual,
wali, or friend, of God, physically and mentally purified of all mundane
desires. Through him, it is believed, flows the divine light (*nur*), grace
(*faiz*), and power of blessing (*barkat*) emanating from Allah. The complex grammar of ritual blessing, which cannot be captured simply by the
word *baraka* (*barkat* in Urdu), is summarised in chapter 11, while the
conclusion reviews various dimensions of saintly charisma.

A striking feature of Zindapir's regional cult is its remarkable vitality,
evidenced by the deep faith and love people felt for their saint and their
willingness to devote their lives to him. This vitality needs to be considered against the background of a more general debate about the 'decline'
of Sufi cults and of charisma more generally in the context of secular
modernity.[7]

Interrogating Weber's notion of charisma, Eisenstadt proposes that he
was centrally concerned with 'the problems and predicaments of human
freedom, creativity, and personal responsibility in social life in general
and in modern society in particular' (Eisenstadt 1968: xv); and it was in

---

[7] For studies that propose the historical decline of Sufi cults see, for example, Trimingham 1971, Gilsenan 1973, Eickelman 1976 and Lindholm 1998. Most of these refer to the
Middle East and North Africa.

relation to the problem of individual freedom and creativity that Weber's notion of charisma, as antithetical to routine and rationalised institutional order was formulated (ibid.: xviii–xix). The disenchantment of the world, the hallmark of modernity, was, in Weber's view, the product of increasing rationalisation, of the growing reach of bureaucratic structures of domination. These structures he typified as permanent, routinised, recurrent, systematic, methodical, calculating, ordered, procedural and rule bound (Weber 1948: 245 *et passim*).

By contrast, Weber saw charismatic domination as highly personalised, intense, expressive and irrational as well as being innovative and creative. The source of charisma was a perception of the unique, extraordinary, supernatural or heroic qualities of the charismatic leader. Leadership was thus based on voluntaristic recognition and authority constituted by inner restraint and personal responsibility rather than external, rule-bound discipline.

There are echoes here of the exemplary autonomy Dumont attributed to world renouncers (Dumont 1957), and of Turner's liminal anti-structure. Indeed, the question of the possibility of attaining personal freedom and ethical subjectivity against modernity's pervasive, imposed disciplines has been revived by Michel Foucault in his work on aesthetic self-fashioning and the possibility of dissent (Foucault 1992: 251, 1983: 211), in Habermas's invocation of the 'life world' (1987) and in other work on new social movements (e.g. Melucci 1989, 1996).

Against the anti-structural interpretation of charisma, which defines it as antithetical to bureaucratic or patrimonial domination, Edward Shils (1965) proposed that institutionalised charisma 'permeates' all walks of life. The source of charisma is the 'contact through inspiration, embodiment or perception, with the vital force which underlies man's existence', a force located at the centre of society (ibid.: 201). The defining features of charisma are intensity, embodied centrality (of values or institutions) and the capacity for ordering.

This capacity for ordering and taming is one associated with Sufi saints (Gardner 1995, Eaton 1993). The widespread belief in South Asia is that wherever they go, Sufi saints bring a sacred fertility to the earth. Just as they sacralised the land in their movement eastward, so too they are now sacralising British soil, the book argues, in their move westward.

Building on Shils's insights, Clifford Geertz interrogates the sacred centrality of sovereign power and its symbolic ordering capacities. Through royal progresses and processions sovereigns mark out their

territories 'as almost physical parts of them' (Geertz 1983: 125), allegori-
cally shaping their dominion according to some cosmic 'exemplary and
mimetic' plan (ibid.: 134). Even in the context of modernity, he argues,
political authority retains its charismatic aura. In precolonial India, Bernard Cohn has shown, Muslim courts gave out tokens of honour, usually
garments, in ceremonial *darbars*, to substantialise the bonds between the
ruler and his princes or notables (Cohn 1983: 168).

There is, however, something intrinsically problematic in situating
charisma at the centre and equating it with state power and its routinised
extensions. For the citizens of postcolonial societies, it is often the opposition between a morally grounded charisma and the ambivalent authority of the state that more accurately reflects the experienced reality of
modernity. What thus needs to be theorised is the nature of charismatic
(saintly) dissent and opposition to the bureaucratic domination of the
state.[8] At most we might extend Geertz's view to argue that embodied
resistance to the centre's values draws on the same fund of charismatic
symbols which the centre attempts to appropriate for itself. Sufi lodges
bear the name of royal courts (*darbar, dargah*). The saint gives caps,
shawls and gowns to his disciples and *khulafa*. In this way, the (discontinuous) dominion of a saint, like the bounded one of a sovereign, is conceived to be almost a physical part of him.

But beyond these mimetic borrowings, the Weberian opposition still
holds true for autonomous Sufi lodges in South Asia.[9] As is shown in
chapters 5 and 6, the capitalist, commodity economy is converted at a
saint's lodge into a good-faith, moral economy through altruistic giving
to the *langar* (food cooked and distributed freely at the lodge), a form of
perpetual sacrifice.[10] More generally, the site of the saint's lodge is set
apart as a space of voluntarism, expressive amity and emotional goodwill, of *sukun*, tranquility and harmony, as chapter 10 reveals. The state
and its politicians, by contrast, are seen as menacing, corrupt, greedy and
unfeeling. They are not truly 'rational' in the Weberian sense since they
bend the rules to their selfish interests, using the instruments of patriarchal domination to achieve their goals. Theirs is a charisma of unbridled

[8] This mistrust of government has been typical of Sufism generally and on the subcontinent in particular (Schimmel 1975: 347).

[9] Many 'old' Sufi shrines have been taken over by the government Waqf department
with a consequent disarticulation of ideology.

[10] E. P. Thompson (1971) first introduced the notion of the 'moral economy' to refer to
the redistributive principles of basic production goods which, he argued, always included
moral assumptions.

power. By contrast the saint's charisma—and his achievement of subjective autonomy and freedom—is the product of his perceived (and projected) self-denial and self-mastery, of love and generosity.

But at the same time, as regional cult theory proposes, social structure is not effaced in Sufi regional cults, just as the mundane realities of politics, economics and social ranking cannot be made to disappear; instead, these structural and ordering elements are incorporated in new combinations, and negotiated in practice. Experientially, nevertheless, the lodge of Zindapir is for supplicants and pilgrims a fleeting sanctuary from the 'real' world, a place of self-discovery and self-fashioning.

The charisma of a saint is embodied in ascetic practices and technologies of the body, and constructed ideologically through a corpus of myths about his miracles. Many of the fables told are themselves about transnational movement, and they are told and retold transnationally. In this sense charisma is both unique and creative, as Weber posited, and yet paradoxically also routine. Sufi cults thus exemplify the existence of a mediating third term between charisma and routinisation, where the rise of charismatic individuals is a recurrent phenomenon, which assumes predictable cultural patterns. To understand how the charisma of a living saint is constructed during his life time and underpins his authority, chapter 4 analyses comparatively the poetics of travelling theories; that is, the way that such myths tell, simultaneously, both a local and a global tale about Sufi mystical power everywhere, and the settlement of Sufis in virgin, barren or idolatrous lands, such as the lodge valley in Pakistan or industrial towns in Britain. Each Sufi cult is distinctive and embedded in a local cultural context. But, against a view of the radical plurality of Islam (e.g. Geertz 1968), the chapter argues that Sufism everywhere shares the same deep structural logic of ideas. These shape the ecological and cultural habitat and local habitus wherever Sufi saints settle. In relation to this, the book asks the classical question first posed by Evans-Pritchard (1937): how do beliefs persist despite internal inconsistencies and evidence to the contrary? What makes such beliefs so compelling and powerful?

VIOLENT MYTHS AND THE PROBLEM OF SYNCRETISM

In the South Asian context, myths of bloody saintly battles with demons, encounters in the jungle with wild animals, or the violent dismembering and miraculous reconstitution of severed bodies, point to a shared Hindu-

Muslim universe of images and tropes, as the works of Bayly (1989), Eaton (1993) and Basu (1998) demonstrate. Yet even when they appear on the surface to be syncretic, the deep structure of these myths remains the same: a Sufi saint gains powerful spirituality by overcoming superhuman ordeals. If the persuasiveness of Sufi myths derives from their familiar localism, the message is one of a Sufi saint's closeness to Allah.

Most Sufi myths in South Asia tell a story of tolerance, inclusiveness and peace. Even in the case of the 'warrior' saints described by Bayly (1989), the majority were Sufis who had established their cults by peaceful means; the warrior myths about them are later accretions, added to an original mythic corpus during a period of extreme political violence several hundred years after these saints' death (ibid.: 190). Other warrior saints were Muslim soldiers canonised after their death as martyrs (ibid.: 200). Historically only on rare occasions have Sufi saints led real battles, usually in the face of extreme external threats. The Grand Sanusi of Cyrenaica coordinated the rebellion against the Italian colonisers (Evans-Pritchard 1949); the Akhun of Swat fought against an Afghani invasion (Ahmed 1976). Where Sufi violence does occur, as in the so-called Hurr rebellion in Sindh, this is often in response to direct provocation (Ansari 1992). Originary saints like Zindapir have a stake in peaceful coexistence and tranquility which enables them to expand their cult networks across a region and to reach different ethnic and religious populations. The very inclusiveness of cult membership and its pragmatic accommodation to different regimes militates against violence.

This promotion of peace is evident also in Hindu regional cults. The Swaminarayan guru appeared in a particularly chaotic period in Gujarati history and contributed to the restoration of peace in the region (Williams 1984: 8).[11] As it expanded, the movement generated several regional cults, each with its own central temple and organisation of voluntary labour, free food and networks of affiliated places.

It is, however, important to recognise the critical differences between Muslim saint-focused regional cults and Hindu guru-focused cults in South Asia. While the *pir* may be an intimate of God, the Hindu guru is believed to be god incarnate (ibid.: 67–71). Unlike the saint, whose burial place becomes a unique site of veneration,[12] the guru-god is reproduced

[11] van der Veer reports, however, on the existence of fighting ascetic sadhu trader-soldiers during the eighteenth century (1994a: 48–9).

[12] In rare instances, a saint's tomb may exist in more than one place. This may happen, as in one case described by Bayly 1989: 200, when the body of the saint is said to have been dismembered into (in this instance) at least six parts.

in concrete images and statues which are replicated throughout his region, in numerous temples and even by the wayside. The central temple, the administrative hub of the cult, may be magnificent in its wealth and effigies but it is not uniquely endowed with sanctity, as is the abode of a living Muslim saint or the grave of a *pir*. Pilgrimage to a saint's *darbar* is thus for a Muslim essential for gaining access to the embodied charisma of a saint.

TRANSNATIONAL FLOWS AND SACRED EXCHANGE

Regionalism and transnationalism in Sufi cults are embodied in flows of pilgrims, nurture, voluntary labour, sacred gifts and ritual objects. Chapter 6 shows the way that these flows of tribute and perpetual sacrifice, characteristic of Sufi cults in South Asia, underpin the organisation of Zindapir's regional cult in and across space, and have enabled the building and expansion of its central lodges in Pakistan and Britain. Through his *langar* the saint is conceived to be the great nurturer, the source of infinite generosity. This is so even though pilgrims know that they themselves are the immediate source of this unending abundance.

The *langar* underlines the fact that Sufi cult centres are sites of sacred exchange. This is equally true of the great pilgrimage centres of Mecca or Benaras. Supplicants arrive with offerings or objects to be sacralised and return home carrying with them a bit of the sacred centre. Such sacred exchanges across boundaries generate movements of exorcism and purification, on the one hand, and connections between distant places, on the other (R. Werbner 1989). The waters of the Ganges (Gold 1988), of the Jordan river or of ab-e Zamzam (the spring at Mecca), the earth of Mwali[13] or of Karbala; gowns, amulets and other accoutrements, crystallise embodied connections between a sacred centre and its extended periphery. The transformation is both metonymic, a joining of substance, and metaphoric or symbolic. Meaning is substantively inscribed by creating contiguities and connections, while inscription is rendered meaningful.

Another transnational movement analysed in the book is that of *jinns or evil spirits*, now said to populate Britain in vast numbers, living 'among the people.' Healing is an integral feature of all Sufi orders, crucial to the redistributive economy of the lodge. The saint, alive or dead, is regarded as a great healer. He is able to see and command invisible

---

[13] Mwali is the South Central African High God cult studied by R. Werbner (see R. Werbner 1989) and others.

spiritual beings, fiery *jinns* and other dark malevolent influences. He can penetrate people's minds and hearts and diagnose their ailments and sufferings. His spiritual power and divine light and blessing permeate his surroundings and all those who come in proximity to them.

A constant, daily stream of supplicants travel to the cult centre in search of healing. Chapter 10 shows that even beyond exorcism and *barkat*, the saint brings to afflicted pilgrims the healing power of *sukun*, a quality achieved through mystical meditation and purification, which pervades his lodge. Not all men claiming to be saints can generate this tranquility, and the chapter also documents the cases of two British disciples who came to be utterly disillusioned with the spirituality and healing power of local British saints and moved to discover the saint within themselves.

THE EMBEDDEDNESS OF SUFI REGIONAL CULTS IN BROADER SOCIAL MOVEMENTS

Much has been written about the Barelvi movement in South Asia that arose in the nineteenth century to defend popular Islam and the veneration of saints from Islamic reformist attacks (Metcalf 1982). Yet there has been little appreciation of how the Barelvi movement is interpolated into the saintly system of regional cults, or how the connection between saints and the *'ulama* is sustained. The key to this relationship, chapter 11 suggests, is the *'urs*, seen as an open, inclusive popular festival. It is through the many thousands of *'urses* held annually at shrines and lodges throughout the length and breadth of Pakistan that Sufi regional cults link into and sustain the wider Barelvi movement. With the global extension of Pakistani centres of migration, the provenance of this symbiotic relationship has also extended. Yet while the *'urs* provides a platform for the *'ulama*, it is also an indexical occasion which reinforces the supremacy and autonomy of living saints and re-enacts the ambivalent relations of interdependency between saint and *maulvi*, shrine and mosque.

Chapter 11 sums up the centrality of the *'urs* as the organisational nexus of Zindapir's translocal, regional and global cult. It views the *'urs* as both a ritual and a giant popular religious festival. It is also the hub of the organisational power of a Sufi regional cult, underpinning its reproduction and enabling its continued geographical extension. These three aspects of the *'urs*: ritual, popular cultural and organisational, are all intertwined.

Having considered the *'urs* as embedded in the broader Barelvi movement and folk popular culture, the chapter goes on to analyse the festival
as a performative ritual moved by the power of blessing to its final dramatic moment. The different phases of the festival, analysed in earlier
chapters, are here shown to be part of a single structured ritual process.
The *du'a*, the final benediction pronounced by the saint over the whole
congregation, is the most spiritually powerful act of the whole ritual. It is
the final transformative moment which follows a series of other ritual
acts. The ritual process of the *'urs* sacralises space and person. Reciprocally, the *'urs* is the moment in which the charisma of a living or dead
saint, embodied in his lodge or grave, is actualised before the whole
congregation.

A major argument of the book, then, is that Sufism is performative and
embodied in ritual practice, even when it appears to construct an abstract,
highly integrated cosmology based on the *du*alism of body and soul. The
'urs is the major Sufi ritual, connecting persons across space, enacting
sentiments of love and devotion in opposition to the material world of
everyday postcolonial life, and forming the hub of a major religious
movement in South Asia itself. Performative ritual as movement in space
is the subject of the next chapter.

3

STAMPING THE EARTH WITH
THE NAME OF ALLAH

JULUS, ZIKR AND THE SACRALISING OF SPACE

JULUS

Twice a year processions of Muslim men wind their way through the drab dilapidated streets of Birmingham, Manchester or London's immigrant neighbourhoods, celebrating anniversaries of death and rebirth. As they march they chant the *zikr*. In chanting thus they not only purify their hearts and souls; they also sacralise and 'Islamicise' the very earth, the buildings, the streets and neighbourhoods through which they march.

Julus, zikr, nazrana, langar, na't, taqrir and *du'a* are the central ritual phases or episodes of both *'Id-milad-un-nabi*, the celebration of the birth/death of the Prophet, and of the *'urs*. The *'urs* starts with the *julus* and culminates in the final *du'a*. Here we are concerned mainly with the significance of the procession, as movement in and through space, and the performance of *zikr* in relation to it.

'Urs: Mid-day, Birmingham, May 1989. We arrive from Manchester, a coachload of men, a minibus of women. The men congregate at the gates of a park, not far from the Dar-ul-'Uloom Birmingham, the religious centre of Sufi Sahib, head of a Naqshbandi regional cult in Britain, first *khalifa* and *pir* of Pir Hazrat Shah, known throughout Pakistan as Zindapir, the 'Living Pir'. Zindapir's lodge, is at *Darbar*-e-Alia Ghamkol Sharif, located in the wilderness of the hills of Kohat, in the North West Frontier Province of Pakistan. We are celebrating the final and most important day of the *'urs*, a ritual gathered to commemorate the death and rebirth of Hazrat Muhammad Qasim, a renowned saint of the Naqshbandi order whose shrine, Mohra Sharif, is up in the Muree hills, at the foothills of the Himalayas, north of Islamabad. Hazrat Muhammad Qasim, 'Baba Qasim', arrived from Afghanistan and established his lodge headquarters in the Muree hills in the late nineteenth century. He died, a very old man,

3. Decorating the lead car for the *'urs* in Birmingham

in 1943.[1] Hazrat Shah, 'Zindapir', was his most illustrious disciple and *khalifa*. Zindapir founded his own lodge in 1951, in the barren and lonely Kohat hills, beyond human habitation. He has built it up, during the past forty years, into a vast regional cult focused on the lodge headquarters in Kohat, and stretching from Karachi in the south to Abbotabad in the north, and from Lahore in the east to Birmingham and Manchester in the far west (see Map 1.1, page 2).

Julus: The men congregate at the entrance to Small Heath park. Elderly venerable men with greying beards and turbans, young energetic men, teenage boys and little children all wearing white traditional Pakistani clothing and green caps. They come from all over Britain—from Derby, Burton-on-Trent, Watford, Manchester, Luton, London, Rochdale and High Wycombe (see Map 1.2, page 3), as well as from Birmingham itself. Each group carries a green or black banner inscribed with golden Islamic

---

[1] Buehler (1998: 172) gives the date of his death as 1960, surely an error from all the accounts I gathered. He lists Muhammad Qasim as one of the major reformist Naqshbandis, a spiritual descendant of Ahmed Sirhindi.

calligraphy, usually with the *kalimah* ('There is no God but God and Muhammad is his Prophet') or other verses from the Qur'an. Leading the procession are several cars elaborately decorated with green, gold and red tinsel, carrying Islamic insignia on a green background, a palanquin of cloth on the roof of one of the cars. Another car carries a loudspeaker. The loudspeaker blares out:

'*Nara-i takbir!*' (Say: He is the greatest!)
'*Allahhu akbar!*' (God is greater!), comes the answer from the assembled men.
'*Nara-i risalat!*' (Say: prophethood!)
'*Ya rasul Allah!*' (Oh Prophet of God!), comes the answer.
'Zindapir!' (the 'Living Saint'). '*Zindabad!*' (Live forever), comes the refrain.
'*Mera pir!*' (My saint!) '*Zindabad!*'
'*Tera pir!*' (Your saint!) '*Zindabad!*'
'*Islam zindabad!*' (Islam live forever) '*Zindabad!*'
'*Darbar-e-Alia Ghamkol Sharif!*' (the Lodge Ghamkol Sharif)! '*Zindabad!*'

Leading the procession is a group of some seven or eight *khulafa*, deputies of Zindapir and of Sufi Sahib, venerable sages with flowing beards. Each *khalifa* wears a black robe, a *juba*, a gift from the *shaikh* in Pakistan, over a white new cotton robe. The black robes are said to signify the state of mourning which is the initial condition in the *'urs*, a sadness associated with the remembrance of a departed saint. Heading the procession is Sufi Sahib himself, one of the most prominent Sufi saints in Britain today. He is a giant of a man, dressed in flowing white and black robes. He carries his head high, his massive white beard covering his face. It is the face of a man who has known the heavy toil of twenty-five years' work in the iron foundries of the Midlands. He carries a long cane and strides ahead of the procession, looking for all the world like a biblical shepherd leading his flock.

It is time to start. I follow the procession in my car, accompanied by the women who have come with me from Manchester, and who are as keen as I am to witness the march from which they are barred. In front of the procession and flanking it on either side are English policemen who follow the march, redirecting the traffic and clearing the way ahead of the marchers. We move past the Dar-ul-'Uloom and continue our way through Small Heath and Sparkbrook towards the Birmingham Central *Jami'a* mosque. As the men march they recite the *zikr*. Melodiously, *'la ilaha illa'l-lah'* (There is no God but God) or, more stridently, *'Allah-hu, Allah-hu'* (God is present). Now and then the chanting is interrupted by the same loud, high pitched calls of the loudspeakers on the cars, to which the marchers' respond with answering refrains:

> *'Nara-i takbir'*
> *'Allah-hu akbar'*
> *'Nara-i-risalat'*
> *'Ya rasul Allah'*
> *'Zindapir'*
> *'Zindabad'* and so forth.

The men march through the streets of Birmingham, through Asian commercial areas, shabby, run-down but teeming with life. Grocery stores advertising ritually slaughtered *halal* meat, their vegetables and fruit piled high outside on the pavements, sari and clothes stores stocked with shining silks and colourful synthetics, Asian traditional jewellery stores with their delicately designed gold earrings and necklaces, Asian sweet shops with their wares piled high in perfect conical towers, Muslim banks, travel agents, restaurants and takeaways. Aromas of cumin, cloves

4. Sufi Sahib leading the *khulafa* dressed in black robes at the *julus* in Birmingham

and cinnamon follow us as the men turn the corner and march into a residential area, tall three-storey terrace houses overlooking narrow streets. Curious bystanders stare at us as we pass, English residents and shoppers, Pakistani women carrying their babies, young men idling on the sidewalk. Now we move into a second commercial area. Then, once again, back to terrace-lined neighbourhoods. The Birmingham Asian ghetto seems to stretch for miles. The procession itself extends for some half a mile, several hundred men of all ages marching along, three or four abreast. It is a three-mile walk. Finally, over the crest of the hill we see the Central Birmingham mosque. Set somewhat apart from other buildings, flanked by a busy thoroughfare, its minarets beckon the tired processionists. We reach the mosque, the march is over.

The women are waiting at the mosque together with the cooks of the *langar.* It is food cooked in the name of God by pure men who perform *zikr* as they cook. They respect the food, it is *tabarruk*, blessed. Like all actions at the *'urs*—the procession, the prayers, the praises of the Prophet, the reading of the Qur'an—the giving of food is a source of *sawab*, merit, transferred to the soul of the pir of Mohra Sharif.

The traders have also arrived and have set up their stalls in the courtyard, displaying a colourful variety of wares: bottles of scent from Saudi Arabia and Pakistan, *qawwali* cassettes of famous singers and groups, recorded *khutbas*, or sermons, of venerable Muslim sages, hagiographies of saints and other books in Urdu and Arabic, pictures of famous saints, Qur'anic and Sufi calligraphy in bold gold lettering, framed in golden frames, ready for hanging in the terrace houses we have just passed. There are foodstalls selling tea and bottled drinks. The traders are there for the profit; they need not be followers of Sufi saints, although many are. They come twice a year on the *'urs* and *'Id-milad-un-nabi.*

At the steps to the mosque the Lord Mayor of the city of Birmingham waits, together with several Muslim city councillors and the Pakistani sub-consul, who is based in Birmingham. The end of the *julus* is also an occasion for the leaders of the order to honour local notables and public figures who, in turn, dignify the festivities with their presence. Despite its cultural and religious specificity the celebration thus allows for the creation of a shared institutional space where Muslims and non-Muslims can assert common public values. The presence of the Lord Mayor signals the order's identification with civic institutions and its interest in cooperating with them. Indeed, the chairman of the order's management committee is closely tied to the Labour Party in the city, and the order has been a recipient of a major grant to build a community centre on its premises.

The *maulvi* (religious cleric) opens the proceedings with a prayer, followed by the Pakistani chairman of Sufi Sahib's Dar-ul-'Uloom committee, a jovial, blue-eyed, spectacled man, an accountant by profession, who makes the opening statement. He thanks the guests for having come on the procession, despite arriving home late last night, after participating in the anti-Rushdie demonstration in London which had taken place the previous day. His opening speech is followed by short speeches by the Lord Mayor, the sub-consul and two councillors. Finally, the *pir* stands up and raises his hand in *du'a*. The congregation below the crowded steps raise their hands silently as he prays. This is the first supplication. It seals the *julus* and opens the mosque proceedings. The second and culminating *du'a* will be later in the night, and it will seal the *'urs* as a whole. That second prayer will be attended not only by the living congregation present at the *'urs* but by the living souls of all those *auliya*, friends of God, saints, who have reached and merged with God and the Prophet, including Hazrat Shah, *faqir* and *wali* of God, Hazrat Muhammad Qasim, the departed saint in whose name the *'urs* is being held, and the departed saints and prophets who watch over the living.[2]

'Urs: Ghamkol Sharif, Kohat, Pakistan, October 1989. Preparations for the *'urs* have been going on for several weeks. As the time of the *'urs* approaches more and more disciples of the *shaikh* arrive to help with voluntary labour. The lodge nestles in the valley, climbing the slope of a hill, surrounded by hills on all sides, a series of stone buildings with internal courtyards, walled enclosures, walled orchards, vegetables gardens and cattle and goat pens. Surrounding it is a perimeter wall, running along the slopes of the hills, protecting the lodge from the leopards which come down from the mountains during the winter.

It is a lovely, prosperous, tranquil scene. The orchards bear apples, oranges and lemons. Tomatoes, cucumbers, cabbages, cauliflowers and chillies grow in well-tended vegetable beds. A fifty strong cattle and buffalo herd grazes in the valley. Chicken and geese honk in their coop. A herd of

---

[2] The presence of the living souls of departed saints at the final *du'a* was articulated quite explicitly by several *khulafa*. Their living presence at the lodge was further indicated by the fact that Zindapir was said by them to commune with the departed saints every morning before attending to the needs of the public. This, I was told, was why he was unable to meet anyone before 11 a.m.

5. The orchards of Ghamkol Sharif

goats bleats on the hills. Wild honey bees have made a hive in one of the trees of the orchard groves. The courtyards of the houses and hospices are surrounded by green lawns and bordered with flowerbeds and shady trees. The beautiful mosque, elaborately decorated in white, green and dark red, its three domes and delicate minarets set against the blue skies and the hills beyond, is a scene of perfection. Two fountains of pure water splash into pools on either side of the entrance to the vast mosque open courtyard, shaded by a giant banyan tree. All is quiet apart from the sound of *zikr* echoing in the mountains and the splashing of the water fountains. Ghamkol Sharif is, perhaps, as close to paradise as a Muslim can get on this earth.[3]

It was not always thus. When the *shaikh* arrived here in 1951 there were only the bare mountains. The *darbar* contains several key land-marks of the *pir's* settlement in this 'jungle' (wilderness). Of these, one is the first cave in which the *pir* settled, located in the hills overlooking the *darbar*. This is where the Prophet first sent him. When he arrived, the

---

[3] On my visit to the lodge in November 1991, I was told a tale of a visitor who had ex-plicitly described the place as paradise. It is noteworthy also, as I mention elsewhere (P. Werbner 1990c: 271–2), that Zindapir himself claimed to have found paradise on earth. He was referring in this particular instance, however, primarily to the abundance of food and gifts at the lodge which he was able to distribute in his lifetime (see Chapter 6).

shaikh shut himself up in the cave for three days and three nights without eating or drinking. Then God said to him: 'I have not sent you here to close yourself up inside a cave. Go out and meet the people.' This cave, now just beyond the perimeter wall, has been preserved as it was apart from a lone electric bulb lighting the interior. It has become something of a shrine and pilgrims to the lodge climb the hill and leave pledges of their requests in the form of pieces of cloth tied to the thorn bushes outside the cave. From here the pilgrim has a perfect view of the lodge and the valley below.

The second landmark is another cave at the heart of the lodge, towering above the mosque and all the other buildings on the slope of the hill. It is reached by a steep staircase. This cave has been converted into a window-less room. Its floor is covered with Persian carpets and its whitewashed walls are decorated with pictures of the *ka'aba* (the black stone at Mecca, believed to be the centre of the universe) and the *shajara* of the *silsila* (the spiritual genealogy of Sufi saints leading to the present saint, Zindapir). Outside this cave is the rock on which the *shaikh* sat and preached to his disciples for many years, before the mosque was built.

There was no water at that time, no electricity, no roads, no orchards, no cattle. The water was carried several miles from a spring on the other side of the hills on donkeys. Before the *shaikh* came there it was the abode of a famous dacoit from the fierce Kabaili tribes which live beyond the hills. This local Robin Hood was said to have robbed the British and stored his booty in one of the caves in the valley. The dacoit's fame lives on to the present.

Many remember those days and the wilderness as it then was. It has taken almost four decades to build the lodge to its present state of perfection. Virtually all of the labour which went into this building has been voluntary, unpaid. Even the electricity and the well were installed by the government free of charge. They were not asked for, they were simply given. But a good deal of the building work, the construction, the extension of water pipes, electricity and sewerage, the building and decoration of the mosque, the planting of orchards—all these have been achieved gradually, year by year, during the weeks preceding the annual '*urs*. This is the time of *intizam*, the arrangements and preparations for the '*urs*.

The *khalifa* who runs these arrangements has taken over the job from his father before him. He is also the *darban*, the gatekeeper of the *shaikh*, who handles the guests and decides how long they will spend with him. He carries the keys to all the locked buildings, storehouses and gardens,

6. Labour of love: Building the perimeter wall at Ghamkol Sharif

supervises the preparation of the *langar* and meals for the guests, the feeding of people during the *'urs* and, indeed, all the preparations for the *'urs*.

The *murids* arrive in groups, many of the helpers about three weeks before the *'urs*. There is a good deal of building going on, and rocks are broken with sledgehammers by hand and carried in baskets on the workers' heads from the rocky hillsides. This year the *murids* are in the process of building a watchtower on the periphery to guard the lodge. The *khalifa* supervising the building work is an ex-army man who comes from a place near Sohawa in Jhelum district. Another *khalifa*, organising the electrical work, is also an ex-army man. He hails from Faislabad and is supervising the decoration of the lodge buildings and hillsides with coloured lights and neon signs, as well as the various extensions needed for the new buildings. Some of the lighting is already in place at the *darbar* from *'Id-milad-un-nabi* which was celebrated last week. The decorative lighting is highly elaborate, with chains of flashing coloured lights, brightly lit coloured signs, spinning neon spoke wheels and a written neon sign in Urdu, '*Allah-hu*', that extends across the hillside. Most spectacular, perhaps, is the decoration of the mosque, each of the three domes lit with chains of light which spin around it.

The working teams are hard at work digging up last year's broad metal *chapati* grills, and giant *tandoor* (clay ovens) for baking *naan*, clearing the ground of rocks and stones so people can sleep on it, connecting new electricity and water lines for the expected guests, extending sewerage lines and building sumps, clearing areas for the coaches carrying the pilgrims. The mosque is being cleaned and redecorated, the elaborately designed iron gates repainted with blue and red flowers by a local 'artist', another *murid*. One of the fountain pools flagging the entrance to the mosque is being whitewashed. The whitewashing of the other has been completed, its waters now a sparkling blue.

People at the lodge perform *zikr* at all times of the day and night. Even as they work, they perform the *zikr*. Some, especially the *khulafa* supervising the arrangements, have not slept for many nights, yet still they continue with this labour of love, performing the *zikr* as they work (on a similar labour of love for a North African logde see Lings 1971: 18–19). The hills echo with the melodic sound of *'la ilaha illa 'l-lah'*. The melody changes from time to time as new melodies become fashionable, but the words of the chant are unchanging. The *shaikh* comes out to inspect the work's progress, accompanied by a group of *khulafa*. Nothing happens in the lodge without his knowledge. He is the ultimate planner and decision-maker.

7. The *langar* of the *'urs*: Feeding the multitudes

We meet two young men from Birmingham. They too have come to attend the '*urs*. They have many wonderful tales of the *karamat*, miracles, associated with the *shaikh*. One tells a story about the *zikr*:

'The people here do *zikr* all the time. Even when they are working they do *zikr*. When I came here the first time, I insisted that I wanted to do some work. So they gave me an area to clean. I was cleaning one of the rooms when I heard someone doing *zikr* in one of the other rooms. But when I looked into that room there was no one there. But still I kept hearing the *zikr*. Then I looked up and saw that there was a pigeon sitting on the edge of the roof doing *zikr*. I had heard that the pigeons do *zikr* here.'

The house we are staying in, with two rooms and a bathroom, running water and drainage, surrounded by a walled garden, was built last year for a party of British Pakistani pilgrims, led by Sufi Sahib, who attended the '*urs*. The house is beautifully furnished, with a three-piece suite, coffee tables, Persian carpets and European-style beds, for this is, after all, what British Pakistanis have come to expect as normal, and the *shaikh* provides only the best in hospitality for his guests.

The preparations continue. More and more *murids* arrive and join the work. It is truly a labour of love for the workers. All speak of their great love for the *shaikh*, of his devotion, his purity and his dedication. He never sleeps and barely eats, all he does is pray day and night and devote his life to God.

The cooking areas are being prepared. Great pots are brought out. Eating utensils are stacked in tall towers. Wood for the *chapati* ovens and cooking is piled high. Another guardroom is being built outside the women's quarters. Canvasses are extended over the whole area, so the women are screened from onlookers on the hills and everyone is under a shade. The cooking area is now fully set up with *chapatis* baking and pots simmering. The *intizami*, the organisers, rush around madly, making sure everything is working.

People are arriving in buses and trucks, in *qafilas*, convoys. Some carry banners which they place around the *pir's* courtyard, as well as banners on the colourful tents they set up. Decorated in green, white and red, the tents are secured on tall bamboo stakes with a wide gap between the walls and the roof. On the ground they lay thin rugs. Although it is October, it is very hot under the sun, and it is getting very dusty.

Everywhere *zikr* is being sung. People sing *zikr* on the trucks when they arrive, sometimes fast—'*Allah-hu*', '*Allah-hu*', sometimes slow and melodious—'*la ilaha illa 'l-lah, la ilaha illa 'l-lah*'. What they sing depends also on the pace of driving or the work tempo. From time to time other prayers blare over the sound system, but the sermons have not started in earnest yet.

The groups continue to arrive. They come from all over Pakistan. Some have travelled for 48 hours, covering 1,000 miles. A city of tents arises in the arid valley, myriads of people, men, women and children gather, an enormous crowd composed of groups from every big town in Pakistan and many of its villages. All have come to attend the *'urs* and receive the *pir's* blessings: they will share in his final *du'a*. There are no processions. They do not perform the *julus*. They have travelled great distances in the name of Allah, traversing the length and breadth of Pakistan. They departed singing *zikr*, first the *zikr* leader, then the answering chorus, and they go on singing thus all the way to Ghamkol Sharif.

HIJRA AND THE SACRALISING OF SPACE

Sufism is conceived of essentially as a journey along a path (*suluk*) leading towards God. In Sufism the human being is a model for the universe, a microcosm of the macrocosm, and the journey towards God is a journey within the person. Very briefly, Sufi Islam posits a complex relationship between body and soul expressed in a spiritual dualism between the *nafs*, the vital, desiring self or spirit, and the eternal soul, the *ruh*. The move towards self-purification is a move towards the transformation of the self, the *nafs*, through a transcendence of bodily desires and needs. By totally denying the self, the *nafs* is purified and 'dies', reaching intimacy during a series of phases with the saint, the Prophet and ultimately God (see Subhan 1960: 77; Rao 1990; P. Werbner 1990b) before, in the case of true saints, returning to instruct the living. In annihilating itself the *nafs* is eternalised. The path is a complex and dangerous one in which the spiritual guidance of an exemplary Sufi teacher who has undergone this journey is essential. In Sufism knowledge is gained through practice rather than intellectual learning, through experience rather than rationality alone (see Lapidus 1984). Divine knowledge is acquired via the heart.

The central ritual practice on this journey is *zikr*. By continuously practising *zikr* a person's *nafs* and his very body are transformed. A young *khalifa* of Sufi Sahib explained to me:

'The way to do *zikr* is through the parts of the body that are *latif* [very fine]. There are seven *lata'if* [sing. *latifa*, points of 'light' on the chest]. First is the heart, *qalb*, but *qalb* is not the heart but the hidden, transformed heart after doing *zikr* successfully. As a result it is inscribed with the name of Allah and filled with the light of Allah. It is like twirling a fire on a string [so that it creates an illusion of a continuous circle of light]. You kill yourself, your *nafs*, and if you succeed in doing so you die, hence at your death, since the Qur'an says you must all die, you do not die, but live again, since you have already died in your life.[4']

'When you do *zikr* you breath in "Allah" and breath out *'hu'*. *'Hu'* means He is present. If you say this long enough and concentrate then your heart begins to beat *"Allah-hu"*, *"Allah-hu"*, *"Allah-hu"*. Hence the way towards knowledge and light is through *zikr*.'

Logos is reality in mystical Sufism, the name of Allah inscribed in the rhythms of the heart and breath *is* God, or divine knowledge (see Nicholson 1921: 93). This from another young *khalifa* of the *shaikh*:

'There are seven points of energy in our body through which the spiritual power of Allah enters the body. If you do *zikr* correctly, and in my case it didn't take long [to learn], then your heart starts doing *zikr* all the time, every moment of the day and night, even when doing other things. Like now, when I'm talking to you.'

Or, as another *khalifa* put it,

'The way to the annihilation/purification of the soul/heart is through *zikr*. In *zikr* you breathe in the word of God, "Allah", holding your breath as long as possible, then breath out, saying *"hu"*. While holding the breath you hear your own heartbeat, and if you perform *zikr* correctly, eventually the heart will take on the chant "Allah, Allah, Allah", so that all the time the heart beats "Allah", "Allah". At this point the heart will burst through, open up the *'arsh-e mu'allah* [the throne of God which divides the world of appearances from the world of eternal realities]. But these are a matter of the *tariqa*. Don't write them down.'

This merging of body and cosmos is the way of purifying and transcending the vital, carnal, selfish self which is recovered as the eternal soul. The constant and continuous practice of *zikr* purifies, 'opens', the seven hidden *lata'if*, the 'light' (or 'subtle') spots in a person's chest and body, to receive the light of Allah (*nur Allah*). The *wali's* purified soul reaches beyond this world of creation (*'alam-e-khalq*) to the world of divine command (*'alam-e-amr*). He penetrates the thousands of screens or veils (*parde*) hiding the world of realities, moving on a journey towards an ultimate illumination, first of the shadows, then the reflections, then the

[4] The theory of the seven luminous *lata'if* was developed by the Kubrawi mystic Simnani in the fourteenth century (Schimmel 1975: 379), and described explicitly in the Naqshbandi order by Mir Dard in the eighteenth century (Schimmel 1975: 174). It is recognised by other Sufi orders as well, although in other orders the *lata'if* are believed to be located in slightly different places on the body. (More generally, see also Schimmel 1994: 13, 148.)

attributes of Allah, and finally His very being or essence (*zat*) (see also Subhan 1960: 61–1).

But Sufi Islam is not only a journey within the body and person, conceived of as a journey towards God. It is also a journey in space. The sacralising of space is not, it must be stressed, simply a coincidental feature of Sufi cultic practices. It is a central, essential aspect of Sufi cosmology and of Sufism as a missionising, purificatory cult. Beyond the transformation of the person, Sufism is a movement in space which Islamicises the universe and transforms it into the space of Allah. This journey, or *hijra*, which evokes the migration of the Prophet to Medina, empowers a saint as it empowers the space through which he travels and the place where he establishes his lodge.

The journey is twofold: on the one hand, into the wilderness, the 'jungle', beyond human habitation, the place of capricious *jinns* and dangerous outlaws, of predatory nature beyond civilisation; on the other hand, towards the land of infidels, *kufristan*, of idolaters, hypocrites, backsliders—the 'unbelievers'. It is these dangerous journeys which endow a Muslim saint with his charisma. He who stays home and grows fat on the land may be rich and powerful; he will never be the founder of a Sufi regional cult, he will never be revered and worshipped as one of God's chosen friends. It is the divine transformation in space which is the ultimate proof of the divine transformation of the person.

About a week after the *'urs* in Birmingham, Sufi Sahib came to Manchester to celebrate *gyarvi sharif* with the congregation at the Dar-ul-'Uloom there.[5] After the celebration and the *shaikh*'s final *du'a* he received supplicants with various problems and ailments, seeking his advice and blessings. I went in to see the *pir* with several other women. When my turn came we talked first of the *'urs* and Islam and he turned to me and warned me:

'In the Qur'an God says: "Islam is my religion." If that is the word of God, should you not accept it? When you come before God on the Day of Judgement he will ask you: "Did anyone tell you about Islam?" And you will have to say "yes". He will ask: "Why did you not become a Muslim?" You will have no answer.'

'You ask about the *julus*. It is written in the Qur'an [and here he quoted a Qur'anic verse in Arabic] that you must do *zikr* when you are standing, when you are walking, when you are lying down. According to the *Hadith*, when you walk

---

[5] *Gyarvi sharif* celebrates the death/birth of Abdul Qadr Jilani, the founder saint of the Qadiri order, considered a key founding figure of South Asian Islam, on the eleventh of every month.

along saying *zikr* then everything, including people and objects and things of nature, will be your witness on the Day of Judgement that you have performed *zikr*, yes, even the stones and buildings.'

I asked: 'Even the earth?'

'Yes, it is said in the *Hadith* that once you have said *zikr* stamping on the earth, the earth will wait for you to come back again.'

Sufi Sahib came to England in 1962. He had known Zindapir when he was still in the army, when he first became a *pir*, and he had shared with him some of the arduous experiences of the wilderness of the Kohat hills during his leave from the army. In the late 1950s there were many people, especially the ex-soldiers among the *shaikh's* disciples, who were going to England to seek their fortunes. It is said by some that Sufi Sahib approached the *shaikh* and asked him if he could go to England. Reluctantly the *shaikh* agreed to part with him. Having agreed, he appointed him to be his first *khalifa* in England. A British Pakistani visitor to the *'urs* in Ghamkol Sharif told me

'I went to England six months before Sufi Sahib. We were together in the army. We came here to the *'urs* in 1961 and I showed him my visa for England. Sufi Sahib promised to join me in six months. But when he was given the *chogha* [the initiatory gown of a vicegerent, also known as *juba*] by the *shaikh*, he changed his mind, he cried and wanted to stay, but the *shaikh* told him he must go.'

Zindapir told me that he had sent Sufi Sahib to England because the people there, the Pakistani labour migrants, did not even know how to pray, they did not celebrate *'Id*, they did not fast on *Ramzan*, they did not perform the *zikr*, they had forgotten Islam. They needed a spiritual guide to lead them on the path of Allah. Before Sufi Sahib left Zindapir made him his *khalifa*. He was one of his earliest *khulafa*, and most trusted companions.

One of the speakers at the *'urs* in Birmingham talked of this mission fulfilled by Sufi Sahib and men like him:

'...Those God-loving people who started the movement to raise the religious consciousness in you [the people present at the Birmingham mosque gathering] years ago enabled you to raise the flags of Islam, not only in the U.K. but all over the world, and especially in the *kufristan* of Europe.'

Whether it is to the land of infidels or into the wilderness, the saint's journey is a lonely journey, filled with hardship. It constitutes the ultimate ordeal. This is why the followers of an 'original' saint like Zindapir or

Sufi Sahib, a 'living' saint, a *'faqir'* (Zindapir's favoured term for describing himself), a *wali* (intimate of God, conduit of the power of God, His spiritual power through a chain of saints), speak somewhat dismissively of the *gaddi nishin*, the descendents of illustrious founding saints, guardians of shrines whose charisma is derivatory and who are seen to benefit materially from the cult founded by their gloried ancestors. They respect them greatly, but they are not 'real' saints. A true friend of God is a man who endures incredible hardship. Zindapir told me:

'When I first came here the land was barren and hostile and it had never witnessed the name of Allah. Yet look at it today, a green and pleasant land (*'abad*— cultivated, populated), all due to the faith in Allah of one man. No one had ever worshipped here since the creation of the world, it was a wild and dangerous place, a place of lions (my son saw a lion). Now the earth is richer in religion than many other places. One man is the cause of it all. One man came here and did *zikr*, and this place became a place of habitation. [Zindapir said this as a rhyme: *'sirf yeh jagah 'abad hay, ek admi ki waja se'* (If this place is inhabited, it is all due to one man.)]'

One of the guest speakers at the *'urs* in Ghamkol Sharif stressed this relation between the love of God and the sacralising of space in the course of his sermon:

'… When a man starts loving Rasul-i Pak [the Prophet] then everything starts loving him. Every part of the universe—the water, the flowers, the morning dawn, the moon, the roses, the green plants—everything starts loving that man. And this is the love of Rasul-i Pak which has given beauty to the flowers and beauty to the whole of the world. And whatever is present here is due to the love of Rasul-i Pak and the love of Allah.'

THE SUFI SAINT AS TAMER OF THE WILDERNESS

Zindapir and other speakers at the *'urs* repeatedly evoked the trope of the Sufi saint as tamer of the wilderness, a trope related closely to another, that of the Sufi saint as bringer of natural fertility. The foundation myth of the *darbar* as told by Zindapir every year at the *'urs* (see chapter 4) is of the successful overpowering by the Sufi saint of the devil, on the one hand, and of wild animals, wild men and the bare wilderness itself, on the other. It is the test of absolute faith (*tawakkul*), the mastery of the *nafs* and its wild, animal-like passions, its desires and temptations. The way to the valley of the cave is thus a concrete embodiment of the battle of the *nafs*. It is the *shaikh's via purgativa* (see Schimmel 1975: 4, 98). This is the first phase in the core myth of the legendary corpus—the triumph over the soul, the inner *jihad* (holy war). As Schimmel informs us:

As soon as every feeling and thought is directed in perfect sincerity toward God, without any secondary causes, neither humans nor animals can any longer harm the mystic. Thus *tawakkul* results in perfect inner peace. The numerous stories of Sufis who wandered 'in *tawakkul*' through the desert without fear of lions or highway robbers, without any provisions, reflect this attitude... (Schimmel 1975: 119, see also Rao 1990: 19; Nicholson 1989: 108–9; and Attar 1990: 158, 164, 273).

Similarly, we are told that Baba Farid chose as his abode a place

...inhabited by backward Hindu tribes. There were *chuls* (deserts) all around. Snakes and wild animals were to be found everywhere (Nizami 1955: 36).

In this place he founded a *jama'at khanah* which was

...the only place under the Indian sun where the Emperor of Hindustan and a penniless pauper were received in the same way... It was an oasis of love in a world of strifes and conflicts (ibid.: 114).

The legends of North African saints' miracles also evoke the mastery of the wilderness:

...a typically Maghribi feature [of such miracles is] that the saint wanders with his disciples through desolate areas and at one point sticks his staff into the ground, whereupon water springs from the ground and lush vegetation appears in the desert. The *zawiya* of the saint is then founded at such an oasis and brings blessing and salvation to later generations (Goldziher 1971: 270; see also Eickelman 1976: 33–4; Meeker 1979: 229–30).

Similarly Clancy-Smith reports that:

In most areas, the presence of springs, and thus the existence of the group and of life itself, was credited to the miraculous powers of legendary holy persons (Clancy-Smith 1994: 31).

A Sufi saint is seen, as Lapidus points out, to be

...directly connected to the cosmos because he participates in the essential forces of rational or spiritual power (Lapidus 1988: 254).

The control of nature is an important feature of a Sufi saint's claim to charisma. The challenge is to recognise that cosmos (*'alam-e-khalq*, the shadow world of becoming), person, and spiritual world (*'alam-e-amr*, the world of realities) are constituted in Sufi thought as three interdependent, ranked, parallel domains. By mastering the spiritual world and reaching its source of power, the Sufi becomes master both of the cosmos and of humanity. In his mastery he not only humanises but also energises the cosmos; he generates both cultivation and fertility. Hence Rao records that the Bakkarwal of Kashmir mythologise their founder saint as 'someone who led directly to the taming of nature' (Rao 1990: 19) and to the establishment of agriculture, a 'Home' and a 'specific Community' (ibid.). Gardner was told that:

Sylhet District has more power than other districts in Bangladesh. The trees and fields are more beautiful. This is because this is the country of the saints. The great saints came here. The soil has more strength, and the fields yield more paddy (Gardner 1993: 6–7).

Such widely held conceptions of saints as bearers of cultivated fertility fit Schacht and Bosworth's argument that according to Sufi philosophy nature is both theocentric—rational yet subject to divine intervention; and anthropocentric—at the service of humankind (Schacht and Bosworth 1974: 352).

The centrality of a Sufi saint's power over the earth and nature is explicitly personified in Sufi theosophy by the mystical rank of *abdal*, part of the esoteric set of beliefs regarding the ranked community of saints. According to this set of beliefs, there are at any one time forty living saints in the world who are *abdals*. These saints, I was told, make the grass grow, give food to birds, and ensure the fertility of the earth (see also Nicholson 1989: 123–4).

Just as saints are internally ranked, as well as being intrinsically superior to ordinary human beings, so too places in Sufism are ranked. Their ranking corresponds to the ranking of the saints who live or are buried there. Thus another speaker, a well-known *maulvi*, speaking in Urdu, told the congregation:

'...[To] the people who are resident in Pakistan and the friends who have come from outside Pakistan: I would like to say clearly that nothing in the universe is equal. Everything has its own status and honour...Even the piece of land where we are sitting now has different honours. For example, not every peak of a mountain is the peak of Mt Sinai [Tur]. And not every piece of land is the land of Madina Sharif. And not all stones have been honoured to become the House of Allah, the *ka'ba* [in Mecca]. And not every domed mosque is Al Aqsa [the Dome of the Rock in Jerusalem]. And not all hills could be the hills of Ghamkol Sharif. People may wonder why the people of Pakistan and people from outside Pakistan have come here after obtaining visas and spending a great deal of money? What have they traveled so far for? All the speeches have been made. What are they waiting for? I know that they have all come here only to share in the *du'a* of Khawaja Zindapir... We know that if we touch a flower it gets crumpled. But I know one thing, that wherever Khawaja Zindapir has placed his foot on the earth, he has turned it into a garden and flower bed... When love makes its place in the heart of man, the world is changed altogether.'

'I will request all of you to place your hearts at the feet of Muhammad Mustafa (Praise Be Upon Him [henceforth P.B.U.H.]) so it be cleaned of sins and desires. Because when my Lord, the sacred Prophet, came on this earth and placed his feet here, the whole land was declared a pure and orderly place—East and West were cleansed [purified]. We the Muslims have been allowed in the absence of water to do ablution with sand or dried mud. Before the coming of the Prophet no person was allowed to do his ablutions with sand or mud and no one was allowed to pray on the earth anywhere they chose. When my Lord Muhammad (P.B.U.H.) put his sacred feet on the earth, the earth was declared a pure place and we were allowed to say our prayers wherever we liked, and to do our ablutions with sand and dry mud. How was this permission given? It is clearly written in the Qur'an: "You may do ablution with dry mud". This earth became pure, not because we cleaned it with soap but because of its relation with the feet of the Prophet (P.B.U.H.).'

'...And oh, audience, if the prayer of a person is accepted because of his contact with the dust which touched the feet of Muhammad (P.B.U.H.) I will say to you that all the *murids* who have come to Ghamkol Sharif should come once a year, if you could, you should come daily, because in the *hijra* of Ghamkol Sharif there is a lover of the Prophet Muhammad. We don't come here to see Pir Sahib. We come here to seek the path of Allah, the path which leads to Muhammad, and to see his true follower, who loves Allah and his Prophet beyond the imagination of any man, and who has been blessed by Allah above all others in this world. We pray to Allah that he should give fortitude and endurance to us, so that we should be able to keep coming to see our Pir Sahib every year and to have his blessings. Amen.'

As Zindapir himself repeated annually at the *'urs*:

'To a person who is an infinite believer and absolute follower of Allah, Allah grants that person great honour and respect in this world. And Allah will bring honour and respect to his grave. Allah will bestow honour and respect on the area where he lived his life, and Allah will undoubtedly bestow honour and respect upon him on the Day of Judgement ...Other people, when they die, no one can distinguish their graves after two years...Allah leaves them when they die. But Allah takes care of His *faqirs* even after their death and bestows infinite honour and respect to their graves, to the places where they lived...'

THE SPATIAL DIMENSIONS OF SUFI MUSLIM INDIVIDUAL IDENTITY

The spirituality of a Sufi *pir* is embodied in the space he has sacralised. His divine blessing purifies his spatial dominion and endows it with sanctity. For Sufi Muslims in Britain, who are followers of Sufi Sahib, Darbar-e-Alia Ghamkol Sharif is the centre of their symbolic universe. The separation and distance between Kohat and Birmingham or Manchester are overcome in their symbolic imagination, to create a single, unitary cosmic order. For these disciples, religious identity derives from their connection to a chain of saints, from Sufi Sahib to Zindapir, to Baba Qasim, who are located within a sacred spatial network. As Pakistani migrants they are linked by love and obligation to relatives and friends whom they have left behind in their natal villages and cities, and by loyalty to Pakistan as a nation. They return periodically to Pakistan to renew these valued relationships. As Muslims and 'brother-disciples' (*pir-bhai*) within a single regional cult they are united in their expression of love for two men: Sufi Sahib in Britain and Zindapir in Pakistan. Their religious identity as Muslims and Sufis is particularised through this love and loyalty, and is revitalised periodically through pilgrimage and celebration at the spaces these holy men have sacralised by their religious activity.

As was stressed in chapter 1, they are members of a single 'regional cult' rather than simply of a Sufi *tariqa*. The distinction is important. The Naqshbandi order stretches from Iraq and Turkey in the west through Iran and Afghanistan to the whole of South Asia. It is only in theory a unitary organisation. As a distinct order it recognises slight variations in Sufi mystical practice on the path towards unification with the Prophet and God. The regional cult built up by Zindapir is, by contrast, a viable organisation with a known hierarchy of sacred centres and sub-centres and recognised chains of authority. It is a known universe of specific communities linked together in devotion of a single man. For disciples living in Britain their various communities are united with all the other communities centred on Ghamkol Sharif, even though the majority of these communities are, of course, located in Pakistan itself.

Regional cults generate specific, individual religious spatial identities. This is because they are fundamentally cults of the middle range (R. Werbner 1977: ix). In certain regional cults a universal God is particularised around sacred shrines and spiritual intercessors, and religious worship is mediated by ascriptive links to spatially known and recognisable communities. In similar vein Eaton has argued that the establishment of Baba Farid's regional cult meant that

> ...a certain tract of the Punjab had become identified with Baba Farid's *wilaya*, or spiritual kingdom, which to his devotees was perceived as having specific geographical boundaries that bordered the *wilayas* of other saints... [This geographical extension] demonstrates how closely the notion of spiritual sovereignty could parallel, in spatial terms, that of political sovereignty (Eaton 1984: 341).

Two common fallacies are evident in Eaton's account. First, he mistakes a cult region for a bounded territory. Second, he assumes a correspondence between ritual and political domains (but for a different view, see Eaton 1978b). As Richard Werbner emphasises, regional cults are not contiguous, spatially bounded territorial organisations; they are spatially discontinuous, interpenetrating organisations linked together through a common connection to ritually sacred centres and sub-centres (see R. Werbner 1989: 245–98). Nor do they correspond to or fit neatly into political territorial divisions.[6]

The particularising of the universal in Sufi regional cults makes the sacralising of space central, as we have seen, to Sufi cosmology. Moreover, the pivotal role of the Sufi saint as sacraliser of space also has important bearings upon our historical interpretation of Sufi reform movements, and for our understanding both of the way Sufi cults have spread into Britain and also of the meaning this extension has had for British Pakistanis.

THE WAXING AND WANING OF SUFI REGIONAL CULTS

To discuss space in Sufism is to comprehend the relations between three dimensions of sociality: power, spirituality and religious organisation. Although the basic outlines of Sufi regional cult organisation are generally known, the social dynamics of cult organisation and the complex relationship between power, space and theosophy are less clearly understood.[7] Sufi regional cults, like regional cults elsewhere, do not remain constant either in the regions they control or in the following and political

---

[6] Buehler (1998: 195), like Eaton, is mistaken in claiming that a saint's ability to exercise control over his spiritual territory 'only extended to the boundaries of this territory, and if a Sufi did not observe the correct protocol when entering the spiritual domain of another Sufi, it could have fatal consequences'. Sufi spiritual territories or regions are not bounded in any simple sense, except perhaps the immediate vicinity of a lodge; rather, they leapfrog over boundaries.

[7] But for excellent discussions see Gilmartin 1979 and Clancy-Smith 1990. See also Clancy-Smith 1994 on the creation of the Rahmaniya order in North Africa.

influence they command. Not all shrines are centres of currently viable regional cult organisations, with their sacred networks of vicegerents and cultic sub-centres. Instead, there is a continuous vying for ascendency between cults and the saints that control them. At any one time there are particular centres which rise to prominence and gain reputation and followers at the expense of others. Sufi regional cults as viable, ongoing regional organisations, 'wax' and 'wane' (R. Werbner 1977; Trimingham 1971: 179), they rise and fall periodically.

This cyclical and recurrent process is evident at the micro-level in any particular locality, as local extensions of regional cults within the broader encompassing *tariqa* are displaced by new revitalised cultic centres or sub-centres, energised periodically through the emergence of a charismatic saint. In any particular locality, there may thus be followers of several living saints at any time, a feature discussed more fully in chapter 7. Although shrines of illustrious saints, once established, remain points of personal pilgrimage and seasonal ritual celebrations, such shrines no longer extend as organisations far beyond a relatively localised area, and cannot continue to control, as the cult founder did, a series of sub-centres, and sub-sub-centres over a vast region.

This cyclical waxing and waning of Sufi regional cults is related to, but should not be confused with, historically specific revivalist movements. As historical movements, Sufi revivalism engaged in different eras and centuries with different religious challenges to its authority, and responded to the particular religious debates and discourses of specific historical moments. In this sense revivalist movements tended in each century to challenge some of the theosophical premises current at the time in Sufism, and some of the shrine practices related to them. The revivalist movements which swept across the Hijaz and North Africa in the nineteenth century, for example (see Trimingham 1971: 105–27; Evans-Pritchard 1949; Clancy-Smith 1990 and 1994), or the Naqshbandi reform movement spearheaded by Ahmed Sirhindi in South Asia in the seventeenth century (A. Ahmad 1969: 40–2; Subhan 1960: 286–95) as well as the Chishti revivalist movement of the same and later period (see Gilmartin 1979), transcended localised cults in setting new standards of religious excellence and a new ideology of ritual practice. In renewing the stress on the *Shari'at* and on the austere practices of fasting and prayer, and in reformulating the relationship between Sufi saint and follower, the impact of these neo-Sufi movements was profound and far-reaching.

In many senses, however, the movements may be regarded as part of a continuous process of renewal and not as radically unique events. Sufi cults are continuously revived through the periodic rise of new regional cults focused upon a holy man who ventures beyond the current boundaries of the established Islamic world and who founds a new centre, generating a regional organisation around it in the course of time. What reform movements share with ascendant local Sufi regional cults is, above all, *a renewal through movement in space*. This makes sense organisationally as well. Old shrines become enmeshed in endemic succession disputes which dissipate the power of the centre and of the current holders of saintly title. Such disputes challenge the moral authority of the centre and its current trustees (see Jeffery 1981; Gilsenan 1982; 240–41; Gilmartin 1984). The shrine retains its sacred power but the current *gaddi nishin* cannot fully recapture its organisational authority.

Hence theosophy, missionary activity and the revitalising of religious organisation are all tied to the high value placed on movement and the sacralisation of hitherto profane space. The most remarkable feature of the Sanusi cult in North Africa, for example, was the Grand Sanusi's periodic movement: once he had established a cult centre, he left it to one of his vicegerents, only to move once again, further and further south, along the oasis trade route across the Sahara (see Evans-Pritchard 1949). He established a major Islamic library numbering some 8000 volumes a hundred miles from the coast, in the heart of the desert. Evans-Pritchard tells us that

Jaghbub, now to become the centre of the Order and the seat of an Islamic University second only in Africa to al-Azhar, was till 1856, when the Grand Sanusi made it his seat, an uninhabited oasis, in which the water was brackish, highly sulphurous, and insufficient to irrigate more than a small area of gardens (1949: 14).

At its height, after the Grand Sanusi's settlement there, it numbered some 1,000 people (ibid.: 17).

The great regional cults in Pakistan today are recently founded: Golra Sharif (see Gilmartin 1979 and Ur-Reheman 1979), Mohra Sharif, Alipur Sharif, Sharqpur Sharif, Jalalpur Sharif and Ghamkol Sharif. Such centres build up an extensive network of cultic sub-centres extending throughout Pakistan, wherever loyal and devoted vicegerents of the original saint have founded branches of the cult. Some of these vicegerents will ultimately found new centres which in time may become the focus of new viable cults, outshining the tired successors of local shrines with their moral and religious excellence. It is, above all, the 'living pirs', those who venture beyond the established order, who endow Sufi Islam with its continued vitality.

JULUS AND HIJRA

I have argued that the charisma of a holy man is objectified and thus proved through its inscription in space. The saint who has traveled beyond place (*la-maqam*)[8] on the Sufi path, and beyond the boundaries of Islam, has in doing so inscribed his charisma on the new place (*maqam*) he has founded, and this very act of inscription constitutes the ultimate proof that he is, indeed, a saint.

But there is a further question that needs to be asked if we are to understand the significance of movement through space for British Pakistanis: why is it that for these immigrants the holding of the *julus* in Britain seems to represent a radical departure from previous practices, a new movement imbued with deep subjective experiential significance?

To answer this question we need to recognise that the *julus* embraces a plurality of meaningful acts. It is of course, as I have argued here, above all a religious act in which the name of Allah is ritually inscribed in the public spaces Muslims march along. Through the chanting of *zikr* British Pakistanis Islamicise the urban places where they have settled, and the towns and cities which are now their homes. In South Asia, religious processions have been identified as important vehicles not only of group solidarity but also of communal riots and anti-colonial protest. Freitag, in particular, stresses the effervescent and performative dimensions of such processions, arguing that through the 'interplay' of sacred and profane space they foster the expression of 'community' and link centre and periphery in a single 'civic culture' (Freitag 1989: 134–5).[9]

Historically, the holding of South Asian Muslim public processions in Britain can be seen as constituting a radical shift in the terms in which Muslim immigrants have come to represent themselves to the wider society. During the initial phases of migration the only public religious signs of an Islamic presence in Britain were the stores and mosques that immigrants built or purchased. Outside mosques, ritual and religious

---

[8] *La-maqam* is an epithet for Allah who is beyond place.

[9] The cultural and political significance of public processions varies widely. The display of dominance in official state processions may be contrasted with potentially explosive religious-communal processions, such as those in Northern Ireland. There are pilgrimage processions (see, for example, Sallnow 1987), annual ritual processions (see Fuller 1980), English miners' processions, memorial processions, and processions which form part of broader rituals of revitalisation, such as carnival processions before Lent. Although all processions may be said to constitute existential displays of power and territorial occupation/demarcation, their significance differs widely in different cultures and localities, and at different historical moments.

activities took place in the inner spaces of homes, which were sacralised through repeated domestic *'Id* and communal Qur'an reading rituals (see P. Werbner 1990a, chs 4 and 5). Sacred Islamic spaces were thus confined within fortresses of privacy, whether mosques or homes, and these fortresses protected immigrants from external hostility, from a dangerous exposure.

When Sufi Sahib first held a *julus* in Birmingham around 1970 he was warned by the *'ulama* that such an assertion of Islamic presence could lead to trouble, exposing marchers to stone-throwing and other attacks. Sufi Sahib, not a man easily intimidated, went ahead with the procession anyway. Over the years it has sometimes been the target of attacks, mainly verbal, from outsiders, but this has never deterred the marchers. The organisers of the processions take pride in the fact that these events have always been peaceful, that they have never become the scene of trouble or violence.

Marching through immigrant neighbourhoods, the processions not only inscribe the name of Allah on the very spaces stretching between and connecting immigrant homes or mosques—they also call Muslims back to the faith. The *julus* is, as one *khalifa* told me, above all an act of *tabligh* (proselytising), of publicly saying to other Muslims: 'Regard us, we are proud of being Muslims, we are willing to parade our Muslimness openly in the streets, we believe that Islam is the last and best religion, containing the true message of God, the whole message, including even its hidden truths, and we are not afraid to show our pride in our religion openly and publicly.' But (he explained) 'we are also making clear that if you want to be a good Muslim you have to choose. You can't "mix" with the English' (or be, in other words, a part-time Muslim).

The *julus*, and the public meetings before or after it, also lend themselves to more overt and specific current political statements about Islam in Britain. A *julus* can become a kind of political demonstration. Not all Sufi groups are willing, however, to politicise the procession itself openly in this way. In the Birmingham processions I observed, the banners carried were in Urdu and Arabic, and were inscribed mainly with verses from the Qur'an. In Manchester by contrast the banners in 1990 were in English, and made implicit references to the Rushdie affair through the demand for a change in the blasphemy laws. Other banners, stating that Islam was a religion of peace, also referred implicitly to the association of Muslims with violence which the Rushdie affair had generated in the public mind.

Whatever the nature of the procession itself, in both cities the meetings held either before or after the procession included invited English digni- taries and officials, and the speeches made in them referred openly to the current political concerns of Muslims in Britain (for a detailed analysis, see P. Werbner 2002: 120–8).

Whether explicit or implicit, once people have marched openly in a place they have crossed an ontological barrier. They have shown that they are willing to expose themselves and their bodies to possible outside ridi- cule for the sake of their faith. Once they have organised a peaceful pro- cession, they know they are capable of organising a peaceful protest. Such processions can thus be seen as precursors to more overt (democratic) political protest.

The banners in English are also part of the missionising activity of Muslims in Britain—the propagation of Islam undertaken by many Mus- lim organisations (see Lewis 1994). The banners appeal to an English audience of potential converts, people who feel that Christianity or secu- larism have somehow failed them and are seeking a new religious truth.

Further, the processions assert the legitimacy of a particular Islamic approach, one focused on saints and their shrines. Historically, this type of Islamic practice has come under attack from other reformist move- ments, in South Asia primarily from the Deobandis, Ahl-i Hadith and more recently Jama'at-i-Islami (see Metcalf 1982). In Pakistan today the processions are, of course, part of a popular national culture; they are shown on public television and no one apparently dares question their legitimacy. In Britain, however, they still represent an act of assertion in a struggle between different Islamic approaches, all competing for local hegemony. Moreover, holding a *julus*, particularly a city-wide one on *'Id- milad-un-nabi*, also attests to the ascendency of a particular Sufi regional cult in a city. In Birmingham, Sufi Sahib holds the processions to which all the other Sufi orders are invited. In Manchester the procession was, until 1991, dominated by members of the Qadiri order whose *khalifa* controlled the central mosque.

Beyond matters of local competition, the composition of the proces- sion is also significant. Whereas *Jami'a* mosques are often built and fun- ded by management committees manned by the wealthy or educated, and sometimes even by external governments, the processions are open to anyone. Many of those who march are members of the Muslim under- privileged or working class. It is they who assert, by marching, their pride in Islam, their self-confidence and power.

Marching through the streets of a British city, then, is in many different ways an assertion of power and confidence. This is why the holding of the processions seems to have a deep subjective experiential significance for those who participate in them.

Finally, and most simply, the *julus* is an expression of the rights of minorities to celebrate their culture and religion in the public domain within a multi-cultural, multi-faith, multi-racial society. Seen thus, Muslim processions do not differ significantly from Chinese New Year lion dances, public *Diwali* celebrations, St Patrick's Day processions or Caribbean carnivals. They are part of a joyous and yet unambiguous assertion of cultural diversity, of an entitlement to tolerance and mutual respect in contemporary Britain. Through such public festivals and celebrations immigrants make territorial claims in their adopted cities, and ethnic groups assert their equal cultural rights within the society.

EMPOWERING MORAL SPACE

Recent deconstructive critiques have argued against a tendency to map anthropological discourse onto social space, so that 'hierarchy' is constructed as epitomising India, 'segmentary opposition' Africa, 'gift exchange' Melanesia, and so forth. So too classical authors (Dumont, Evans-Pritchard, Malinowski) derive their authority, it is claimed, from their defining association with these 'totemic spaces' (Appadurai 1986; Strathern 1988) of anthropological knowledge. What is perhaps missed in this deconstructive critique is the fact that mapping knowledge onto culturally constructed spaces is also a practice of anthropology's subjects.

Like anthropologists, the people we study construct topographies of high and low value, good and evil, truth and falsity, in social space. For Muslims, a complex geography of sacred knowledge-places with its centre in Mecca, has been propagated since medieval times. The believed location of different forms of Islamic knowledge and spiritual blessing has impelled Muslims to travel in search of these elusive truths to key places in the Islamic world, whereas a visit to those places of knowledge serves to legitimise different (and sometimes competing) religious leaderships in the Islamic periphery (for a comparative discussion, see contributions in Eickelman and Piscatori 1990). Hence, as with anthropology, so too in indigenous ideologies, totemic cultural spaces of knowledge also map, *ipso facto*, unequal global power relations and contested moralities. Space and place are thus widely conceived of, whether in the groves of academia or the rapidly diminishing forests of the postcolonial world, as metaphors for, and metonymic extensions of, culture, moral virtue, identity, truth, hegemony and subordination.

Given the complex symbolic connotations which topographies of space and place are endowed with, it is to be expected that the conquest of space, its inscription with a new moral and cultural surface, will be regarded as an act of human empowerment. The present chapter has discussed such a contemporary and historical process of religious spatial 'conquest' effected by a transnational Sufi regional cult centred in the North West Frontier Province of Pakistan and extending into Britain and other parts of the world as a result of international labour migration. I have argued that in Sufi cults, associated with an impetus to expand is an ideology of supra-human spatial and earthly transformative power which constitutes and proves the charisma of Sufi saints.

It is important to consider the theoretical subtext of my argument. If alien cultural spaces are, as Fabian has argued (Fabian 1983), perceived as bounded and enclosed and hence apparently distanced in time as well as in space from the contemporary world, so that the space of the 'West' comes to be opposed to the space of 'Islam' as separate, bounded and historically distant, it is equally the case that the very same spaces ('Western', 'Islamic') may be conceived of by Muslims, from another perspective, as contemporaneous, expansive and 'open'. This implies a dual spatio-temporal orientation. On the one hand there is the past in the present (the pre-Islamic 'West', a 'pure', 'Christian' England) that defines and encloses the cultural space of the alien other, beyond the boundary, constituting it as separate and distant. On the other hand is the potential future expansiveness of this very same space ('Islamic' Britain, the Islamicising West) that reconstructs it as open and fluid. In refocusing on border zones in this way we are, in effect, looking at what is powerfully contested but also shared in the here and now.

Post-Second World War migration from Pakistan to Britain has entailed a breakdown or de-territorialisation of former bounded (national) spaces, a reversal of demographic flows (from the colonies to the centre), and an active reinscription of the spaces fragmented by the migration process. As Gupta and Ferguson (1992) propose, global disintegrations of space are followed by acts of re-integration or re-territorialisation; in these, newly defined spaces generate novel constraints. Pakistani migrants to Britain have in many senses, as I have argued elsewhere (P. Werbner 1990a), appropriated space both in its commodified form and through the ritual transformation of home spaces into moral spaces. Cityscapes have also been colonised by these immigrants through the purchase of houses and businesses and the gradual invasion of whole residential and commercial districts.

Alongside these territorial encroachments has been an expansion of Islamic religious movements of various shades (for an account see Lewis 1994; Ahmed and Donnan 1994). Among the South Asian Islamic sectarian groups in Britain, Sufi orders predominate, and it is these orders which most actively work to sacralise alien cityscapes—the 'land of the infidels'—and reconstitute this land as moral space.

To understand this empowering potential of Sufism, the tendency towards movement in space has to be understood as an intrinsic feature of Sufi cult organisation, and a source of renewed charismatic authority. Hence the chapter has shifted back and forth in both space and time in order to demonstrate the hypothesis that the moral conquest of alien space is a test of charismatic authenticity which legitimises the rise of new 'living saints'. One may cite also an emerging literature demonstrating a similar process of spatial sacralisation by saintly cults which has occurred in modern Israel following the migration of North African Jews to the country in the 1950s (see Weingrod 1990; Ben Ari and Bilu 1992).

It is critical to distinguish between the mere pragmatic capturing of new spaces and acts of ritual sacralisation which are perceived to be essentially transformative of the substance and quality of lived-in space. Or, to put the matter differently, we need to ask, not only how new spaces are sacralised but also how sanctity is embodied in a new place. The Islamic encroachment into European spaces has been widely documented (see, for example, Lewis and Schnapper 1994). Arguably, what is perceived by many Europeans as most threatening about this encroachment has been the realisation that, like most migratory movements, the movement of Muslims into the West has also been associated with new ritual inscriptions upon old spaces (see Metcalf 1996).

Apart from the obvious growth in the number of mosques, more subtle inscriptions are evident. In France, for example, Senegalese migrants transform the spaces of municipal male hostels into temporary saints' lodges (Ebin 1996) or sites of sacrifice (Diop 1996; Brisbarre 1999), while in Germany the Turkish Alevis create spaces for ecstatic celebration (Mandel 1996). In sacralising spaces, Muslims also root their identities as Muslims in a new locality and embody the moral right of their communities to be 'in' this new environment.

Central to the present chapter has been the argument that the sacralising of alien Western spaces by Sufi disciples is not haphazard: it is an ordered, culturally predictable process typical of Sufi regional cults now turned global. Regional cults are characterised by a nodal organisation of hierarchically ranked sacred centres and sub-centres, linked across space rather than enclosed within territorial boundaries. A further feature of such cults, as we have seen, is that cultic centres are perceived to be religiously powerful places to which sacred journeys or pilgrimages are routinely made.

Typically, regional cults cut across boundaries, whether of community, nation or ethnic group, and generate their own sacred topographies, often in tension with national and local centres of temporal administrative power. Hence also the expansion of such cults normally takes the form of leapfrogging across territory, even national boundaries. In Sufi Islam, this process is carried out by migrating holy men who sacralise new centres, linked to the founding centre, and who now and then establish new regional cults around them.[10]

The sanctity of space is to some extent a matter of degree: while the headquarters of Sufi saints, their *darbars* or *dargahs*, are permanently transformed into sacred sites imbued with the saint's charisma, the sanctity of urban spaces is created and recreated by Sufi followers who march periodically through the streets of their cities. This marching, I contend, has to be grasped as a performative act, an act of metonymic empowerment, which inscribes and re-inscribes space with sanctity. At the same time the Sufi processions may be conceived of as 'texts', carrying messages produced by Sufi followers through occasional public displays of collective identity (on this process of occasional visibilisation see Melucci 1989: 70–1).

To stress the metonymic requires, however, also that we recognise the ritual place of Sufi urban processions within a complex liturgy of ritual acts performed on the occasion of the *'urs*, the 'wedding' or mystical union of a saint with God. In avoiding the textual metaphor, I am not denying the rich multivocality of the procession; rather, I want to stress the active inflection, the question of 'Who has the power to make places of spaces? Who contests this? What is at stake?' (Gupta and Ferguson 1992: 11). With this problem of agency and power in mind, this chapter has considered the procession itself.

[10] See, for example, Clancy-Smith 1994 on the creation of the Rahmaniyya order in North Africa.

As Pakistani Muslims have migrated beyond the boundaries of their natal countries to create Muslim communities in the West, they have also created fertile ground for new Sufi cult centres. In Britain, all saints are 'living' saints. Through *hijra* they have become the original founders of a new order in an alien land. In marching through the shabby streets of Britain's decaying inner cities, they glorify Islam, they stamp the earth with the name of God. If, like Sufi Sahib, they are powerful vicegerents of a great saint, they retain their link to the cult centre, they pay homage to it, go on pilgrimage to visit it, marvel at its beauty, and share in the powerful godliness of its keeper.

To establish these new diasporic centres, linked by ties of personal loyalty to 'home', these Muslims have expanded the totemic spaces of Islamic knowledge and spiritual power. Today the Muslim *'umma* (community) encompasses 'the West' in a transnational network of Islamic scholars and religious leaders. By making places out of spaces, Sufi saints have decentred and recentred the sacred topography of global Islam. New peripheries, whether in Africa, Asia or England, converge ultimately on the epicentre of the Islamic universe—the sacred *ka'ba*, navel of the earth.

Once a year, pilgrims from Britain led by Sufi Sahib meet pilgrims from Pakistan, led by Zindapir, in Mecca on Hajj. Zindapir provides free food to all needy pilgrims to the Hajj and it is Sufi Sahib's responsibility to organise the *langar*. Two men, friends and companions of old who have been separated for a quarter of a century by 5,000 miles of land and sea, meet annually at the sacred centre of Islam, part of what has become through the process of migration a global sacred network generated by a belief and love of one man, following a divinely ordained mystical path.

4

KARAMAT

THE LEGENDARY CONSTITUTION
OF A LIVING SAINT

WORLD RENOUNCER, WORLD RENEWER

Hazrat Shah, Zindapir, the 'living saint' was a man who achieved saint-hood in his lifetime. This means, in effect, that he was a living legend. His life, as told by him or about him by his disciples, has been the life of a friend of Allah, and as such it has been a life motivated by and moved teleologically through the guidance of divinely inspired dreams and visions. Every event in the *shaikh's* life has religious significance. The personal joys and crises that motivate the lives of ordinary men—mar-riage, bereavement, birth, love, wealth, happiness—although known to his disciples and often appearing to be (from a Eurocentric perspective) turning points in his career—are regarded by them as having no causal effect upon his moves and decisions. They are mere coincidences, to be brushed aside and ignored. He has been guided, like all Sufi saints, only by religious imperatives known to him through visions and dreams (Schimmel 1975; Kakar 1982; Ewing 1990b).

As is customary, the *shaikh's* sayings (*malfuzat*) and deeds have been of enormous importance to an inner circle of close disciples. They have repeatedly tried to gather some of the key narratives documenting his life and miracles into a 'book' to be printed and widely circulated, but the *shaikh* has always withdrawn his permission at the last moment, offering no explanation. As a man who continuously stresses the infinity of his generosity, abundance and knowledge, it seems likely that he is reluctant to be reified and contained in the finite confines of an object-book. As we shall see in chapter 12, this rejection by him of all written texts came in the end to represent a serious anthropological dilemma. In similar vein he allows no pictures of himself to be circulated, fearing people may 'worship' his circumscribed image. His charisma thus remains personal and immediate, actively flowing from his very presence, and the legends about him are circulated by word of mouth. As a result, many different versions exist of the same landmarks in his saintly career. His disciples exchange these narratives, citing authorities who were 'there' to prove that the version they know is the correct one, while simultaneously believing and embracing all the different versions which are, in any case, concrete details aside, mere structural variations of each other.

After the *'urs* in 1989, I sat with some of the *shaikh's* devoted disciples in the summer house at the lodge. The disciples had written a short biography of the saint and the lodge, a copy of which they presented to me. I refer to this document as the 'official version' (O.V.). Sitting in the summer house, surrounded by lush greenery and the buzzing of insects, they tried to reconstruct for me the biography of the *pir*.

LINEAGE

> Pir Hazrat Shah Sahib, known as 'Zinda Pir Sahib', was born to Pir Ghulam Rasool Shah Sahib Akhwandzada in Jangal Khel, Kohat, who was himself a *khalifa* of Hazrat Adde Sahib (Swat). Pir Sahib [Zindapir] belongs to the family of Hazrat Khwaja Nizamuddin Ghaznavi (Afghanistan), a great saint. Pir Sahib Zakori Sharif (Dera Ismail Khan) also comes from the same family. Khwaja Nizamuddin Ghaznavi himself descends from the family of Hazrat Abu Bakr Siddique (may Allah be pleased with him), the first Caliph of Islam. (O.V. p. 1).

As we shall see, some of these details were later disputed and remained shrouded in ambiguity throughout the rest of the research. Zindapir's closest disciples had constructed a 48-generation genealogy of Zindapir but this was later rejected by the saint. Zindapir's patrilineal grandfather, Pir Sana Barsha, was said to have a shrine in Kohat, as does Mullah Ibrahim, an agnate five generations from Zindapir Sahib himself (see Figure 4.1, p. 64). The apical ancestor of the Kohat *khel* (lineage) was Azam Din. Azam Din's father was Nizamuddin Ghaznavi of Afghanistan, mentioned in the official version. Nizamuddin's father, Dalil Baba Al Maru Shaikh Nurani Sahib, also has his shrine in Afghanistan. Beyond Nizamuddin the genealogy takes the form of a simple line of pedigree including 37 or 38 names leading to Abu Bakr, the first Rightful Caliph and Companion of the Prophet.[1]

Zindapir's innate heritage of divine grace from his family is indicated in a tale told of a close relative of the *shaikh*. When the *shaikh* was a

---

[1] Descent from Abu Bakr is common among Naqshbandis.

young boy, his paternal grandfather's brother's son, Abdullah, was a
faqir at Jangal Khel. His power was revealed by the miraculous fact that
the jackals never damaged his cornfields. Zindapir Sahib, the researchers
told me, would visit him regularly as a boy to talk about his family background, having found out that his ancestors had moved from Arabia and
Afghanistan to Pakistan in order to spread Islam. He wished to emulate
his forefathers.

The family of Zindapir, the disciples told me, had lived in Jangal Khel
for seven generations. His father was a practising saint who migrated to
Delhi, India, where it is believed that his *mazar*, grave, is located. He left
his family, never to return. He had five sons and two daughters. He never
came back to his village; I was told, 'just like the *pir* himself'. The father
of Pir Abdul Latif Zakori of Dera Ismail Khan, another shrine in the
Frontier, died when his son, the present incumbent *pir*, was very young.
Hazrat Shah's father took his place and was the *gaddi nishin* for some
time, until the boy grew up. It was then he left home and went to India.

On my visit to Pakistan in 2000 I was told that one of Zindapir's half-
brothers had paid a surprise visit to the lodge. It emerged from his tale
that Zindapir's father had migrated from Delhi to Ajmer, remarried and
fathered several more children. One of the sons had heard of the fame of
Ghamkol Sharif and had come from India to visit it.

THE SAINT'S SPIRITUAL GENEALOGY

The official version prepared by the disciples continues: Pir Sahib is the
last disciple of the last *khalifa* of the great Naqshbandi saint, *Khwaja-e-
Khwajagan* (Master of Masters) *Ghaus-e-Zaman* (the 'Sustainer', highest
ranked saint of his time), *Mujaddid-e-Waqat*, (the 'Renewer of the Era'),
Hazrat Khwaja Muhammad Qasim Sadiq, popularly known as Babaji
Mohrvi Sarkar, *Darbar*-e-Alia Mohra Sharif, in the Muree Hills. Hence,
the official version continues, '*Darbar*-e-Alia Ghamkol Sharif becomes
more elevated and unique in status with the dual relation to its origin
(both genealogical and spiritual), i.e. to Hazrat Abu Bakr Siddique (May
Allah be pleased with Him).'

The *silsila* ('chain' of Sufi teacher-disciples) of Zindapir is printed in
different forms and displayed in framed pictures in several key rooms in
the *darbar*. The saint's vicegerents (*khulafa*) and disciples also possess
copies of this *silsila* in its poetic form, praising the lives and qualities of
Naqshbandi *shaikhs* (see pp. xiii–xvi). The poetic rendition of the order's

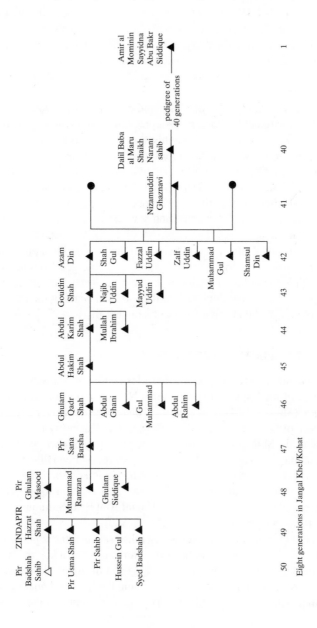

Figure 4.1: Disputed agnatic descent (*shajara nasb*) of Hazrtat Shah, indicating main descent groups in Jangal Khel, Kohat, and pedigree line to Abu Bakr, the Prophet's first companion (a second version leads to Ali, grandson of the Prophet)

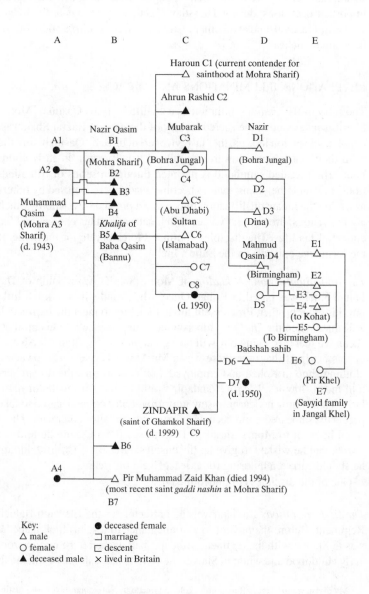

Figure 4.2: Affinal relations of Zindapir

silsila, reproduced here in the opening pages of the book, is recited on all important occasions, during Thursday night *zikr* meetings at the lodge, on the *'urs* festival, and at all other festivals held at the *darbar* or in one of its many branches.

REVELATIONS, ILLUMINATIONS AND MIRACLES

The story of the *shaikh*'s initiation as a khalifa by Baba Qasim of Mohra Sharif is a key one in the sacred history of the *darbar*. Hazrat Shah was, the official version tells us, the 'last' vicegerent of Baba Qasim before the saint died, but his path towards sainthood was foreseen in early childhood. His revealed sainthood is narrated through a series of 'illuminations' in which the young man to become a saint is recognised by others as having the innate qualification to become a *pir*, and 'revelations' which are the visions, dreams and voices which determined his choices and the course of his life.[2] The disciples continued to elaborate for me some of the formative episodes in the Saint's life.

The first illumination. A *khalifa* of Mohra Sharif, *Faqir* Sahib of Daj Ismail Khel, was based in Kohat. Once, when Zindapir was still a little boy, his elder brother, Pir Hussein Shah, took him to meet the *faqir* sahib at Kohat. When the *khalifa* sahib saw the young boy he told his brother: 'I can see that this young boy will be a great *faqir* in the future. Take care of this boy!' At that time there was a Mr Anwar Hussein who owned a clothing shop in Kohat, and employed a tailor who was, the researchers told me, a 'low-level *faqir*'. Zindapir would go to visit this tailor regularly. This is how he learnt to sew uniforms. Later on he decided to take part in the same trade, and became an army master tailor-contractor. Then, when he went to Mohra Sharif in 1942 to see Baba Qasim, he told the *shaikh* that he wished to give up his business. But Baba Qasim told him he should carry on tailoring for at least five more years.

One of the disciples continued the tale.

The first revelation. Zindapir was a contractor for the Eleventh Baluch Regiment. Before the *bai'at* (vow of allegiance to a saint) took place he was in Sialkot with the regiment. Zindapir had wished to be a *faqir* from early childhood and while in Sialkot, he went to see a shrine of Imam Ali

---

[2] My classification here differs a little from that made by Sufis themselves who distinguish between miracles (*karamat*), inner visions (*kashf*) and divine revelations (*ilham*).

Ul-Haq, an illustrious Sufi saint, and entered into *chilla* (forty day seclusion). He stayed in the *darbar* for eight days in order to ask where he should go to do *bai'at*. It was there that the Imam was revealed to him and told him he should go to Mohra Sharif. It was in response to this revelation that he went to Mohra Sharif.

The second revelation. Zindapir went to Mohra Sharif. He says that before going to Imam Ali Haq's *darbar* he had never considered going there. At the time he went to Mohra Sharif, Baba Qasim was a very old man, and he was no longer accepting *bai'at*. His son, Pir Nazir Ahmad Qasim, had taken over from him (Figure 4.2). The son of Nazir Ahmad, Gulbad Shah, took Zindapir to his father, Nazir, who was the *gaddi nishin* of Mohra Sharif. Zindapir entered Pir Nazir's inner sanctum with various other supplicants. The other supplicants took *bai'at* but Zindapir just stood there. While he was standing there, he says, he heard a voice in his right ear. The voice told him that he should give *bai'at* to Khwaja Qasim, not to his son, Pir Nazir Ahmad. The *shaikh* says he looked around but he could see no one who could possibly have spoken. So he left the room. This was the second revelation.

The second illumination. The *pir* of Bohra Jangal, Pir Mubarak (his brother-in-law) was at Mohra Sharif at the time. Zindapir told him he would not give *bai'at* to Pir Nazir sahib but only to Pir Nazir's father, the great *shaikh* himself. When he heard this, Pir Mubarak went in to see Baba Qasim, his grandfather, and told him that there is a man outside, Hazrat Shah, who would like to give *bai'at* to him. Baba Qasim called Zindapir in to see him and received his *bai'at*, and, at the very same instance, he also gave him the *khilafat* (vicegerency). This was the second illumination: the instant recognition by Baba Qasim of the supreme spiritual qualities of Hazrat Shah, and the passing to him of the power of sainthood in a matter of seconds.

Was Hazrat Shah already a *faqir*? Of course. If he had not been such a good person, he would not have been sent to Mohra Sharif from Sialkot.

The third illumination. In reality, this illumination preceded the second told here in time. There is a story, which I heard several times on other occasions, told about Zindapir and Baba Qasim, which happened before he became a disciple. At that time Zindapir used to visit Mohra Sharif. He was standing among a group of men when Baba Qasim came out of his room. He looked directly at him (although he did not know him at the time), pointed to him and said: '*Is larke ki chabi men bahut rotiyyan hain.*' (I can see that this young man's *chapati* basket will be full of food). This sentence is interpreted by the *shaikh*'s disciples as signifying that Zindapir was singled out by Baba Qasim, who recognised instantly, without knowing him, that he would be a *shaikh* of enormous stature, the *ghaus* or *qutb-e-madar* (Axis Mundi) of his time, and that his *langar* would be the most generous of all.

The formal chain of *pir-murids* and the continuity it implies is celebrated on every '*urs* festival and objectified in the reading of the *shajara sharif* on all ritual occasions, but is rarely dwelt upon by the *shaikh* himself. It was only in response to a direct question that he spoke of Baba Qasim. I asked the saint what he had learnt from Khwaja Muhammad Qasim, his predecessor and teacher? 'What I know, I know from God,' he replied. But, I persisted, could he say what the saint had taught him? He learnt many things, he said. Was he also generous? 'Yes', he replied, 'His generosity was like a strong wind (*tez hava ki tarah*)'. This marvellous image encapsulates, as we shall see, all that the saint values most.

It was during his time as a master tailor-contractor for the (British) army that Zindapir first established himself as a saint. It was here that his first public saintly miracle occurred.

The first karamat[3]. The Eleventh Baluch Regiment had its headquarters in Abbotabad, although the regiment was regularly transferred from place to place. There came a time when the regiment was stationed in Qazi Bakr in Gujrat, and during its stay there, Zindapir would go outside the regiment's perimeter fence, and pray on the banks of the canal every night. The second-in-command of the regiment, Major Iqbal, lived near the base and one night he went home to see his relatives. As he was passing the canal he saw someone, dressed in a white *chaddar* (sheet) praying, and he recognised the man. When he returned from his visit home, he

---

[3] This tale, like many of the others presented here, was told in English, and my account is constructed on the basis of my notes. All the morality tales told by Zindapir were in Urdu and were translated orally into English at key intervals. I was not allowed to tape these tales or to take notes in the saint's presence, and had to recapitulate his narratives directly after our lengthy meetings. However, he told the same tales, almost verbatim, again and again. The final supplication made by the saint was recorded on tape for two years running and translated in full into English. Most legends about him were told in English by disciples, a few were told in Urdu, often in casual conversations recorded by me later in notes and reconstructed here. The 'official' typewritten account is in English.

found an order awaiting him from headquarters, transferring him to Quetta in Baluchistan. Major Iqbal did not want to go to Quetta so he went to see Zindapir, and asked him to pray, to say a *du'a* for him, beseeching Allah that he should not be transferred. To his request Zindapir responded: 'Why come to me? I am only a tailor. Don't disturb me and let me get on with my work!' Major Iqbal said: 'If you don't say a *du'a*, I shall tell the whole regiment that you are a *pir*.'

Until this time Zindapir Sahib had kept the fact that he was a saint, and that he performed *zikr* by the canal every night, a secret. Zindapir said to the major: 'Don't tell anyone. Just collect your luggage from the railway station and come back here.' There was only one train a day from Gujrat to Quetta, but Major Iqbal collected his luggage and missed that train. The very same evening he received a telegram from his general headquarters in Rawalpindi, announcing that he had been promoted to a lieutenant colonel and that his transfer was cancelled. Instead of him, the previous colonel had been transferred to Quetta.

All these things, his closest disciples told me, have been confirmed by the *shaikh*, they are told by the Pir Sahib himself.

This first *karamat* by Zindapir took place after he had taken *bai'at* at Mohra Sharif, and, it was thought, after Partition in 1948. Baba Qasim died in 1943. Between 1942, when he took *bai'at* and became a *khalifa*, and 1948, he kept the fact that he was a saint a secret and practised in secret, I was told. Yet he already had many disciples inside the unit, like Sufi Sahib, the incumbent *khalifa* and saint in Birmingham. It is said that he performed his first *'urs* in Abbotabad in 1947 (hence the forty-fourth *'urs* took place in 1991). But this was his first public *karamat*, and the news of it spread through the army like wildfire, so he became known as a great *pir*.

The story of this first *karamat* made Zindapir famous and there are many variations of it, each as detailed and replete with circumstantial facts as the others. According to one variation, which I heard from several persons in Islamabad, the saint was asked by the major to sew him a uniform. When he came to collect his uniform he found that Hazrat Shah had sewn him a colonel's uniform. He complained: 'I asked you to sew me a major's uniform. Why have you sewn a colonel's uniform instead?' Zindapir insisted: 'Take the uniform.' That very evening the news came from headquarters that the major had been promoted to a colonel.

Although this is not the authoritative version, it points to Zindapir's fame throughout Pakistan, and the knowledge that he had become a great *pir* while serving in the army.

Another version, with an impeccable line of authorities (*isnad*), was told to me by a person who had heard it from Sufi Sahib and, with slight variations, by another early disciple, now a retired brigadier. According to the first of these two versions, Sufi Sahib and Hajji Mustafa, two of the saint's earliest and most loyal disciples, were sergeant and sergeant-major in the unit in which Zindapir was a tailor-contractor. The commanding officer of the regiment was transferred and the second-in-command, a major, was notified that a colonel who would arrive the next morning and take command of the regiment would replace him. The arriving colonel had been the major's junior and he was thus very upset by the news. He discussed his predicament with his trusted NCOs, Sufi Sahib and Mustafa, and they advised him to go to their *shaikh*, but not to tell the *shaikh* who had sent him. They gave him detailed instructions on how to behave. When he arrived at the *shaikh*'s tent he asked to be let in and the *shaikh* invited him in. The major entered and closed the tent flaps behind him as he had been instructed to do. He sat down on the ground in front of the *shaikh*. Then he said: 'I have a request but first you must promise to fulfil it.' The *shaikh* replied, 'Whatever do you need from me? I am a mere contractor!' The major said: 'I know that you are a *shaikh*.' So Zindapir, seeing the major was very upset, promised to fulfil his request. Then the major asked him to pray for him. The *shaikh* prayed a *du'a*. The next morning a telegram arrived from headquarters informing the major that the colonel had been transferred elsewhere and that he had been promoted and was to take command of the regiment.

According to the second version of this account, the major sat in Zindapir's tent for three hours, until the telegram arrived.

The second karamat. In another army 'miracle' tale, also attributed to Sufi Sahib, Zindapir was asked to sew uniforms for the regimental brass band which had been selected to represent the Pakistan army in a brass band competition of Commonwealth nations which was to perform in England before the king. This was in 1949. On the evening before the final inspection parade the uniforms were not yet ready. When he discovered this, the colonel in charge became agitated and accused Zindapir of failing to fulfil his contract. But the saint merely locked up shop for the night and went home. The following morning all the uniforms were ready and pressed, brass buttons shining, ranks, braids and names all in place, perfectly fitted. The commanding officer who arrived to inspect the band was duly impressed, and heaped praise on the regiment.

Hazrat Shah, I was told, did not call himself Zindapir at that time. But there were five or six living saints who died around 1940, and no one succeeded them (Mohra Sharif, Muree; Alipur Sharif, Sialkot; Shekhupura Sharif, Shekhupura; Jalalpur Sharif, Jhelum; Golra Sharif, Rawalpindi; Idgah Sharif, Rawalpindi). He was the only real saint left so people started calling him 'Zindapir'.

We see here a series of meetings with key holy men, visions, voices and finally a *karamat* concerning a superior army commander, all leading up to the *shaikh*'s emergence as a living saint. His innate qualities were recognised by *faqirs* and saints, both as a child and as a young man. He sought to be a *faqir* but visions guided him as to where to go and whom to turn to. In the course of this legendary early life, some of the moral themes guiding later events in his life emerge: he is the great feeder, the beneficent nurturer and infinite giver; and in confrontation with secular power and authority he always emerges supreme by virtue of his spiritual power. The tales thus weave the specific and the paradigmatic into a single authoritative tapestry.

Both the themes and the teleological development of his career continue in the next episode in his life. Here I return once more to the official version, only correcting dates when necessary.

Hijra: the founding of Ghamkol Sharif

The third and fourth revelations. 'Pir Sahib proceeded to perform his first Hajj in 1951 from Abbotabad, following a specific call (*basharat*) from the Holy Prophet.' He says: 'When I was returning from Hajj, I prayed at Roza-e-Mubarak, the mosque over the grave of the Holy Prophet (Peace Be Upon Him), at Madina. I said: 'Where should I go and live?'

The third revelation appeared to Zindapir in Abbotabad. It was a mystical vision seen during meditation, *muraqaba*. He heard the voice of the Prophet at night, and the voice instructed him to 'Come and see me [i.e. the Prophet].' So he took leave from his job with the army to go on Hajj. This was in 1951. In those days the trip to Mecca was an arduous journey by ship, lasting several weeks. At Medina, Zindapir Sahib himself told me, while he was praying at the Prophet's grave he saw in his vision a sign: 'Ghamkol Sharif' alongside another sign, 'Kohat', plainly written. He also saw a vision of the place where the *darbar* is now located, though he had never been to that place before. (The *darbar* is located about a

mile-and-a-half outside his natal village, Jangal Khel, in a little valley of
low trees surrounded by bare hills.)

According to one version of this story, a vision appeared before his
eyes while praying and a voice told him to go to that place. Still he did not
understand. Then a verse from the Qur'an appeared: 'You should sit on
this stone' and besides it a further sign inscribed with the words 'Ghamkol
Sharif'. No one, according to one of his *khulafa*, knows what these words
mean, not even the *maulvis*. But he was given this name by the Prophet
(P.B.U.H.). In fact, 'Ghamkol' is mentioned as the name of one of the
passes to the valley of Kohat in an early British survey, *circa* 1900, but for
disciples, this historical detail would be unlikely, in any case, to diminish
the force of prophetic revelation. This was the fourth revelation.

The fifth revelation. On his voyage home by ship, he felt that his right
arm had extended so far that it reached out into other countries and many
people were under his hand. So he knew that his followers would come
from many countries beyond Pakistan—from China, Africa and England.

The year 1950 was one of tragedy in the life of the *shaikh*. According
to his son, his wife and one-year-old daughter both died that year, and he
was left with a four-year-old little boy. The life and career of an ordinary
mortal might well have been affected by such a tragedy. A Westerner
might be tempted to think that he renounced the world in despair because
of this tragedy, but this would be to misunderstand the sacred historical
causality that, in his view and that of his disciples, guided his decisions.
Zindapir's life was determined by sacred revelations, not by personal
tragedies, and it was the vision he had in Medina that caused his next
move.

Yet he himself draws a symbolic contrast between two kinds of 'marriage'. Repeatedly, he stresses his credo of world renunciation as captured by the aphorism: 'The world and religion [*dunya te din*] are like two
sisters. If you marry one, you cannot marry the other.' He adds that 'If
you turn your back to the world you will face God' (*dunya ki taraf pith
kare ton khuda ki taraf mun hota hey*).

By the time he returned from Hajj to Abbotabad, I was told, he had
decided to leave the regiment and his old life as a master tailor. He
resigned and spent only a few days in Abbotabad. It is said that when he
left, the whole of the Baluch Regiment came out to bid him farewell,
flanking the way from Abbotabad to Khota Khabr, several miles away.
The army provided a jeep and as he was driven along, the regiment stood
to attention and saluted him.

The third karamat. The story of his arrival back from Hajj is the subject of another miracle tale. This particular tale was told to me by a disciple who had known Zindapir in Abbotabad, and had risen to the rank of brigadier-general and later, secretary to the cabinet. The brigadier had not only accompanied the *shaikh* on his first trip to the *darbar* valley, but he continues to be his companion every year on Hajj. This was his tale:

'When the *shaikh* came back from Hajj I went to meet him at Rawalpindi railway station. I expected a greeting party of about fifty people so I made arrangements to have food prepared for fifty. When we arrived at the station we found that 600 people had turned up to greet the *shaikh*. I was very worried about the food, but when the *shaikh* arrived he told me: "Don't worry! Dish it out!" So I just dished it out as he had told me to, and the food was enough for all the people there, with a little left over.'

Shortly after his return to Abbotabad, Zindapir went to visit Jangal Khel, his natal village. Some say there was a death in the family of a close relative, possibly a brother. He spent some time at Jangal Khel, living in the graveyard. Today there is a small mosque at the site where he stayed. I was told that after he had been there for several months, supplicants began coming to visit him and there was a great crush of people at the graveyard. So one day he quietly got up and walked away, accompanied only by a few trusted companions. That was in 1952.

The following account represents the central mythological episode in the *shaikh*'s achievement of sainthood. It is a tale of renunciation, poverty, patience and trust in God before the final achievement of divinely inspired knowledge, blessing and fulfillment.

The core myth

The fourth karamat. Zindapir left the graveyard on foot with his companions. One of his companions had a bag of flour. Zindapir Sahib, while walking, felt a burden. He turned back and saw his companion carrying the flour. He said: 'What is this?' The man said: 'It is flour to make *roti* (bread). It will last two-three days.' Zindapir said: 'And after that, what shall we do? Who will feed us then? Throw it away and we shall go in the name of Allah.' This morality tale implies a *karamat*: Zindapir and the *darbar* have never lacked food, even though he arrived in the valley empty handed. The source of the food is Allah Himself.

The fifth karamat. According to the story told annually by the *shaikh* on the final day of the *'urs*, the valley to which the Prophet sent him was inhabited by thieves and robbers (*daku* or dacoit) led by a famous robber, Ajib Khan. Wild animals prowled this wilderness. When the *shaikh* left his village, he took with him only a clay water pot, a jug for performing *wazu* (ablution) and a prayer mat (*musala*). He sat at the cave entrance where the robbers kept their booty. According to one version of the legend, the robbers began shooting at him but the bullets did not touch him. In wonder, they came up to him and vowed to reform their ways, and became his disciples.

In relation to Ajib Khan, a story is told about a British commander who led his troops on a raid of a tribal village behind the hills, raping the women. In retaliation, the dacoit kidnapped the young daughter of the British commander and kept her in the very cave the *pir* later settled in (this was before the *pir's* arrival). The daughter's name was Alice. The story spread and another *pir* from the other side of Kohat had the robber arrested and the girl released. There was a court case in which Alice gave evidence that Ajib Khan had treated her with great kindness, so much so that he was released without punishment. In 1988, it seems, Alice, now an old lady, came back to Kohat to visit a school friend. In interviews she gave to the media, she recalled the kindness of that famous robber-leader.

The tale of the *shaikh*'s journey by foot to the valley is told annually by the *shaikh*, as we have already seen, at the end of the *'urs*. Another version, told by the brigadier, tells of a more contemporary kind of journey:

'…it took us more than three hours, traveling by Vauxhall and jeep, to make our way to the cave. We had to build a road, fill the gullies, as we went along. When we got to the cave there was nothing—no trees, only small bushes. That night I just slept on the ground. Someone had brought a rolled up blanket for the *shaikh*. We cleared the cave for him. All he had was a Qur'an. The next day we went off. That was in October 1952.'

The first morality tale. The *shaikh* recalls: 'Colonel Sultan Ali Shah Sahib, district Khatib Kohat, asked me: "Did you come here all alone?" I replied that Allah Almighty was with me. "How can I survive alone?"'

The official version continues:

'Ghamkol Sharif was an unknown barren valley before the arrival of Pir Sahib, and it was impossible to pass through the valley even in broad daylight. The close proximity to the tribal area made the valley even more dangerous. There was no habitation. The valley of Ghamkol Sharif would not have been so greatly blessed by Almighty Allah if Pir Sahib had not come to live in it.' (O.V.: 2).

This is the tale of his arrival, told by the *shaikh* himself in his final sermon at the *'urs*. On his journey the *shaikh* encountered not God or the

Prophet, but the Devil himself, *Shaitan*, whom he must battle with before he can found the House of Allah. The reference to Satan appears, however, allegorical rather than actual. The sermon stresses once again that the *shaikh* was not a free agent—he was compelled to come to the *darbar* against his personal will, and yet at the same time, it required an act of immense will to fulfil the commands issued by God and the Prophet.

The foundation myth of the *darbar* is told year after year, with only slight variations, by the *shaikh*, his trembling voice audible in the absolute silence that descends on the congregation:

'To all the congregation and disciples present. It was not at all my wish to come to this place. [I speak the truth because] if anyone God has blessed and who is His *faqir*, if he tells a lie, it is just as if he became a *kafir* [an infidel, a non-believer]. A sinful person can tell lies but not a *faqir*. For a *faqir* changing his religion and telling a lie are the same. [So I speak the truth:] It was only the absolute order of the Prophet (P.B.U.H.) that I should proceed to this place. And if now this place is inhabited, it is due to the express order of the Prophet (P.B.U.H.). *Nafs* and *Shaitan* both said that I should not come here. There was not even enough water for a sparrow (*chirriya*). Ajib Khan used to divide his booty in this area. There were not even trees here. The place was barren and arid. Only God was here. At that time the *nafs-shaitan* [devil in the soul/heart] did their best to stop me from coming here. They argued that the people are already my disciples and why should I go there? What is the need to go there? I told the *Shaitan* that I must obey the Prophet (P.B.U.H.). Then I offered two *rak'at nafl* [optional canonical prayers] and we set out on our journey from the graveyard. And during the whole way to the cave the *Shaitan* was trying his best to betray us, to tell us we should not go ahead. When I reached before the cave that was shown to me [in his vision in Medina] I prayed to Allah the Magnificent and the Merciful: "Oh Allah! I have come only for you here, and now I am your guest." And because of this infinite and absolute faith this place is established and fully developed. [Or, in his 1991 sermon: "With the grace of God, this place is more generous (*sakhi*) than any other."] I have not asked anyone for subscriptions or donations, and neither did I ask for donations to build the mosque and establish this place...'

'Nobody had bowed before Allah on this earth before I came to this place; even sparrows did not live here. When we came here there was water on the other side of the hill. I would like to narrate further that the people of my village came to me and they said to me that I should migrate to Bonapir's shrine which is on the other side of the hill, where there are already established arrangements, and plenty of water is also available there. I told them that I have come here only for the sake of Allah and I don't want to leave for the sake of water. And the water here is also brought here by Allah and we have also been blessed with water by Allah.'

This is a tale of successful overpowering by the Sufi saint of the Devil, on the one hand, and of wild animals, wild men and the bare wilderness itself, on the other. The way to the valley of the cave is thus a concrete embodiment of the battle of the *nafs*. The fact that the cave is located a mere two miles from his natal village, on village land, is regarded as irrelevant by his followers and does not obviate either the courage and arduousness of the journey or undermine the validity of the imaginative conception of the valley as a mysterious unknown territory, discovered by the saint following his vision of it in Medina.

This is the first phase in the core myth of the legendary corpus—the triumph over the soul, the inner *jihad*. The second mythic phase, following the achievement of *tawakkul*, is a period of total seclusion and isolation. This brings us to the sixth revelation.

The sixth revelation. After the *pir* arrived in the place he had seen in his vision in Medina, he secluded himself in a cave overlooking the present *darbar*, halfway up a hill, for three days and nights. This, according to the official legend, is where the Prophet first sent him. According to our guide, Saeed Anwar, the *shaikh* shut himself up in the cave for the period without eating or drinking. Then he heard the voice of God saying: 'I have not sent you here to close yourself up inside a cave. Go out to meet the people.'[4]

As mentioned, one of the caves has been preserved as it was. This has become a shrine and pilgrims to the lodge climb the hill and leave pledges of their requests in the form of pieces of cloth tied to thorn bushes outside the cave. From here the lodge and the valley below present an idyllic view.

For many years the *shaikh* and his companions lived in one of the three caves in the area. Many people would come to visit the *shaikh* and he preached to them from a rock outside one of these caves, just as his vision in Medina instructed he should do. To begin with, there was no water, so water had to be carried by disciples on donkey back over the hills from the spring at Jangal Khel, or by supplicants seeking the *shaikh*'s blessings. This brings us to the third mythic phase.

The seventh karamat: *the encounter with nature.* The most significant evidence for the power of the *shaikh* over the natural world is the transformation he has brought about in the lodge itself: from a deserted wilderness to a place of cultivation. The discovery of water in the lodge is represented as a miraculous gift of God and exemplifies this spiritual

---

[4] This event duplicates the life of the Prophet who also secluded himself in a cave before hearing the voice of God.

8. The cave where Zindapir spent the first three days at Ghamkol Sharif

power over nature. It was told to me by one of his first disciples and companions:

'There was a blind disciple at the lodge and he began to dig a well, just outside the mosque. Some people searching for oil came by. They had with them sophisticated seismic instruments. They told the *shaikh* that according to their instruments, there was no water there, at the place where the blind disciple was digging. The *shaikh* asked: "How do you know?" They answered: "Our instruments show it." The *shaikh* queried: "Who made the instruments?" They replied: "They were made by men." The *shaikh* said: "But the water here is shown to me by God." They continued with the digging of the well and found a plentiful source of water, enough to supply the whole lodge and all its visitors.'

Recently, an electric pump has been installed with a water tank high in the hill providing water pressure.

A different tale is told by the Brigadier:

'There were eight *charsa* [cannabis] smokers who were digging the well. They dug down to 39 feet and there they struck hard rock. A water diviner was brought along. He declared that there was no water there. But the *shaikh* said: "I know there is water there, running from the hill—this way down [pointing]. I know, because I have performed my ablutions in it [i.e. in a vision]." So I [the brigadier] said: "We can blast through the rock with dynamite." Which is what we did. The

9. The miracle of water: The pure pool outside the mosque at Ghamkol Sharif

water below was so abundant that it flowed up to 30 feet. That happened in March 1953 or thereabouts. The *shaikh* had lived in the cave for six months before the water was discovered.'

The brigadier added that the cannabis smokers gave up their habit and became disciples of the *shaikh*.

The discovery of abundant water concretises the final phase on the Sufi journey, the achievement of gnosis, *ma'arifa*. The *shaikh* knew of the presence of the water, had bathed in it ritually in his mystical vision, and its concrete discovery thus objectified the flow of divine knowledge and all that emanates from it: water, fertility, abundance, generosity, the concrete objectifications of divine grace.

The *shaikh* stressed repeatedly that no harm will come to his visitors at the *darbar* from the wilderness beyond its perimeter. There are lions in the hills, but they don't attack the goats, or disturb the lodge. There are snakes, but they don't bite, and if they do, their bite does no harm. The honey bees do not sting when the honey is drawn from their hive. The *shaikh* lives in complete harmony with nature. He explained that when he breaks his daily fast, he drinks some sweet drink and then pours the rest on the ground for the ants; he does not allow the killing of ants and the use of poisonous powder, he just puts flour over their holes so they change their place. This is because they were created by God and God listens to them. If you step on them they cry out. Once he made a sacrifice of a buffalo which was weak and then, instead of giving the meat to the people, the disciples threw it beyond the boundary wall of the lodge for the wild animals. There are doves above his room, birds of peace. He himself is a vegetarian.

In 1991 a new watering trough was built for the buffalo and cattle herd of the lodge, at the far end of its perimeter. Every evening the *shaikh*'s son fills the trough with water for the wild animals who come down from the hills at night to drink.

In line with his control over nature in its wildest forms is also the *shaikh*'s domination over the *jinns* who inhabit the wilderness. The hills surrounding the valley of Ghamkol Sharif are, the disciples say, full of *jinns*. They come down to the lodge to perform *namaz*, the five daily canonical prayers, at the mosque. They are all disciples of the *shaikh*. When someone comes here who has been afflicted or possessed by a *jinn*, the *jinn* leaves that person forever because it wants to remain in the *darbar* with the *shaikh*.

There are many different kinds of *jinns*, I was told: some are Hindus, some are Christians, some Jews, some Muslims. They are all followers of the *shaikh* and he has his *khulafa* among them who spread Islam to the others. They are capricious, wild spirits, unless harnessed by divinely inspired spiritual power. The *jinns* at the *darbar* guard its perimeter wall and make sure it remains safe.

Can the *shaikh* see them? Of course he can. He has been given the power and full protection of God and the Prophet. One of his disciples told me that he knew the *jinns* were there because he had heard them singing *zikr* at night in a special voice, coming from the hills west of the lodge, when everyone was asleep. He would call me to hear them. (Unfortunately, I forgot to remind him to do so.)

His ability to exorcise *jinns* also stems from his domination over the devil, and the whole hierarchy of devils. A person possessed or afflicted by *jinns* must breath in smoke from an amulet on which the five names of the devils are printed. According to the exegesis I was given at the *darbar*, the burning of the amulet causes the devils to urge the *jinns* to leave the person because they are burning and being consumed (by the saint's powers).

The healing powers of the *shaikh* are linked both to his control over wild animals, and of *jinns* who possess people. Many stories are told about this curative power. Once, for example, a snake bit someone in Lahore and the *pir* sent water he had blessed to him, which cured him instantly. On another occasion, I was told by a woman doctor, a loyal disciple of the *shaikh*, someone was bitten by a snake in Kohat nearby and was critically ill. A relative came to the lodge and the *pir* gave him, the messenger, water on which he had blown a blessing (*dam*) to drink. At that very instant the snake-bitten man in Kohat recovered. To cure is to change the course of nature. Hence the ability to cure is objectified by the *shaikh's karamat* in which he demonstrates his mastery over nature and his ability to affect the natural course of events, to see beneath the opaque surface of materiality, to anticipate or change the future. The ordinary causality which determines the ordinary lives of men or women 'in the world' is transcended by the saint, an individual endowed with divine grace. He can only achieve this transcendence, however, by placing himself outside and beyond the world, rather than in it.

This, then, is the sacred story of Zindapir, his arrival and founding of Darbar-e-Alia Ghamkol Sharif. According to the official version, Zindapir was born in 1910–12. He became a *khalifa* in 1942, at the age of thirty, while he was still attached to the army as a tailor. He is thus an 'army *shaikh*' and many of his most faithful *khulafa* and disciples serve or have served like himself in the army. He held his first *'urs* festival in Abbotabad in 1947. He left the army in 1951 to go on Hajj and shortly after this, in 1952, he founded his own lodge, at the proverbial age of forty. For the past forty years he has built up the lodge and his following throughout Pakistan.

The core myth of the *darbar* is that of a world renouncer. The legends about the saint's life focus on his self-denial and asceticism, his battle with temptation, the miracles he has performed and the encounters with politicians or *maulvis* in which he invariably gains the upper hand, and which are discussed in the next chapter.

The legends are of an ordeal overcome: when the saint arrived, there was no water, no electricity, no roads, no orchards, no cattle. Many remember those days and the wilderness as it then was. It has taken almost four decades of voluntary labour to build the lodge to its present state of perfection. This voluntarism draws upon cultural premises about religious service and sacrifice. It is these which have enabled the material development of the cult organisation, based almost entirely on voluntary donations, but conceived of as emanating from the saint's generosity and divine blessing.

A good deal of the building and construction work has been achieved in the weeks preceding the annual *'urs* festival, and in anticipation of it. The *'urs* is the moment when all the disciples gather together for the saint's blessing. It is also the period of organisational mobilisation and physical construction.

The first construction in the *darbar* was its mosque, and the official version describes the mosque in poetic hyperbole:

The grand mosque of Darbar-e-Alia Ghamkol Sharif is a manifestation of the magnificence of Islam. The construction of the mosque was done under the day-to-day guidance of Pir Sahib. It is so beautiful, balanced and symmetrical that it leaves a spectator lost in wonder. The beauty of the mosque is magnified on moonlit nights, and keeps onlookers spellbound. The call for prayer echoes from the carved minarets of the mosque in this barren valley, which fortifies the faith, gives satisfaction to the heart, and tranquility to the spirit. The voice of *afzal-u-zikr* [virtuous, gracious *zikr*], *'la ilaha illa 'l-lah'* remains continuously in the air round the clock. This very *zikr* has become the identity symbol of Darbar-e-Alia Ghamkol Sharif. By the sweet anthems of *zikr* and its attractive calls, lost people are drawn towards Ghamkol Sharif to renew their promises and adopt the straight path with new determination (O.V.:3).

Zindapir himself told me: 'Have you seen the *darbar's* beautiful mosque? It is all built by the faith in God, not by money sent from England or anywhere. If you believe in Allah, and do *zikr* and say—there is no one but Allah, there is only Allah, and Allah is [*Allah-hu*], then Allah will give you honour and respect [*izzat*], and the place you live in will be honoured and respected.'

KNOWLEDGE AND COMMONSENSE

The plots of Sufi legends are predictable and repetitive. At the same time, the coexistence of many versions of legends about the same saint, seen together, may generate surface factual inconsistencies and contradictions. It is, however, the fable that travels, and hence it is the impact of this fable that needs to be considered as it encroaches into quite different and distant cultural and economic environments.[5]

---

[5] I draw here on Said's notion (1984) of 'traveling theories', Becker's notion (1979: 217) that plots are prior to narrative as implicit knowledge, and Aristotle's notion of the fable as plot in the *Poetics*.

An understanding of the authority of 'nomadic' dominant narratives depends, critically, on a recognition that contradictory commonsense beliefs are not inconsistent through and through: *ad hoc*, unmethodical and contradictory explanations are usually deployed in the defence of paradigmatic 'theories', a core of *consistent* propositions which come to be naturalised and taken-for-granted and are, in being so, also commonsensical. The fan of secondary elaborations at the margins of such commonsense paradigms serves to defend and reproduce their coherence.[6]

This has practical implications: rather than merely adapting to different environments, a transplanted Sufi fable of perfection generates a powerful symbolic field wherever it encroaches. Like capitalism or modernity, Sufism is a distinct discursive formation which shapes the very cultural habitat and habitus it invades, while being authoritatively constituted by its everyday familiars.

In regarding Sufism as a discursive formation, I start from the assumption that discourses are not simply negotiated between equals, but are persuasively imposed in any given social context by the socially or culturally powerful. Although Sufi Islam in South Asia is the product of peaceful missionising, it nevertheless accompanied the Muslim conquest of India (see Gilmartin 1988). Contemporary Sufism draws upon culturally recognised sources of power. Such sources may be, as in the case of Zindapir, symbolic and non-verbal ways of bodily self-representation, through which a person marks himself out as an extraordinary, unique individual; an individual who is, simultaneously, an archetype of a culturally recognised category of similarly unique individuals.

Equally critical is the fact that discourses of legitimation, mythic 'charters', are grounded in valorised social relationships. The relations between Zindapir and his followers are extensions of other socialities. His disciples are not only *pir-bhai* (saint-brothers); they are also consociates in other contexts: many serve in the same army or police units, are employed in the same civil service departments, are workers in the same factories (both in Britain and Pakistan) or are neighbours and kinsmen living in the same villages, towns or cities. Continuing contact, migration and pilgrimage link these far-flung members. Equally importantly, members of each branch share relations of sociality and amity which transcend formal occupational relationships. Like Sufi orders in the Ottoman empire, Zindapir's regional cult has expanded through occupational

---

[6] This is a possible reading of Evans-Pritchard's argument (1937) on Azande witchcraft; see also Kuhn 1962; Horton 1970; and for a different view, see Geertz 1983.

channels. This means that both saint and disciples have a vested interest in the powerful continuity and legitimacy of saintly charisma.

It is, above all, the concreteness of the myths which makes them authoritative. Religious certainty stems from the embeddedness of a paradigmatic, structural logic (in this case of Sufism as world renunciation) in the indexical particularities of place, time and person (Ewing 1990b; R. Werbner 1989, ch. 1), and its validation through visible and continuing moral achievements (Lambek 1990). Hence, as I argue also in the conclusion, a global logic or common sense is valorised through its concrete localisation and embodiment in myths and effective demonstrations of power, morality, and social-cum-material investments. This emerges clearly in the legends narrating key turning points in the saint's life.

The moral message of all the different versions of the legend of Zindapir's emergence as a saint is the same: the saint's knowledge transcends place and time and as such, his authority surpasses that of any powerful warrior, ruler or bureaucratic order and is global in its reach, penetrating the inner hearts of men, the outer limits of the globe and even what is invisible or beyond normal human knowledge. Although the saint's lodge at Ghamkol Sharif is now the centre of his sacred dominion, Zindapir stresses repeatedly that he is merely a guest there, in the House of God. In abandoning his natal home in Jangal Khel and divesting himself of all his prior worldly possessions, and even of his name (few know his real name), he has, in effect, disengaged from any specific place or locality. He protects and nurtures his disciples wherever they are: working in the Gulf, living in Britain or serving in the Pakistani army. His knowledge is not merely signalled through an ability to foresee the future, see and control invisible *jinns* and other malignant spirits or know what is in men's hearts wherever they are; it is a concrete manifestation of divine grace, indicated by his power over nature.

In the mythic corpus, the most significant evidence for this spiritual power, *ruhaniyat*, has been the transformation the saint has brought about in the lodge itself, from a deserted wilderness to a place of cultivation.

The inconsistencies of detail found in the mythic corpus are regarded as quite irrelevant by the saint's followers. So too is the fact that the *shaikh* left the army and came back to his natal village just after the death of his wife and child. These events, from a Western perspective the likely cause of deep trauma and radical rupture, are regarded by disciples as irrelevant details. The fact that the valley is very close to his natal home, that its name was reported in the *Punjab Gazetteer* at the turn of the

century, or that the lodge is located on village lands—significant facts
from a scientific perspective—are regarded as irrelevant to the illumination in Medina in which the *shaikh* saw a strange place inscribed with an
unknown name, and was told by a voice that this would be the location
for his future lodge.

Equally insignificant, it appears, is his recent arrangement of a marriage between his grandson and a daughter of the most distinguished
Sayyid family in his natal town (see Figure 4). Such personal details are
not deemed to challenge his public denials of the importance of pedigree,
wealth, village connections, caste, or prophetic lineal descent. Few wonder why he refuses to discuss his own lineage in detail. (Despite numerous probes, I was never able to verify the genealogy first given to me. It
seems that the *shaikh*'s family are Sayyids, coming from a group of lesser
status in his village than the high status Pir Khel group, but there is some
ambiguity surrounding his genealogical descent, whether from Abu
Bakr, which would make him a Siddiqui, or from the Prophet directly,
which would make him a Sayyid.) Similarly, each of the legends about
him, like the tale of his first public *karamat*, are accepted by his disciples
as self-evident truths, even though, as we have seen, there are several
alternative versions of most of these central legends and these, empiri-
cally speaking, could not possibly all be true.

Seen together, the mythic corpus surrounding a Sufi saint can be analysed in processual terms as depicting his personal transformation as he
moves towards the ultimate achievement of gnosis and superior spiritual
authority (see Rao 1990). Even in the case of a living saint like Zindapir,
where mundane facts are known to many, and the less credible details of
the legends could (in theory) be checked or questioned, such a challenge
never occurs. This is because the beliefs generating the legends include
also the secondary elaborations which uphold their validity. Indeed, over
time, disciples' tales about their saint's miraculous powers multiply, surrounding the primary legendary corpus set out here with a further set of
secondary legends. Their personal dreams and visions of the saint, his
encounters with the Prophet or his empowerment of their lives, further
enhance his charisma.

Zindapir's tales and legends, repeated annually in his final speech during the *'urs* festivals, and in numerous conversations with and between
disciples, all serve to sacralise the voluntary labour and contributions
which have gone towards creating the *darbar*. Hence, we can argue more

generally that the symbolic and organisational unity of Sufi cults springs from the supreme value accorded to world renunciation and otherworldly asceticism in Muslim society. This unity is sustained by myths and legends which link key tropes: the divine predestination of the Sufi saint, his journey, central lodge, grave, asceticism, generosity, miraculous deeds, vast following, and supreme spiritual power.

The very uniqueness of the saint, proved in practice by his extraordinary asceticism, demands that his choices and actions, as embodied symbolically in the primary mythic corpus, be seen as transparently selfless and sincere. Above all, disciples insist that the humdrum, human, familiar motivations and aspirations which dominate the lives of ordinary mortals are quite irrelevant to an understanding of their saint's life. Personal tragedies or ambitions are both discounted. Usual yardsticks of judgement are suspended in favour of a world of teleologically inspired acts of supreme courage, selflessness and faith.

5

WILAYAT

AXIS OF THE WORLD

AXIS OF THE WORLD

The *shaikh* has arrived. He never leaves again. From this point onwards the nature of the legendary narrative changes. The first part of the *pir's* life was that of a traveler, a person seeking divine grace and guided by revelations. Once he reaches Ghamkol Sharif, the place where he has built his lodge, he ceases traveling altogether. He leaves his room only to perform *namaz* in the mosque or to inspect the preparations for the annual *'urs* festival. Otherwise he goes nowhere, not even to visit his son's house in the lodge itself, or his natal village nearby. His only visible journey is the annual pilgrimage to Mecca. He is a fixed point of stability in a fluctuating universe. People undertake pilgrimage to see him, to consult him about illness, to ask for amulets, medicine and *du'a* (supplication or benediction), to seek his advice, to participate in *zikr* meetings, or to attend the annual cycle of celebrations. Hence the tales he tells about himself from this point onwards are morality tales of encounters in the lodge or Mecca with the stream of guests, supplicants and pilgrims who visit him both daily and annually, and partake of the free sacred food (*langar*) provided at the lodge.

As he sits in his room, cross-legged, the saint's charisma is a tangible ambience, as my first encounter with him highlights:

We are summoned to meet the shaikh in his inner sanctum. The room is covered with a bright red elaborately patterned Persian carpet, and the *shaikh* sits in the right-hand corner, cross-legged and reclining, satin and brocade cushions piled behind him. A white *chaddar* flows over the saint's legs, creating an island of whiteness around him, and his head is bound in a white turban with a further white *chaddar* flowing from it and framing his face. He wears a *juba* over his white clothes.

It is the face, however, that draws the visitor to the saint. It is a striking face with high cheekbones, a long, aquiline nose, very light eyes and a wide, delicately carved mouth. Although he is not tall, his head is that of a large man. His long white beard is finely combed, but the most arresting aspect of the *shaikh* is his brightness, the mobility and expressiveness of his face, with its quizzical amused look or sweet, innocent, almost child-like smile. He sits very still, his hands unmoving on his lap, and now and then lapses into meditation. His voice is low, the voice of an old man.

Dividing the room in half is a low wooden barrier with a small gate in its extreme right. The women coming to consult the *shaikh* usually sit behind this barrier. He meets them in groups. Across the room, about six feet away, is a second pile of cushions and a space for honoured guests who sit, as I invariably did, facing the *shaikh*, within the enclosure. It is while sitting thus that he told me the morality tales which constitute the corpus of his teachings. These are the *malfuzat* which his disciples have attempted to record for posterity.

The moral tales or legends the *shaikh* tells serve to underline the spiritual power of a true *faqir* over nature or the wilderness, on the one hand, and over temporal and religious scholarly power and authority, on the other. Hence, the superior power of divinely inspired spirituality over the natural world, over temporal or secular authority and over 'external' religious knowledge is the common thread running through these morality tales. They are tales known to many of his disciples, and the *shaikh* tells them as exemplary stories to his visitors, including the anthropologist. I turn therefore now to the legends exemplifying the power of the shaikh's spirituality.

THE ENCOUNTER WITH TEMPORAL POWER

The saint repeatedly makes the point that powerful temporal politicians are forgotten after their death while the power of God's friends persists forever.

Some of the morality tales the *pir* tells about his encounters with powerful politicians and foreign dignitaries appear in the official version of the *shaikh*'s life, and some were told or repeated to me by the saint himself, in a series of meetings which usually took place late in the evening. In combining these tales into a single account, I have sorted them out thematically, in order to highlight the moral lessons intended by the stories.

Many high ranking visitors come to visit the *shaikh*, including foreigners. He stresses repeatedly that he treats all who come to him, *badshah* (king) or *garib* (poor person) alike. He asks no one his or her name. The current prime minister of Azad Kashmir, Sikandar Hiyat Khan, visited the *darbar*, he told me, for the first time when he was chief minister of the province. He came with a member of the national assembly, Sardar Mustafa, who had already visited the *darbar* several times before. Sardar Mustafa said to Sikandar: 'For the past three years I have visited this place but the *pir* sahib has never asked my name.' He asked the *pir*: 'Why is this?' The *pir* replied that 'When you remember the name of Allah you need not remember any other name.'

In this tale the *pir* stresses, as he does repeatedly, that he needs no favours from those who visit him. He is a giver, never a taker. Thus he commented on another visit:

'The prime minister of Kashmir came to me here, but I do not try to get help from ministers and such people, only from God. Everything else is *shirk* [infidelity]. People come to me from different faiths—Hindus, Muslims, Christians. They are all welcome. When the viceroy of India visited the shrine of Khwaja Ajmeri he saw all the people coming there—Hindus, Muslims, Sikhs. After his visit he said: "India is ruled by two governments—the British government and the government of Khwaja Ajmeri, and the second one is the greater power because it rules over people's hearts."'

Another morality tale of this type appears in the official version:

Once an uncle of the minister of finance, Mian Muhammad Yasin Khan Watto, came to *Pir* Sahib. He was suffering from a serious illness, and had returned from England, diagnosed as incurable. Pir Sahib cast *dam* on him and said: "Let him eat the *langar's* food and he will be cured." Once healed, the minister asked the *pir* if he could make him, the minister, his disciple, allow him to cast *dam*, and provide the food for the *langar* for three days. Zindapir said: 'You will provide for the *langar* for three days but what will happen after that? I cannot make you partner, *sharik*, with God. Nor will I make you my disciple or allow you to cast *dam*.'

The pretensions of politicians whose temporal powers, unlike the spiritual powers of a saint, are finite, are repeatedly exposed in these morality tales.

A similar tale was told by Rab Nawaz, a senior *khalifa* of Zindapir, after the saint's death.

'There was a very rich man who came from the nearby tribal areas. He arrived at the lodge with a lorry packed with sacks of bank notes. The *pir* told him he could not accept the money because it was false. The man protested that he was a businessman and had earned the money honestly. The *pir* said to him: "But you have

not paid *zakat* [an annual Islamic tax of charity to the poor, widows and orphans].
Take your money away and don't come back." The businessman never returned.'

Once, Rab Nawaz recalled, a minister of water affairs came to the
lodge to tell the saint that he had arranged all the permits for digging a
well and building a water tank, and that he himself would carry out the
work. Zindapir told his *murids* that the work would have to be completed
before the minister returned, so the lodge would incur no obligation to
him. Within eighteen days the building of the tank was completed, even
though it was a very large tank. By the time the minister returned, the
work was done.

In his encounters with politicians the *shaikh* presents himself as tough
and definite. Politicians who aspire to acquire some of his powers must
confront the fact that they cannot compete with the divine spiritual power
with which he has been endowed.[1]

The official version records the various dignitaries who have attended
the *'urs* festival or have come to seek blessings from the saint: the former
commissioner of Kohat, the former deputy director of intelligence, and
even the British police commissioner of Birmingham, who attended an
'urs festival in Birmingham. Others are mentioned by the *shaikh* himself,
or by his followers. Ayub Khan's sister and family had come the previous
year from Haripur, Hazara, with a convoy of fifty buses. They come
every year. On my second visit, in 1991, I was told 'off the record' that
the highest elected politician in Pakistan today had come to see the saint
before the elections and presented him with a cheque for a large sum of
money. The *shaikh* refused the money and suggested that the politician
eat from the *langar.*

As the official version puts it, 'Not only millions of people from every
nook and corner of the country participate [in the *'urs*] but also high military and civilian officials.' All these men come to seek the *pir's* blessings.'

Again and again the generosity of the lodge, its fertility and abundance
are stressed in the morality tales. Once the Nawab of Bahavalpur came to
the lodge and while he was there he asked for an orange. The *shaikh* gave
him two boxes of oranges to take home with him from the *darbar's*
orange grove. The Nawab said he was amazed to see how peaceful the
darbar was, even during an *'urs*; that no one was carrying a gun, although
in the Frontier everyone carries guns. (While the *shaikh* does not object

[1] For similar tales of encounters between Sufis and temporal leaders see Attar 1990;
Schimmel 1975: 347; Geertz 1968: 33–5; Gilsenan 1973; Crapanzano 1973: 30–56,
esp. 48.

to men carrying guns, he does not allow them to fire into the air during the 'urs, as used to be the custom, even as a celebration, because, he says, this scares the congregation. The fear became more acute since the war with Afghanistan and the presence of Afghan *mujahiddin* and a large refugee camp nearby.)

Once a chief of police, CIP, went on pilgrimage to Mecca. When he returned he said: 'In Mecca I was a nobody, but Zindapir was feeding thousands of people.' Again and again, it is the *shaikh*'s ability to provide nurture on a daily and annual basis to all who come, the infinite flow of nurture from an unending source, which makes it impossible for secular politicians to compete with him, and which proves that his following is much vaster than that of any politician. He told me: 'I do not worry where the money comes from to feed the people, I just believe in Allah.'

That Zindapir's fame has spread beyond the confines of Pakistan is made evident in another Hajj morality tale, told by a faithful disciple of the *shaikh*. Once, when Begum Zia (General Zia's wife) went on Hajj, she asked King Fahd of Saudi Arabia to introduce her to a great *shaikh*. King Fahd sent her to Ghulam Rasool in Medina, known by his nickname 'Biliwala' because he used to feed hundreds of cats. Biliwala said to her: 'Why have you come to me? There is a great *shaikh* here in Medina from your own country.' 'Who?' she asked. 'Zindapir. Go to Mecca, to such-and-such a place, and ask for him.' Now Biliwala had never met Zindapir, but the two recognised each other's greatness by their spirituality. Begum Zia found Zindapir's hostel in Mecca but the gatekeeper was inexperienced and did not recognise her. He told her the saint was resting and could not be disturbed. Then Sufi Sahib arrived and recognised the visitor. He told her to come with him and brought her in to see the *shaikh*. When he met her, the *shaikh* said: 'You did not come directly here, you were sent here.' She said: 'Yes, Ghulam Rasool sent me.'

We see here another feature of the *shaikh*'s relations with politicians and important civil servants or army commanders. While he will not accept monetary donations from them, he nevertheless treats these dignitaries with the utmost deference, deviating from his usual routines of fasting and meditation, and according them privileged and private access to him. Just as he denies the importance of these visits and asserts that he asks no one's name, so too, simultaneously, do the visits prove that he is indeed a great and spiritually powerful friend, *wali*, of Allah (on this Sufi respect for worldly hierarchies see also Ur-Rehman 1979, esp. ch. 4).

Yet there is no doubt that he has consistently refused to get involved publicly in political elections. God, he says, is not elected, and to become a Sufi you don't need to be elected. Politicians come to him and ask him for his support but he always denies it. Once, he told me, a local politician cheated in the elections and then, following his victory, came to visit him, the *shaikh*. The politician wanted to put two of his political opponents in jail. The *pir* said to him: 'Even though you were elected by cheating, now that you have been elected, you must work for the good of the people, and not imprison those people who are against you.'

'The politicians,' he said, 'come here for *du'a*, and I say a *du'a* for them, but they still have the thoughts of politicians—by coming to me they are making a demonstration to the people that they respect me, in order to gain their support.' 'Why don't you like them?' I asked. 'Because they tell lies [*jhut*].' I asked if he could see into people's thoughts? He said: 'If after the *asar* prayers [the third of the day] you say a sentence from the Qur'an, *surah ikhlas* [the third surah from the end] and repeat it one thousand times, you will know what will happen tomorrow.'

In another Hajj morality tale, Zindapir told me that there was a group of important dignitaries from Kohat. They were offered *langar* at Mecca for three days during Hajj but then it occurred to the *shaikh* that they might think he was offering them food because he wanted something from them. So he called them to him and explained that he never goes to Kohat so he needs nothing from them.

When General Zia convened a meeting of *shaikhs*, Zindapir was invited to attend, but he refused to go. Politics, he explained, was not the way of the *faqir*. So too Nurani, leader of one of the Barelvi religious parties, came to seek his support but he said: 'I believe in God and God does not need votes and does not get elected.' He gave Nurani 2,000 rupees (thus signaling the latter's inferiority) and let him go.

There was once a *shaikh* in Swat, I told him, who became a ruler during the British colonial period. He had not heard of this but commented that this would only be possible to protect religion, not for any other (secular) purpose.

Could a *faqir* not influence politicians to improve their ways? No, he answered, if it ever enters the head of a *faqir* to want to influence politics he is no longer a *faqir*. Later in our conversation, however, he returned to this question and told me: 'Once the Emperor Jahangir was brought handcuffed before the Mujaddid 'Alaf-i Thani. His captor told the Mujaddid: "If you like, I will behead him." But the Mujaddid instructed the captor to release the prisoner, while admonishing the emperor to mend his ways and believe in God and the Prophet.'

In addition to the morality tales told by Zindapir himself, several miracle tales of the encounter of the saint with temporal authority were told to
me by Rab Nawaz, his most beloved *khalifa*, poet and chronicler of the
saint. These were told after his death in 2000:

'President Ayub Khan created the Waqf department and someone, a general, was
sent from there to investigate where Zindapir got all his money from. It was sus-
pected that he was printing counterfeit currency. When the general came in to see
the *shaikh*, Zindapir told him to lift up the corner of the prayer mat in his room.
The general lifted up the prayer mat and immediately fainted. He had to be taken
outside. I was there with a group of soldiers. When he regained consciousness I
and my fellow soldiers [all *murids*], despite our lowly rank, were so consumed
with curiosity that we dared to ask the general why he had fainted? He told us that
when he lifted the carpet he saw convoys of lorries packed with money all moving
towards the *darbar*, and two streams running alongside the road, one of silver, the
other of gold.'

Clearly, this was the end of the Waqf department's attempts to investigate
the finances of the lodge.

If the authority of the saint is above that of temporal rulers, it also
recognises no temporal political, ethnic or religious boundaries. His tolerance towards members of other religions is stressed in many of the
morality tales he tells. He continually stressed that the 'true' Islam does
not discriminate between men of different creeds and faiths. It was the
Sufis, not the *'ulama*, who had brought Islam to the subcontinent.

WILAYAT: THE SPIRITUAL DOMINION OF THE *SHAIKH*

Critical to an understanding of the spiritual power and sovereignty of the
shaikh is, as we saw, his love for, and domination over, the natural world
and all that is in it. Paralleling this is his love and dominion over the
human world, including men and women of all faiths, from the poorest
beggar to the most elevated politician or the most respected of learned
scholars. The dominion springs from a single source: his faith in God, his
asceticism and generosity. Thus the morality tales about this dominion
over the natural and human domains are essentially interwoven, and I discuss this enmeshment below. The separation here of different categories
of morality tales is necessarily, then, an artificial one, for the sake of analytic clarity, but the tales need to be seen as a single, related totality.

The encompassment of all of God's creatures is also the basis for his
tolerance of non-Muslims. The *shaikh* believes that the true spirit of

Islam is tolerant, unificatory and universal, and that it is the learned scholars who have created divisiveness and abandoned this spirit.[2] His universalistic message was signified by constant references to God and the love of Allah, in preference to the stress on the Prophet or specifically Islamic symbols.

THE ENCOUNTER WITH FOREIGNERS AND NON-MUSLIMS

During my visits to him the *shaikh* continuously stressed that he expected no reciprocity from me for the generous hospitality he had extended to me. He will never be a guest in my house, he assured me. He treats me this way because I am a human being, *insan*, I am God's creature, for the sake of Allah, irrespective of whether I am a Muslim, a Christian or a Jew.

What is a *faqir*? A *faqir* is a friend of Allah. He does things only for Allah. Even if he is offered 100,000 rupees on the one hand, or to eat nothing for God's sake, he would choose to stay hungry. If a *faqir* loves the people, he only loves them for the sake of Allah, not for himself. It is like the fan in his room. Once an Englishman came from the British High Commission in Islamabad. He said: 'I have a nice house in Islamabad, full of comforts, yet I feel so peaceful when I come here. Why is that?' The *shaikh* replied: 'The fan is blowing cool air for me, but if someone is sitting in the room with me, he too will feel the cool breeze. So too Allah is here for me and you share in his light. Allah says that if you want to find me, you must first find my friend, you must find *mera banda* [my man, my servant, the person who does *bandagi*, prayer].'

The *shaikh* said that usually women sit behind the barrier where they cannot touch him. He never shakes their hand. Why not? Because it is *guna*, sin. But once a white woman doctor came from Islamabad and he shook her hand because she is a Christian (for her it is not a sin).

The *shaikh's* tolerance is repeated in many of the moral tales he tells. He explains: 'I respect all people whatever their religion because they are human beings. In fact, once a Christian came here and he was given food before the Muslims so that he would not think they regarded him as inferior.' An American came to see him and asked why Pakistan helped the Afghan refugees? The *shaikh* replied that Pakistanis and Afghans believe in the same God, and so too do Christians, but the Russians (i.e. the Communists) do not believe in God.

---

[2] I never, for example, heard him speak out against Shi'as either, although there had been anti-Shi'a riots elsewhere in the North West Frontier Province (Talbot 1998: 339–40).

Once, a team of doctors from the United Nations working with Afghan refugees in Kohat came to visit him. The leader was a Christian doctor, himself not a believer, yet later he asked if he could bring another doctor friend. All are welcome at the *darbar*, the *shaikh* said, irrespective of religion, and he treats them all the same: 'I gave the visitors food even though it was *Ramzan* and I myself was fasting. I said they should eat. I fast, but every person who comes here, rich or poor, gets something to eat.'

My own visit was an occasion to prove once again his universal acceptance and tolerance, irrespective of faith or creed. On the last day of my visit to the *darbar* in 1991 he called me to him and said: 'You have stayed with us for three weeks and during this time you have slept on a bed, in comfort. We know that you are Jewish. While you have been here you have seen many Muslims come and all have slept on the ground. Would you get such good treatment even from your own husband? And where else in the world would you find such peace? Nowhere!' On my departure, I was showered with gifts, including wild honey, perfume, suits of traditional clothing in the most exquisite fabrics, and gifts for my husband. As in the case of important politicians and civil servants, the gifts objectified the *shaikh*'s ultimate transcendence and the miracle of his generosity.

Zindapir stressed repeatedly that what he does, he does for the love of God and God alone. Some time ago a Japanese team came to the *darbar*, headed by a Mr Hiroshima, a famous climber who had conquered Mount K-2 in the Karakoram range of the Hindu Kush, the second highest mountain in the world after Everest. The team consisted of scholars from a Japanese institute with an interest in Sufism. They asked the *shaikh*: 'What is the significance of the dome on the graves of *pirs*?' The *shaikh* replied that the dome is only for *auliya*, friends of God, not for generals, heads of state or kings. It is a sign (*nishani*) of a man of God, a friend of Allah. On the occasion of this visit, Hajji Ibrahim, a devoted disciple of the *shaikh*, invited the visitors for tea, Japanese style, and spoke to them in Japanese. He had worked for a Japanese firm in the Gulf and he utilised his experience to entertain the guests in a fitting way. Thus each guest to the *darbar* is honoured according to his customs—an English visitor is provided with a bed, the Japanese with the appropriate kind of tea.

Once, the *shaikh* recalled, three young Englishmen came to the *darbar*. Two had already converted to Islam and one was converted in the *darbar* by the *shaikh*. When they met the *shaikh* on Hajj one of them put the question to him: 'Should I stay with my mother who is still a Christian, or leave her?' The *pir* said that he should keep on living with his mother and should serve her and take care of her. 'You should treat her with the respect due to her as a mother.' The Prophet, he said, told a man who had converted to Islam and whose father was an old man and a devout Christian: 'You should take your father to the church door, wait for him outside while he prays, and then accompany him back home.'

On the last day of my stay in the *darbar*, following the *'urs* in 1991, I went to bid goodbye to the *shaikh*. He looked particularly ethereal, thin and pale, his eyes darkened, and he smiled a sweet, innocent smile. He stressed once more that all he did was for the love of God alone and no one else. He knew I was a Jew (*yahudi*). If a Jewish and a Muslim woman came before a Muslim judge to be judged, and he put the Muslim woman in the shade, then the judge was not a Muslim. Muslims, Christians and Jews have the same God, but he, Zindapir, does not like the Russian Communists (in Afghanistan) because they don't believe in God. During *zikr* people mention only one name—the name of Allah.

By appealing to God, Zindapir transcends Islam to reach out to all people of faith. In doing so, he underlines his own transcendence, the reach of his dominion. He also asserts the difference between the mystic's knowledge of the inner truth of Islam with its broad, tolerant, universal message, and that of the narrow-minded *'ulama*. Thus, interwoven with the encounters with politicians and strangers are also encounters with the *'ulama*.

THE ENCOUNTER WITH RELIGIOUS SCHOLARS AND *'ULAMA*

Zindapir is greatly respected by the *'ulama* and there are many tales and moral stories exemplifying both this respect and his spiritual dominion as a Sufi *shaikh* over *'ilm*, the 'external' knowledge and learning, of the *'ulama*.

During the *'urs* festival I attended in 1989, a famous Egyptian *qari* (a cantor who is also a *hafiz*, who has memorised the whole Qur'an) came to the *darbar*. He came to give a sermon, intending to continue on his way to Rawalpindi, where he was supposed to give a sermon the next day in the President's house or mosque, but when he saw the lodge and all the people gathered there, he telephoned Rawalpindi to say that he would not be able to attend the meeting the next day, because he had decided to stay until the end of the *'urs*.

During the final session of the *'urs* festival in 1989, the first *qari* to recite was this *qari*, while the second was Benazir Bhutto's *qari*, Khushi Muhammad. Another *maulvi*, Aziz Ullah from Dina, gave the final sermon. He had given a sermon at the *darbar* some years before in which he had glorified the *shaikh* and extolled his virtues. Zindapir Sahib, I was told, was angered by this adulation and told the learned *maulvi*: 'You should talk about God and the Prophet (P.B.U.H.); these people already know about me!' Henceforth for several years the *shaikh* had refused to allow the *maulvi*, despite his reputation, to give sermons at the *darbar*.

The *shaikh* says; 'To be a *faqir* who pleases God one needs patience and endurance—*sabr*, not like Jama'at-i Islami [one of Pakistan's reformist religious parties]. It requires one pinch of salt as *'ilm* and the rest is all the flour [*atta*] of *'amal* [good deeds].'

I asked him about the Day of Judgement. He smiled broadly and said 'Ah, that is when the *faqirs* will have all the power, not the kings and *maulvis*. The tombs of kings don't get *izzat*; only the *auliya* get respect in their lives and in death their respect grows and grows... There was once a *shaheed* [martyr] of *jihad* whose grave was uncovered by chance. They found him still alive; he had turned over on his side and was covering his face. Once the *ziyarat* of a famous *pir* was dug up—they found his body quite perfect like on the day he died. How is this possible? These things are "above thought" [*khayal ke uppar*], beyond understanding.' He will write it all out for me, not as the *maulvis* explain it.

He said that the people who do *bai'at* with him, whom he receives *bai'at* from, want to have a connection with God. The hand he gives them is the hand of Allah. He cannot refuse them. He said 'Look at all these educated *'ulama*, some of them, even their wives don't obey them!' He quoted a *Hadith* 'God's *auliya* talk with the mouth of Allah, see with the eyes of Allah, walk with the feet of Allah, hear with the ears of Allah, hold their hands out with the hands of Allah. God said: "I become the hands, tongue, feet, ears of that man."'

The *pir's* credo, told again and again through different morality tales is summed up by him in the following aphorism: 'If you love God, the people [*makhluqat*] will love you; if you believe in God, people will start believing in you; if you remember yourself, then you cannot remember Allah.'

He told me: 'You have met A. [referring to a British Muslim "saint" who established himself in London, but had previously been a *maulvi* in Pakistan]. They are the *maulvis*. *Faqirs* are people who believe only in Allah and do not depend on people.'

He said that while undoubtedly God will send the *'ulama* to paradise, *jannat*, after the Day of Judgement, God gives the blessings of paradise to his *fuqara* (plural of *faqir*) on earth. This is shown by his ability to give generously of God's bounty to all who come to see him. On another occasion he told me that Abdul Qadr Jilani had once remarked that he did not want the Day of Judgement to come, even though he knew he would go to paradise, because it would mean that he would have to stop worshipping God. For Zindapir, paradise is already here, in the act of worshipping.

The *shaikh* said: 'A well-known *maulvi* from the Punjab, near Lahore, came to see me and asked if he could be my disciple. I said to him: "You are a scholar and when you become a disciple of a *pir* you will have to submit yourself absolutely to him." I showed the *maulvi* my white headscarf, this one here, and said: "If I say it is black, will you agree that it is black? But if you say, according to your knowledge, that it is white, then you cannot be my disciple." The *maulvi* accepted this condition and became my disciple, and later I made him a *khalifa*.'

At the end of my visit in 1989, having first overwhelmed me with gifts, the *shaikh* said:

'You won't find any *maulvi* who can give like this, only a man of God. There was a *maulvi* here for the *'urs* and I gave him 400 rupees and a white headscarf. A *maulvi* can't show you the path of Allah. If I give you all this it is not because I want something from you. I will never come to England. It is to make God happy. God does not care if you are a Muslim or become a Muslim. Tell me truthfully, is there anywhere in Europe where you could feel so safe and secure and peaceful as you do here?' 'You see,' he said, 'this is the House of God. You know it is the House of God because of the peace that is here.'

'Another *maulvi* asked me: "What is the difference between a *maulvi* and a *faqir*?" I answered: "A *faqir* knows that one *rak'at* [genuflection during the canonical prayers] is sufficient for the whole of a man's life" [the exegetic meaning of this is that a *pir* is so pure that he does not need to perform his ablutions between prayers as ordinary men do]. This particular *maulvi* was very learned, he had written many books. On a visit to London he said: "The sayings of Zindapir are so profound that I could write many books about them."'

By implication Zindapir's wisdom is above textual knowledge. The oral narrator surpasses the learned scholar. The morality tales prove that the *'ulama* respect the saint as a man of true knowledge and infinite generosity. Yet if these tales illustrate his refusal to recognise the rank and status of the learned scholars, in practice the saint treats these famous scholars as he does politicians and civil servants, with the utmost deference.

Although he did not dwell on it with me, I was told by disciples that the Tablighi Jama'at movement, which preached against *pirs* in the nearby Afghan refugee camp, was anathema to the saint. But he did not—at least in my presence—single out any particular group of *'ulama* for greater derision. It was the class of *'ulama* generally that he disdained.

Often, as I sat and listened to the *shaikh*, in the early evenings or late at night, during the long sessions in which he told these morality tales, groups of men would arrive in convoys of cars or vans to visit him. They would stand outside the entrance to his room, forming a semicircle and singing *zikr* while they waited. Sitting inside we could hear their haunting song, and the *shaikh* would say to me: 'Do you hear them singing? They are saying one Name, and one Name only' (i.e. the name of God).

If the love of God is the source of the saint's spiritual power, this love is transformed into a transcendent, unbounded love of humanity and nature, of God's creatures and creations. Herewith is contained the deep, hidden truth of Islam which the saint imparts to his followers, a truth which the scholarly sermons of the *'ulama* are unable to penetrate or capture.

Zindapir is thus a 'true' saint, a man whose spiritual dominion extends over *'ilm*, the 'external' knowledge of the *'ulama*, and over all forms of temporal power. The legitimacy of this legendary corpus, itself legitimising the *specific* authenticity of the saint, is grounded in a *general*, abstract, metaphysical, translocal religious theory, a theosophy of knowledge-power which is discussed in chapter 9.

CONCLUSION: THE COMMONSENSE STRUCTURE OF ASCETIC SPIRITUALITY

The weaving and interweaving of morality fables about politicians, strangers, Muslim scholars and afflicted patients by Zindapir all serve to exemplify his transcendence and elevation above ordinary mortals, his domination over nature, temporal power, 'external' religious knowledge, and a humanity which recognises no religious or political boundaries.

Through the morality tales surrounding his encounters with politicians and his rejection of their offers, Zindapir underlines his superior power and *izzat*, as objectified in the generosity of the blessed food distributed freely at the lodge (the *langar*). Yet the fact that these politicians come to him with bribes and offers serves to confirm his high status, while proving simultaneously his renunciation and rejection of worldly power and wealth. Similarly, scholars disdained for their narrow, superficial and divisive knowledge of Islam, nevertheless confer legitimacy to the intellectual profundity of the *shaikh*.

It is because he wishes to tell these tales of exemplary encounter without appearing to boast about his fame (thus demeaning his authority by making it dependent on worldly recognition) that the saint weaves different types of tales into a complex tapestry. If he tells of the visit of an important politician, he follows this tale immediately with one about his care for a poor orphan, or his healing of a nameless supplicant. The mythic narrative structure depends on the interweaving of different types of legends and morality tales, which, juxtaposed, deny the potentially subversive messages contained in some of the legends while stressing their moral lessons.

The most important validation of all the legends, myths and morality tales is the saint's extraordinary self-denial. He fasts all year round during the daytime, and manifestly has no personal desire for material objects or luxury food. He is said never to sleep and he prays constantly, day and night. Fasting is not only an important component of his mystical asceticism; it is also seen by his disciples as final proof that the legends about him are all true. He is a man who does not seek money, wealth or secular power, as imposters do. He is God's conduit for food given away in the *langar*, but he proves his own detachment, his world renunciation, by eating sparingly, and avoiding delicacies like meat, milk, butter or *ghee*. To emphasise this disinterestedness, he forbids the display of collection boxes in the *darbar*. His asceticism remains the cornerstone of his continued and expanding influence for, like the potentially subversive countermessages contained in the political encounters, the very expansion and development of the lodge also contains a possible subversive countermessage.

Disciples know, of course, that the *shaikh* has substantial property, several new cars, a large house, money to provide an education for his grandchildren, and so forth. But these worldly trappings are regarded as embodiments of God's grace, a divine blessing which proves that 'their' *pir* is endowed with respect and honour unrivalled in the land. Disciples gloss over his accumulation of personal wealth because he has shown that he personally has no interest in the world of consumer items. He proves this by the simplicity of his existence, his abstinence and bodily self-denial, and by his evident generosity and care for his disciples.

The *shaikh* asks for no money yet there is always enough. As he told me, so great were the quantities of food and flour brought as offerings (*nazrana*) by the pilgrims to the *'urs* festival that there was enough to supply the *langar* and feed everyone for half a year.

Although the saint is regarded as a great healer, this is not the side of his life he chooses to emphasise. The greatest *karamat* of his life, and one which he continuously refers to, is that of the *langar*. The miracle of the *langar* is constituted by his refusal to accept money from supplicants, rich and poor alike. Indeed, he often gives money to those in trouble. No one is ever asked for a contribution. There are no collection boxes at the *darbar*. And yet the *langar* is there in a never-ending supply.

The miracle of the lodge and *langar*, and the *shaikh*'s generosity, are arguably the miracles of deeply enshrined customs. The *shaikh* never demands. He has no need to demand, for he trusts in the flow of customary donations, of food and services, provided as *khidmat* for the sake of God. His absolute trust is repeatedly rewarded. Before the *'urs* festival volunteers arrive to work tirelessly providing labour for the sake of a communal project. During the *'urs* convoys of disciples arrive from all over Pakistan, bearing sacks of grain and beasts for offering and sacrifice. Cantors arrive to lead the prayers in Arabic. Learned scholars arrive to preach their sermons. Poets arrive to sing their praise songs (*na't*) for the Prophet. No one is summoned; no one is paid. Entertainment and intellectual content at the *'urs*, like the food of the *langar*, are donated. The abundance is created by followers and disciples.

Yet despite their practical knowledge of the effort they themselves have invested, and the contributions they have personally made, the disciples continue to regard this abundance as a miracle. In a sense they are right: it is the miracle of selfless custom observed repeatedly (by themselves, as well as by others) in a world where their experience has taught them that selfish interest, political manipulation, and greed reign supreme (see Lindholm 1990; Ewing 1991). The fact that this selflessness is inspired by the love of a Sufi saint proves his divine grace. He transforms ordinary selfish human beings (like you and me) into people willing to make enormous personal sacrifices, to work day and night without sleep, to dirty their hands doing the most menial and back-breaking tasks, all for no pay, but for the sake of a transcendent cause.

6

LANGAR

PILGRIMAGE, SACRED EXCHANGE
AND PERPETUAL SACRIFICE

PILGRIMAGE AND SACRED EXCHANGE

An important feature of pilgrimages, it has been argued, is that the symbolic transformations pilgrims undergo effect a sacred exchange between
two symbolic worlds, and mediate the contradictions between those
worlds (see R. Werbner 1989: 261–2; 296). During pilgrimage, pilgrims
shed their mundane persona, often through metonymic giving to the poor
or at a sacred site, while they return bearing symbolic substances imbued
with the sacred power of the ritual centre. Hence, for example, Huichol
Indians in Mexico go on annual pilgrimage to their sacred centre of
Wirikuta in order to return reborn and bearing with them the peyote
needed to revitalise their world (Meyerhoff 1974). In the Kalanga cult of
the high god of Mwali, the 'hot' ash of the old year is rubbed on the back
of a female klipspringer which is released into the mountains where the
rain washes off the ash, bringing coolness. Paralleling this act, Kalanga
adepts of the cult bring back from the oracle centre the dust they roll in
when 'tied' in possession by Mwali. The dust is only washed off when
they reach their natal homesteads, bringing coolness, fertility and prosperity to the earth.

A focus on sacred exchange in pilgrimage reveals the limitations of
theories which stress merely the experiential dimensions of pilgrimage.
Of these theories, that of Victor Turner on pilgrimage as 'anti-structure'
and 'communitas' powerfully captures an important dimension of the pilgrimage experience, while glossing over the fact that pilgrimage is a
highly structured process of metonymic (and not just metaphoric) transformation. The view proposed here is that pilgrimage is both 'anti-
structure' and 'counter-structure'. The counter-structural features of
pilgrimage refer to the fact that pilgrims expect not only to undergo a
spiritual renewal but a renewal of personhood through contact with the

101

sacred, and a renewal of community through the bearing of what has been in contact with the sacred home, into the structured mundane world. These transformations of personhood and home often require a highly structured and elaborate series of symbolic acts. Some of these acts may be in the form of transactions with ritually designated persons. Hence in Benaras, as Parry (1989) has shown, pilgrims must unload their 'sins' in the form of gifts to Brahmins before they can purify themselves.

This type of apparently interested exchange leads Eade and Sallnow to describe metonymic exchanges effected at pilgrimage centres as 'self-interested exchanges between human beings and the divine' (1991: 24). '...this market ideology,' they argue, 'embraces both the miracle and the sacrificial discourses' (ibid.). However, they recognise that

...lay helpers are enjoined to set an example in self-sacrifice to other pilgrims by giving freely of their time and labour [in the] spirit of the 'pure' gift...For a strongly salvationist religion...it is questionable whether the notion of purely dis-interested giving can be anything other than a fiction (ibid.: 25).

Hence, Eade and Sallnow refer to this type of sacred exchange frequently associated with pilgrimage as 'sacred commerce' (ibid.).

In the spirit of this interpretation, studies of Islamic pilgrimage have repeatedly stressed the intercessionary role of the saint who mediates between supplicants and God. Pilgrims make offerings at a saint's tomb in the name of the saint in order to return imbued with the saint's cha-risma or *baraka* (blessings, *barkat*), containing the curative powers and abundance they desire. This type of dyadic sacred exchange seems on the surface to be relatively simple, and has been explained as modeled upon supplicants' everyday experiences of secular power as being based on dyadic chains of patronage (Eickelman 1976).

Sacrifice more generally has also often been conceived of in relatively simple terms as a sacred exchange between man and god with the victim acting as mediator (Hubert and Mauss 1964). Subsequent research has, however, begun to explore the extreme complexity of the symbolic trans-formations involved in animal sacrifice as analysed in particular cultural settings (see de Heusch 1985; R. Werbner 1989: ch. 3; also P. Werbner 1990a: ch. 5).

The reduction of processes of sacred exchange in pilgrimage to mere dyadic interested reciprocity, however disguised, obscures the highly structured and complex set of symbolic operations which bring about the desired transformation both in the moral persona of a pilgrim, including his or her acquisition of the desired sacred substances to be taken back on the journey home, and of the community (R. Werbner 1989). Within this process, animal sacrifice is a key moment which has to be set in relation to other symbolic acts.

The present chapter argues that the *langar* at a Sufi saint's lodge may be regarded as a form of perpetual sacrifice which is a key symbolic moment of substantive or metonymic exchange during pilgrimage to a saint's lodge. As such, it structures both the routine organisation of the lodge and the wider organisation of the Sufi regional cult focused upon it. In its generative organising capacity, it also structures gender relations and makes women integral to the process whereby God's blessing is objectified at the lodge.

My interpretation of the acts of sacrificial service, and the act of sharing in a sacrificial meal at the lodge, also stresses the need to unmask a self-interested discourse in order to reveal the central experience of altruism and humanism which energises Sufism. My argument thus reverses a common sociological tendency to seek material interests beneath the surface of apparent altruism. In Sufism, a discourse of contractual market relations and patronage is used by supplicants to 'explain' their relation to the saint, alive or dead. Given an Occidental tendency to seek individual self-interested motives behind an apparently altruistic façade, this Sufi allegory of interested exchange may easily be accepted at face value, as a 'true' explanation of supplicants' motives. Similarly, the occasional unmasking of individual saints as exploitative charlatans or sexually promiscuous seducers of innocent female supplicants is seen as proof of the manipulative nature of Sufism.

THE HAJJ AS A GLOBAL TEXT OF MUSLIM PILGRIMAGE

To fully understand the Sufi *langar*, however, it needs to be understood in the context of other forms of pilgrimage and Islamic sacrifice, on the one hand, and the sacred exchanges accompanying such pilgrimages—of voluntary service, ritual substances, social identification and powerful blessing—on the other.

For Muslims the Hajj, the global pilgrimage of Muslims to Mecca, is the ultimate pretext for all sacred exchanges during pilgrimage. My research on the Hajj was conducted in Manchester through discussions with returning Hajjis who, in telling me of their journey in minute detail, relived the experience of the Hajj while reflecting, at my request, on its significance. Part of the same ritual pilgrimage, performed outside the Hajj month, is known as *Umra*.

10. An offering for the *langar*

Seen as sacred journeys, the counter-structure of the Hajj and *Umra*
rituals achieve the desired symbolic transformation in the person of the
pilgrim through a series of significant alternations and reversals in time.
Starting from Mina, the place of Abrahamic sacrifice, on the eighth day
of the month of Hajj, the pilgrims are moved back in time on the ninth
day at the valley of Arafat, which is both the beginning and end of time.
Thus I was told by a Qadiri *khalifa* in Manchester: 'We believe that when
Adam and Hava [Eve] were sent down to earth they met together near the
ka'aba at the Mountain of Mercy at Arafat.' One pilgrim thought that
Adam and Eve weren't sent down together. Adam was sent to Arafat, Eve
to another place. So they met at Arafat. This was the place where Adam
asked for forgiveness after he was tempted by the devil and ate from the
forbidden fruit.

But Arafat is also, as several pilgrims told me, the place of the Day of
Judgement, the end of time. The same woman continued: 'People go to
Arafat because Muhammad went there [remembering] Arafat. On the
Day of Judgement all the people will gather there. All the people will rise
from their graves and run towards Arafat on the Day of Judgement.'

The Qadiri *khalifa* went on to explain the link between Adam and Eve
and the holy *ka'aba*, rebuilt according to tradition by Abraham and his
son, Isma'il, after the binding of the son.

'Before Ibrahim and Isma'il there was just desert there [at Mecca], no stones or bricks. Then we believe that after they met with each other and, being forgiven by Almighty God, they needed a place of worship on earth. Almighty God had appointed the angel, Jibreel, to build a place for Adam and Eve to worship. And he came down with his angels and built a place of worship for them and their descendents. There was a house there but the society was not as today—the people were still living in caves. The house was demolished during the storm of Noah [the Flood] to the ground. But still its foundation was there. When the Prophet Ibrahim and Isma'il his son came there from Egypt, they received a revelation to build up this house again. The Prophet Ibrahim again prayed to Almighty God to guide him to the place where he should build the house. God instructed Jibreel to put a cloud upon that place and revealed to Ibrahim to dig around the shadow of the cloud. And when the Prophet Ibrahim and Isma'il were digging round the corner of the cloud they were amazed to find the foundation already laid down underneath. They stopped digging and raised the house there.'

The *khalifa* continued:

'We believe that the whole Hajj is Sufism—simplicity ...under the heaven—total submission. I went to practise Sufism there [at the valley of Arafat] even though the heat was quite intolerable. The sun burns the sins. The sun is like water: both bring purification. Over there you don't fast. People do eat but very little. Why is the night so powerful? At night [in the valley of Muzdaliffah where the pilgrims go in the evening after Arafat] it is quiet, there are no distractions. You do remember your children and family but no other love except the love of God and His Prophet. Naturally, on Hajj the attention is only on God and the Prophet, no one else.

'When we arrive at Mina we still carry the burden of the city. We perform five prayers at Mina (over the whole day). During midday at Mina we first experience trouble, difficulties, hardship, but we're still not very exhausted, we still have [physical] resistance. Then we perform the next prayer, and the next prayer. We wear only two sheets and roam almost bare feet (we wear rubber sandals). The next day we move to Arafat. This is the most important day and a test of one's faith because now you are living entirely without a roof over your head, food or any facilities. This is again Sufism, because now a person's spirit is free from all the dirt of materialism. The soul is becoming more and more powerful because over there people pray, they cannot cut their nails or trim their hair or their beards. They cannot make any physical changes in themselves. Just as when they were born and their nurse put them into sheets, and when they go to their graves they will go in sheets. Sufis believe everyone is equal—even a king is equal to others. King, slaves, and servants—all have the same dress.'

The sacrifice of the *'Id*, commemorating the binding of Isma'il by his father, Ibrahim, which takes place on the tenth day of the Hajj, after the return from Arafat to Mina, is framed by several encounters with manifestations of the Devil, who are represented by three pillars in the valley of Mina. The first encounter takes place just before the sacrifice. Following the sacrifice and the pilgrims' performance of the *Umra* ritual, there is a further, double encounter with each of the three devils.

This reversal of the original time sequence of the sacred qur'anic (and biblical) narratives is not accidental, in my view, but part of the process through which the pilgrim gradually sheds her or his sins by moving backwards in time, and becomes as pure and innocent (*ma'sum*) as a newborn infant. The pilgrim starts this symbolic journey dressed in two white sheets, likened to the shrouds of the dead, that is, at the end of life, but these are transmuted in the course of the ritual into the sheets wrapping a new baby. After the sacrifice commemorating the binding of Isma'il, the pilgrim's head is shaved or clipped and he is reborn as a new person.

The Hajj ritual is highly elaborate. From the valley of Arafat where the pilgrims spend a day under the baking sun, they move to the valley of Muzdaliffah where they spend the night and where they collect forty-nine tiny pebbles. Returning to Mina for the second time on the tenth day of the Hajj, they cast one lot of seven pebbles onto a single devil-pillar, that of Aqaba. They then perform the *qurbani* (animal sacrifice) and eat the meat. Finally, they shave their head or clip their hair (in the case of women). Once they have completed the sacrificial meal, they can put on their usual clothes and all taboos are lifted, except for prohibition on sexual intercourse.

On the eleventh day of the Hajj, following the sacrifice, the pilgrims move to Mecca to perform the Meccan ritual. This ritual, also performed on its own throughout the year when it is known as *Umra*, highlights the time reversal of the narrative even more clearly. The movement during Umra is from *tawaf*, the circumambulation of the house of God which is believed to have been rebuilt by Ibrahim (Abraham) and Isma'il after their re-unification; in the second phase, the pilgrim moves to the sacred spring, the Zamzam, which Hajara (Hagar) discovered had sprung from the heel of Isma'il as he lay wailing in the sand when they were banished into the desert by Ibrahim; here the pilgrims wash and drink the water; the final stage of the Umra is *sa'i*, the running back and forth between the two hills of Saf and Marwa which recalls Hajara's agonised running in search of water for her baby boy after the banishment. The movement is thus backwards, from death towards purification like a baby.

Having completed the Meccan episode, the pilgrims then return on the twelfth and thirteenth days to Mina once more for a final stoning—this time of all three devils. Altogether in the post-Meccan stoning, the pilgrims cast forty-two pebbles, fourteen on each of the pillars over two days. The pilgrims start from the pillar farthest from Mecca and end with the Aqaba pillar which is the nearest. In the original narrative, Ibrahim (some say Isma'il) encountered these three devils before the binding of Isma'il. During Hajj and *Umra* the multiple stoning of the devils (except for the first stoning) occur after the sacrifice, reversing the original narrative. Finally, the pilgrims return to Mecca for another re-enactment of the Meccan ritual. The Hajj thus lasts 3 + 3 days and is built on an alternation between the *Umra* ritual at Mecca and the Hajj sacrifice at Mina, each of which is repeated twice (Hajj/Umra/Hajj/Umra = Mina/Mecca/Mina/Mecca). Arafat is the place of exposure to the sun and intense heat. Muzdaliffah, which follows, is exposure to complete darkness, night. Arafat is said to be the holiest site and people believe that whatever prayer is said there will be accepted, any sin will be forgiven. They cry to ask for forgiveness, to purify themselves.

The Hajj is thus a moral allegory which can only be understood in relation to its sacred pretexts, the binding of Isma'il and the banishment of Hajara. The sequence of acts, moreover, brings about a series of identifications with exemplary persons. The key identifications elicited are two: with Ibrahim and the ordeal he faced in having to sacrifice his son; and with Hajara, his wife, and the ordeal she faced in wandering with her son in the desert, with no water to quench his thirst. The mythic narratives of these two exemplary persons are structurally identical. In both, a parent is asked to sacrifice his/her child for the sake of God without losing faith in God. In both, God intervenes miraculously at the final moment to save the child from certain death. The pilgrims enact this dual ordeal during the Hajj and *Umra*.

Islamic traditions stress the voluntarism of these ordeals: Isma'il knew in advance, pilgrims told me, that God had ordered Ibrahim to sacrifice him and told his father to obey God's will. Hajara too accepted the edict of God. Hence one pilgrim explained:

'Mina is where Ibrahim sacrificed Isma'il. The pillars are the places where the devil tried to stop him. The first devil was small, the second medium and the third large. Isma'il said to Ibrahim: "Tie my legs and put my face away [from you] so that the affection [you feel for me] won't stop you [from fulfilling God's will]."'

She explained about Ibrahim's ordeals that 'Whomever Allah likes most he tests more than others.' Hence Hajara was sent into the desert in order that water be found and the *Ka'aba* rebuilt.

The identification with a woman is significant. A woman pilgrim who had just returned from Hajj explained to me that the story of Isma'il and Hajara was very important to her as a woman. When she was there and performing *sa'i*, she said, she reflected on what an effort Hajara as a mother had made for her son. Just as all the pilgrims, both male and female, identify with Ibrahim, a male, so too they all identify with Hajara, a female.

The Meccan pilgrimage creates other key identification. Pilgrims invariably explain that they perform the Hajj in this particular order because this is the way the Prophet performed it, they are merely retracing his footsteps. When they visit Arafat, one pilgrim told me, they stand where Adam stood on Mt Jabal Rehemat to ask God for forgiveness. 'In Arafat Adam asked in the name of the *kalimah* [There is no God but God...] for forgiveness, so we go there to ask God's forgiveness for our sins.' 'The Hajj,' he continued, 'belongs to the Prophet Ibrahim as does the *'Id*. There are two *sunnat* [rules of behaviour based on the example of the Prophet's life as given in the *Hadith*], Ibrahim's and Mohammed's. It moves from Adam to Ibrahim. The Prophet did the same [when he performed the first Hajj].'

Although the transformation effected in pilgrims is fundamentally a spiritual one, nevertheless pilgrims return from Hajj bearing with them sacred tokens—bottles of water from the holy spring, the Zamzam, as well as dates, rosaries and shawls. They sprinkle this water on people back home, spreading the blessings they received (for similar metonymic transfer in Turkey see Delaney 1990: 520).

One woman pilgrim told me:

'When Hazrat Mariam [the mother of Jesus] had labour pains she closed the palm of her hand, and the patterns were imprinted on the ground. There is a plant called Hand of Mary which I brought back from Mecca. You put it into water at delivery [of a child] and it opens up, and you give the water to women to drink. It helps with labour pains. At *Umra* you cut the hair, it's a *sunnat*, like when you shave the hair of a newborn baby. We give the weight away in silver or gold as *sadqat* [alms given to avert misfortune].'

The making of *qurbani* during the Hajj is thus a moment in a sequence of structural transformations which effects the movement of pilgrims on Hajj towards blessed innocence, a state embodied in the sacred water and dates they carry home with them.

Sacrifice is a key moment of transition in this process. In saints' lodges and shrines in South Asia, this moment is expanded and magnified to become the central trope of the lodge, binding together the moral ideas of mystical Sufism with the organisational agendas of the lodges as centres of far-flung regional cults. Sacrifice in Islam as performed during the Hajj is a moment of ordeal and release, in which a person's faith in God is tested. One of the key features of the *'Id* sacrifice on the Hajj is that both the sacrificial slaughter and the prayers accompanying it are multiplied a thousand times. In explaining the Hajj, Sharif Ahmad, a distinguished British *'alim* (man learned in Islamic law and sciences) in the Deobandi, reformist tradition, told his congregation:

'When one person asks blessings alone from his God, he shall get the blessing. But if many people ask for blessing all together, they will get manifold blessings. The bigger the congregation is when they ask for blessings, the more blessings Allah will give them, and in the whole world there is no gathering of human beings asking for Allah's blessings as large as that of the Hajj. And this gathering only takes place on the Mount of Rehemat and in Arafat, nowhere else. And on the day of Hajj millions and millions of people, on the same day and with the same intention, call out to their God. So the blessings of God come running towards them. This state, this atmosphere, and this situation cannot be found on any other day, any other time or any other situation.

'The time of Hajj is the time of blessing. On that day if a person asks for blessing with a true heart, he will get a river of blessings and will be purified. Such a person will feel so pure, as though he was just born from his mother's belly.'

What is stressed here is mediation with God not by a single man but by the community of believers, united in their intentionality and all focusing on Allah. While for Sufis the mediation of the Prophet and of saints on the Day of Judgement is a cornerstone of their belief, this mediation is itself mediated by the ability of these saints to mobilise the multitude in a shared ordeal. Like the sacrifice, the day in the valley of Arafat, exposed to the heat of the sun, is regarded as a test of faith.

To develop this point in relation to sacrifice at saints' lodges in India and Pakistan, let me begin by describing the annual sacrifice as a cultural performance held in Ghamkol Sharif, the lodge of Zindapir, as it nestles in its little valley in north-western Pakistan.

PERPETUAL SACRIFICE

The annual sacrifice on the *'urs* at Ghamkol Sharif is a major event. In 1990, 95 goats, 13 sheep, and 17 cattle and buffalo were slaughtered over a three-day period, the equivalent of over 3,000 kilos of meat, distributed to 20,000 or more pilgrims and supplicants. In preparation for this annual feast local high class Sayyid women, of wealthy families, along with a large number of women from other respected families throughout Pakistan, clean and scrape thousands of clay dishes, hundreds of flat bread baskets, about twenty to thirty giant clay pots and an equivalent number of iron *chapati* stoves (*loh*). The latter accumulate a layer of rust over the year and need to be scraped and polished in readiness for the thousands of *chapatis* that are to be baked on them during the major three-day festival. Once cleaned, they have to be re-installed in the earth and the women—again I must stress their wealthy, high-caste origins—use heavy iron picks to dig up the dry earth in order to install the ovens. After they are installed, the women smear the surface around the ovens with mud. The labour of the women is an act of *khidmat*, or, as Zindapir stressed to me repeatedly—it is all done out of *mahabbat*, the love of God. The women explain that they work for *sawab*, merit, and for God's forgiveness, *Allah mo'af kare*.

11. Women preparing the ovens for the *'urs* at Ghamkol Sharif

While the women, wash, scrape and polish, the men invest their voluntary labour in piling up vast quantities of wood in preparation for the
enormous quantities of food to be cooked.

The occasion of the sacrificial feast is the *'urs*, the commemoration of
the death/rebirth of Zindapir's Sufi master, Baba Qasim. Every year on
the *'urs*, the valley of the lodge fills with disciples coming in convoys
from all over Pakistan. They bear with them tributary gifts for the saint,
nazrana, and offerings for the *langar*. The food is pure, I was told, because it is cooked by men of pure heart who chant *zikr* as they cook.

The *langar* during the *'urs* is the high point of a continuous flow of
food provided at the lodge by the saint all year round. Because it never
ceases, this food may be conceived of as a perpetual sacrifice, a sacrifice
that provides an apparently endless supply of sacrificial meat each day
throughout the year. To appreciate the sacrificial nature of the *langar*, the
need is to conceptualise first, however, the difference between everyday
Islamic ritual slaughter, *halal*, and ritual sacrifice, since nominally in
Islam all *halal* animals slaughtered are a sacrifice.[1] In Pakistan, intentional ritual sacrifices are set apart from routine *halal* slaughter by additional ritual customs related to particular festive occasions—the *'Id,
'aqiqa* at the birth of a child, or sacrifices of exorcism and expiation
known as *sadqat* (P. Werbner 1990a: ch. 4). The question is: how can one
speak of *perpetual* sacrifice; that is, quotidian sacrifice, sacrifice as a
routine of daily life?

The answer to this question lies in a key difference between ritual
slaughter (*halal*) and perpetual ritual sacrifice at a saint's lodge. At the
saint's lodge, sacrifice involves an act of conversion. The conversion is
from the cash economy to the moral economy, the good faith economy,
and the gift economy. Unlike ordinary commercial *halal* slaughter, a ritual sacrifice is the slaughter of an animal freely given, removed from the
cash nexus of commercial buying and selling. This means that a purchased animal must be transformed through rites of sacralisation before
it can be sacrificed or defined as an offering. Among Pakistanis this sacralisation is usually achieved through a communal reading of the whole
Qur'an in a cooperative gathering, or through a special specified prayer
of dedication—such as the *'Id* morning prayer—which takes place before
the slaughter of the animal or the cooking and eating of an offering of
vegetarian food.

[1] for a comparative account of Islamic sacrifice see contributions to Brisbarre and
Gokalp 1993, and Bonte et al. 1999.

It is in the light of this distinction between commercial *halal* slaughter and ritual sacrifice that the slaughter of animals at the lodges of Sufi saints in Pakistan can be regarded as perpetual sacrifice. This distinction also highlights a difference between the *langar* of a living saint and that of some of the older shrines in South Asia, such as Data Ganj Baksh in Lahore, or Bari Imam in Islamabad, where the *langar* is mediated by commercial cooking. A pilgrim buys a portion of rice (say a pot) from one of the many cooking stalls leading to the shrine. She or he then donates the food to the shrine, from where it is distributed to the poor by employees of the Pakistan Waqf department. The *pir* in his grave is believed to mediate the transaction, but its commercial origins remain transparent in that it creates a clear division between the rich and poor. Only the poor eat the food of the *langar* at these shrines. Even the queuing up for food is unpleasant and degrading and the food given out is very basic, consisting of rice only.

By contrast, the *langar* of Zindapir is freely given and is open to everyone, rich and poor alike. Wealthy visitors and not only the poor are expected by the saint, as the legends in the previous chapter make clear, to partake of the *langar*. It is thought to contain miraculous healing powers. It includes sacrificially slaughtered meat or chicken, pilau rice and *chapati*, as well as a sweetened rice dish, and it usually is very delicious.

Crucially in this case, the source of the *langar* is the living *pir* himself. The question of whether or not he has used voluntary labour and contributions in cash or kind to sustain the *langar* is secondary. He personally controls the slaughter and cooking of the *langar* and it is thus he who directly nurtures the multitudes. This is why the rich and the powerful are willing to partake of the *shaikh's langar*.

The ethics of feeding and providing shelter consolidate the moral relations between saint and disciple, and between disciples among themselves. They are crucibles on the path to God which forge enduring human ties between visitors to the lodge. Many of the volunteers preparing the *'urs langar* work without pause claiming, if asked, that they do not even feel tired. This, they say, is the miracle of the lodge and the *pir*. The voluntary labour underpins the distributive and redistributive economies that maintain the lodge as an ongoing concern. It ensures that a remote place, away from major centres of population, can stage a large-scale, three-day feast of such magnitude.

All the animals slaughtered for the *langar* are freely given by pilgrims, disciples and supplicants—none is purchased. Moreover, the sacrifice takes place in a space which has been sacralised by continuous prayer.

The saint is said never to sleep but to spend all his time meditating and praying. The lodge itself is a place of *zikr*—the remembrance of God, the incantation of God's name. The sound of *zikr*—*Allah-hu* or *la ilaha illa'l-lah*—both individually and communally sung—echoes continuously through the valley. The men who slaughter and cook the animals for the *langar* do so as a meritorious, freely given act, an act of selfless service (*khidmat*). All the labour in the lodge is freely given in the name of God. Hence the lodge is a space set apart from the commodity economy, and capitalist logic does not hold there. As we have seen, during the *'urs* the convoys of trucks and buses coming from the different villages, towns, factories, army barracks or work places throughout Pakistan and beyond it, from Britain where Zindapir's order extends, bear with them not only animals but sacks of flour, bags of rice, large containers of clarified butter (*ghee*) and money donated for the purchase of food for the *langar*. These staples and animals, like the cash and the voluntary labour, are freely given. Perpetual sacrifice and other forms of offering are in this respect identical.

While all the pilgrims share the *langar* at Ghamkol Sharif and all are equal before God and the saint, Islamic sacrifice in South Asia is nevertheless framed by a semiotic of inequality, a feature of what I have termed hierarchical gift economies.[2]

ISLAMIC SACRIFICE AND SOCIAL HIERARCHY

The hierarchical nature of South Asian Islamic gift-giving is clearly expressed in the ideas and practices surrounding Muslim sacrificial giving. Gifts to God, including animal sacrifices and offerings of food and money, are always unilateral—given without expectation of return. Yet the direction of this gifting is highly significant. Gifts to God are directed either 'downwards', to the poor, in the form of *sadqat*, or 'upwards', as religious tribute to saints and holy men, whether alive or dead. Alternatively, offerings are made to communal causes such as the building of a mosque. In similar spirit donations are made directly to the *langar*, the communal distribution of food at a religious lodge or celebration.

Saints, regarded as descendants of the Prophet or his close companions, are almost invariably members of the highest Sayyid or Siddiqui Muslim castes. Members of these castes, I was told, will not accept *sadqat*, but only

---

[2] On hierarchical gift economies see P. Werbner 1990a, ch. 8; 1990c and 1996b.

nazrana. The remains of communal meals held after religious gatherings (usually fruit or cooked food) are distributed as *tabarruk* among the people to be taken home; the food is sacrificial and dedicated and hence it cannot be thrown away. Again, I was told that Sayyids, and certainly the *shaikh* himself, are not offered and do not usually accept *tabarruk*.

In accord with this distinction between gifts to God via the poor and gifts to God via a superior, pure religious intercessor (a saint), Pakistani Muslims also distinguish between different forms of animal sacrifice: *sadqat, qurbani*, the *'Id* sacrifice, in which a portion is given to the poor and the rest shared among kin and friends conceived of as equals; and *zabh/zibha*, in which an animal is given as a tribute at a saint's lodge and is usually shared out as *langar* (see Figures 6.1 and 6.2).

The hierarchical nature of religious giving was made evident to me in Pakistan by Zindapir who described himself as a *faqir* and explained 'A *faqir* is the friend of Allah. Even if he is offered one lakh [100,000] rupees or nothing to eat for Allah's sake, he would choose to go hungry.' The *faqir*, he said, denies himself while giving to others: 'This is the way of a *faqir*. He fasts all day while making sure that everyone else is given food.' Remarkably, the saint gives not just at his own lodge. Hence Zindapir explained: 'I have arrangements to host people wherever I go, all over Pakistan and even all over the world. Wherever I go, whether here [at the lodge] or in Mecca, Allah provides the *langar* and hospitality for my guests.' Here Zindapir is referring to his regional cult, the network of satellite lodges distributed throughout Pakistan and Britain which also provide *langar* for visitors. On the annual Hajj, Zindapir distributes *langar* in Mecca. This *langar* is organised and funded by his vicegerent in Britain—Sufi Sahib, the saint in Birmingham, himself the centre of a regional cult with satellite centres in nine British cities. The money for the Hajj *langar* is donated by British Pakistanis while the pots and utensils are kept by disciples of Zindapir living in Mecca who are labour migrants working in Saudi Arabia.[3]

Explaining his remarkable generosity, Zindapir told me:

'I have to be generous because this [the Lodge, Mecca] is not my house. It is the house of Allah. I too am a guest here. It is easy to be generous in someone else's house. If it were my own house, it might be hard for me to part even with a glass of water.'

---

[3] Sufi Sahib also collects donations for feeding the pigeons on Hajj in the name of disciples who remain behind in England. He handles two funds: the *langar* fund and the pigeon fund, keeping meticulous records of the donations to each one, I was told.

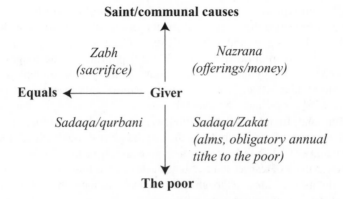

Figure 6.1: The structure of sacrificial giving

We see in this statement the close identification of the saint with Allah, his proximity to God. But it is also a commentary on the identification between the saint and the community. Commenting on the difference between himself, as a *faqir* and friend of Allah, and the *'ulama* he said: 'Allah will undoubtedly take the *'ulama* to paradise on the Day of Judgement. But Allah gives paradise to his *faqirs* on earth. I can give all the blessings of Allah.'

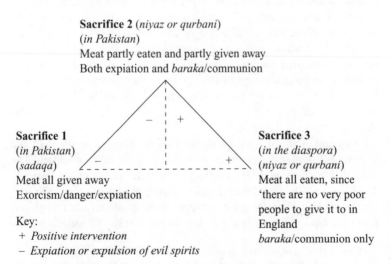

Figure 6.2: Sacrifice and offering in the context of migration

Zindapir repeatedly reminded me of the enormous crowds his *langar* has just fed during the *'urs* festival and the vast number of gifts of money and cloth he has bestowed on his followers and the needy. The *'urs* is said, somewhat hyperbolically, to draw 300,000 pilgrims to the lodge, all of whom are fed by the saint. By contrast, *'ulama* are mere employees. Zindapir told me: 'Only yesterday I paid a *maulvi* 400 rupees [at the time about £15] for giving a sermon at the mosque.'

The saint, friend of Allah, most elevated and closest to Him, asks for nothing except from Allah. He is the infinite giver through whom flows the bounty of Allah to his followers below him. If he takes, it is only as tribute, a mark of respect and gratitude made towards him by his followers. By contrast the *'ulama*, although undoubtedly pious men, are mere receivers, dependent on human generosity, employees of low status and honour.

Mediation with God is thus achieved either by giving to the poor, or indirectly, via a tribute to a saint who, in turn, is expected to use the tribute, if it is a sacrificial animal, for the *langar*; thirdly, by giving directly to the *langar*, for the sake of the people, *makhluqat*, all of creation. In Pakistan, and throughout South Asia, most major Muslim shrines and lodges have *langar* arrangements at festivals and often daily.

In Britain, the *langar* is provided for the celebration of the *'urs*, of *'Id-milad-un-nabi*, and during monthly rituals commemorating the birth/death of Abdul Qadr Jilani, regarded as the founder of all the Sufi orders in India. These monthly rituals are known as *gyarvi sharif* and are held in most of Zindapir's satellite lodges and mosques throughout his regional cult. In addition, during the month of *Ramadan*, food and offerings are distributed daily at the mosque branches of Zindapir's Sufi order in Manchester and throughout Britain. In all these instances the food is donated and its cooking is voluntary. In Britain, unlike Pakistan, the immolation of the animal is entrusted to the Pakistani butcher who slaughters them at the abattoir.[4]

At Ghamkol Sharif, by contrast, animals are donated on the hoof and one of the disciples slaughters them, assisted by several companions. The same disciple acts as chief sacrifier for the lodge on all major festivals. The *langar* at Ghamkol Sharif is open twenty-four hours a day to all supplicants and pilgrims, from the very poor to the most elevated and powerful in the land. Zindapir is a well-known *pir*, and he is regularly visited

---

[4] There appears to be very little sentimental value attached to the act of personal slaughter, and similarly, people do not appear to attach much value to the appearance of the live animal. The choice of the animal, like the slaughter itself, is entrusted to the butcher.

by top civil servants, army brigadiers and generals, and even politicians. Regardless of status, all are expected to partake of the *langar*. To partake of the *langar* is to partake of the blessings of the *shaikh*, the divine blessing, *faiz*, which endows him with *baraka*; and indeed, the *langar* objectifies this perpetual source of saintly divine spiritual power.

The hierarchical nature of South Asian giving does, however, imbue even the *langar* with some ambiguity. At Zindapir's lodge there are, in effect, two *langars*. One is an open, general *langar*, and the other is run by his son's wife. Many of the most respected guests are fed from this more exclusive *langar*, although *chapatis* usually come from the central *langar*. The Sayyid women with whom I spent the *'urs* in 1991 had brought their own food with them for the festival, and ate almost nothing from the central *langar*, although they denied that this avoidance had any significance, beyond a matter of taste preferences.

The *langar*, conceived of as perpetual sacrifice, is the key organising feature of Sufi lodges in South Asia. Such lodges are centres for the collection and redistribution of food on a vast scale. Virtually all the activity of the lodge is geared to this continuous provision of ritually sacred food. Ghamkol Sharif has its herds of cattle, goats and other small stock, its orange groves and fruit orchards, its vegetable gardens, as well as storage rooms for grain, rice and *ghee*, brought by supplicants or purchased with their donations. Gifts of camels and horses, and of exotic and beautiful wild birds and animals, as well as of goats, sheep and buffalo are not unusual. Many are dedicated to the *langar* and cannot be used for any other purpose.

The saint himself is a vegetarian who regards himself as the protector of all living creatures. Killing ants and any other creatures, however minute, is prohibited within the lodge area. This is also true of his conduct during the Hajj, I was told. As we have seen, a special water trough has been constructed by the saint's son for the wild animals that descend from the hills at night, while the legends about Zindapir recount his conquest of the wild. He can cure poisonous snake bites, honey bees in the lodge are said not to sting, and wild animals do not invade the lodge or attack its inhabitants. The saint is conceived of as the source of natural fertility and his command over nature is a metaphor for his command over his *nafs*.

Yet his abstention from meat underlines once again the hierarchical logic informing sacrifice. As a perpetual giver he cannot take. The unilateral nature of gifting would be compromised if he took of what was given

him. God is the ultimate source of both food and life which flow from
Him downwards, into the world of ephemeral creations.

Sacrifice is a tribute to God just as *nazrana* is a tribute to the saint. The
offerings or tributes are meritorious acts of respect, but neither God nor
the saint need the gifts offered them. Need implies a lack and hence
imperfection. The saint is an exemplar of the perfect man, *insan el kamil*.
Just as God needs no sustenance from man, so too the saint needs sustenance from God alone. The saint gives generously and accepts tribute
which he himself does not consume but redirects to the *langar*—and
hence ultimately to the whole community. He fasts all day and is a vegetarian while being the source of meat.

Why do people give to the *langar*? They do so in fulfilment of a vow
(*niyat*) or to seek merit, but also as an act of identification with an unbounded Muslim community. By contrast, the giving of *nazrana*, even if
the expectation is that the tribute will ultimately be redirected to the
langar, is much more simply an expression of love and respect for the
saint by his disciples, or of gratitude, with the added assumption that God
loves those who love his *auliya*. Although giving *nazrana* may be construed as meritorious and efficacious, it is not an act of sacrifice, unless
we recognise the identification of the saint as the exemplary person with
the community. It is the saint who sacrifices, when he dedicates the animal donated to him to the *langar*. Sacrifice is necessarily mediated either
by the poor or the community. It is an act of expiation, and—in the case of
sadqat—of exorcism of afflicting spirits (see Figure 6.2). The poor are
not conceived of as scapegoats—since they need the meat for their sustenance and survival, it is assumed it will do them no harm.[5]

THE ENCOUNTER BETWEEN THE GOOD FAITH
AND BAD FAITH ECONOMIES

To fully understand, however, why people give to the *langar*, or why they
devote their time and labour to voluntary work at the lodge, we need to
recognise the contrast that they and the *pir* draw between the greed and
corruption of the 'world' (*dunya*) and the purity of the lodge as a place of
true religion (*din*). The postcolonial reality of contemporary Pakistan is
seen by pilgrims as one of mendacious politicians, of greed, selfishness
and violence. Even the politicians themselves acknowledge this reality:

[5] In this sense the poor, like the saint, differ from the priests of Benaras described by
Parry (1989).

the celebrations of fifty years of Pakistani independence, which took place in August 1997, were an occasion for political leaders to beat their breasts in public about the endemic corruption and social divisions afflicting their nation. To lead the good life of a Muslim in this world is, people say, virtually impossible. Only *pirs* can therefore guarantee God's forgiveness for their followers on the Day of Judgement.

Hajji Karim, Zindapir's vicegerent in Manchester, and my companion and guide during my 1989 visit to Ghamkol Sharif, told me: 'People believe that on the Day of Judgement they will appear before God as a group and the *pirs* will speak for them and ask God to forgive them, and they will then be forgiven and go to heaven.' 'They know,' he continued, 'that if they stood alone before God they would definitely not go to heaven.' 'Why not?' I asked. 'You are a good man, why should you fear God's judgement?' 'Because this is not an Islamic country and it is very hard to be a good Muslim here.'

Zindapir repeatedly explained that he refused to get involved in elections because, he said, 'God is not elected, and to become a Sufi you don't need to be elected' (i.e., a saint is not chosen by the people but by God). The corruption of politicians and large *zamindars* (landowners) is associated also with an unbridled hubris: they believe that their wealth can buy anything, even God's approval. As we saw in the previous chapter, Zindapir is fond of telling stories of politicians who have wanted to supply the *langar* with vast quantities of food or money, and whom he has refused, arguing that 'I cannot make you partner [*sharik*] with God.'

The paradigmatic tale which illuminates the place of the lodge as the sole source of God's boundless nurture is contained in the founding myth of Ghamkol Sharif, recounted in chapters 3 and 4, in which the *shaikh* instructs a disciple to throw away the sack of flour he is carrying and trust in God. This story, like others, stresses the finitude of men's resources, whatever their wealth or power, set against the infinity of God's capacity to feed the world. Wherever he goes, Zindapir regards himself as dwelling in the House of God. On one occasion he was invited by an important Saudi politician to stay at his home in Jeddah, but he replied: 'When I visit the House of God, I am the guest only of Allah.'

As mentioned in the previous chapter, on my visit in 1991 I was told confidentially that one of the leading political figures in Pakistan had visited the lodge and had wanted to write Zindapir a cheque for a very large sum of money. The saint refused the donation and instead, offered the politician and his entourage food from the *langar* to eat. If it even

crosses the mind of a saint to influence politicians, he told me, then he is
no longer a *faqir*.

The evidence for the superiority of saints over politicians is proven,
Zindapir repeatedly asserted, by the honour given to saints' shrines after
their death:

> 'The tombs of kings do not get *izzat* (honour); only those of *auliya*. The men to
> whom God gives respect in their lifetimes, in their death their respect grows
> and grows. Like Data Ganj Baksh in Lahore [the shrine of the eleventh century
> Sufi saint Hujwiri]. If you go to the emperor's tomb [Jahangir] you will find no
> people there. But at Data Ganj Baksh there are thousands of people all the
> time.'

Again and again it is the *shaikh*'s ability to provide nurture on a daily and
annual basis to all who come, from an unending source, which the morality tales stress. It is this which makes it impossible for politicians to compete with him, and which proves that his following is much greater than
that of any politician. This world of generosity and giving as constructed
by the saint is the one pilgrims enter into when they arrive at the lodge,
bearing their gifts for the saint and the *langar*, in what may be conceived
of as an imaginative as much as a real journey.

Yet, paradoxically, as we saw in the previous chapter, just as he denies
the importance of the visits and honours granted him by state officials
and politicians, so too, paradoxically, do the visits prove that Zindapir is
indeed a great and spiritually powerful *wali* of Allah. And despite the
constructed ideological opposition between the lodge and the world, the
growth and success of the lodge have profited from official goodwill.
Land, telephone lines, water, roads, transport, have all been provided free
through official channels and Zindapir takes great care, in reality, not
to offend politicians. Moreover, there is a symbolic economy of gifting
which pervades pilgrims' and supplicants' relations with the saint.

In exchange for the gifts of money, perfume, flour, animals, rice and
clarified butter given to the *pir* as *nazrana*, or donated directly to the
langar, the saint gives his close disciples white chiffon headscarves, embroidered praying caps and perfumes. These he draws, with the almost
magical gesture of a conjurer, out of the treasure house of objects he
accumulates in his room, buried in the silk and brocade cushions on
which he reclines. He distributes salt and amulets to the supplicants who
visit him, along with *du'a* and *dam*. He also donates money generously to
the poor and needy who come to him with requests for help. I myself was
showered with gifts: several clothing outfits, jewellery, perfume and a

handbag from the *shaikh*'s son's family; four large bottles of honey collected from the lodge's beehives, a lovely white, finely woven cotton headscarf of a type usually reserved for disciples, a beautiful length of silk cloth and a box of sweets (*mithai*), all to take home with me to England, gifts from the *shaikh*. My attempts to reciprocate were of little avail. The gifts personified the saint's generosity but, even beyond that, they proved his supreme elevation above the anthropologist and, indeed, any educated, non-Muslim Westerner.

EXPERIENCING THE GOOD FAITH ECONOMY

Stressing the communal dimensions of sacrifice and gifting highlights the limitations of Eade and Sallnow's view, according to which much of the activity at saint's lodges is a matter of 'sacred commerce.' Such a conception denies, moreover, the experiential dimensions of voluntary labour and sacrifice, particularly in the case of close disciples of the saint. Most of the women who work as volunteers in preparation for the *langar* of the *'urs* say they are seeking merit but in reality the transformation they experience appears to be both far more immediate and far more complex.

For three weeks before the *'urs* both men and women begin arriving at the lodge to contribute their voluntary labour to the preparations for the festival. Much of the building of the lodge takes place during this period, including the extension of water pipes, drainage, and electricity. New hostels are constructed for pilgrims. The women arrive daily, increasing in number as the festival approaches. They come from throughout the Frontier and even from Lahore. But a core of women comes from neighbouring Jangal Khel. Most of the women are, as already mentioned, from the high-ranking Sayyid family which is the largest, wealthiest and most important in Jangal Khel, now a small town of 20,000 inhabitants. Members of this large family are scattered throughout the world, occupying professional positions as doctors, engineers or pilots. They hold, and held in the past, many of the top administrative positions in the town. They own large houses and the women who run these have servants to assist them. Yet these very same women are willing to take on the most menial, dirty, unpleasant tasks, hard, tiring, physical labour, and live in crowded conditions, sleeping on mats on the floor if they come from some distance, in preparation for the sacrificial feast of the *'urs*. During the *'urs* they also help supervise the visits of women supplicants to the saint.

The contrast between this intimacy with the *shaikh* and the cold distance of stranger-supplicants is evident. Every day and late into the

12. Women preparing the *langar* for the *'urs* in an English town

evening the saint is visited by both male and female supplicants. They sit at some distance from him. Both men and women expose their faces, the women drawing their veils above their heads. The exposure underlines the belief that the saint transcends sexuality. His persona combines male and female qualities—the gentleness, love and tenderness of a woman, the power, authority and honour of a man (see also Kurin 1984).[6] He communicates very briefly with the supplicants, addressing them in short, distant tones. Once they have explained their problem to him, he usually instructs them to perform their daily prayers, sometimes throwing an inscribed paper amulet in their general direction or (in the past) salt. At other times, he instructs them to collect amulets 'outside'. Once he has heard a whole round of supplicants (he takes in about ten at a time) he raises his hands in *du'a*. Even in these brief interchanges, however, the symbolic transference appears to be very powerful. One can only speculate that for the supplicants his immense healing power derives precisely from

[6] The belief that this professional distance is abused is widespread, fuelled by tales of the excessive sexual appetite of saints (see Lindholm 1990: 33) and periodic scandals. The power of the cultural ideal of saints as world renouncers is evidenced, however, by the fact the women continue to unveil before the saint. In the case of Zindapir, his reputation was quite immaculate.

13/14. At Ghamkol Sharif: *above*, cooking pots and wood piled high in anticipation of the *'urs*, and *below*, cooking the *langar* for the *'urs*

his gendered ambiguity: he combines maternal and paternal qualities: he is a maternal father or a paternal mother, protective yet authoritative.[7]

His relationship to the women preparing for the *'urs* is radically different. Every day during the weeks of preparation for the *'urs*, the saint visits the women at their work. They greet him *'asalam-u pir'*. There is no bowing or scraping. He does not allow it. They smile at him, an elderly man limping along slowly since his knees have been causing him some trouble. It is clear that the women are very fond of the saint.

After work each day the women workers come into the saint's inner sanctum to receive his blessings. During these meetings he prays a *du'a* for them. The meetings are marked by their atmosphere of intimacy. To most women supplicants the saint is a distant charismatic figure, fearful and awe inspiring. His face as he distributes amulets or prayers is expressionless, his tone matter of fact, verging on abruptness. The vast majority of his male disciples treat him with respect. The saint is a remote figure, revered, feared and respected. His commands are instantly obeyed. Grown men tremble at his anger and sink into despair. He is treated as a king or prince. On their visits to his room women supplicants sit behind a low wooden barrier to prevent them from reaching too close to him.

This remoteness contrasts with his relationship with his close disciples, those who work on the preparations for the *'urs*. The women disciples who assist in the preparations for the sacrificial meal of the *'urs* treat him with the freedom of companions. The *shaikh* clearly enjoys the company of these women, and they entertain him with anecdotes of amusing incidents and gossip, including the odd behaviour of the anthropologist which he finds particularly amusing. The women are an invaluable source of information to him about what goes on beyond the confines of the room in which he meditates. They are also privy to a good deal of information about his family and private life to which others have no access. They say they fear him but in practice, what they mainly express is their fondness for him.

During my visit to the lodge in 1991 Zindapir's son's wife was undergoing throat surgery in England. On the day of the operation the close women disciples visited the saint. Earlier he had been to pray in the northern guest house for the success of the operation. The women disciples kept trying to comfort him by discussing the details of his son's wife's condition. But he kept sighing and lapsing into long silences, then

---

[7] Whether healing is achieved through transference is debated by Kakar (1982) and Ewing (1984). See also chapter 10.

renewing the conversation. They too would lapse into sympathetic silence. This went on for about forty minutes. As time passed with no news of the operation from England, the whole lodge entered into a state of worried expectation. Eventually, at 9.30 p.m. in the evening, the telephone message arrived, informing the saint that the operation had been successful.

I tell this story to underline the clear connection between sacrifice and moral amity. If sacrifice in Islam hinges on the existence of inequalities, of a category willing to define themselves as 'poor', it nevertheless also encompasses notions of moral responsibility within a moral community. The *langar* objectifies the moral community embodied by the saint himself as a figure of infinite generosity. This underlines the fact that in Islam voluntary labour, donations, offerings and charity merge with sacrifice. All these acts are vehicles mediating the relationship between person and God. In all, moral space is extended, objectified and personified, while the identification between person and community is revitalised.

It is remarkable that in many ways the *langar* at Sufi Sahib's Dar-ul 'Uloom in Britain differs rather little in organisation and ideology from the *langar* in Pakistan, except for the fact that as yet, it is not a perpetual sacrifice. The same discourses and practices characterise both *langars*. The resemblance underlines the transnational nature of Zindapir's order. British branches of the saint's regional cult, like the branches of the cult in Pakistan, provide *langar* for the same major Islamic and Sufi holidays and festivals, just as the branches in both countries send tribute to the *shaikh* himself. As we have seen, the ultimate objectification of this diasporic transnationalism is through the *langar* provided annually by the order during the Hajj, a kind of perpetual sacrifice at the global centre of Islam.

One might still object that supplicants' actions are nevertheless based on a calculus of exchange. If we deploy familiar religious terms such as penance and salvation, we may easily mistake the work of the women and men for what they explicitly say it is—a calculating act of service before God for the purpose of accumulating merit. So too, offerings and sacrifices, whether directly to the saint or to the *langar*, can be understood as they are apparently intended: as acts of dyadic reciprocity in which a favour is sought from the saint or from God in return for an offering. The saint's gifts to pilgrims—white cotton scarves and white embroidered hats for his disciples, gowns for his *khulafa*, amulets and salts for supplicants, may all be seen as items in a simple relationship of dyadic reciprocal exchange.

If, however, as I believe, these ideological statements tell only a very partial truth, then the need is to consider what the sacred exchange effected in the pilgrimage to the *'urs* is. At first glance, there is no elaborate sacred reversal in the *'urs* which may be said to parallel and comment upon those of the Hajj. Reversal does occur, however, because the *'urs* is an annual event which creates a recurrent sacred return in time.

A key feature of Ghamkol Sharif is its sacred peripherality (Turner 1974). The lodge was built outside any established settlement, very gradually, over many years, in what was previously an uncultivated valley. The men and women who return annually to work for the *'urs* have participated in this gradual transformation of the lodge. Each year they retrace the footsteps both of the saint and of themselves in prior years as they move beyond the boundaries of their settled communities. Metaphorically, they move back in time by journeying once again to the lodge in order to be renewed. As they work they often recall the early days of the lodge. The women's gossip during the long working hours is in itself a work of making history, reliving the myth of the lodge's establishment.

The same is true of all the pilgrims who visit the lodge annually. The journey to the lodge is a movement back in time in the sense that it repeats an earlier journey. In his final supplication for the sake of the community, the saint recalls his own first arduous journey to the lodge. Indeed, as we have seen, he repeats the story of this legendary journey almost verbatim every year. The assembled crowd wait for this final *du'a*, the request for God's blessing, the peak moment of the three-day ritual festival. Yet as in the Hajj, the supplication is more than the voice of a single individual: it is the sum of all the silent prayers of the multitudes present, even if it is embodied in the trembling tones of the saint. So too the sacrificial feast is perceived to be more than the multiplication of individual acts of sacrifice. It is an achievement of a community that has stepped outside the world. As in the Hajj, pilgrimage to Ghamkol Sharif is a fleeting act of world renunciation in which the pilgrims identify with their saint. In the sermon cited earlier, delivered in Rochdale on the day of the Hajj, Ahmad Sharif told his congregation:

'While the real test of faith is faith in the world then...If someone wants to renounce this world, it is possible for him to do so on Hajj; a pilgrim, as long as he keeps on his *ihram* [the two sheets the *Hajji* wears], is a *faqir* of God.'

The food of the *langar* eaten in this extra-mundane world differs in every respect from the sacrificial *halal* meat of the everyday.

This may be taken to imply that the annual pilgrimage to Ghamkol Sharif is a text (in the Ricoeurian sense) enacting Eliade's myth of eternal return to a point of original creation. It may also be taken to be a reiteration of Turner's view that pilgrims to a sacred centre experience a sense of communitas in which the boundaries between individual and community are obliterated. The *'urs* is a cultural performance which can be analysed from different perspectives (on this see Weingrod 1990). Beyond individual calculus or communitas, however, I want to stress a further point: pilgrimage to the *'urs*, and especially the voluntary labour vested in preparation for it, are texts which are at once personal and performative. Each pilgrim re-enacts his or her own text, her or his annual visit and contribution to the growth of the lodge. Each personal text reflects on all the prior personal texts, as a series of reflexive memorials of positive action. In addition, each personal text also allegorises the shared pretext of the saint's first journey to the lodge, itself an allegory of the texts of the Prophet's migration and return to Mecca, for which Ibrahim's test of faith by sacrifice, and Hajara's ordeal in the desert, searching for water for her infant son, are the ultimate pretexts. Hence also, for example, the text of the *'urs* in Britain echoes that at Ghamkol Sharif while being uniquely British. These acts of identification imbue the sacred exchange at a saint's lodge with moral meaning in the world. The gifts, amulets and blessings, charged with saintly charisma, which are carried back from the pilgrimage, have to be understood as tokens of moral renewal energising this mundane world of the here and now in which pilgrims live their daily lives.

An example of this sacred exchange across boundaries, embedded in voluntary labour and communal blessing, is the story told to me by Rab Nawaz, the annual *intizami* of the *'urs*. During the *'urs* Rab Nawaz never stays still for one moment. Caught in a whirlwind of activity, he smiles apologetically at chance encounters, saying he is *masruf*, busy, before rushing off to solve some minor crisis or instruct the builders. He claims not to sleep or eat during the weeks of preparation.

Every year after the *'urs* is over, he told me, when he gets back home, he soaks the work clothes he wore during the *'urs* and during the weeks leading up to it in a big bucket of water. Once all the dirt has been soaked out, he sprinkles the dirty water over his fields so that the crops will grow in abundance.

The *langar* at saints' lodges in South Asia has been a taken-for-granted, background reality in the literature on Sufi cults, trivialised in that literature as merely a 'communal kitchen' and often mentioned only in passing. Against that, the present chapter has shown that the *langar* of a living saint is the organisational core of Sufi regional cults and the geographies of saintly charisma such cults generate during their heyday. The *langar*, I have argued, is to be grasped as the embodiment of voluntarism, whether in labour or kind. The great *degs* (pots) of the shrine of Mu'innudin Chishti at Ajmer, donated by the Mughal emperor, Akbar, and his son, Jahangir, and seemingly containing an endless supply of rice, may be said to symbolise this flow of generosity for the whole subcontinent (see Moini 1989).

At Ghamkol Sharif, the *langar* establishes the Good Faith economy as an experiential reality of the lodge, and as a contrastive reality to the mendacity of politicians and greedy calculus of modern capitalism in a postcolonial society. Sacrifice at the lodge echoes the sacrifice of the Hajj and notions of redemption, renewal and purification associated with that sacrifice. Yet unlike the singularity of the Hajj sacrifice, the *langar* of Zindapir is a perpetual sacrifice which frames the lodge in the ambience of nurture and protectiveness. As the food flows from the *pir*, so too, pilgrims believe, does God's *faiz*, to nourish his disciples.

7

MURIDS OF THE SAINT

MIGRATION, OCCUPATIONAL GUILDS AND
REDEMPTIVE SOCIALITY

THE ARMY SAINT

All night long the *qafilas* kept arriving, churning up clouds of dust in the darkened valley. They came from all over the North West Frontier Province and the Punjab, from Azad Kashmir and even beyond, trucks, vans, lorries, buses, minibuses, each elaborately decorated with intricate colourful drawings and patterns, the vast majority bearing the name of Zindapir in bold letters. As many as twenty-three had come from the arms factory near Rawalpindi; there were four from Azad Kashmir, four from Tarbela

15. The *qafilas* arriving for the *'urs*

129

dam, twenty-five from Haripur, four from Abbotabad, sixty from Bannu, Peshawar, Nusheira and Shikr Dera, more than hundred from the towns and villages of the Punjab. Three separate groups had come from Rawalpindi alone, four from Lahore. Altogether, I counted on the first day of the 1989 *'urs* 220 buses and trucks, each with capacity for sixty passengers, as well as some thirty vans. They had travelled long distances to attend the festival. Throughout the three days, a perpetual stream of local vehicles continued to move back and forth down the narrow, winding road leading to the *darbar*, ferrying individual passengers and families from Kohat. Many had arrived by aeroplane, train or bus. And as the moment of the *du'a* on the third day approached, it seemed that the whole town had descended onto the little lodge, packing the narrow valley with vehicles of all shape, colour and description.

Each truck or convoy carried *pir-bhais* and *pir-behens* (sister-disciples). Their relations are defined as deeper and more enduring than those between kinsmen. Saeed, *khalifa* and utterly loyal right-hand man of the *shaikh* until his untimely death at the age of thirty-five in 1996, told me:

'The *shaikh* always tells us that whenever *murids* meet, you must think that I am between you. Between real brothers there is marriage, there is land and there is wealth [*rishta, zamin, daulat*], but not between *murids* [i.e., between disciples there is nothing but love].'

In his study of the Nunari of the Punjab, Richard Kurin makes a similar observation when he distinguishes between cultural notions of collective solidarity based on turbans (agnation and descent), skirts (marriage and alliance) and spirit (allegiance to a single saint):

In this model of the *qaum*, the spiritual ties which bind members are thought to be everlasting and eternal with especially great relevance to the afterlife. They are ties that occasion not the alluring heat of blood ties but the cooling shadows of blessedness. Such ties are generally associated with kindness, tranquility and peacefulness... (Kurin 1990: 108)

As Philip Lewis (1984: 12) points out, *piri-muridi* relations are

...deeply rooted in traditional Pakistani society. Parents often expect their children to follow a pir, preferably their own. In village society someone without a pir may well court ostracism since 'it is believed that he does not have a source of spiritual guidance and his sins cannot be written off on the day of judgement' (cited from Reheman 1979: 68). In Urdu the adjective '*be-pir*'—literally 'without pir'—means vicious, pitiless, cruel, without sympathy etc. (taken from Platt's dictionary).

How do you recognise your *murids?* I asked Zindapir, since he claimed repeatedly never to ask his disciples their names or where they came from.

'If a man is thirsty, will he not find the well of water?' he replied. 'A *pir* takes care of his *murids*. The *murids* are like goats, they nibble grass wherever they find it, but he won't leave them unprotected and unfed.' In other words, a *pir* does not keep lists of his disciples but when they need him he is there, he knows when they are in trouble wherever they are.

The Sufi *shaikh* is a shepherd to his scattered flock and his sacred dominion reaches wherever they are. Evidence from South Asia shows that Sufi regional cults often extend widely beyond the central shrine's immediate locality, and interpenetrate into one another. In a study reported by Adrian Mayer (1967: 164), 100 Multani city respondents acknowledged 56 *pirs* between them, while the same number of villagers acknowledged 27 *pirs*. Among the Nunari, Kurin reports, villagers followed two key local saints in the Sahiwal region. Discipleship runs in families but, as Kurin reminds us, it can also cut across families if and when disputes arise between brothers (1990: 108). Eaton shows the wide distribution of 1,654 disciples of a single saint, Hajji Muhammad Naushah, whose shrine is located in Gujrat district. By 1965, however, 97 per cent of all followers were concentrated in three adjacent districts (Gujrat, Gujranwala and Shekhupura). Yet a few years later small numbers of *murids* were surfacing in Faislabad, Multan, Muzaffargarh and Peshawar, extending once again the reach of the cult's sacred dominion (Eaton 1978b: 79–81).

Eaton makes the further point that although disciples clustered by *zat* and *biradari* (caste and local intermarrying kin group or lineage), no single group or category dominated the cult's following. Indeed, he argues, 'The Naushani shrine and order serves to knit together a wide number of endogamous cultivating groups, giving them a common religious focus at the popular level' (ibid.: 85). This integrative function stands in marked contrast to potential village cleavages and class antagonisms (ibid.: 87).

The mediation of cross-ethnic, inter-caste and cross-regional divisions is a central feature in regional cult theory (R. Werbner 1977, 1989). There are cases, as Gaborieau documents, in which saints become patron saints of a particular occupational group (1983: 302–3), but these are relatively rare. Against that exclusivity, Saiyed echoes other scholars when he contends that it is through Sufi shrines that 'the subcontinent saw the best part of Hindu-Muslim integration', and that it was 'the personal and spiritual influence of various saints that... allowed for the peaceful coexistence

of the two communities for several centuries on the Indian subcontinent
(Saiyed 1989: 242). Although van der Veer has argued that current antagonisms between Hindus and Muslims in contemporary India have dimin-
ished and politicised the spirit of Hindu-Muslim fraternity at Sufi saints'
shrines (van der Veer 1994), there are parts of India where even today
Hindus and Muslims participate harmoniously in joint celebration, as at
the *'urs* of the saint of Nagore-e Sharif in Tamil Nadu (Saheb 1998; see
Werbner and Basu 1998b: 19–20; Liebeskind 1998). It is certainly very
common for occupational, *biradari* or village clusters and confraternities
to join together as disciples of a single saint, often over great distances.

The catchment areas—the sacred dominions—of Sufi regional cults
are thus marked by their instability and by the fluctuating range of devotees drawn to them. Elizabeth Mann reports on a minor shrine which
emerged in Aligarh in the 1940s and, over a short period, challenged and
greatly exceeded in popularity the shrine of Shah Jamal, a long established Chishti saint. The Sufi saint and world renouncer who revitalised
the minor shrine lived, she argues, 'Within living memory, [and] stories
of miraculous events are fresh in the minds of devotees who witnessed
them at first hand' (Mann 1989: 163). Since his death in the 1960s, inten-
sive building activities have greatly expanded the shrine.

Quite distinct from the fluctuating fortunes of medium-level shrines of
this type are the universally venerated great shrines of the Subcontinent
such as those of Mu'inuddin Chishti of Ajmer or Data Ganj Baksh of
Lahore. At the other extreme are shrines of minor *pirs* with restricted local
village followings, some of which may even be nameless (Werth 1998).

The bonds of spirit between disciples of a single Sufi saint often consolidate and mediate *biradari* or village ties; but they may also form the
basis for new friendships forged away from home, in the absence of family or community, and they may introduce parochial villagers to the glo-
ries of shrines located well beyond their district and even province. In
such cases, being a disciple comes to acquire many new and complex
meanings. This is true for the devotees of Zindapir's regional cult. To
explain the cult's vast catchment area, we need to look for its genesis in
relations between soldiers, migrants and city dwellers living away from
home, and their continued ties to their rural communities. It is thus the
intersection between labour migration and village or urban roots which
explains, as we shall see, the spatial patterning of the *shaikh*'s sacred
dominion and the reach of his cult.

Zindapir is, above all, an army saint. His career started as a tailor-
contractor in the army where his early circle of companions was forged.

Sufi Sahib, who created his own regional cult centred in Birmingham was, as we saw, one of these companions. Rab Nawaz, one of his trusted *khalifa*, told me that until white hairs appeared in the *shaikh*'s beard, he and all the *khulafa* wore khaki. It was only when his beard turned white that they began to wear white gowns. Even after becoming a practising *faqir*, Zindapir spent time in Abbotabad not far from the army base where he had worked, and he continued to recruit army followers. Ghamkol Sharif, the lodge he founded when he left Abbotabad, is located only a few miles from Kohat, a large British garrison town which was taken over by the Pakistan army at independence. The lodge's reputation as a place of local beauty attracts a constant stream of curious visitors. Many of his *murids* told me how they first visited the lodge while stationed in Kohat. On seeing the lodge, they were overwhelmed by its gloriousness and the spirituality of its *shaikh*. Later they became his *murids*.

The story told me by one *murid* exemplifies this intersection between army, labour migration and village roots:

'I took *bai'at* in 1969. I come from near Tarbela Dam in the Frontier. Many people had told me about the *shaikh* and a friend suggested that I take *bai'at*. Since then I have brought many *murids* here, and I come here for the *'urs* with three or four lorries every year. I am a *qafila* leader, the leader on the Tarbela side. When I did *bai'at* I was in the army. Now I am a pensioner, I retired in 1976. Today I am a farmer. I have performed the Hajj five times, because after I retired from the army I went to Dubai with Ibrahim [another *murid*] and then to Saudi Arabia [as a labour migrant]. My name is Hajji Ghulam Muhammad and I am a stonemason. I am the person who built the perimeter wall around the *darbar.*'

It needs to be remembered that while many of Zindapir's *murids* are soldiers, it is as civilians that they join his cult. The moment they enter the space of the lodge, they shed their military persona. Even in army barracks, when they perform *zikr* they create a space apart. Nevertheless, the fact that they are *pir-bhai* as well as comrades-in-arms serves to deepen relations of amity between them. The camaraderie they forge in one context spills over into the other to create multiple relations of enduring obligation and trust. It counters formal relations of hierarchy in bureaucratic and military settings.

PROXIMITY TO THE *SHAIKH*

Sufi disciples in modern South Asia have been analysed from a number of different perspectives. These include relations of loving intimacy for a

living *majzub*, incapacitated by old age (Frembgen 1998), of embodied
magical connection to a very powerful saint, alive but distant, which
Landell Mills argues personifies all relations between self and other
(Landell Mills 1998), and of ecstatic love and 'madness' in a Siddi healing cult (Basu 1998). A classic issue explored by Pinto (1995) is the emotional bond which develops between a saint and his disciples over time
(see also Nanda and Talib 1989). Since Sufi saint cults are healing cults,
many have also stressed the malevolent dimensions of saint-disciple relations, and the chicanery, the sexual and the financial exploitation perpe-
trated by living saints or their descendents (Sherani 1991; Malik 1998a)
on gullible supplicants.

On the whole, however, less consideration has been given to the way
close proximity to a saint affects relations between disciples themselves,
or the way disciplehood permeates contexts of modern employment
beyond a saint's lodge. In a fine article, Katherine Ewing has suggested
that being a Sufi disciple endows men with the capacity for autonomous
decision-making and personal independence in bureaucratic contexts
(Ewing 1993). In the present chapter I explore this question as part of a
broader attempt to probe the complex subjectivities of the *murids* of
Zindapir, a man who, during his lifetime, wielded considerable spiritual
power over those close to him. A key question, then, is why 'modern' men,
soldiers, factory workers, civil servants, bureaucrats, politicians, continue to feel attracted to Sufi saints. In what ways does being a *pir-bhai*
endow the lives of such men with a redemptive sociality.

As we have seen, most disciples are introduced to the saint by friends,
co-workers or kinsmen. It is this which creates the pattern of interconnec-
ted communities—*biradaris*, occupational guilds and neighbourhoods—
typifying the organisation of Sufi regional cults. But this points to a paradox: first, how is it that being a Sufi disciple is experienced as a highly
personalised and individualised choice despite the fact that most disciples belong to families or larger social collectivities, all initiated to the
same saint? And second, how is it that this relation of discipleship is
experienced as socially and subjectively empowering and voluntaristic
despite the fact that, paradoxically, the relationship requires, in theory
and often in fact, complete submission and self-denial?

Central to my argument is the fact that the experience of subjectivity
differs for different categories of disciples in line with their normal
spatial proximity to a living saint. The distinction is between, first, ordinary disciples who see the saint intermittently, either annually on the *'urs*

festival, or more frequently, at most once a week, for *zikr* prayers which are usually held on Thursday evenings in saints' lodges in South Asia, or in army bases, factories and villages—indeed, wherever a *zikr* circle emerges.

Second are his *khulafa* who have been promoted from the first stage (*martaba*) on the Sufi path, who have a special connection to the saint and who are perceived to have acquired some mystical forces. These *khulafa*, in the Naqshbandi order which I studied, were 'sent' by the saint to remote places to found local branches of the order, and were thus located most of the time beyond the lodge. Among them, Sufi Sahib, the *khalifa* originally sent to England by Zindapir, was the most powerful and independent, a *pir* in his own right. Although a very close companion of the *shaikh* during his rise to sainthood in Pakistan, for more than twenty years after he first came to England Sufi Sahib never set foot in the lodge. He developed his own close circle of *murids* in Britain.

Finally are the disciples who live in the lodge itself and who have dedicated themselves, either permanently or temporarily, to serving the saint. Some of these are also described as *khulafa*. These are the disciples who live in closest daily proximity to their *shaikh*.

The story of a distant *khalifa* is instructive. Living in deep Sindh he has become, like Sufi Sahib, a *pir* in his own right. The *khalifa*, a very dark, chunky, solid man with a large belly and a bright face, told me he had been a tax collector, a *potidar*, in deep Multan, on the edge of Sindh. In 1965 he had a dream in which he saw the *shaikh*. Then, in 1974, a friend brought him here (to the *darbar*) and he found the man in his dream. In 1976 he was made a *khalifa*, given the *khilafat* and told to go and find a site to practise in Sindh. He visited three places and eventually chose a place in a village or area where there were both Muslims and Hindus. The village already had a *murid* of the *shaikh* living there. He travelled there by train, with no money, so he went third class. Since the train was packed, he sat on his haunches for thirteen hours, from midnight until 1 p.m. the following day. When he arrived a man from Lahore with whom he had got friendly helped him to carry his suitcase. In the village the *murid* of the *shaikh* had vacated his house for him, but he met with a lot of opposition from local people.

By this time he was married. He had married a girl from the village. Initially, he went to see the *shaikh* to ask permission to marry a girl from his own family but the *shaikh* said, 'No, you won't be able to be a *khalifa* there if your wife is from the Punjab.' Then, while he was still in

Ghamkol Sharif, at the *darbar*, he saw in his mind's eye a vision of a Sindhi girl he knew back at the village. She was a daughter of a *murid*. He asked the *shaikh* about her and the *shaikh* said, 'Yes, she is the one you should marry.'

When he was having trouble in the village he had a dream one night. In his dream he saw a place, outside the village, some way away. He found that place and built a hut there. Gradually, he expanded the place and now they are building a mosque there.

As we shall see, there are other such stories about Zindapir's *khulafa* who struck out on their own and, like Zindapir himself, became the hub of new sub-centres. Such *khulafa* living at a distance are treated with immense respect. Some, among them several still serving in the army, fulfil important roles in the preparations for the *'urs*.

Whereas *khulafa* living at a distance are organisers in their own right, in the lodge itself Zindapir holds absolute sway. Nothing is done (certainly nothing new) without his permission (*ijazat*). As a researcher, this meant for me that I could show no initiative, not even visit the nearest town, without his *ijazat*. On my visit to the lodge in 1991, I surveyed the supplicants visiting the *shaikh*, interviewing them about their reasons for the visit and obtaining brief personal biographies. On the second day of this interviewing, rumours began to circulate in the lodge that people (that is, the supplicants) were 'complaining'. On hearing the rumours my helper and guardian, Hajji Ibrahim, who had dedicated many years of his life to serving the saint in the lodge, panicked in case he had transgressed an unwritten rule and would thus invoke the wrath of Zindapir. He said to me: 'I have done 30 years of work here, and then, if the *shaikh* is angry with me, it will all be wiped away in one second!'

As his anxiety increased, he became a broken man. He looked utterly crushed and defeated, and was also suffering from a stomach upset, heartburn and diarrhoea. Pinto (1995: 299–314) describes the heartbreaking crisis of a *murid* living at the shrine of Nizamuddin who had begun to acquire some charismatic powers in his own right, and was punished by his *pir* for his supposed hubris by having his hair cut off and his beard shaved, his duties awarded to another *murid*, while he himself was subjected to various other forms of hazing. In his despair the *murid* wanted to die or alternatively, to leave the *darbar* forever. But he found himself trapped in a relationship that had lasted too long. He had nowhere to go, and eventually he persuaded himself that this was a trial set by his *pir* to advance him on the Sufi path.

During my visit to the annual celebration of the *'urs* in 1989, my purse was stolen. My companion from Manchester, a respected *khalifa* of the saint, was called to the *shaikh* and reprimanded for not adequately looking after me, a foreigner with no appreciation of local dangers. It was obvious to me that the theft had been entirely my own fault, and I made this clear to the *pir*. I did not blame anyone: I had been warned, and despite that I had been careless, mainly because the lodge was so very peaceful until the arrival of the crowds for the festival.

But my explanations were to no avail. The saint regarded me as his responsibility, entrusted to his care, and anything at all that happened to me was therefore construed as reflecting on his *izzat* and the honour of the *darbar*. He therefore reprimanded my companion, Hajji Karim, very sharply.

For the next few days, Hajji Karim walked around like a shadow, depressed beyond words. His hopes of 'promotion' on the Sufi path had, he felt, suffered a terrible setback and he was in deep despair. To lose the approval of the saint was to lose a lifetime of devoted good works. This the saint could achieve with a mere gesture. Yet the Hajji Karim I had known in Manchester was an active, decisive man, able to contend with the rough and tumble of local community politics and the intricacies of municipal bureaucratic regulations.

Any unusual requests in the *darbar* needed the saint's *ijazat*. If this took three days (because the saint was busy, or I had no direct or indirect access to him) so be it. To me, the fieldworker, this was a constant source of frustration. I had wanted to video the preparations for the *'urs*, I had asked to see the register of disciples in a book supposedly kept, I was told, by a *khalifa*. Repeated requests were to no avail. I asked why the *shaikh* did not allow videos or the publication of a book about him. In exasperation at my obtuseness, one of the *murids* closest to the saint said to me: 'It is just his order. You are not supposed to reflect on his orders, you just obey him. When he gives an order, you do not ask him "why?" or "what is the reason?"'

On another occasion, when I wanted to visit the graveyard where an ancestor of the *shaikh*, also a saint, was said to be buried, I was told that I would be attacked by *qalandar*, wandering ecstatics who frequent saints' tombs in Pakistan. Women were not allowed in the graveyard, I was informed. Once again the *shaikh*'s close *murids* admonished me:

'Why do you want to know these things? We never ask the *shaikh* permission for the same thing twice. Even Badshah Sahib (the saint's son) would not do that.

Anyone in a position of responsibility must inform the *shaikh* before leaving the *darbar*, especially members of his own family. When he orders, you obey. You don't ask questions. You never ask why. You never ask for an explanation.'

In the end, I never did see the register on that visit (I did see it later, by chance), never climbed to the top of the hill where one could look beyond and see Jangal Khel, the natal village of the *shaikh*, or the path marking the route the saint had taken on his first journey to the lodge. I never took that video film. Nor did I continue with my casual interviewing of suppli- cants (since I did not wish to jeopardise Hajji Ibrahim's chances of going to paradise). I did, however, finally get to go to Jangal Khel, travelling on the road around the hills, after several women had repeatedly approached the saint to get 'permission' for my visit to their homes.

Close daily proximity to the *shaikh*, as for those working in the lodge, can be oppressive, while for *murids* living at a distance being a disciple can be experienced as liberating and empowering. The approval of the saint is a prize of immense significance while his disapproval can cause strong men to crumble. Those working in the lodge thus compete for the saint's approval and proximity to him. Anyone threatening to displace them in their established role is subjected to intense gossip, and gossip in general—which might reach the saint—is experienced as very threaten- ing. Except during the annual Hajj to Mecca, the *shaikh* spent almost all his days and nights at the lodge in his room, apart from brief forays to the mosque or to inspect the preparations for the *'urs*, and it was to this inner sanctum that gossip flowed towards him from all his disciples working at the lodge.

In these circumstances of competition for proximity, anything out of the usual is experienced as highly disruptive. Hence, perhaps not surpris- ingly, my visit as an anthropologist was felt by key disciples to undermine their place in the established hierarchy at the lodge, a fact I elaborate on in the conclusion. Gossip is the daily fare of disciples living permanently or semi-permanently in the lodge. The saint's esteem and praise are so highly sought after that jealousies are barely disguised. My guide and assistant on my second visit, Hajji Ibrahim, told me that A. had been say- ing 'bad things' about Sufi Karim, the *khalifa* from Manchester. When I asked why, he said he did not know. He then volunteered, and repeated this to me the following day, that he did not trust anyone in the *darbar* or know whether they were telling the truth, except the *shaikh*, his son and his nephew, the latter being a minor saint in his own right who was visit- ing the lodge at the time from a small shrine in Gujrat to stand in for the *shaikh*'s son and daughter-in-law who were away in England. Hajji Ibrahim was responding also to the malicious rumours about his complicity in my interviewing of supplicants, or inadvertently providing me with secret information. This had clearly upset him greatly.

The closest *murids* share daily in the *faiz* of the saint, they literally bask in this divine light emanating from him. For some, like Saeed, a young *khalifa* who was an important mover and shaker in the little community of the lodge, the saint filled his world. At the time of my visits in 1989 and 1991, he wanted nothing but to remain in close proximity to the *shaikh*. He told of his first encounter with the *shaikh*:

While I was still doing my higher secondary education I had a wish in my mind that I should become a *murid* of some good *silsila*. I was searching for a proper place when my elder brother, who was in the army and was stationed at Kohat, told me that there is a Pir Sahib there. I come from Tahsil Sohawa near Jhelum. There is a *khalifa* there of Ghamkol Sharif (you should go there and meet him). Whenever somebody spoke the name of Ghamkol Sharif in my presence tears would start rising to my eyes, despite the fact that I'd never seen the *shaikh*. After some time I came to Kohat and when I entered Darbar Alia Ghamkol Sharif it was the time of the *zohar* [midday] prayers. The *darban* Mr Nawaz Haq told me that I should say my prayers first and then I would be allowed to meet the Pir Sahib. When I went to the mosque, and we were standing there waiting for the prayers to start, I looked around me and saw many elderly *khulafa*. I saw them all and said to myself in my heart that if any one of them is the Pir Sahib then I have come to the wrong place. However, I said my prayers and when I finished, I saw the man with the green *juba*. When I saw Pir Sahib I started shivering, I kept on shivering until Pir Sahib entered his *astan* [lodge]. Then I was allowed to see him and I requested permission to do *bai'at* which was granted to me. When the people went away there were three or four people who were still sitting with Pir Sahib and he told them they should say their prayers regularly. Immediately the thought crossed my mind, that since I am [already] saying my prayers regularly, what will he say to me? The *pir* smiled and looked towards me and said: you should pray regularly for *tahajad* and *ishrak* [optional prayers in the last quarter of the night, additional to the five regular canonical prayers]. That night I attended the *zikr* and then again I met Pir Sahib next morning at 10 a.m. After the meeting, when I was coming out of the door, the *pir* looked towards me for a while. Then I went back to my house in the village. But I was restless, and after spending 20–22 days there I made up my mind to come forever to this place. Since that time I have been living here. That was in March 1977.

With his charismatic good looks, enormous energy and commitment, and evident intelligence, Saeed was obviously one of a very select circle of close companions of the *shaikh*. But for some of the older, less educated men serving at the lodge, close proximity required high levels of self-disciple and self-abnegation, and yet was also associated, as we have seen, with mutual suspicion and jealousy.[1]

For people coming into contact with the *shaikh* more intermittently he is a far less oppressive and more liberating figure than for those living in close proximity. This is true even of disciples like Hajji Ibrahim himself who had felt sustained and empowered by the saint during the periods he spent working away from the lodge. Two incidents illustrate this transnational empowerment.

THE GLOBAL POWER OF THE SAINT

Hajji Ibrahim's experiences reflect the global spread of transnational Sufi cults and its impact on the careers of individual devotee labour migrants. Hajji Ibrahim was a villager with relatively little education who had served in the Pakistani army before retiring on a pension in 1974. He had taken *bai'at* while still in the army, in 1964, and used to work at the *darbar* for six weeks during his annual two-month leave from the army. Between 1974 and 1979 he lived in the *darbar*, first working as the *darban* of the *shaikh* for three years, and then as a driver for Badshah Sahib, the saint's son.

When A. left in high dudgeon during my second visit to the lodge in 1991, Hajji Ibrahim became my main informant. His command of English, although ungrammatical, was quite impressive. To my query, since I knew he was relatively uneducated, as to where he had learnt to speak English, he explained: 'I learnt it,' he told me, 'while I was working in the Gulf.' 'In the Gulf?' I wondered. 'But didn't you tell me that you were working for a Japanese firm there?' 'Yes,' he answered, 'of course.' 'Well, how did you learn English then?' 'I learnt it from the Japanese,' he replied. 'The Japanese? But they also don't speak English. How did you manage?' 'We used dictionaries,' he explained, as though this should have been quite obvious.

On another occasion we were chatting about the saint and the large number of foreign visitors he hosted at the *darbar*. 'The saint,' he explained, 'likes to entertain each person according to what he is accustomed to. In your case, for example, he has given you a comfortable bed to sleep in. The Japanese are very interested in Sufism. Once there was a

---

[1] Saeed died tragically of a heart attack a few years later.

Japanese delegation that came here to talk about Sufism. At that time I was the *shaikh's darban*. I served the visitors green tea without sugar, exactly as I knew they liked it. They were delighted and amazed. Once in the Gulf,' he added, 'I cured a Japanese of a very bad headache by blowing *dam* on him.'

Despite his humble origins Hajji Ibrahim is a cosmopolitan traveller with a good deal of international experience. His first labour migration trip followed an instruction by the *shaikh* to go to Dubai to earn money for his family. This instruction was issued, it seems, after Hajji Ibrahim's wife had been to see the *shaikh* to ask advice about her financial difficulties, since her husband was working at the lodge in a voluntary capacity, earning no wages.

While in the Gulf, Hajji Ibrahim not only learnt to speak English, but also Arabic and even a little Japanese. When he started working in the Gulf, he told me, he was not competent as a builder or an electrician but by mustering the *tasawwur* (image) of the *shaikh* before his eyes, he acquired the requisite skills. His encounters with the Japanese were complex. At one point he left the firm he was working for in Dubai at short notice after he had obtained a valuable visa permitting him to go on Hajj. His application to the firm for leave was refused. At the time, he was a supervisor, and both site engineers were away in Japan on leave so he was responsible for 250 men. The manager told him: 'If I let you go all the Muslims working here will want to go too.' Hajji Ibrahim, so he told me, consulted a Pakistani friend who was working for another company. The friend advised him to forget the money and go on the pilgrimage anyway. 'This is a great opportunity for you to go on Hajj,' he said, 'you may never get another one!' So Hajji Ibrahim went off on Hajj without handing in his notice, for fear that the company might take away his passport. He just left, 20 days before the Hajj. In Mecca he stayed with a Pakistani *khalifa* of the *shaikh* based permanently in the holy city.

When the *shaikh* arrived in Mecca for the annual pilgrimage, Hajji Ibrahim was terrified he would be angry with him for deserting his job. He did not come forward to greet the *shaikh* but the latter noticed him hiding behind the door and called him in. Even though the saint knew nothing of his desertion he said to him: 'Ibrahim, you have done the right thing. You preferred God to money. Do not worry. God will look after you.'

Hajji Ibrahim was afraid to go back to his company. He spent a whole month searching for another job in Dubai, staying with a fellow cult member, but to no avail. Then, one night, at the end of the month, the saint appeared to him in a dream. He told him to go back to his old company, to go there at 2.30 p.m. sharp, just after lunch. He found out later, he told me, that the company was about to strike him off the books the following day, and to have him deported. He arrived at 2.30 and all the workers—Indians, Bangladeshis, Japanese and others—greeted him. 'Hello, Hajji Ibrahim' (stressing the 'Hajji' bit, since he'd been on the pilgrimage to Mecca). At the office all the Japanese were there except the manager, who was late. They were pleased to see him but they advised him to wait in the meeting room so that the manager wouldn't encounter him straight away when he returned, since the manager was, they said, very angry with him. They promised to tell the manager that he was waiting for him in the meeting room.

Finally the manager arrived. He told Ibrahim: 'I cannot employ you any longer. You were solely responsible for 250 men, and you abandoned them.' 'But,' Hajji Ibrahim explained to me,

'I had the *tasawwur* of the *shaikh* in front of me [in my inner vision] and this gave me courage so I answered: "You refused me permission to go on Hajj when I already had a visa, and all the Muslim workers were laughing at me." The manager thought for a while, and told me to wait. Eventually he called me to him and told me his company had just started a new project in Baghdad. He promised to send me there. I knew the Japanese manager of the new site, Mr Kato, who was away for a few days in Japan. When he came back I met him to discuss the move to Iraq. He wanted to put me in a lower position than I had before, under an ex-gang leader of mine who had meanwhile been promoted. But I still had the *tasawwur* of the *shaikh* before my eyes, so I refused. In the end they gave in. They promoted someone else to assistant engineer and made me a supervisor instead of that man. Then the company paid my wages and sent me back to Pakistan for a month. I came straight here, to the *darbar*, to see the *shaikh*, even before going home.

'When I first came in to see him, the *shaikh* said to me: "Now you are going to Baghdad—first Mecca, now Baghdad. You are a very lucky man. Your company is located close to Abdul Qadr Jilani's tomb, just one stop by minibus. You will work in the company in the daytime and clean the tomb at night." You see, the *shaikh* knew everything, even though he has never been to Iraq. As Iqbal [the great nationalist Punjabi poet] says, "God's *wali* can take two-and-a-half steps and see the whole world."'

While he was in Baghdad, Hajji Ibrahim's wife joined him there for a while, and the two of them both worked as volunteers cleaning the shrine of Abdul Qadr Jilani.

Hajji Ibrahim does not belong to a landowning caste. One of his sons is a watchmaker in a small Punjabi town. But two of his sons have recently married cousins (wife's sister's daughters) in Amsterdam and have moved to the Netherlands. In 1991, when these conversations took place, they were waiting for their passports to be released, and then they would be allowed to bring their parents over to the Netherland. Hajji Ibrahim regarded these marriages as a blessing granted him by the saint as reward for his labours.

One day, discussing the issue of 'promotions' on the Sufi path, I asked Hajji Ibrahim whether he did not resent his position as a mere *murid* despite the long years of unpaid service he had put in at the lodge since he retired from the Pakistan army. 'No,' he said, 'I *have* been promoted,' and he explained that the saint had given him permission to blow *dam*. 'But could you not become a *khalifa?*' I persisted. 'After all, you know Arabic and can even lead the prayers.' Hajji Ibrahim then revealed to me a secret dream. 'Perhaps the *shaikh* will send me to the Netherlands,' he said, 'to found a branch of his order there. He did have a *khalifa* there before who was sent over from England, I think, but the man proved to be a failure, and has now left. So Amsterdam is the only place which is now "empty" (that is, has no branch of the order, despite the large number of Pakistanis living there).

'In addition to Pakistanis, you know, there are lots of Turks and Arabs in Amsterdam. The other *khalifa* did not speak Dutch or Arabic,' he told me. 'But what about you? You don't speak Dutch either,' I said. 'Dutch is very easy,' Hajji Ibrahim replied, 'it's just like Punjabi.' At this unexpected reply, I burst out laughing, but I had to admit to myself that for a man who had learnt English from the Japanese, as well as fluent Arabic, while working on a building site, learning to speak Dutch was likely to be a relatively small challenge.

Hajji Ibrahim is a devoted Sufi and an evidently pious Muslim. He would not have been given his job back had his piety and sincerity not been recognised by his Japanese employers. But his story is also a tale of transnational Sufi religious empowerment. He is locked into a transnational network, not of relatives and family but of *pir-bhai*. A *pir-bhai* advises him to seize the opportunity and go on Hajj. He stays in Mecca with the *khalifa* of the order. He meets the saint he left behind in Pakistan at a recognised meeting point of the cult in Mecca, when the saint comes for the annual pilgrimage. He then lives with another *pir-bhai* while seeking alternative employment. Finally, in Baghdad, along with his wife, he spends the days working for wages and the nights working for the love of God at a saint's shrine. Away from the saint's lodge the *shaikh*'s presence becomes for disciples a source of courage[2] and companionship, mutual loyalty and solidarity.

For Hajji Ibrahim, 'home' is condensed in the image of the saint whom he musters before his inner eye whenever he needs courage to confront superiors and foreigners or to learn new tasks. That image is always with him, wherever he is. His experience of overseas travel is thus not one of alienation but of triumphant mastery, rooted in his localised faith in his saint—which is, simultaneously, very much also a faith in Islam as a world religion. Hence, one of the most exhilarating aspects of his migration experience for him was the sense of Islam as a boundary-crossing global faith. His work at the tomb of Abdul Qadr Jilani in pious service to God confirms his identity in his own eyes as a cosmopolitan who is at home everywhere just as God is everywhere. So too, the pilgrimage to Mecca, which he performed subsequently several more times during his stay in the Middle East, provides him with an experience of membership in a global community. He is determined to share in that experience, even at the risk of losing a valuable job.

Although he is a simple man from a poor background and with little formal education, Hajji Ibrahim clearly feels that the experiences both as a Sufi and a labour migrant have transformed him. He is competent now in the traditions of others. He knows the Japanese intimately, has observed their minutest customs. By the same token, he has also observed the customs, habits and idiosyncrasies of Indians, Bangladeshis, Arabs and Iraqis. He appears to have had close cross-cultural friendships. His confidence is such that learning Dutch is regarded by him as a small matter, almost like knowing Punjabi—which is his mother tongue. But when he considers moving to the Netherlands, it is nevertheless from the vantage point of his most valued identity as a Sufi. If he moves there, it will be with the mission to found a branch of his order there. He will utilise the Arabic picked up in the Gulf to create a cross-national Sufi community of Pakistanis, Turks and Arabs. He knows he can do that, since he has lived with Muslims from other countries already.

The world is mapped by him in terms of his Sufi order. Holland is an empty place, a void, since there is no branch there. His perspective as a Sufi member of Zindapir's transnational regional cult shapes his cosmopolitanism and provides it with a sense of order.

[2] On this see also Nanda and Talib (1989).

INDIVIDUAL SUBJECTIVITY AND DISCIPLEHOOD

The subjectivity of disciples both mirrors and contrasts with the subjectivity of Sufi saints themselves as world renouncers. Dumont, following Weber, contrasts the Protestant concept of the 'individual *in* the world' with the Hindu concept of the individual as world renouncer, or the 'extramundane individual' (1957: 52). His analysis illuminates the symbolic logic of world renunciation in a caste-based society in which temporal and spiritual power are separated and legitimised by a rigid hierarchical ideology. Within this holistic system world renunciation allows space, he argues, for individual innovation. Paradoxically, then, the renouncer 'finds himself invested with an individuality which he apparently finds uncomfortable since all his efforts tend to its extinction or its transcendence' (ibid.: 46). Furthermore, Dumont stresses, 'the renouncer does not deny the religions of the man-in-the-world'; nor, importantly, does he deny the holistic social structure associated with this worldly religion (ibid.).

This paradox is evident also in Sufism or popular Islam. Zindapir was described to me quite explicitly, in his own words and those of his followers, as a man who had 'turned his face away from the world', and had, by virtue of this self-denying asceticism and internal purification, achieved a unique individuality. As world renouncer he was believed to have a direct connection with God which endowed him with immediate and comprehensive knowledge. This knowledge was not derived, as one of the saint's trusted deputies—an elderly man—repeatedly stressed to me whenever we met on the narrow paths of the lodge, from the literate study of theological treatises or Islamic *Shari'at* law (*'ilm*), but from an immediate mystical experience of the divine (*ma'arifa*). Hence the saint in Islam is unique in being a religious innovator, not bound by the strict letter of the Islamic law, able to interpret the 'spirit' of Islam through his transcendent understanding of the inner meaning of religion.

This innovatory individuality, having parallels, as Dumont points out, with liberal ideological constructs of individualism, goes along, however, with an endorsement of worldly, *Shari'at*-based Islam for the saint's followers and disciples, and an acceptance of worldly hierarchies (see also Lindholm 1998). As possessor of spiritual power, the saint's place is at the apex of this hierarchy. He is regarded as superior to any temporal ruler and his divinely sanctioned superiority is usually underlined by genealogical descent from the Prophet Muhammad or his first Caliph, although the importance of this genealogical connection is often publicly denied by the more reformist-minded saints. By contrast, the individuality of disciples, whether scholars, legal experts or laymen, as autonomous decision-makers is totally submerged and denied in the presence of the saint. Theoretically, and often in practice as we have seen, they must obey him, with his superior inner knowledge, however absurd and irrational his directives may appear on the surface to be, since it is believed that he possesses transcendent ethical insight which recognises the ultimate rationality of the apparently irrational.

This is not to deny, of course, the commonsense, quotidian rationality and moral knowledge of individual Sufi followers or the existence of worldly hierarchies. As we have seen, in practice the saint accords special treatment to men and women of high status. From a philosophical perspective, however, total obedience to the saint necessarily implies a denial of any notion of the individual as the locus of a transcendental rationality and ethical knowledge. Indeed, the way to mystical revelation on the Sufi path is through the denial ('killing') of the *nafs* achieved by the disciple merging himself with the saint, and ultimately with the Prophet and God. As we have already seen, this abjection or submission is articulated in pragmatic terms by the notion of *ijazat* and the rejection of even the possibility of questioning unexplained or apparently irrational decisions. In Sufism the universalism of men's equality before Allah is displaced by a stress on exemplary personhood: the saint, *wali*, is a rare individual. Followers are, as if to compensate for the saint's unique individuality, expected to be obedient non-thinkers; 'like a corpse in the hands of its washer' is the oft-cited Sufi saying. Self-denial is a crucible on the Sufi path to true knowledge, to be realised, it is believed, only through total submission to the guidance of the saint (see Ajmal 1984).

The theory of the individual, *insan*, as subject in Sufi Islam is a dualistic one. According to this theory, most men are motivated by their *nafs*, their carnal, desiring soul, which animates their being during their lifetime. The *nafs* is the source of individual agency, but it is also regarded as selfish and hedonistic. By contrast the *ruh* is a source of spiritual individuality which exists prior to the birth of a person and survives his or her death, to be rewarded or punished in heaven or hell on the Day of Judgement. In Sufi mystical theory, *jihad* is the battle between these two sources of individuality—the carnal and the spiritual. The Sufi saint is the person who has killed his *nafs* by turning towards God—that is, he has submerged his individuality as a desiring and active human being, but in doing so he has released his *nafs/ruh* from its dark cage and thus achieved a transcendent spiritual individuality which makes him an agent and conduit of God's power and blessing, even after his death (on this in detail see Rao 1990; 1998, ch. 2; P. Werbner 1990b). He is *insan-el kamil*, the perfect man (see Nicholson 1963: 163–6).[3] Hence, the usual notions associated in Western discourse with 'the individual'—autonomy, agency, uniqueness, equality—have very specific, non-Western connotations in Sufism, and interact in constellations quite different from any theory of western individualism. What is privileged is not common sense 'rationality' but a higher, divinely inspired rationality, associated with divinely endowed powers.

THE DILEMMAS OF A SAINT

Yet just as those *murids* living in close daily proximity to the saint are minutely observed, so too is the saint himself. It is not easy to be a full-time saint and I could only admire Zindapir's utter professionalism and dedication to his role as a *faqir*. It was said that he never slept and that he ate very little, a dry *chapati* with some vegetables, no meat or butter. He saw visiting disciples until the very early hours of the morning. During the *'urs*, an endless stream of pilgrims came in groups into his sanctuary, often pushing and shoving in their attempts to reach close to him. These crowds would have daunted a much younger man, let alone a man in his eighties as he then was. Yet he never faltered. He accepted his followers, men and women, young and old, with a distant stoicism. He even had time to joke with the close disciples who worked hard to keep the crowds in order. Perhaps only his tireless *darban* knew whether he sometimes snatched an illicit nap or was tempted by a delicacy. But if he did, he divulged nothing.

---

[3] Muhammad Iqbal, the great Punjabi poet-philosopher of Pakistani nationalism, although a Sufi initiate inspired by Sufi thought, condemned the Sufi idea of the perfect man as 'apt to destroy human personality' and lead to 'stagnation'. In his view 'the personality which has developed his inward possibilities in full, and is united with God in a union of will… is able to be the spiritual ruler of the world' (Schimmel 1963: 367–8). Iqbal was greatly influenced by German vitalist philosophy, and especially Nietzsche (Schimmel 1963: 323–6). But, according to Schimmel, Iqbal was not a humanist of 'man *qua* man, but of man in relation to God…not man as measure of all things but as a being that grows the more perfect the closer his connection God is, …neither as an atheistic superman who replaces God' (as Nietzsche would have it) 'nor as the Perfect Man in the sense that he is but a visible aspect of God with whom he is essentially one—but man as realizing the wonderful paradox of freedom in servantship' (Schimmel 1963: 382). This contradictory logic nevertheless serves to underline the gulf separating Sufism from Western modernism.

Sufi Sahib, the head of the order in Britain whose headquarters were in Birmingham, was a rather different character. A very large, powerful man, he had left the Pakistani army as a sergeant and accompanied Zindapir on his journey to the lodge. In Britain, he had worked as a labourer in a steel foundry on twelve-hour night shifts for many years. He was an organisation man who had succeeded in establishing branches of the order in quite a number of British towns and cities. This was achieved through hard work and dedication and his reputation as an honest man until the early 1980s was quite impeccable.

16. *Du'a*: Sufi Sahib arriving at London Heathrow airport, after a journey to Mecca

In Birmingham, Sufi Sahib had bought a piece of property in the inner city, and over thirty years, he gradually established his dominion over a whole tract of land, as he purchased house after adjacent house. Part of this land was the site of a smallish mosque housed in a wooden structure. This is where he and his closest disciples performed regular *zikr*, and where these disciples, the majority young men born in Pakistan who had grown up in Britain, discussed *tasawwuf*, Islamic mysticism, endlessly among themselves, sometimes consulting him, at other times reading voraciously in books on mysticism available in English or Urdu. Sufi Karim was one such disciple, later sent to Manchester to set up a branch of the order there. Although initiated directly to Zindapir he was dedicated to Sufi Sahib who had rescued him and brought him into the sanctuary of his circle when Karim's family turned against him as a young teenager, following his father's death.

In building up his empire Sufi Sahib relied on the chair of his mosque management committee, a charming and highly intelligent accountant with excellent links to the Labour Party and the City Council in Birmingham, which for some years has had a large number of Pakistani councillors.

It was in the early 1980s, one of Sufi Sahib's *murids* recalled, that the idea of building a purpose-built mosque was first mooted. And it was the mosque that revealed the saint to his followers in a new light. Until that time he had been the object of great devotion, a charismatic figure who was always greeted with adulation. This continued to be the case for more distant disciples. But for those closest to him, Sufi Sahib's willingness to raise money, as they saw it, by unethical means,[4] caused an irredeemable rift. As one of his close *murids* at the time told me (I paraphrase our conversation):

I became aware of things, as did the other *murids*, since I sat on the management committee of the mosque and was involved in putting together various applications to the council. By 1986 things had begun to come to a head for me. There were discussions among us about whether Sufi Sahib was aware of what was going on around him. Because he was much admired, it was generally thought that he didn't know. Eventually Shaikh B., a very knowledgeable *murid* who had studied Islamic studies, approached him to ask whether he knew that there was cheating going on. He was greeted with an angry response. Sufi Sahib told him that this was a *kufr* government and the cause was a good one, the building of a mosque. We then approached the Maulana, like Sufi Sahib one of the earliest of Zindapir's *murids*. We asked him if this was right according to the *Shari'at*? He replied that it was. But we *murids* could not accept that the *Shari'at* could just be infringed in this way.

---

[4] The chair of the management committee of the order, in his capacity as chair of an affiliate organisation, along with three other Muslim groups, was accused by the press of attempts to defraud the Further Education Funding Council of the West Midlands of over a million pounds by claiming fees for 'phantom' evening classes which never took place (*The Observer*, 5 Mar. 1995, pp. 1–2; *Birmingham Evening Mail* 15 Dec. 1995; see also the Birmingham *Daily and Express* 4 May 1995, and *Times Educational Supplement* 14 Feb. 1997). The chair defended his innocence to the press and cooperated in the police investigation. No charges were ever brought against him, I was told by the detective constable handling the case for the crown court with whom I spoke in January 2000. He continues to chair the *tariqa's* management committee.

Far from being a world renouncer, the saint had revealed himself to his disciples as a man all too firmly entrenched in the world with its dirty politics and corrupt practices. One by one, the closest circle of disciples began to leave the order. They had been happy in the old hut with their small *zikr* circle, the *murid* told me. The envisaged mosque, rather than glorifying the order, had corrupted it for them. Some joined or set up branches of other Sufi orders in Birmingham. Perhaps the last to leave was Hajji Karim himself, who quarrelled with Sufi Sahib some time in 1994 after disagreeing over the educational policy of the Dar-ul-'Uloom in Manchester. Only one *murid*, much disliked by the others according to my interlocutor, remained and colluded with the various money-making schemes. But he too suffered an emotional breakdown. For all the other *murids*, the decision to leave was traumatic.

In building the mosque, Sufi Sahib used the income from his property as well donations from followers and sympathisers. I was present at the laying of the cornerstone to the mosque in which £ 200,000 was raised for the mosque in less than half an hour. But, in addition, the relations he and his chairman had built up over the years with Birmingham Metropolitan Borough, before it was dissolved, and with the dominant Labour Party ruling Birmingham City Council, became major sources of regular income for the organisation. A grant from the Metropolitan Borough was used to build a new community college on Sufi Sahib's land, which was then leased back to the local authority with substantial monthly rent. The college provided much needed training in sewing and design. It also served as a centre for senior citizens and a club for the disabled, and it was let out for weddings and other functions.

Other projects funded by the authorities included a job club, an A-level access college with very good records of attendance by young Asians, and an employment centre. All these were legitimate enterprises which brought in a substantial income while at the same time they also enhanced Sufi Sahib's reputation as a community leader concerned with the predicaments of the elderly and the disabled, as well as of local Asians facing tough competition in the educational and labour markets.

There are several ironies in this tale. The first is that Sufi Sahib, like Zindapir a reformist saint, had taught his young disciples to respect the morality of the *Shari'at* too well. He no longer held absolute charismatic authority over them. They were, in the end, unwilling to believe that breaking the law and cheating the state (as they saw it) were permissible. These were young men who had gone to school in Britain. Clearly, they could not treat the state as merely an alien presence. They had become too English, in a sense, as well as being very devout Muslims, and could not simply embrace the view that the usual yardsticks of morality did not apply to the British state because it was not Islamic. We need also to remember, as Gellner points out, that the cult of submission in Sufism is very deceptive and cannot be taken at face value. 'It is precisely because organisation is normally so very weak,' he says, 'that the doctrine of discipline is so very exaggerated' (Gellner 1972: 205).

The typical Sufi order is a loose and dispersed federation of holy centres, where the minor ones balance the losses inherent in submission against the advantages gained from the spillover of prestige from some famous centre (ibid.).

The second irony is that in the long run the departure of this loyal circle of early disciples mattered rather little. Sufi Sahib built a magnificent mosque, an architecturally designed building in Barelvi style, beautifully inlaid with white and green marble, glittering chandeliers, and wonderfully decorated red and green gilded domes. Much of the building work was done with voluntary labour, just as it always had been in Ghamkol Sharif, Zindapir's lodge. Although the scam, almost a million pounds for 'phantom' classes which were never held, was uncovered by the Education department at the nick of time and some of those associated with this scam brought to court, Sufi Sahib's order has prospered. I was told that during *jum'a* (Friday prayers) the mosque is packed and that the *zikr* circle, which once used to include at most twenty men, now included more than one hundred.

REDEMPTIVE SUCCESS

Whether a saint retains the unquestioning devotion of his closest disciples, then, does in the end depend on his exhibition of the qualities that epitomise his saintliness for them. Blind obedience to the saint does exist, as my research in Pakistan highlighted, and it is often caricatured and condemned by Muslim critics of saintly traditions. But ultimately, for more educated and informed disciples, it is implicitly conditional. By contrast, educated disciples who are more distant geographically from the saint are unable to scrutinise his daily conduct so closely. For them, the appearance of godliness is enough for the saint to legitimise their worldly success.

One of the least understood features of Sufism in South Asia is why it remains attractive to apparently Westernised, high ranking civil servants, army officers, politicians, businessmen and professionals, as well as to large numbers of relatively uneducated villagers. Sufism, at least Reform Sufism, appears to appeal to the educated and powerful, as well as the vast mass of low ranking followers.

This continued elite attraction to Sufi orders stems, I found, from a peculiar understanding of worldly success and predestination in popular Islam. A key role of the saint is believed to be his ability to act as mediator for his disciples with God on the Day of Judgement, asking forgiveness for them and thus assuring that they go to *jannat*, paradise. Disciples are, in other words, dependent upon the saint not only for grace in the world, but for eternal salvation. This leads to the further belief that worldly achievements are divine rewards for obeying the edicts and instructions of the saint regarding religious observance and daily practice, which include the multiple repetition of specific religious litanies (*wazifa*) allocated by him alone. As bringer of divine blessing, he is believed to be able to change the course of nature, to sway the will of God, and thus to affect the predestined movement of the universe. This assumption is at the root of the repeated stories by disciples about the miracles performed by the *shaikh*. Hence if, after their initiation, disciples succeed in their businesses, in arranging marriages for their children, in obtaining job promotions, in passing examinations or tests, in finding work as labour migrants—in short, in any of their endeavours, they interpret this as a sign of God's blessing conferred upon them via their saint. The saint's own vast accumulation of wealth is similarly regarded. The beauty of the mosque in Birmingham made Sufi Sahib a great man for most disciples. Discipleship thus constitutes a legitimation of personal worldly success. The gloriousness of Ghamkol Sharif proved Zindapir's spirituality and chosen status as *wali* of Allah.

For low caste peasants or urban workers too membership in the cult is a source of status. They derive their personal standing vis-à-vis others from their connection with an illustrious saint, and regard themselves otherwise as social nonentities. In this sense the respect accorded to Zindapir by high level politicians and civil servants or army officers is not only useful for pragmatic purposes, but perhaps even more significantly, it confirms the saint's elevated status in the eyes of the many villagers who form the main body of his disciples, and brings together the high and the low in a single 'family' of 'disciple-brothers'. The vicarious status derived from membership in an 'important' order of this type was seen by these disciples, I found, to confer a meaningful and dignified gloss upon their lives. They were proud of their saint and proud to be associated with him, while the cult's daily, weekly, monthly and annual rituals imbued the routines of their daily life with a transcendent significance.

In general, then, autonomous religious individuality-cum-knowledge— the direct personal access to God valorised by the Protestant Puritan sects—is regarded as a rare achievement by Sufi disciples. Nor do they share an explicit notion of predestination which Weber argued was so fundamental in Calvinism. As in Calvinism, however, worldly rewards and achievements are believed to be signs of divine approval and bless-ing, and thus also guarantors of election and salvation. This goes along, I found, with instructions by the saint to his disciples to practise self-denial and self-discipline in their worldly activities—in other words, to observe worldly asceticism—and with an affirmation of the value of hard work, obedience and respect for authority, all of which tend, of course, to lead, as in the Puritan case, to worldly success. In sum, then, non-individuality and self-denial do not entail a diminution of the will to succeed in worldly matters, and indeed, have an elective affinity with it—they facili-tate and legitimise this success.

CONCLUSION: THE CAMARADERIE OF DISCIPLEHOOD

Ultimately, Sufism is a fundamentally voluntary relationship. We cannot understand the subjectivity of Sufi disciples unless we recognise the vol-untarism inherent both in the dyadic relation with a saint, and in the rela-tions between saintly disciples. Being a *murid* is liberating to global migrants far from home who can muster the image of their saint in their inner eye, but it is also liberating through the relations between *pir-bhai*, the fraternity (and sorority) of saintly disciples. Zindapir's followers are drawn mainly from three types of organisation: the army and the police, large government works departments, and villages. It seems quite rare for people as isolated individuals to become disciples. Although I did meet a number of such people, the story of initiation on the whole followed, as we have seen, predictable lines: a person dreams of seeing an old man or a beautiful place, or passes by chance near the *darbar*. The encounter is one of almost accidental good luck or 'discovery'. Either way, on reach-ing the lodge or encountering the *shaikh*, the person realises that this is the place he or she has always been seeking. After some hesitation, per-haps going away and coming back a second or third time, the person decides to take *bai'at*. But then, when one probes further, one discovers that close relatives—a father, a brother, members of the village, co-workers, colleagues or fellow soldiers—are all disciples as well. Discipleship, in other words, runs in families or occupational guilds.

The significance of this journey which turns out not to be a journey on closer look, is the voluntarism it implies. Even though whole villages, arms factories, public works departments, police units, army regiments, may follow a particular saint, as they follow Zindapir, nevertheless the relationship is an elective one. You choose to become a disciple; your relationship to a saint is conceived to be dyadic. What the stories of epiphanies and dreams-come-true show, above all, is the sense that disciples have that their relationship with the saint is not only unique but voluntaristic, an expression of their deepest subjectivist desire and hence a sign of freedom par excellence. Rather than being enslaved, then, to the saint in a relationship that extinguishes their persona, the relationship is experienced as liberating, just as the voluntary work performed by disciples in the *darbar*, or the food they donate to the *langar* are experienced as crucibles, tests of personal capacity which are thus empowering.

The story one *murid* whom I encountered hard at work with a team of builders building new modern flush toilets for the women's quarters, exemplifies this process. Mr Saghir had had a dream (*khuab*) in which he was building a stone wall in a place surrounded by hills, with a very beautiful mosque and garden. A *shaikh* came by while he was working and praised him. He did not know where the place was or who the *shaikh* was. He recounted the dream to his friend and the friend, already a *murid*, suggested that the person in his dream might be Zindapir, the *shaikh* Ghamkol. So, the disciple told me, he came to Ghamkol Sharif and met the *shaikh*, and the first thing the *shaikh* asked him to do was to start building a wall. He realised then that this was the *shaikh* of his dream. So he became a *murid* and his whole village, located about thirty kilometres south of 'Pindi, all became *murids*, 500 strong. He was the first *murid* in his family.

At the time of his dream he was working on a building site and he was only a mason. Now he is a contractor with a truck and car, he has built offices and big houses, his company puts in tenders for major building projects. He and his brother, who are partners, built Badshah Sahib's house free of charge and they have done a good deal of the other building work in the *darbar*, including the courtyard wall of the house in which I was staying. Recently, they brought all the tenting for Badshah Sahib's son's wedding in the *darbar*.

For men away from the saint, and often working away from their families, the support networks of other disciples enable them to resist arbitrary authority, as Ewing (1993) argued. The saint is an (absent) source of moral empowerment, as we saw in the case of Hajji Ibrahim. But this absence is strengthened by the co-presence of other disciples who often meet, usually in the evenings, to recite *zikr* together, as several disciples in public works departments and the army told me. 'We sit around in the evenings and I give them tea and sweets, and we chat and do *zikr* and it creates friendship between us, all the *pir-bhai* are very close. I make all the arrangements for the *zikr* meetings,' a *murid* who is a recruiting officer in the army, told me.

Another *murid*, an officer in the army, claimed that there were lots of other disciples of Zindapir in the army—fifty per cent of his unit are disciples, he said, and since he retired with a pension he has recruited followers from his village. He started by doing *zikr* in the mosque on his own, and now there are forty-two disciples in the *zikr* circle. 'When the *shaikh* tells someone to start *zikr* in the mosque then many people join if they see that it is good,' he said. 'What benefit do disciples in the army get by following Zindapir?' I asked, with Ewing in mind. He replied that the *shaikh* instructs people to tell the truth and be dutiful and hardworking so this is a great help (in performing one's duties as a soldier). What would happen if one had a bad commander who gave a wrong order? He replied that if there is a bad officer who gives a bad command, his command should not be followed because God is watching.

Hajji Ibrahim, himself an ex-soldier, also stressed that the *shaikh* teaches obedience and hard work but he seemed less certain as to whether one should disobey a bad military order. Especially in the army, he argued, orders should be obeyed, good or bad. But our interlocutor, himself an officer, viewed the matter differently. Bad commands, he felt, should not just be obeyed blindly.

I asked another *murid* working as a plumber in the Ministry of Works in Islamabad if there were any other *murids* at his place of work? He told me that two or three buses come from government offices to the *'urs* each year. *Murid-bhais*, he said, help each other and visit each other and do *zikr* together. In Islamabad there are five mosques where they meet regularly in turn and do *zikr* and *gyarvi sharif*, each time in another place. In 'Pindi there are possibly as many as eight different mosques. They get together, do *zikr* and eat together after work, and there is a feeling of *mahabbat* (love). Even some of the *murids* of other *darbars* come to their *zikr* sessions, because they don't have their own sessions.

Disciples of the *shaikh* thus set themselves apart as morally superior, and their ascetic values endow their physically difficult jobs with a moral gloss. Just as medieval guilds were attached to Sufi saintly orders in the Ottoman empire (Trimingham 1971: 233–4), we find in modern Pakistan a rather similar phenomenon, surprising perhaps in the context of a capitalist, modern nation-state, and relatively submerged and invisible to the public eye (since there are quite a number of diverse types of collectivities from which Zindapir draws his disciples). The complex subjectivity generated by voluntarism, submission, an 'imagined' dyadic relationship and real collective camaraderie, are some of the defining features of Sufism in South Asia today. One may find an echo of this mixture in the literature on the Murids and Hausa traders in West Africa. Only further comparative research on contemporary Sufi cults in other Muslim societies, such as Turkey or North Africa, will tell how widespread this phenomenon still is.

So too in Britain men working in the same factory or living in a single neighbourhood may become devotees of a particular saint. They meet in *zikr* and meditation circles, go together on Hajj or *Umra*, march together in processions on *'Id-milad-un-nabi* or the annual *'urs*, help cook the *langar* for special occasions and in general participate in a world of voluntarism beyond the mundane drudgery of daily life.

Hence we see that, paradoxically, voluntarism and submission, liberation and total obedience, self-denial and worldly success, are combined in shaping the subjectivities of both Sufi saints and their disciples. Obedience to the saint is not in the end unconditional; so too the saint, while preaching obedience and respect for hierarchy, empowers his disciples to disobey superiors if they feel moved by what they regard as a higher moral imperative. Becoming a disciple is the result of personal voluntarism, even if a person is simply following a family tradition. How far on the Sufi path an individual may choose to journey is ultimately up to him or her. But in all these matters, as I have tried to show here, close physical proximity to a saint shapes the quality of relations between disciples as well as their understanding of the saint himself.

8

KHULAFA

LIFEWORKS ON THE SUFI PATH—THE POET, THE STRUCTURALIST AND THE ORGANISATION MAN

INTRODUCTION: REPLICATING THE CENTRE

For the visitor and pilgrim, the central lodge of a Sufi regional cult generates an illusion of utter uniqueness and total dominance. In reality, however, the exemplary centre replicates itself throughout a Sufi saint's sacred dominion through scores of deliberate and conscious acts of mimesis. In different parts of the Punjab I encountered men who, in their manners, dress and minute customs, reproduced the image of Zindapir, along with the ethics and aesthetics of the cult he had founded. Such mimesis needs to be read as the outward expression of the intense devotion and love that senior *khulafa*—emissaries of the saint beyond the central lodge—feel for their *shaikh*. Their evident devotion is in accord with Sufi theory which places love at the heart of mystical Islam: the love of God, the love of the Prophet and the love felt for the *shaikh*. A Sufi *murid* is a desirer, a lover. In Sufism such love demands total identification with one's *pir*, and is associated with an act of self-denial which is a precondition for the achievement of mystical unity and gnosis.

Babaji Gyarhvinwala,[1] Zindapir's *khalifa* in Lahore, an elderly man who has dedicated his life to building up his urban lodge, told me that the same principles and order (*nizam*) practised in the *darbar* had been instituted in his place. So much so that people who entered his room found themselves in doubt: 'Is it he, or is it Zindapir? What is this?' 'This is because of the *tasawwur* of my *shaikh*,' he explained. 'Just like Pir Sahib,' he continued, 'I never go anywhere nor do I answer the telephone. I just sit in my room and let the people come to me.' Expressing the classic Sufi idea of *fana fi'l shaikh*, annihilation in one's *shaikh*, he continued:

'When a person loves someone he assumes his form. My love of the *shaikh* has made me in his image. As you yourself are witnessing, we do *zikr* here in

---

[1] A nickname by which he is widely and fondly known locally.

157

exactly the same way [as at Ghamkol Sharif]. What else could be better than this? You have been there [at Ghamkol]. When I sit here, I do not find me in myself, I find my *shaikh* in me...Now when I look carefully at my hands, sitting here, [I wonder], where are my hands? These hands are surely Pir Sahib's hands, where are mine?'

Another *khalifa*, the poet Rab Nawaz, has built the mosque at his lodge as a replica of Ghamkol Sharif, only smaller, out of respect, as he explained. Rab Nawaz was the organiser and building supervisor of the original mosque at Ghamkol and is a man of very fine aesthetic sensibilities. His lodge buildings, shining white in the midst of the lush, green fields of the Punjab, are planned with meticulous attention to form and decorated in plaster with beautiful intricate patterns. Like Babaji of Lahore and Tauhid Shah of Sialkot, Rab Nawaz too wears a green gown over a white robe. With their white turbans under flowing white *chaddars*, and long white beards, all three *khulafa* bear an uncanny resemblance to Zindapir as they sit cross-legged behind low wooden barriers in their richly carpeted rooms. It is here that they receive disciples and supplicants. Like Zindapir, all three refuse to have their photographs taken. The walls of their rooms are hung with pictures of holy places, Mecca and Medina, Sirhind, Ghamkol Sharif. Like Zindapir, the *khulafa* recline back on brocade cushions. Like him, they distribute *ta'wiz* and say *du'a*. Like him, they are generous with their gifts to the anthropologist.

In every one of the lodges I visited the distinctive sound of the *darbar's* melodious *zikr*, the hallmark of the central lodge, pervades the atmosphere creating an illusion that one is actually there, at Ghamkol. All three *khulafa* are addressed by their *murids* as Pir Sahib. All three hold an annual *'urs*, although these are said to be smaller than the one at the central lodge. All three offer a continuous, free *langar* to supplicants and disciples. Yet they recognise their dependence on the saint and their place in the hierarchy of Zindapir's organisation. In the central lodge they are merely *khalifas*, deputies, as the grandson of Zindapir reminded me. Nevertheless, it is the dedication and voluntary work of these men, sent by Zindapir to establish lodges in different parts of Pakistan, which has built up the saint's regional and global cult to its present national and international scale.

Along with this extraordinary mimetic resemblance, each *khalifa* also fosters his own distinctiveness, his own special way of being a Sufi. In this chapter I want to consider the lifeworks of key Sufi *khulafa* of Zindapir living in Pakistan and in Britain. My aim is to highlight how these men, privileging contrasting Sufi ideological and ethical ideas, have set themselves lasting projects by which to glorify their order and Sufism more generally, while at the same time creating a personal legacy.

Judging by my own encounters with him and the accounts of intimate *khulafa*, Zindapir himself refused during his life to dwell in detail on the particularities of Sufi doctrine and cosmology. His chosen path was the ethical Sufi way based on practice, the path of the *faqir* or ascetic. He preached—and practised—generosity, obedience, self-discipline, dedication and love. He presented himself to the world as a world renouncer and lover of God. This, despite the fact that in many ways he was man of action with considerable organisational skills who had built up his lodge and order from almost nothing to their present impressive regional and global scale. Zindapir was an eloquent speaker but, as we saw in chapter 5, he chose to speak in parables and aphorisms, through morality tales or exemplary stories rather than through philosophical speculations. For aspiring Sufi cosmologists like Hajji Karim, this reticence about Sufi theory was a source of intense frustration. Perhaps unusually even among Zindapir's *khulafa*, he was determined to explore the whole universe of Sufi conceptual realms. But each *khalifa* elected to weave Sufi concepts into his personal experiences and chosen path in unique and distinctive ways.

While drawing broadly on Sufi ideas, Zindapir's senior *khulafa* were especially familiar with the *maktubat* (letters) of Shaikh Ahmed Sirhindi.[2] Ahmed Sirhindi, known also as 'Mujaddid-i Alaf-i Thani' (the Renewer of the Second Millennium) was a highly complex and somewhat ambiguous historical character whose life and writings are open to many different and often conflicting interpretations (see Friedmann 1971, ch. 9). While he elaborated and developed Sufi cosmology and theosophy even beyond—and in argument with—their original formulation by Ibn 'Arabi, Sirhindi also stood out as a strong proponent of strict *Shari'at* observance. Although arguably a Sufi above all else (see Friedmann 1971; ter Haar 1992), he famously involved himself in the affairs of the Mughal state and defended the dominance of Sunni Muslims, their purity and ascendancy, in relation to Shi'as, Hindus, and other religious groups in South Asia (ibid.; Rahman 1968: 77–81).

---

[2] Ahmed Sirhindi was a Sufi reformer and important early seventeenth century figure in the history of the Naqshbandi order in India. For excellent discussions of the life and thought of Sirhindi see Rahman 1968, Friedmann 1971 and ter Haar 1992.

Zindapir's order was not a Naqshbandi Mujaddidi order explicitly dedicated to Sirhindi's chosen path. It did, however, follow reformist Naqshbandi traditions in banning instrumental music and, like other reform Sufis, it laid strong emphasis on *Shari'at* observance. But Zindapir followed his own *murshid*, Baba Qasim, in creating public space for vocal religious singers at the *'urs*, and he continued to take pride in the melodic *zikr* of the lodge, relegating the silent *zikr* (*zikr khafi*) recommended by Sirhindi to a single phase in the lodge's *zikr* ritual.

Sirhindi remained in other ways, however, an important figure in the order's symbolic imagination. When I asked Zindapir, for example, whether he did not think he should influence Pakistani politicians to improve their ways, he invoked Sirhindi. His initial response was to claim that if it just entered the mind of a *faqir* to want to influence politics he would no longer be a *faqir*. If the thought just crossed his mind! No, the *shaikh* told me, I am here, and my *langar* is available to everyone, *murid* and non-*murid* alike.

Later on, however, the *shaikh* returned to my question, recalling Sirhindi's encounter with the Emperor Jahangir (see Chapter 3).[3] This hagiographical parable highlights the prevailing view of Sirhindi as an influential, indeed dominant, Sufi saint in the Mughal court, while stressing his ultimate rejection of the violent path associated with temporal politics. In Britain, strict Islamic reformism typical of Naqshbandis elsewhere in the Muslim world has been a growing tendency evident in the stance adopted by Zindapir's most senior British *khalifa* and some of his disciples.[4] For other *khulafa*, however, both in Britain and in Pakistan, it is Sirhindi's Sufi philosophy, the complex cosmology and theosophy he elaborated, which has most captured their imagination.

Babaji Gyarvinwala explained, for example, the movement from *murid* to *murad*, from the lover and desirer to the beloved and desired of God, much in the way that Sirhindi does (ter Haar 1992: 40, 91–3, 158):

When the connection becomes perfect and complete [*mukammal*] then you see God's reward. Intense worship [*riazat and 'ibadat*] keeps the connection [*talak wasta, nisbat*] with God. Those who are *murids* [lovers, desirers], can never

[3] This exemplary fable, although bearing little historical validity, was one I heard more than once. On the whole Zindapir did not give historical examples but he did tend to compare unfavourably the tombs of emperors like Jahangir to those of saints.
[4] On the prominent involvement of Naqshbandis in the state and its politics in Turkey, Syria and Central Asia see the contributions to Özdalga (1999).

become *dalil* [God's intimate, exemplar or proof of God's friendship]. Only the *murad* [the beloved and desired], can become *dalil*. When someone worships God and does *riazat* [to the exclusion of all else] then he becomes [desired by Allah] *murad*.[5]

Another tale about Sirhindi told by Babaji highlights why the true Sufi saint always remains in his lodge. Once, he told me, when Sirhindi was standing in the company of his disciples, they saw the *shaikh* take a step forward, then withdraw his foot; he then took a step in the opposite direction and once again, withdrew his foot. This happened a third and fourth time. Wondering at this strange behaviour, his disciples finally asked him: 'Your Honour, what is the matter, why do you keep stepping forward and withdrawing your foot?' Sirhindi replied that there are three types of ranked *faqir*: the person of *karamat* who can cross the earth in two-and-a-half steps. He moves from place to place, visiting his *murids*. The person of high rank (*maqamat*) can cross the earth in a step-and-a-half. He only visits select places. And finally, the *faqir* who has achieved the rank of utter steadfastness (*istiqamat*). If this *faqir* lifts his foot, there is no place on earth for him to put it down; he can cross the earth in half a step and so he has no need to go anywhere. He remains fixed in one place. This is the place where he sits and this is the place where he is buried.

The tale is one of global Sufi reach and power. Through it Babaji connects himself both to Sirhindi and to his *pir*, Zindapir, famous for never leaving his lodge except to go to Mecca on Hajj once a year.

In many ways, Babaji is a typical example of a *khalifa* who stresses practice. Indeed, he spent some time detailing for me the *crores* (millions) of *darud sharifs* and *lakhs* (hundreds of thousands) of other prayers 'collected' by him and his disciples over the past year in honour of Zindapir and the central lodge.[6] He is not unlike the majority of Zindapir's *khulafa* who privilege practical worship (*'amal, 'ibadat*) over philosophical speculation, and concentrate on building up their lodges. While a few have raised their eyes beyond such restricted horizons in order to seek their own unique ways of articulating their mystical faith, the most charismatic and spiritually powerful among the *khulafa* is remarkable for being above all an extremely effective organisation man.

---

[5] Sirhindi proposed that in the Naqshbandi *tariqa, jazba* (attraction) precedes *suluk* (wandering): 'Only then is the Sufi "loved" (*mahbub*) and 'desired' (*murad*) by God, which makes him eminently suitable to act as Shaykh' (ter Haar 1992: 92–3).

[6] 1 *lakh* equals 100,000. A *crore* equals 100 *lakh*, i.e. 10 million.

THE ORGANISATION MAN: BUILDING A SUFI ORDER
IN THE LAND OF THE INFIDELS

'Sufi Sahib Ghamkolvi who is living in the land of infidels'—so the
monthly Pakistani magazine *Mouhafiz-e-Haq* (Feb.–Mar. 2000: 7–9)[7]
opens its account of Zindapir's senior *khalifa* in Britain—is like 'the perfect saints who spread Islam in India' (here the magazine cites some
famous examples), 'taking them out of the darkness of infidelity and
lighting the candle of God's and the Prophet's oneness. So too in Britain,
from the land of Birmingham a fountain of unity [*tauhid*] and Prophecy
[*risalat*] has spread all over Europe where preaching and printings
quench the thirst of Muslims.'

   The article, entitled 'Zindapir's Miracle in Britain', goes on to stress
Sufi Sahib's qualities as a man of practice and religion (*din*) with outstanding results: 'The Ghamkolia mosque not only benefits the Muslims

17. Devotion to the saint: Sufi Sahib greeted by a disciple on his return
from Mecca

---

[7] The article is in Urdu, and was translated by my research assistant, Mr Munir Choudri.

of Britain,' the magazine tells us, 'but it also gives pride to all British people of the Prophet [*Ahl-e Sunnat*, i.e. Barelvi followers].'

Sufi Sahib, at seventy-seven still a giant of a man, well over six feet tall, with a powerful presence, survived three years in a German prisoner-of-war camp during the Second World War, before meeting his *pir* in Abbotabad in 1945. For the next seventeen years he served as a soldier[8] in the Pakistan army while serving his *pir*, helping to found and build the central lodge at Ghamkol. This long and intimate association with Zinda-pir during the founding years of the order has endowed Sufi Sahib with an almost mythical status. The days and weeks he spent at the lodge in the company of his *shaikh* at a time when it was still a wild, uncultivated place, are regarded as a source of immense spiritual power. During those years he was a close companion, helping to bring up Zindapir's small child, Badshah Sahib, when he lost his mother at a tender age.

By the time Sufi Sahib migrated to Britain as a labour migrant in 1962, at the age of thirty-five, he was well established as a trusted companion of the *shaikh*. According to his own account, when the *pir* appointed him a *khalifa* to Britain he was filled with self-doubt: 'I am only an ordinary person. How can I perform such an important task?' he asked. Zindapir replied with his usual conviction that since he was embarking on God's work, God would help him. In Britain he encountered Pakistanis who never prayed and did not even know the location of the mosque or *qibla* (direction of prayer, towards Mecca). He describes the first *'urs* in Birmingham:

There were two other *pir-bhais* in Britain. The three of us celebrated the *'urs* with a *mahfil* [musical gathering] which lasted half an hour... We made a mosque in one room of our house. When we held the Friday *jum'a* prayers there for the first time we were only seven or eight people...Later we began to do *zikr*...in 1964 we began to perform *zikr* regularly...Now with the blessing of God we have a mosque, a community centre, ten houses which are the property of the mosque, and a printing press (ibid.).

He also noted the order's Dar-ul-'Uloom in Manchester and the school in Birmingham for *hafiz qur'an* which had so far trained over forty young boys to memorise the text of the whole Qur'an.

---

[8] I was told he was a *subedar*, most likely a Non Commissioned Officer, given his lack of English. See also Draper (1985: 55). Geaves, who interviewed him and one of his close *khulafa*, reports that he was an instructor in the signals section (Geaves 2000: 119). *Subedar* usually refers to a Junior Commissioned Officer, a rank instituted by the British army for Indian soldiers above sergeant major and below regular commissioned officers from the rank of lieutenant upwards.

I visited Sufi Sahib's Golden Hillock complex in Birmingham in 1994, when the building of the mosque was still in progress. By this time he had created an impressive array of institutions on his property: a community centre, funded by Birmingham Metropolitan Council to the tune of £ 400,000, which housed a training college for industrial sewing machinists, a wedding and community hall and (in 1998) a centre for the elderly and disabled. Users of the hall were not charged a fee but were asked to make a donation to the mosque. The older terraces in the complex had been entirely refurbished and now housed an employment centre which included a job club for the unemployed, a pre-vocational training centre, information technology training, typewriting, youth training, and English language courses. An Advice Centre employed two men and there was also a pre-university Access course with an excellent attendance record. Paid workers included a mix of young British Pakistani disciples and English instructors. Upstairs, in one of the buildings, was a hostel for the young boys learning to be *hafiz*. The concentration of services for Asians in a single complex was impressive, providing training in needed skills, and helping to motivate men and women lacking in self-confidence, and to cushion their access and entry into the labour market. This was very much an English way of being a Sufi—acquiring charitable status, establishing a management committee and voluntary organisational structure, serving the community.

The story of the building of the new mosque as told by Sufi Sahib is one of astute and miraculous negotiation with the city council. Initially, he acquired some terrace houses and a large hut which replaced the downstairs living room of his house as the order's mosque and *zikr* meeting place. Then, in 1985, his management committee applied to the Council for additional parking space. The Council offered an adjacent area of thirty-five derelict terraces. What did the Council intend to do with the rest of the houses? Did it have any other project in mind? 'Since this place was allocated by God to be a mosque,' Sufi Sahib commented, 'the City Council told us "if you build a mosque on this area we will sell the land to you for a third of the price." We fell silent for a minute but then we thought: a non-Muslim is offering us a place for a mosque and yet we are hesitating... we sat together and talked the matter over among ourselves and realised that this is the best place in which to build a mosque. We then drew up a plan and presented it to the city council. When they saw it, the English started to laugh: how could we build such a big mosque? They laid down a condition that if we failed to build a mosque in eighteen months, they would confiscate the land. We accepted their terms and, by the grace of God, the very day we were given the land, work began. ... We completed the mosque in four years. The mosque has 56 pillars, each 45 feet in diameter' (ibid.).

Fund raising for the mosque involved a major drive. Sufi Sahib and his disciples traveled on weekends to every town and city in Britain, and contributions came as well from Europe, from Iraq (which contributed £ 5000) and from Islamic Relief (Saudi Arabia) which gave £ 11,000. All the rest of the money, several million pounds sterling, was donated by ordinary people. 'When people say I built this mosque I say, No, I did not build it, the Muslims built it.' The chandeliers alone in the central hall cost £ 75,000 each. 'I am the son of a farmer and have been all my life a factory worker. This is all due to the blessing (*karam*) of God.' And he continued: 'My *pir* has never been to this country [England] but there are fourteen cities where, every week, *zikr* gatherings are held, and every month, *gyarvin sharif* is celebrated [in his name]. So too the '*urs* [to commemorate him] is held in fourteen places' (ibid.).

This extension of Zindapir's regional cult to England has, in large measure, been the achievement of Sufi Sahib's tireless organisational work, along with his determination to emulate his saint. Much of the building work at the mosque was done with voluntary labour, cutting the costs substantially. The example set by Zindapir clearly motivates him. Like his *pir*, he says, he never asks *murids* their names. This is because, as the *pir* told him: 'If you keep water, those who are thirsty will find you.' The *pir* also instructed him never to visit the homes of *murids* as this might arouse jealousy or impose expenses on the *murid* that he cannot afford, thus causing inconvenience rather than blessing. Like Ghamkol Sharif, Sufi Sahib's mosque is open to everyone. Like Zindapir, he has never, he says, delivered a sermon (*taqrir*). Even the performance of *zikr* is regarded as a miracle (*ijaz*) of his saint: in the early days they had had to defend the *zikr* against detractors, but now *zikr* is performed everywhere in Britain.

He describes the new mosque as a 'wonder of Islamic art for Muslims and non-Muslims alike.' Whenever groups come from abroad, he says, the city council sends them to see the mosque. They are told: this mosque was not built with human power but with the spirituality of the saint of Ghamkol Sharif.

In conclusion, Sufi Sahib mentions with pride that the processions on '*Id-milad-un-nabi* and on the '*urs*, which started in 1973, today attract

18. The mosque of the brotherhood in a large British industrial city

thousands of followers of Ghamkol from all over the country, besides thousands of others who join in the march. During the two days of the celebrations, *'ulama* preach the virtuous deeds of the Prophet and *na't* singers sing his praises, much as they do at Ghamkol, while the *langar* is freely distributed. Besides this, thousands of booklets are printed and distributed free of charge, so that 'non-Muslims can understand Islam and our own people know the meaning of the true faith. All this is because of the *faiz* of Zindapir' (ibid.).

With this, the magazine interview ends. It reveals Sufi Sahib to be in many ways a sensitive and humble person, conscious of his connection and indebtedness to his *pir*. This sense of humility is echoed by a thesis written about him and the order in Birmingham in the early 1980s (Draper 1985: 26). Draper reports that Sufi Sahib often claimed that his status was low, and denounced himself as having no spiritual value. Out of the context of public display, Draper says, he revealed a 'humility and melancholy at certain times in contrast to other moments of apparent transcendent serenity'. This is 'in contrast to the personality image which many external critics consider him to manifest, claiming that he is arrogant and self-deluded', and it also contrasts with his large physical build which 'reinforces the image of authority that many feel he possesses' (ibid.). As his power and influence have grown, so too, I found, has the volume of such denunciations. The *pir* is said to have become more like a *maulvi* than a *pir* (i.e. more concerned with exoteric matters than with Sufism), to have lost his way, to lack the spirituality of a saint, to be interested only in money or in self-glorification, so that when he invites *'ulama* to orate at the *'urs*, it is only so that they can praise him.

Draper (who for a while was a *murid* himself and is still a Sufi follower) notes the *pir's* 'sense of humour and joviality which never extends into triviality but functions as a means of reducing tension... In many ways,' he says, 'this sense of humour is the source of his charisma' (ibid.). When I first read this passage it surprised me: I had never seen the humorous side of Sufi Sahib's personality, which he clearly reserved for his closest disciples. There is no doubt, however, that the majority of followers both in Britain and in Pakistan respect him very highly, and that he has a reputation for being scrupulous in handling religious donations. It was he, after all, who organised the annual *langar* of Zindapir at Mecca, on Hajj, and he was thus widely known even to Pakistani disciples. After 1988, he began to attend the *'urs* at Ghamkol regularly, and to dominate the all-night *zikr* there. He led the *zikr* prayers in March 2000, after the saint's death, much as he always does in Birmingham, with incredible vigour.

There is little doubt that Sufi Sahib had become a significant religious figure in the Islamic Barelvi landscape of Britain. The magnificent mosque he has built and the fund raising drive he initiated, which appealed to all Muslims even beyond the Ghamkolia order, made him a national public figure outside Birmingham and Zindapir's regional cult. That he called the mosque Ghamkolia and acknowledged his continued deference to Zindapir and his family were thus significant acts of voluntary humility. In turn, the family of Zindapir respect his authority in Britain. Yet they feel uneasy about the fund raising drive. Unlike Sufi Sahib, Zindapir had built his lodge almost entirely with voluntary labour, not through public appeals. Unlike Zindapir, Sufi Sahib has also always permitted open expressions of adulation towards his person from disciples, a form of veneration which Zindapir rejected and repeatedly tried to stop.

The ambiguity of authority was stretched to its limits by the death of the saint. Sufi Sahib was, after all, recognised to be his most charismatic *khalifa*. At the first *'urs* after the saint's death, in October 1999, it was Sufi Sahib who was asked by the saint's son to say the final *du'a* in place of Zindapir. It was he who led the *zikr* (the following year this was changed).

Such interregnums inevitably highlight ambiguities in authority. There is no doubt, however, that Sufi Sahib proved through his actions his continued loyalty and generosity towards the saint and his family. For one thing, he visited Ghamkol at least four times during 1999–2000: first, to see the *shaikh* who was already very frail and ill; then, to attend the funeral; then, to attend the *'urs* in October 1999; and finally, to attend the *'urs* in March 2000, the first to commemorate the death of Zindapir. This was on top of a trip to Mecca and Medina for *Umra* during *Ramadan*.

Such tireless devotion from a man of that age suffering from diabetes and other ailments, undoubtedly proved his deep sense of love and commitment: the journey to Pakistan is long and tiring, an overnight flight and endless queues at Islamabad airport. During his sojourn at the lodge, Sufi Sahib stayed up night after night, energetically performing *zikr*. He showed his solidarity with the family through these gestures of devotion, and on each occasion he brought with him a large entourage of disciples and followers from England. For the family at Ghamkol and the Pakistani *khulafa* who were trying to manage a very difficult transition following the saint's death, the public support given by a person of such charismatic authority, deeply linked to the history of the lodge, who had traveled long distances from a faraway land to be at the lodge—such support was clearly of great symbolic and emotional significance.

Like Zindapir Sufi Sahib was a supreme organisation man. Unlike him, the increase in his organisational power seemed to generate suspicion and resentment among some of his closest disciples, along with accusations that he had lost his spiritualisty (*ruhaniyat*) and grace (*faiz*), and had become too materialistic and religiously dogmatic. He never learnt to speak English and most English converts who came to him ultimately found him too 'Pakistani' and abandoned the order (see Draper 1985). He clearly harboured deep suspicions against the 'infidels' (i.e. the non-Muslim citizens of the UK) in the midst of whom he had made his home and who are, after all, the majority in Britain.

His rejection of non-Sunni Muslims is a strand in the Naqshbandi tradition which can be traced to Sirhindi, but it was not the way chosen by his *murshid* (Sufi teacher), Zindapir, who, like Baba Qasim before him, was renowned for his religious tolerance and universalism.

Sufi Sahib also resembled Naqshbandis elsewhere in fostering very good relations with local government and with the *'ulama*. At the same time he was without doubt one of the most successful Sufi *pirs* in Britain in attracting young, British born, Pakistani men as disciples, and this cohort was utterly loyal to him. As one such follower told me, these young followers would willingly go through fire and water for him. More than anything, he clearly loved surrounding himself by his young male disciples, eating, sleeping and doing *zikr* in their company, much like a scout leader or the army man he once was. Sufi Sahib was, above all, an extremely sociable, indeed gregarious, man, a mover and a shaker, not the kind of Sufi who isolates himself in contemplation and meditation.

FOR THE LOVE OF MY *PIR*: POET, SUFI AND LOVER

Being an organisation man does not preclude an ability to reach inner fountains of love and emotion. Sufi Rab Nawaz, one of the most senior and perhaps the most beloved *khalifa* of Zindapir, has been for many years the organiser of both the annual *'urs* and of all the building projects at the central lodge. A *subedar* in the Pakistan army, he is widely known as the *intizami*, the chief organiser. Yet he is also a poet, and the chronicler of Zindapir's life and the history of the lodge.

Rab Nawaz is a man with no enemies. With his ready smile and twinkling eyes shining with an inner generosity and integrity, I met no one who did not profess to love him. He, in turn, loved his *shaikh*, deeply, and alongside him the *shaikh*'s family, his son and grandsons.

The Sufi path is conceptualised in Sufi literature in terms which are both moral and cognitive or epistemological. A Sufi on the path undergoes a transformation in personal ethics linked to a denial of the self (*nafs*) through annihilation in one's *shaikh* and, after him, in the Prophet and God. This transformation is conceptualised in notions such as *tauba*, repentance, or *tawakkul*, trust in God. In a sense, the ethical path, however difficult, is an achievable way to travel which does not demand that the initiate experience mystical visions, or access transcendent realms of knowledge. It simply demands self-denial, trust, concentration upon and devotion to one's *shaikh*. Interpersonal loyalty and feelings of deep affection between disciple and *shaikh* are enough to give the initiate a sense of real achievement, of peace and tranquility, even happiness. Much depends on the personality of the initiate and his or her capacity for self-sacrifice and unquestioning loyalty and faith.

19. The poet and loyal *khalifa* of Zindapir at his own lodge

For the Sufi lover, the presence of his *shaikh* is deeply empowering. The spirituality, *ruhaniyat*, of the *shaikh* is believed to make him a conduit of God's grace, *faiz*, in the world. *Faiz* in Sufism is conceived of as a divine light flowing from teacher to disciple. Sufis on the path are less concerned with *barkat*, blessing for multiplication and growth, or with *karamat*, miracles, and more with gaining access to *faiz*. To absorb *faiz*, which is like a nurturing light, demands a receptiveness on the part of the initiate. His heart must become like a reflective mirror, open to light. This has physical and cognitive dimensions. But at the phenomenological level, the experience of absorbing *faiz* is much simpler: it is an experience of love, of utter absorption in and receptiveness to one's *shaikh*.

The economy of *faiz* thus has both experiential and physical-cum-cognitive dimensions. Alongside the ethical, an alternative conceptualisation of the Sufi path lays more stress on hidden, transcendental knowledge and physical-cum-mental exercise. A complex cosmology charts the sacred dominions and realms which the soul (*ruh*) can potentially reach through self-purification and intense concentration. The cosmology

posits an absolute parallel between macrocosm and microcosm so that
exercises which effect the purification of the body/microcosm are simultaneously expected to lead to gnostic knowledge of the unseen sacred
realms of the macrocosm.

The path of knowledge is obviously for most people a difficult path to
travel, not only because mystical experiences are not that easy to come by
but because the expectation of what these experiences should be remains
rather obscure. The Sufi macrocosm has already been charted by Sufi
thinkers such as Ibn 'Arabi or Shaikh Ahmed Sirhindi as a series of
ascending spheres or realms of intimacy assigned to different prophets or
saints, but the contents of these transcendental dominions are quite vague.
Dreams of meetings with the Prophet, for example, or miraculous revelations, while considered a sign of spiritual power, do not constitute these
eternal realms *qua* sacred spaces of knowledge. The realms remain rather
abstract and theoretical. To try to penetrate them, followers of Zindapir
drew on many different Sufi manuals and philosophical works, the most
authoritative text for them as Naqshbandis being that of Sirhindi's *Maktubat*, his collected letters.

Sufi Rab Nawaz appeared knowledgeable about Sufi theory. A picture
of the mausoleum at Sirhind hangs on the wall of his room and he
referred to Sirhindi several times during our meetings. Esoteric Sufi concepts repeatedly appear in his poetry but in the final analysis, his deep
satisfaction with his life as a Sufi appears to be derived from the love he
feels for his *shaikh*. His sense of reaching gnosis is very much that of
being absorbed in love. I return to this *khalifa* and his works in the final
chapter. Here I want to analyse the way he expresses Sufi ideas through
his poetic odes or praise poems (*qasida*) in honour of Zindapir.

In the *qasidas* Zindapir is given the highest rank: he is described as
'*murshid* of the highest station ('*ali maqam*) who has achieved and highest office (*sarre daftar*) in the assembly of saints, who is the knower of
God's secret (*sirr*) and favourite of the Almighty's essence (*zat kibriya*)[9].

> You are the *ghaus*, and the saints' pole [*qutb* wali],
> You are the *ghaus*, and the revealed pole [*qutb* jali],

The *pir* is described as the highest ranking *wali*, the *ghaus* and *qutb*,
rankings defined by Sirhindi. In the technical terminology of Sufism *sirr*
and *zat* are among the highest stages on the path. The poet describes the
pir as one who trusts (*tawakkul*) in the way of God, a reference to an

---

[9] Throughout the poems, words that rhyme, and plays of word, are underlined.

Khulafa

ethical station on the path, with patience (*sabr*), respect and willingness (*raza*). *Sabr* is a further stage while *raza*, God's will, desire or contentment (ter Haar 1992: 139), is the final stage on the ethical Sufi journey. Such themes appear repeatedly in the poems.

> Whom you wished with the Truth [*haq*] joined [*mila dya*],
> O Lord of Ghamkol.

Haq, the truth, reality, is not simply a reference to God but also to *haqiqat*, the most elevated ontological sphere.

Yet the ultimate truth of the saint is an ethical, moral truth:

> O *Murshid* of the highest station
> Where the poor knock on the door,
> You raise the destitute,
> O Lord of Ghamkol.

Zindapir is feeder of the poor and protector of the destitute. Feeding, however, is also a metaphorical quality of divine grace. The image of grace as nurturing and flowing is made explicit in a number of poems:

> My begging bowl [*qasa*] fill to the brim [*bardo*] with grace [*faiz*]
> The master [*sarkare*] of Ghamkol,
> As a beggar [*gadagar*] I come [*kare aya ho*] to your lodge,
> Man of Ghamkol [Ghamkoli].

> The rain of light [*nur ki barsh*] falls [*barsti*]
> Here night and day,
> Place [*kuche*] of the master,
> What a place of the master!

> How many are the almighty's rewards [*inam-e-bari hai*]?
> A river of grace [*faiz ka dariya*] is flowing [*jari hai*],
> Snatching [*luthi hai*] the bounteous [*fyazi*] ladle [*barbakar*],
> Your grace is recited in every land

> Abundantly fill, fill [*bhar bhar kar*] the multitudes [*sab ko*] with drink [*pila*],
> Yours is [*hassil hai*] Qasim's flagon [*liva*],
> As long as I live [*ham dam*] I'll keep repeating [*ditta raha hun*] the slogan
> [*sada* = sound, voice, echo],
> Your grace is recited in every lane.

The drinking place [*mekada*], says the poet (a reference to paradise) is revealed as the place of his master.

The *qasidas* express longing and pain, as well as the love of the *shaikh*. When he explained to me the source of his poetic inspiration, Rab Nawaz said that the *pir* had blessed him with love, passion and heartache (*mahabbat, ishq aur dard*). He speaks of himself poetically as being in sadness and pain day and night. Yet recollection of his *pir* makes his troubles and afflictions vanish. The saint opens up his heart's bud, his innermost essence.

In another poem the poet appeals to his *pir* to intercede with him on the Day of Judgement. Here too Sufi concepts are interwoven into what is essentially a love poem:

> For God's sake, on the Day of Judgement [*waqt-e nazah*],
> Look after me [*karni nighabani*],
> Nawaz is your destitute [*benawa*] servant [*khaddam*],
> Pir of Ghamkol.
>
> Even though my robe [*daman* = skirt] is empty [*tahe*]
> From good [*husna*] deeds ['*amal*],
> The attraction [*jazba*] of a beautiful faith [*husne aqidat*]
> Is in your madman [*diwane*].
>
> Without example is your gaze [*tawajjuh*],
> Conveying [*ke tofel*] blessings [*barkat*], it creates
> A throbbing desire [*tarap*] to give my life for you [*jan nisari*]
> In your intoxicated lover [*mastane*].

Tawajjuh, the intense concentrated gaze of the *pir* exchanged with his disciple is in Sufi Naqshbandi understanding conceived of as a way of transmitting grace to the disciple (see also Schimmel 1975: 237; ter Haar 1992: 64). The theme of intoxication repeats itself again and again in the poems. The poet speaks of the eyes of his *pir* as flowing with enchanted wine (*sharab-e qasmi*). Elsewhere he speaks of losing one's senses (*behosh mastana*) and being possessed (*wajd-e khaish*). The *pir* is the saviour and guide of the poet, who rescues him from the danger of extreme intoxication or sense of loss:

> Caught in a dangerous whirlpool [*girdab-e-bala*] is my boat [*kashti*],
> The end (*mine*) is near (*qarib*) now to my life (*hasti*),
> You come and boot it (*lagado*) with just one kick (*toker*),
> Your grace is recited in every lane.

Here the poet evokes the image of a whirlpool (*warta*) in which the intoxicated Sufi gets caught and is saved by his *pir* (ter Haar 1992: 100). He told me that when he is in that 'other world' of poetic inspiration, 'drowning in love', he nevertheless retains the sense of propriety which compels him never to step outside the *Shari'at*, thus articulating a fundamental

Naqshbandi axiom that total and permanent absorption in God is a lesser
achievement than absorption and return.

Such esoteric imagery is scattered throughout the poems. In the end,
the poet says, while there may be *lakhs* of Sufis and travellers (*saliks*),
ascetics and devotees, who all want special closeness to the *pir*, for him it
is enough just to dwell in the presence of his *pir*.

Like other Sufis he describes his heart as 'imprinted' (*naksh*) by his
pir. So too, he invokes the imagery of the heart '*at* peace' (*itminan*). In
Sirhindi's thought the heart at peace is the entry point to the final stage on
the Sufi journey when the soul has crossed the universe to reach ultimate
knowledge (ter Haar 1992: 49, 56, 139):

> The heart [*qalb*] is filled
> With these talks [*kya kya bat*] of tranquility [*sukun*],
> The heart at peace [*itminan*]
> Is the remembrance [*azkare*] of Zindapir.

> You are the venerated [*mabood*]
> Whose shadow [*zil-e*] is eternal [*baqa-e*].
> Your lustre [*jalwa*] is my final goal [*maqsud* = desire]
> The vision of [*didar hai*] Zindapir.

The aim of the Sufi is to uncover his essence as shadow of God's attributes (ter Haar 1992: 95, 97) before subsisting (*baqa*) in God. Elsewhere
the poet speaks of 'circumambulating' the *pir* 'like the *ka'ba*'. In Sirhindi's
though *haqiqat-i ka'ba* is the highest rank (Friedmann 1971: 14). The
saint is the centre of the poet's universe.

One of the poems, presented here in full, explicitly draws together a
number of Sufi themes:

> Honourable Pir Alive [*Pir Zinda*]
> Who awakens the ways [*sunnah*] of the Prophet [*jaga rehe hain*],
> God's people who are scattered
> With God are assembling [*mila rehe hain*].

> We take his hand,
> The Prophet's hand we feel [*par rehe hain*],
> He draws us to his robe [*daman*],
> To the Prophet's robe we are drawn [*la rehe hain*].

> The longing [*mutashna*] of a lifelong thirst [*kamo ki tashnagi*]
> The master's [*murshid*] grace [*faiz*] quenches [*bujha rehe hain*].
> The seekers [*talibane*] of the true God [*haq*]
> A holy [*irfan*] wine [*sharab*] are drinking [*pila rehe hain*],

The searchers [*talashe*] whose purpose [*mudda'a*] is God (*haq*)
Are lovers [*talib* = seekers] who seek God's contentment [*raza*].
His manifestation [*azme*] of shining [*jalwa*] love [*mahabbat*]
Now their destination [*manzal*] are reaching [*par rehe hain*].

Where can I dare [*jurat*] gaze [*nazar*]?
Who could bear [*taab*] his lustre [*jalwa*]?
The lustre of Mujaddid Alaf-i Sani,
In his image [*surat* = shape] we find [*par rehe hain*].

You have told [*bata*] us the formula [*nuskhe*] of God's remembrance [*zikre*],
Created [*dada*] the taste [*chaske*] of the Prophet's love [*hube*],
The naked ['*asiyan*] heart's blemishes [*daghdabe* = spots]
Your kindness [*karam*] erased [*mita rehe hain*].

No matter where we are he watches over us,
This is your faith, Nawaz,
It is certain he is listening [*sun rahe hain*],
As his praises [*madhad*] we speak [*sunnarahe hain*].

I have not tried here to analyse the poetic aspects of Rab Nawaz's poems. My aim has been to show how Sufi concepts are interwoven into the personal experiences of the poet:

The image [*tasawwur*] in my heart day and night is of Zindapir,
The remembrance of Zindapir is day and night,
The name of Zindapir has become an incantation [*wazifa*].

The poems, seen together, point to the poet's familiarity with Sufi concepts. They form a taken-for-granted lexis in which to express his emotions. But the poems do not systematise these concepts analytically; they draw upon them selectively to highlight love for the *pir* or to extol the *pir*'s greatness.

THE INTELLECTUAL, AND THE STRUCTURALIST QUEST FOR GNOSIS

This type of fragmentary deployment of Sufi cosmological images is quite usual in the literature on Sufism. It tends to disguise the deep structural logic of Sufism, interrupting it with flowery, highly elaborate poetical and ethical interpretations. It was thus unusual to meet a Sufi dedicated to showing the highly systematic logic of Sufi cosmology as expounded by Sirhindi and others. Indeed, it was the chance meeting with this self-conscious structuralist which first enticed me as an anthropologist to study Sufism and Sufi orders.

If Sufi Sahib stressed '*amal* above all else, and Rab Nawaz expressed his love for his *pir* in ethical terms, another English *khalifa* of Zindapir, Hajji Karim, sought ultimate knowledge of transcendent, eternal spheres. He was not satisfied with '*amal* which did not open up the gates to gnosis, nor did the experience of love for his saint delude him into thinking that he had experienced true mystical revelation. Having mapped out all the Sufi conceptual schemata systematically, on the basis of his readings, he was seeking the specific key which might unlock the experiential and epistemological gates to this universe. Idle talk of love or idiosyncratic references to Sufi terms were of no interest to him. He was a seeker for the truth (*haqiqat*) beyond the ephemeral world of experience. His inability to reach this world filled him with sorrow. After Zindapir's death in 1999, and even before it, he began to seek another *murshid* who might guide him to spheres of divine knowledge which his *shaikh*, the *shaikh*'s son and Sufi Sahib, had all failed to guide him towards. He took textual

20. Two *khulafa* of Zindapir seated in the enclosure where a *pir* receives supplicants and disciples

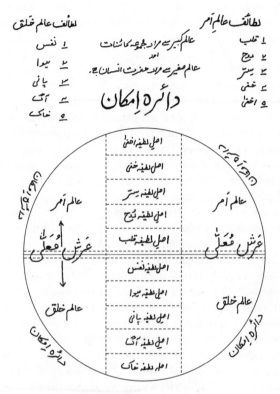

Figure 8.1: The circle of God's realities as represented by Hajji Karim

constructions of Sufi cosmology to be a literal description of a reality out
there. In the following chapter I disclose a version of Sufi cosmology as it
was told to me in detail, over a series of meetings, by Hajji Karim. In
advance of presenting his theory, I present it first in Urdu diagrammatic
form so as to highlight its aesthetic symmetry (see Figure 8.1). The
diagram, as will be explicated in the next chapter, highlights a series
of oppositions and homologies: between body and cosmos, the ephemeral versus eternal worlds, carnal versus eternal soul, exoteric and esoteric,
saints versus prophets, shadows versus truth, attributes versus essence,
body lights versus body matter, all in ascending, hierarchical order.
The movement is upward, through sainthood to prophethood, from the
shadows through the attributes to the essence, and then back again, to

incorporate on the way down the base body and achieve a final physical transformation. In these parallels worlds of microcosm and macrocosm, body and cosmos, the mediators are, on one side, sainthood/the throne of God, and on the other, the human heart. Each mediator participates in both higher and lower world. In Sirhindi's thought, represented by Karim in a series of spherical diagrams, each world reached opens up new worlds but the generative principles remain constant throughout.

What are we to make of such indigenous structuralist models? Structuralism has been the subject of powerful critiques from interpretivist and poststructuralist approaches. The question of how to incorporate a structuralist myth into a poststructuralist analysis is one at which I hinted in chapter 4 and return to in the conclusion. It is worth noting, however, that most critiques of structuralism have been less than persuasive. Geertz's interpretivist analysis of the Balinese cockfight (1973) is easily open to a structuralist re-analysis which shows that the ethos of the cockfight is generated by a series of oppositions between the demonic and the temple cult, as Geertz himself implicitly acknowledges (on this see P. Werbner 1997). Bourdieu's analysis of Kabilyia society (1977), despite his attempts to introduce individual agency and power into his model, remains locked in a structuralist analysis of Kabile institutions and mythologies. In the present instance a speculative mystical philosophy presents itself as an accurate science. The bricoleur is not an experimenter, as Lévi-Strauss recognises (Lévi-Strauss 1966). Because it is entirely speculative, Sufism is not bound by empirical realities. Nevertheless, the language and logic of science lend it authority and verity despite the fact that in many ways it is a highly tentative set of propositions, so that Sufis ultimately must rely on image and representation rather than on scientific evidence to make their claims.

Before going on to present Hajji Karim's structuralist analysis in detail, I want to end with a portrait of another *khalifa* of Zindapir and Sufi Sahib, a modern scientist who has embraced Sufism as a way of life.

THE ENGLISH SCIENTIST

Dr Alam Din, Zindapir's *khalifa* at Pennine, a small town in Derbyshire, is a prominent scientist working at the cutting edge of current research in genetic therapy. He has a full time permanent research post at a prominent British university. Dr Din is a youngish, slim man, about forty, sporting a dark beard and glasses and dressed in modern casual clothes. He speaks softly, in measured tones, at times breaking into a mischievous smile or grin when he suddenly becomes quite English. He grew up in England, arriving from Kashmir as a boy of about nine. Like Zindapir, he seems able to switch from a tone of deep piety to witty, cuttingly critical remarks. With his genuineness, integrity, quiet assurance, natural modesty and willingness to take risks and act independently, his persona radiates charisma.

Dr Din's father was a *khalifa* of Zindapir and a recognised minor *pir* in his own right. After his death, Dr Din took over his responsibilities as *khalifa* and juggles these with his full-time job as a scientist. He made little attempt, however, to describe Sufism to me as a scientific theory. Instead, his stress was on identity and identification:

'Here in England our link to Zindapir was always mainly spiritual and I feel that this spiritual connection has actually increased after his death. I feel his presence all the time, he supports me, I am nothing without him.'

The first time he met Zindapir was after his father's death and burial in Mirpur:

'...the first time my eyes fell on him it looked as if I had come back to see my father. Hazrat Sahib looked exactly like father, with a sideways view, and I thought, I've come back to my father. And that was [intended] for my peace of mind, to say that your father has not left you, he is still with you, but now physically in Hazrat Sahib's body [in other words, the saint created the resemblance deliberately in order to comfort him] ...and therefore, you know, Hazrat Sahib is not only my *shaikh* but my father figure. And so Hazrat Sahib gave me the responsibility of the *khilafat* that my father had; that was something beyond imagination.'

He then told me of an admonishing letter sent to him by Zindapir following a scientific meeting he had attended in Switzerland where he omitted to observe some of the prescribed daily prayers. This miraculous knowledge from a distance strengthened his faith: 'I feel that, you know, he is there any time I need him, he's watching over me.' He also told me of his good fortune in getting his present post, having been passed over for another, apparently superior job. Although his present job had started at a lower level, it was followed by rapid and multiple promotions. He attributed this to God's will. The connection to the *shaikh* gave him the will to continue with all the events of the order, the weekly *zikr, gyarvi, milad, 'urs*, consistently, without gaps.

There were some rumblings from other disciples when he got the *khilafat* from the *shaikh* at a very young age. 'I got the *khilafat* when I was thirty-three and I also got my PhD when I was thirty-three.' The branch in Pennine was built up slowly by his father and at first, even the performance of *zikr* was greeted with criticism. But from the very start he had loved doing *zikr* and never missed the Friday *mahfil*, even when he was student in London.

'After *zikr* you physically feel very tired, if you've done it properly, but mentally and spiritually you feel very enlightened, you feel as if a burden has been taken off you, you know, and it broadens the mind, it opens it, you start, you have a problem, you think about it and the answer comes to you. Afterwards, yes. Yes, it helps you to find solutions yourself.'

I asked: 'It's a very deep form of contemplation?' To which Dr Din replied:

'Oh yes, it is the only worship that automatically becomes worthy of acceptance. In prayer, when you are prostrating in front of Allah and you've made your *niyat*, your intention, and during prayer, *namaz*, it is impossible to have your mind and tongue and heart united in what you're doing. Usually, most of the time, almost invariably, your mind is thinking about something else and your tongue is saying something else and you don't know where your heart is. So that kind of worship is not worthy of acceptance. In *zikr-Allah* you have no choice: you are shouting at the top of your voice, "God is Great", and you are sitting in darkness, removed from distractions, you cannot shout at the top of your voice without having your mind, your tongue and your heart united, and those are the conditions for getting your worship accepted—when your mind and your heart and your tongue are united in the same [activity].'

He admitted that he had not even reached the first step on the Sufi path but at the same time, his *shaikh* had given him *tawajjuh* that

'…even decades of worship can't take you there. That is the difference, that is why I feel I am lucky, because other people do worship for decades before they reach this stage when they can get the attention of their *shaikh*.'

He knew he had this 'attention' after he was reprimanded by Sufi Sahib during Hajj for supposedly backbiting against another *khalifa* who was acting as *darban*. Dr Din felt mortified and tried to persuade Sufi Sahib to come with him to the *shaikh* to explain that this was not his intention, but to no avail. Sufi Sahib refused. Eventually, he mustered up his courage and went to see Zindapir on his own. He told the *shaikh* that he had really meant to praise the *darban*. Zindapir looked at him and said, simply, 'I love you.' He just said, 'I love you', and he, Dr Din, believed him. Zindapir knew what was in his heart. How could Sufi Sahib believe his intention was bad? He, Sufi Sahib, is not a proper *pir*, he cannot see into people's hearts.

21. A *khalifa* leading the *'urs* in a small English town

He is a shy man, he said, but now he finds himself greeting strangers. And people come to him for healing from all over: Nottingham, London. He makes no claims but they still come. Sometimes there are queuęs outside, every night, even in winter. He even has permission to initiate disciples. His aim is to bring the true message of Islam to England, not the one promoted by fundamentalists. He runs Friday *jum'a* prayers at the hospital. In this context he gave me a short summary of the four stages of Sufism (TSWF): *Tauba* (repentance), *Saf* (purification), *Wali* (friend of God), *Fana fi'l-la* (annihilation in God, the complete merging with God). The first stage is to be lost in the *daman* (robe), the being, the body of the *pir*, then the Prophet, then God.

Like most *murids*, Dr Din feels loved and chosen by his saint. For him the *shaikh* is his father incarnate, his spiritual guide, his protector and comforter in the absence of a real father who died when he was quite young. His Sufism is for him a source of identity and conviction which complements his role as an English scientist and anchors him deeply in his local community, giving him a role, a standing and a mission. And yet one didn't feel, in talking to Dr Din, as one did talking to Rab Nawaz, that he missed Zindapir the *man*. The *shaikh* remained an exemplar, an emblematic figure, an imaginary—all of which continued to exist and to give him strength.

Each of the men considered here: Babaji, Sufi Sahib, Rab Nawaz, Alam Din and Hajji Karim, embarked on his own life project partly through intense emotional identification with his saint. Only Hajji Karim constructed this project in purely intellectual terms. In the following chapter I present Hajji Karim's Sufi theory in detail as he told it to me himself.

9

NAFS

THE JOURNEY OF THE SOUL AND
THE QUEST FOR MYSTICAL REVELATION

Hajji Karim told me:

'We Sufis believe that the power of prophecy—*nabuwat*—passed with Muhammad (P.B.U.H.) and the three generations after him who still knew him. After that came *wilayat*, the mystical power, the reflection of *nabuwat*. This shadow is known only to a select few.

'It is generally believed that a human being is made of four *'unsar*, elements, [fire, water, air and clay] but in fact, he is made of ten elements. The other six are *nafs* [vital soul/spirit], *qalb* [heart], *ruh* [eternal soul], *sirr* [secret thing], *khafi* ['silence', more secret], and *akhfa* [the most secret].[1] These ten elements originate in the universe. A human being is the essence, concentration, encapsulation, of all these elements. He reflects in miniature the whole universe [the 'great universe', *'alam-e-kabir*, the macrocosm]. We see ourselves and think we are nothing. But each human being contains within him powers which, if opened up, enable a man to see the whole universe created by God. A human being is an *'alam-e-saghir*, a 'small universe'—he mirrors the whole universe within him. He is a picture [image] of God's creation. A person can leave the world of appearances, of ephemeral creations [i.e. the empirical world of the senses], if he knows the way; and he can reach out to the eternal world.

'A human being is designed so that in his chest are spaces for the entry of divine lights. We call these spaces *lata'if*. A *latifa* (sing.) is something very fine. The *lata'if* are located on the body (see figure 9.1): the first, *latifa-el-Admi* [of Adam], is located just under the heart; the second, *latifa-el Ibrahimi*, is the *ruh* which is located on the right side of the chest, under the right breast; the third, the *latifa* of Moses, *sirr*, is located just above the heart; the fourth *latifa*, of Jesus, *khafi*, is located on the right, above the breast, above the *ruh*;

[1] Buehler (1998: 105–7) translates these as Soul (*nafs*), Heart (*qalb*), Spirit (*ruh*), Mystery (*sirr*), Arcanum (*khafi*) and Super-Arcanum (*akhfa*). I prefer to translate *ruh* as 'soul' since the *ruh* bears strong similarities to the Christian soul that survives after a person's death. In Christianity there is no concept equivalent to *nafs*, which is both the breath of life and the desiring, active ego of an individual.

Figure 9.1: The seven bodily lights (*lata'if*)

the fifth *latifa*, that of Muhammad (P.B.U.H.), *akhfa*, is located at the centre. Prophecy is at the top, sainthood at the bottom [i.e. the *lata'if* are ranked with *akhfa* being the most superior]. The sixth *latifa*, the *nafs*, is located in our *tariqa*, Naqshbandiyya, at the centre of the forehead. The seventh and final *latifa, latifa qalbia*, is composed of the four elements: air, water, fire and clay. It may start anywhere in the body and flow outwards to clean the whole body.

'These are the seven treasures in the human body. The first five *lata'if* parallel the eternal world, *'alam-e-amr*, while the *nafs* and the four elements parallel the ephemeral world of creations, *'alam-e-khalq*.

'To further understand the meaning of these divine lights you have to know that Sufis believe that the universe, seen through the inner eye of the heart (*kashfi nazar* or *batni nazar*) appears as a circle—*da'ira mumkinat*—the circle of possibilities of creation. It is divided into *'alam-e-khalq* and *'alam-e-amr*. *'alam-e-amr* refers to the moment of the creation of the world. God said *kun* ('be!') and everything was created. The whole of *'alam-e-amr* is just one word. It was created by a single order, directly, without intermediaries (*bil wasta*) in one command, and is complete. By contrast, the lower world, *'alam-e-khalq*, is continuously created until the end of the world. This world, the "sun world", has day and night, weeks, and so on, but the upper world is timeless. God created the cosmos, the earth and sky, in six days, so it is not *kun*. People are still coming and going [being born and dying]. This is creation over time.

'In the middle of the circle of possibilities is an arch, the *'arsh-e-mu'allah*, the throne where God sits (though of course, He does not really sit, He has no body). The *'arsh-e-mu'allah* is the division between the two worlds. The human heart, *qalab*, reflects this division in *'alam-e-saghir*, the small universe, that of a human being. Mirroring the *'arsh-e-mu'allah*, the *qalab* separates between the five (superior) chest lights and the other five *lata'if*. It divides *'alam-e-saghir*, a human being, as the *'arsh-e-mu'allah* divides *'alam-e-kabir*. The *'arsh-e-mu'allah* is not a line; it is a place, it has twelve pillars, although what kind of a place it is we cannot know. It is the divine light at the centre of the universe. We know that it rests on the roof of Paradise. Paradise and Hell are both beneath the throne of God, and dividing them, *barzakh* [lit. "bridge" or "intermediary"], is a place known as *ehraf* (limbo). Below them are the sun and planets. *'Alam-e-khalq* is also known as the world of the senses, *'alam-e-nasut*.

'*Mujaddid-i Alf-i Thani* [the 'Renewer of the Second Millennium', Ahmad Sirhindi] said that a human being is a small universe. When Allah made human beings, he used his full power to place the *lata'if* of *'alam-e-amr* in their chest and caused these *lata'if* to be in love with the human body. This is because God wanted human beings to become complete and comprehensively inclusive of *'alam-e-amr* and *'alam-e-khalq*. That way a human being would be entitled to be called *'alam-e-saghir*.

'Above the throne of God are the five worlds which are the origin of the *lata'if*. First is the place of the heart, *maqam-e-qalb*, the origin of the *latifa* of the heart, which is also known as *'alam-e-malakut*, the Angelic World. The divine light of *latifa qalb* is yellow and it is round like a circle and very bright like the sun under the feet of the Prophet Adam. Like all the other *lata'if, latifa qalb* becomes alive with the *zikr* of *ism-e-Allah*, the name of God. At this point a divine light, yellow in colour, enters it and then starts to expand. Later, it starts to rise towards the *'arsh-e-mu'allah* and reaches above it to its original place. In this *latifa* a person acquires revelation of *kashf-ul-qalub*, the knowledge of what is in people's hearts.

'Above *latifa qalb* is the original place of the second *latifa, latifa ruh*, or *'alam-e-arwah*, the World of the Souls, created at the beginning of time. This is also known as *'alam-e-jabrut*, the world of divine decrees and spiritual powers. To reach *'alam-e-arwah* one must first purify the *qalb*. *Latifa ruh* is finer than the heart, one step closer to God. It is red, bright and round like a circle under the feet of the Prophet Ibrahim. When the divine light enters this *latifa* it starts to expand and reaches beyond the *'arsh-e-mu'allah* to its original place. In this *latifa* a person acquires revelation of *kashf-ul-qabr*, knowledge of graves.

'Beyond this world is the original place of the third *latifa, sirr*. This is the world of *sifat ka saya* [the Shadows of God's Attributes] also known as *'alam-e-lahut*, the divine nature revealing itself. *Latifa sirr* is white, shaped like a circle and very bright like the sun under the feet of the Prophet Moses. This is the stage in which a person's existence passes into Allah. According to *Mujaddid-i Alf-i Thani*, this is the stage of intoxication, *sukr*, in which a person is empowered by *galib*, love. The place of *jazba*, absorption in God's divine light, is in this *latifa*.

'Above this world is the original place of *latifa khafi*. This *latifa* reaches the world of *sifat*, also known as *'alam-e-bahut*, the Hidden World. The divine light of *latifa khafi* is black, round and bright like the sun under the feet of the Prophet Jesus. It rises and expands towards its original place on top of *latifa sirr*. In this *latifa*, a person's human attributes, *sifat-e-bashriyat*, leave him so that he is pure beyond other human beings and can hear the angels' prayers. *Mujaddid-i Alf-i Thani* says that at this point a person reaches a state of minor amazement, *hairat-e-sughra*, in which the omnipresence [*shahud*] of God is evident of its own accord [*khud ba khud*]. This is the point at which the curtains of divine light vanish and the traveler gets a taste of the final stage. It is distinctive of Naqshbandiyya and is also known as *hazur Naqshbandiyya*, presence before God. For the *talib-e-haq*, the seeker of God, this stage of amazement is like that of a novice tracing out the way to his final destination [*maqsud*] to reach God.

'Finally, above *latifa khafi* is the divine essence itself, *zat*, the original place of *latifa akhfa*, placed in the middle of the chest and known also as *'alam-e-hahut*, the Most Hidden. The divine light of *latifa akhfa* is green, round and bright like the sun under the feet of the Prophet Muhammad (P.B.U.H.). Like the other *lata'if*, it becomes alive with *zikr*. According to *Mujaddid-i Alf-i*

Thani in this *latifa* a person becomes one with God, in a state of non-existence [*'adam*]. It is also called *haq-ul-yaqeen*, or *tauhid*. *Maqam jam'-ul-jama'* is in this *latifa*, implying a double plural, inclusive of *fana* and *baqa*. It is also called *wajud-e-'adam* [entry into the existence of non-existence] in which a person sees nothing external except God. It is also called *farq badd-al-jamma* [separateness after togetherness] and *maqam-e-takmil* [the Place of Completeness].

'The last two spheres are the domain of prophecy, *nabuwat*, the *wilayat ambiya* which reach out to God's true reality itself, *haqiqat*.

'The five chest lights reflect the five worlds of *'alam-e-amr*, above the throne of God. The other five elements—the *nafs* and *latifiya qalbia* [which is collectively composed of air, water, fire and clay], reflect the world of creation, of continuous becoming, *'alam-e-khalq*, below the throne of God. *Latifa nafs* is placed in the middle of the forehead. The divine light of this *latifa* is dusty coloured, round and bright like the sun. Through *zikr* it expands to its original place below the *'arsh-e-mu'allah*, the lower half of the universe. This world is called *'alam-e-nasut*, the World of the Senses. Later, this *zikr* is more affected by *zikr nafi asbat*, the *zikr* of proof, *la ilaha illa 'l-lah*. In this *latifa* the whole human body begins sucking in the divine light and a person feels he is in front of God. Until this *latifa* is fully purified permanently, a person can never feel the taste of this divine light.

'*Latifa qalbia*, which includes the four elements making up the human body, begins from the middle of the head and brightens up the whole body, from the hair on one's head to the tips of one's toenails. There are 360 main blood supply lines in the body. The *faiz* of this *latifa* circulates in these so that the whole body begins doing *zikr*. It has a powerful effect which cannot be described in writing. This *latifa* is the fountain or source of divine light [*mamba'faiz*], it fills the body with *faiz*.[2] Some people suck too much *nur Allah*, divine light, and become *majzub*, lost in divine meditation. The *latifa qalbia* is also known as *sultan-ul-azkar*, the King of Prayers.

'The four elements of *'alam-e-khalq* each have their original place in one of *'alam-e-amr*'s *lata'if*: *qalab* in *nafs*; *ruh* in air; *sirr* in water; *khafi* in fire; *akhfa* in clay. The *fana* and *baqa* of each *latifa* of *'alam-e-khalq* has its origin in *'alam-e-amr*: air in *ruh*'s deeds [*af'al*] of proof [*sabut-i-yya*]; water in *sirr*'s deeds of personal splendour [*sha'n*]; fire in *khafi*'s attributes [*sifat*] of negation [*salb-i-yya*, i.e. God's non-attributes]; clay in *akhfa*'s attributes of splendour and comprehensive dignity.[3]

---

[2] Buehler (1998: 117–18), one of the very few authors to recognise the centrality of the notion of *faiz* in Sufi theosophy and practice, translates *faiz* (*fayd* in Arabic) as divine effulgence or grace which sustains earthly life. Buehler describes *faiz* as the 'enabling energy' that Sufis utilise to connect the human microcosm through the *lata'if* to other parts of the macrocosm. He adds that 'electricity provides an appropriate metaphor for this divine energy'—a metaphor I heard used only once, by a Qadiri *'alim* in his speech on the final day of the *'urs* at Ghamkol Sharif.

[3] Buehler (1998: 111) translates this last source of *fana* as 'comprehensive synthesis', *sha'n-i jam'*.

'All God's creations are in the circle of possibilities. By purifying the chest lights, opening them up to divine light, a man can see the whole universe (*kashf*, see with an inner vision), he can open himself up to a knowledge of the whole of *'alam-e-amr*. *Mujaddid-i Alf-i Thani* explained this journey and said that when the five *lata'if* of *'alam-e-amr* are completed, those of *'alam-e-khalq* will be automatically completed in tandem, and with it the circle of possibilities. Of the destination of *fana fi'l-lah*, this is only, however, the first step.'

THE GENERATIVE STRUCTURE OF SUFI COSMOLOGY

The journey of the soul as described so far by Hajji Karim reveals the generative structural logic of Sufi cosmology. The system can be seen to be based on a series of homologies: between opposed worlds—of Command and Creation, eternal and ephemeral—on a horizontal axis, and between macrocosm and microcosm, cosmos and person, cutting across these worlds on a vertical axis. The cosmos is thus divided into two analogous and opposed pairs. The worlds of Command and Creation parallel each other within the microcosm and macrocosm, and each is separated by analogous mediators, the person by the heart, the universe by the Throne of God.

Each resulting quarter contains five ranked homologous spheres of divine intimacy or points of light in ascending order, and each is associated with certain qualities: differently coloured lights, prophetic appellations and achieved states of being. The movement of the person is, via work on the body, i.e. the microcosm, from sphere to sphere of the macrocosm in ascending order: initially the movement is within the world of command, followed by a parallel movement in the world of creation. In the Naqshbandi case, the second world of ephemeral creations is said to follow 'automatically' once the world of command and its spheres is completed, and thus requires no further work. The principle is one of recursion, of spiralling return but at a higher level. This recursive principle of repetition and gradual accretion occurs as the soul moves from sphere to sphere.

The fact of repetition is obscured in the cosmology by a multiplication of terms. Each phase and sphere has its own name and qualities. Phases can also be elaborated through the notion of degrees of divine being, from *'zat'* (pure being) through *sifat* (attributes) to the 'shadow' (*zil*, reflection) of attributes and even, as we shall later see, the shadow of shadow of God's attributes.[4]

---

[4] Corbin (1969: 218) notes that the Sufi science of the imagination is also the science of mirrors. As the science of the *speculum*, he says, it takes its place in *speculative* philosophy. The shadow (*zil*) is a reflection, not in the sense of being dark but as a projection of a silhouette or face in a mirror (ibid.: 191).

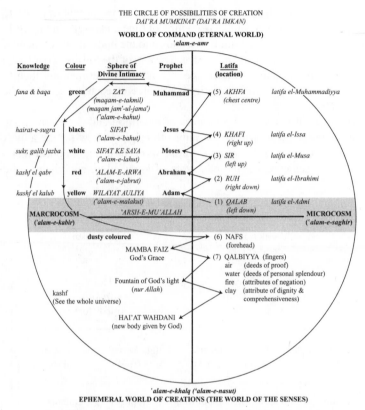

THE CIRCLE OF POSSIBILITIES OF CREATION
DAI'RA MUMKINAT (DAI'RA IMKAN)

WORLD OF COMMAND (ETERNAL WORLD)
'alam-e-amr

Knowledge	Colour	Sphere of Divine Intimacy	Prophet	Latifa (location)	
fana & baqa	green	ZAT *(maqam-e-takmil) (maqam jam'-ul-jama') ('alam-e-hahut)*	Muhammad	(5) AKHFA *(chest centre)*	*latifa el-Muhammadiyya*
hairat-e-sugra	black	SIFAT *('alam-e-bahut)*	Jesus	(4) KHAFI *(right up)*	*latifa el-Issa*
sukr, galib jazba	white	SIFAT KE SAYA *('alam-e-lahut)*	Moses	(3) SIR *(left up)*	*latifa el-Musa*
kashf el qabr	red	'ALAM-E-ARWA *('alam-e-jabrut)*	Abraham	(2) RUH *(right down)*	*latifa el-Ibrahimi*
kashf el kalub	yellow	WILAYAT AULIYA *('alam-e-malakut)*	Adam	(1) QALAB *(left down)*	*latifa el-Admi*

MARCROCOSM *('alam-e-kabir)*   'ARSH-E-MU'ALLAH   **MICROCOSM** *('alam-e-saghir)*

dusty coloured   (6) NAFS *(forehead)*

MAMBA FAIZ
God's Grace   (7) QALBIYYA (fingers)
air   (deeds of proof)
water   (deeds of personal splendour)
fire   (attributes of negation)

Fountain of God's light
(nur Allah)   clay   (attribute of dignity & comprehensiveness)
kashf
(See the whole universe)

HAI'AT WAHDANI
(new body given by God)

'alam-e-khalq ('alam-e-nasut)
EPHEMERAL WORLD OF CREATIONS (THE WORLD OF THE SENSES)

Figue 9.2: Journey of the soul: The first and second stages

Several crucial features of this system have to be noted here. First, the movement is cognitive and experiential rather than ethical. No mention is made of repentance, forgiveness, trust and other key ethical stages on the Sufi path. These are tagged on almost as an afterthought in the final phases of the journey. If love is mentioned, it is within an economy of light or divine grace in which it refers to a physiological, cognitive and ontological state of being suffused or nurtured by light emanating from God. Light is thus the key operator of the system: levels and intensities of light refer to levels of achieved gnosis. Light is transferred via the different spheres of being to the person.[5]

[5] Thus Corbin (ibid.: 191) argues: 'Light is the agent of the cosmogony, because it is the agent of Revelation, that is to say, of knowledge.'

Second, the ontology of the system is based on the notion of return to origin.[6] A soul is created at the beginning of time and dwells in the world of souls, *'alam-e-arwah*, until it descends into the body at the moment of birth and loses its original knowledge. The aim of the Sufi is to return the soul to its prior state of knowledge in a mystic's lifetime, and then to exceed this state. So too, the origin or source of each sphere is in the sphere above it.

The recursive structural principles of repetition and accretion, along with the ontological principle of return to origins, allow for the almost infinite expansion of the system. At one moment it might appear that a person has achieved the ultimate state of knowledge, annihilation and

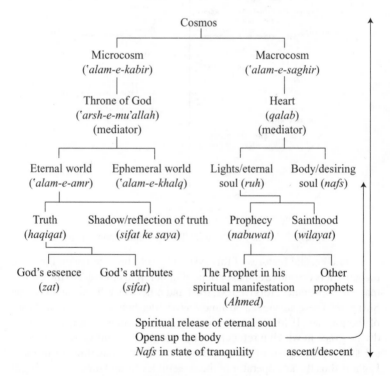

Figure 9.3: Structure of the cosmos

[6] This is the principle of *ta'wil*; etymologically, the 'carrying back' of a thing to its princi-ple, of a symbol to what it symbolises (Corbin 1969: 11); the transmutation of everything visible into symbols, and symbols into essences (ibid.: 13).

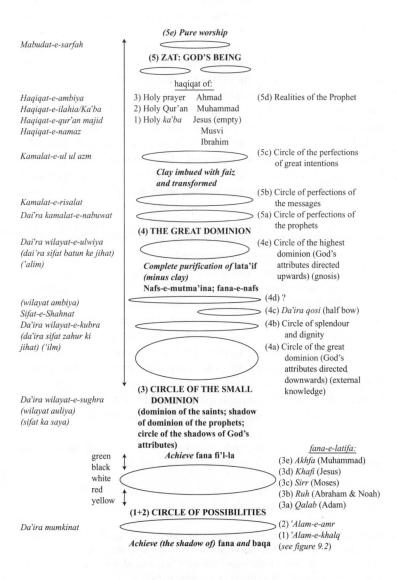

Figure 9.4: The further elaboration of the system

subsistence in God. But then it turns out that this is only the first round and that select persons can repeat the process at a higher level several times over, each time ascending further towards God. In this Naqshbandi version of Sufism, no matter how close one gets to the final destination, God's pure being, the gap between man and God remains, in principle, unbridgeable, however infinitesimal this gap might become.

The movement from sphere to sphere or, in the later stages, between sub-spheres within a single sphere, may be visualised as the ascent of a mountain. The climber aims for the mountain peak but when it has been scaled it turns out to have been only a lower peak, a plateau. In the distance the climber can see the rising peak of the mountain still to be scaled. But, of course, once the traveler has scaled that peak, another appears on the horizon. This is a three-dimensional image which is difficult to present in a two-dimensional diagram. This is why Hajji Karim presented his cosmological scheme diagrammatically as a series of circles. Like a video game, a wedding cake or a mountain range, each circle only becomes visible once the circle below it is completed.

Hajji Karim cited from Naqshbandi sources, *Mushaikh-e-Naqshbandia, Ma'arifa-e-Ladunya* and the *maktubat* of Sirhindi to authenticate his theory, but the systematic construction of the cosmology and its associated ontology was his own endeavour, the result of research into these sources. Like Lévi-Strauss's *bricoleur,* he used the bits and pieces he extracted from the sources to construct a perfectly coherent structural order. On the basis of his reading of the sources he composed a handwritten account in Urdu, complete with diagrams, which he translated at my request into English, and which I helped him to type and edit. The present account is based on conversations we held over a ten-year period, augmented with extracts from this translation.

To appreciate his understanding of Sufi cosmology fully, let us return to Hajji Karim's narrative, as told in his own words.

THE PRACTICE OF SUFISM

'In order to achieve the first stage of knowledge on the Sufi path a person seeks annihilation in his Sufi *shaikh*. We call this stage *fana fi'l-shaikh*. Through *fana fi'l-shaikh* the small universe is revealed. Once a man sees this sphere, the circle of possibilities is revealed to him.

'But Sufis do not simply want to study God's creations; they wish to study God Himself, His power and creativity. In order to do so they must move beyond this circle, they must break out of *'alam-e-amr* into the third sphere.[7] To do so a person must seek annihilation in the Prophet, *fana fi'l-rasul*. The third sphere, located above and beyond the universe, is the sphere of the shadows of God's attributes, *sifat ka saya*, also called the Circle of the Small Dominion [*da'ira wilayat-e-sughra*].[8] It is *wilayat auliya* [the Dominion of Saints], the shadow of the Dominions of the Prophets. There are five dominions: they are, in ascending order, the dominions of Adam, Abraham and Noah, Moses, Jesus, and finally, the *wilayat muhammadiya*, that of the Prophet Muhammad. Through continuous Sufi practice a person can finally achieve knowledge of this third sphere. The divine lights coming from heaven have different colours: green (*akhfa*), black (*khafi*), white (*sirr*), red (*ruh*) and yellow (*qalb*).

'To achieve knowledge of this third sphere, the Dominion of the Saints, beyond the Sphere of Possibilities, is known as *fana fi'l-la*—the heart has killed itself in God. The heart has forgotten everything; hence it has direct connection with God's power. The person who has achieved knowledge of this third sphere is the lowest person able to teach [*pir*]. You see, persons have thoughts which are scattered everywhere, concerned with different things. Once the heart is in its original place it forgets all other thoughts, it cannot think bad thoughts, it is, in a sense, dead.

'There are five stages in this journey: *fana-e-latifa qalb, fana-e-latifa ruh, fana-e-latifa sirr, fana-e-latifa khafi, and fana-e-latifa akhfa.* According to the sources, when, in the fifth and final stage of this saintly sphere, the *salik* achieves subsistence in God—he assumes the ethos [manners and morality] of Allah. According to the *Maktubat* (pt. 1: 60) once the traveler has 'strolled' through the Small Dominion, true *fana* begins and the *salik* reaches the *wilayat-e-kubra*,[9] the Great Dominion, the dominion of the prophets. Except for prophets and angels all other creatures are created from the sphere of the shadow of attributes, the small dominion. And it is here that the shadow of the name of God is originally appointed to each person. But this is not, according to Sirhindi, the original or full name of God, but a fragment only.

'The *shaikh* in Pakistan has reached all five *wilayat*, saintly dominions. To reach them may take a few moments, or a lifetime of constant practice. It requires great spiritual attainment, otherwise their light is too dangerous, it can harm the person not fully prepared for it. The *pir* knows if a person is ready to embark on the journey just by looking at the person, he has inspiration or revelation from God [*ilham*]; otherwise, he can seek *istakhara*, indirect signs (a form of divination). There are two forms of *istakhara*: either the saint reads a passage from the Qur'an and then falls asleep. At the start of his sleep he sees colours and signs which he can interpret as positive or negative. Certain colours such as green and white are positive; others, such as black, red or

---

[7] Presumably, it is the third sphere because it follows both the eternal and the created worlds, seen as two spheres.

[8] Buehler (1998: 122) translates this stage as the 'lesser intimacy.'

[9] According to Buehler (1998: 123) the 'greater intimacy.'

yellow are negative. The other method is to read the opening *surah* of the Qur'an and repeat the words (after the third or fourth line) again and again while praying. In this wakeful repetition, the head will tilt either to the left or the right and this will indicate whether the answer is positive or negative.

'The third sphere, *wilayat-e-sughra*, is in the shadow of the Prophet (P.B.U.H.). All the other spheres are no longer in the shadows. Above this third sphere of *sifat ka saya* are the actual original *wilayats* of the great prophets: Adam, Abraham, Moses, Jesus and Muhammad. This is the sphere of the *wilayat ambiya*, the dominions of the Prophets. These dominions are only reached after a person has reached *baqa bi'l-lah*, subsistence in God, sight, vision with the inner eyes. The fourth sphere, beyond the third sphere of the *wilayat* of saints, reaches to the original powers of God. This sphere is divided in two halves: *da'ira wilayat-e-kubra*, Circle of the Great Dominion, and *da'ira wilayat-e-'ulwiya*, Circle of the Highest Dominion. Revealed only to select persons who follow closely in the footsteps of the prophets, the first is the sphere of *sifat* directed downwards, towards the universe and known also as *da'ira sifat zahur ki jihat*, the Circle of Visible or external Attributes' side; and the second is of *sifat* directed upwards, towards God, and is know as *da'ira sifat batun ki jihat*, the Circle of the Hidden Attributes' side. The contrast is between '*ilm*, external wisdom, and '*alim*, omniscient wisdom, the hidden knowledge of God. Sirhindi (*Maktubat*: 260) described these as the two wings of knowledge and said that he needed both to fly towards God. In flying, he says, he drew on the three elements: Air, Water and Fire. This sphere is the *hijab*, the veil, of *zat*, God's being. The side facing downwards is *zahir*, visible, the part facing upwards is *batin*, hidden. The latter is the sphere of God's *sifat* directed upwards, towards God Himself—His qualities, powers, attributes. This is the circle in which the great angels were created, but unlike the prophets, they cannot rise above it.

'Once the soul has journeyed beyond the fourth sphere it has completed the purification of the five divine chest lights, the *lata'if*. At this stage the soul achieves *baqa bi'l-lah*, subsistence in God. According to *Mushaikh-e-Naqsh-bandia*, the *salik's* meditation [or contemplation], *muraqaba*, fulfils the qur'anic verse, God is nearer than the jugular vein; God's unity [*tauhid-i shauhudi*] appears and it is evident that all creations are mere shadows which do not exist in their own right.

'The final sphere is that of God's being, *zat*. Between the second sphere, '*alam-e-kabir*, and the third sphere, that of the Shadows of God's Attributes, is a curtain through which the souls can discern the shadows. Even to see these shadows the soul must cross '*alam-e-kabir*. The shadows are the reason [*sibab*] for the creation of the universe [to embody the glory of God's attributes], a feature which becomes evident in the fourth sphere.

'From then onwards begins the transformation of the *nafs* itself. Between the Visible Attributes directed downwards of the fourth sphere and the Hidden Attributes directed upwards, towards God Himself, are two-and-a-half further circles: *sifat-e-shahanat*, the Circle of Splendour and Dignity. Which is the origin of the first circle, and *da'ira qosi* (a half bow), which is the origin of the second and third[10] circles. In this circle, the soul performs the meditation of love, *muraqaba-e-mahabbat*. In completing all the circles of the fourth sphere, the soul achieves *nafs-e-mutma'inna*, total satisfaction, total peace (Qur'an, The Dawn, *ayats* 27–30). According to Sirhindi (*Maktubat*: 260) with the perfection of the four elements ('*unsar arba*') the soul is intoxicated, *sukr*, in a stage of absorption [*istiqraq*]. But with prophecy the soul gains sobriety and understanding. The *nafs* which is *mutma'inna* [totally at peace] has no power or desire to cross God, and it devotes itself entirely to obeying His commands. Without God's pleasure it has no will or intention. At this point, the *salik* is honoured with the truth of Islam; he sees to great distances; he reaches true *fana-e-nafs*, transcending an earlier state which was merely the shadow of *fana*. The traveler feels his own weakness and non-existence in the presence of God. God's *faiz* moves, Sirhindi says, from the forehead to the chest; a person's chest is opened and he rises to sit on the throne of the kingdom and govern the rest of the *lata'if* of '*alam-e-amr*, overpowering and over-whelming all previous stages. Beyond this there are no more curtains. From then onwards the soul is totally directed towards God's pleasure, *raza*. This is also where sainthood ends and prophecy begins. The *zat*, God's being, is directly behind the Sphere of the Hidden Attributes directed upwards, namely the Circle of the Highest Dominion.'

THE ELABORATION OF THE SYSTEM

We see here how the system comes to be highly elaborated through the principles of repetition and accretion. Whereas the third sphere simply duplicated the second, going through the five *lata'if* once again, the fourth sphere was said to contain four-and-a-half circles, ranked according to the principles of origin and ascent. States of being such as *fana* already achieved at the lower spheres are repeated, but are said to be more 'real'. Nevertheless, this sphere too was said to complete the five *lata'if* and, by the end of the fourth sphere, three of the four physical elements. The tendency of the system towards increasing elaboration is magnified in the fifth sphere in which the soul is said to reach God's being or exist-ence, *zat*.

Beyond the Circle of the Hidden Attributes of God, attributes which Sirhindi says the *salik* comes to recognise as both part of and separate from God, the movement is to the fifth sphere, that of God's being

---

[10] As far as I can tell, one circle is left unnamed in the translated extracts. Perhaps the dis-tinction between *sifat-e-zaida* (attributes of procreation) and *shahnat-e-zatia* (essential splendours) which are said to make up the circle of *isma-o-sifat* (names and attributes) rep-resents this duality. The translation of the extracts is unclear at this point.

stripped of all its attributes. This sphere includes a large number of circles and realities. First of these is *da'ira kamalat-e-nabuwat*, the Circle of the Perfection of the Prophets. It is followed by *kamalat-e-risalat*, the Perfection of the Messengers, and *kamalat-e-ul ul azm*, the Perfection of Great Intentions. This is the stage in which the *salik* is said to be given a new body and in which clay (*khak*), the distinctively human and final element, chief of all the elements, is imbued with *faiz* and transformed. This is also the phase in which qur'anic letters and mysterious notations or punctuations are illuminated and given meaning.

A well known feature of Sirhindi's thought was the claim that while this was the domain of prophecy, true followers of the Prophet could get some share in its perfections, without, however, exceeding the prophets or becoming prophets themselves. Again, the recursive principle of replication and ascent is evident. The perfections of prophecy are said to relate to earlier perfections as the infinite to the finite, a drop of water to a river (*Maktubat*: 260). Sirhindi says that when he completed this journey it clearly appeared that if he took one step further he would step into pure non-existence. He explains, addressing his son:

'Oh, my son. From this matter do not think that the phoenix ['*anqa*] is hunted and the legendary bird [*simurg*] is snared in the net. Because God is far away, and he is very far away. Being God far away does not mean there are curtains in the way. Because all the curtains have been removed but in accordance with the proof of His greatness and magnificence. Which means He is beyond comprehension [*idrak*] and unfit for religious ecstasy [*wajdan*, rapture, frenzy]. Because God is Being, existence. He is near in His being, but in the sense that He is unfit for frenzy, He is far' (*Maktubat* 260).

This paradoxical set of statements, namely that one can reach God's being, witness His magnificence, become His bosom friend, yet He is far, is distinctive of Sirhindi's thought and it explains why the journey of the soul is in principle never complete. It also explains the continuous elaboration of the system. After the three prophetic perfections, the path to God is said to bifurcate. One way is through the Realities of the prophets, the other through the Realities of God. The path chosen is said to depend on the saintly guide, *shaikh-e-kamal*. The ultimate reality (*haqiqat*) is *haqiqat-e-muhammadi*, that of the Prophet, the source of divine light and mediator or gatekeeper between the traveler and God. All other prophetic and angelic realities are said to be mere shadows of this reality. It is the source of all creation, the hidden treasure, and its moving force is love. The Realities of the Prophets leading to Muhammad are *Ibrahimi* (Abraham) and *Musvi* (Moses). The final stage of Muhammad is the stage of pure love.

Here a further elaboration occurs in Sirhindi's thought (*Maktubat*: 94, 96, 99, 122). The reality of Muhammad is revealed as two: the two *mims* in the name are said to refer to 'two collars', the Prophet's human and spiritual sides or 'individuations' (Friedmann 1971: 15). The elimination or annihilation of one collar, the human, after 1,000 years, has left one reality empty (to be filled in the future by the Prophet Isa, Jesus) and the other reality, entirely focused on God, transformed into *haqiqat-e-ahmadi*, the Reality of Ahmad (with the two *mims* removed). Here the Prophet becomes the *mehbubiat*, the pure beloved of God, and thus complete, no longer the lover. Above this is *mabudat-e-sarfah*, the Stage of Pure Worship. To travel there is to travel with one's eyes alone, accentuating the separation between God and worshipper.[11]

This phase of pure worship can be reached also via the second path of the fifth sphere which Sirhindi names *haqai'q-e-ilahia*, the Reality of God. For the first time, the mystical system is breached by an extraneous discourse through the introduction of dominant, pious orthodox Islamic symbols in place of the ranked prophetic dominions, divine qualities, colours and body elements which have operationalised its structure so far. There are echoes here of Ibn 'Arabi's theosophy in which the *ka'aba* is said to be the cosmic centre of the universe (Corbin 1969: 52–3). The three circles of this second path are (i) *haqiqat-e-ka'aba rabbani*, the Holy *ka'aba*, which is said to be a fixed curtain of divine light, the origin of all fixed points, the subject of prostration and adoration (*Maktubat*: 76); (ii) *haqiqat-e-qur'an majid*, the Reality of the Holy Qur'an, which is said to be the beginning of God Himself; and (iii) *haqiqat-e-namaz*, the Reality of Prayer, the absolute source of all origins and the ultimate shelter and asylum (*Maktubat*: 77).[12]

The unbreachable chasm separating God and Man in Sufi thought generally and Sirhindi's in particular thus creates the potential for almost infinite elaboration of spheres and sub-spheres, ranked realities and origins of origins, shadows and names of shadows.

Sirhindi's thought can, and clearly has been, looked at from a variety of perspectives (see Ahmed 1999: 182–90; Rahman 1968; Friedmann 1971; Schimmel 1975: 366–70; ter Haar 1992; Buehler 1998). What is remarkable is the single-minded tenacity with which Hajji Karim has extracted those passages from Sirhindi's and other Naqshbandis' writings which

---

[11] Thus according to Aziz Ahmed (1999: 187), Sirhindi makes the distinction between *'ilm al-yaqin*, the false knowledge claimed by ontological monists, and *'ayn al-yaqin* (the eye of truth), the true knowledge claimed by phenomenological monists.

[12] Buehler's (1998: 124) diagram is inaccurate at this point.

highlight Sufi cosmology and its generative structure. Remarkably also, most of the key concepts that he identifies as central to the cosmology are missing from other scholarly analyses of Naqshbandi thought (but see ter Haar 1992 and Buehler 1998).

It is important to bear in mind that for Hajji Karim the cosmology he has constructed is a literal description of a real journey, one that he personally has so far failed to travel. Surrounded by men who, as he sees it, have little interest in such esoteric speculations, he conveyed to me his deep sense of frustration and isolation. His disappointment with Zindapir's inability or unwillingness to set him on the path has impelled him to search for another guide, but all that he has encountered so far, he told me, has been ignorance. Most people, even those calling themselves *pirs*, have not even reached beyond the first stage, he said. Later, after the *shaikh*'s death in March 1999, Hajji Karim renewed his search for a saint that would unlock for him the key to mystical transcendence. He 'discovered' such a person far in the north, near Hazara, and was hopeful that he would guide him towards visions and revelations. Later, however, he told me that this man too, although more intellectual than Zindapir, could not help him reach the worlds of knowledge he sought.

Let me continue with Hajji Karim's verbal explanations of Sufi cosmology.

THE ARROGANCE OF THE SOUL

'The original powers of God, starting from the third sphere of the shadows of God's attributes, are revealed only to select persons, the *mujaddid* [renewers]. Every one hundred years there is a *mujaddid* of a hundred years who can hear the voice of the Prophet (P.B.U.H.). Once in a thousand years there is a *mujaddid* of a thousand years, a man of great achievement. The last renewer of this kind was Shaikh Ahmed Faruqi, *Mujaddid-i Alf-i Thani*, the founder of the Naqshbandi *tariqa* [in India]. He is buried in Sirhind. Since then 400 years have lapsed. The original founder of the order was Khwaja Bahauddin Naqshband. He prayed to God and God showed him the way to reach Him. The next *Mujaddid* of 1,000 years to come will probably be the last. He is the *Imam* Mahdi. When he comes he will first have to contend with a claimant to power from the line of Israel. He will fight with him three times and fail. Then Jesus will be brought down from heaven by angels. We believe that Jesus never died but is still alive in heaven; one of the guards replaced him on the cross. God feeds him in heaven. Jesus will help the Mahdi and a man called Dajall with one eye to overcome the pretender. Then the *Imam* will die and Jesus will reign as a Muslim king for forty years (others say seven years, we cannot be sure). Some say he will marry and have children. When he dies he will be buried in Madina besides the Prophet (P.B.U.H.). This will complete the next millennium. His death will signal the coming of the Day of Judgement.

'The challenge in Sufism is to overcome the arrogance of the soul, *gharur takabar*, which is equivalent to thinking the soul, the self, is God. The *nafs* is where all evil things grow.[13] The heart [*qalb*] is where all good things grow. It is the first to reach out to God. *Nafs* belongs to Sufiya only. When a person points to himself, saying "I" or "me", in 'Arabic "*ana*", in Urdu "*men*", that is the *nafs*. In Sufism one must break the *ana*, fight the *nafs*, know that one is made by God. A person who comes into the world thinks he is everything. The *nafs* is pride, arrogance, vanity. The *ruh* is related to air, *sirr* to water, *khafi* to fire and *akhfa* to clay. The four elements are the curtain between a human being and God's *zat*. According to the *Mujaddid-i Alf-i Thani*, the *nafs* is a curtain between the person and God's attributes. When this curtain is removed then everything is done for the sake of Allah. After that what remains are not human curtains but only curtains of divine light. God Himself can never be seen.

'Having purified the *nafs* and passed through its spheres, the *ruh* reaches the next sphere which is that of God's attributes directed towards God. This is the *wilayat mulaika*, or *wilayat mulai Allah*, or *'ulwiya*, the angels of God. It has three *wilayat* [which parallel it in the body, below the throne of God]: air, water and fire. In passing through this sphere a person purifies these three elements in his body. This sphere is *batun*, a curtain [*batin* is behind the curtain] screening the *zat*, God's Being. The sphere of the *zat* itself is the sphere reached only by the prophets. It is the sphere where the final element of the body, clay, is purified and transformed. This is the place of the *haqiqat* [realities, truths, 'perfections' original powers]. The *zat* contains three *haqiqat*: *nabuwat*, including all the minor prophets; *risalat*, including the more prominent prophets, and *ul-ul azam*, the inner *haqiqat* of the great prophets (Muhammad, Moses and Abraham). At the bottom is *da'ira khulat*, the circle of friendship, of *haqiqat Ibrahimi*. Above it is *da'ira mahbubiyat haqiqat-e-muswi* (of Moses). The *haqiqat* of Muhammad is divided in two: *da'ira mahbubiyat haqiqat-e-Muhammadiya*, and above it *da'ira mahbubiyat khals* (pure) *ahmadi* (Ahmad, the name of the Prophet). This is one pathway leading from *ul ul Azam* to the *zat*, which is known as *haqai'q-e-ambiya*. The other pathway is called *haqai'q-e-ilahia*. This sphere is divided into *da'ira haqiqat-e-ka'aba rabbani*, above it is the sphere of reality of *qur'an majid* and finally, the sphere of reality of *namaz*. No prophet can go beyond these spheres; these are the final spheres of creation from which they can stay before the Creator, God.

'So you see, in the purification of the *nafs*, one goes through four stages, from sinfulness [*amara*] to satisfaction [*mutma'inna*]. You can never satisfy the *nafs* in this world. To do so you have to reach the fourth sphere of *sifat* and it is these attributes that finally break the sinfulness of the *nafs* and enable you to reach the highest sphere, that of God's being [*zat*]. This final stage is *nafs*

---

[13] The sinful soul is known as *nafs ammara*.

mutma'inna. At this point the *nafs* becomes *ma'sum*, innocent like a new-born baby, and inviolable, protected, *mehfuz*, safe from external temptation. The *auliya* are not innocent to begin with and only become so at the final stage of this *haqiqat*. The purpose [*maqsud*] of a human being is to reach a protected place before he dies. Once the clay element of a person is purified he is transformed entirely, he receives a new body, *haiat wahdani*, from God.

'The eternal souls [*arwah*, plural of *ruh*] were created a long time ago, before Adam was born. Adam was the last creation. The souls live in *'alam-e-amr*. Here they are *latif*, very fine, they can see God, they are in *mushahida*, observers, witnesses, but behind curtains [*parda*]. They come down one by one and enter human beings at birth. The *ruh* can see God before birth but once it is brought down [into the world of becoming] it forgets God as it gives life to the body. It comes into a dark body, a body is dark. In *'alam-e-arwah* the soul could see and understand the creation of the universe. When it goes into the dark, it cannot see anything. It gives life to the body but its own qualities are lost. The soul is locked like a bird in a "cage" [*pinjara*]; when it entered the foetus in the fourth or fifth month it loses all its brightness and memory of its vision. The body is clay and dark. At the moment of entry into the body the soul is *fana*, dead, finished. All the souls going into the body experience this darkness with the exception of the few chosen in advance, like the souls of the prophets or of the very greatest saints. All the others have to practise to recover the memory of God they have lost.

'The angels too are a creation of God. Yet they remain the same. They do not eat, sleep, reproduce, live or die. They cannot progress morally or improve themselves. Angels simply fulfil the duty ascribed to them at the moment of creation. By contrast, a human being can progress, become better. The *ruh* is composed of *sifat-e-taraqi*, attributes of progress—it has the facility to improve or elevate itself, but only on condition that it enter the body, which is made up of the four elements. The *ruh* dies when it gives life to the body. Hence it needs to return to its origins to be elevated. No one can achieve this without the guidance of a qualified man, a *pir*.

'The difference between a *shaikh* and an ordinary man is that the *shaikh* is a person who has taken his *ruh* out of this world before he dies. He has opened the curtain between *'alam-e-arwah* and earth and taken his soul there. With practice, and the blessings of the Prophet (P.B.U.H.) and God, he crosses the *sifat ka saya* while still in his body—a good person's *ruh*, his *nafs* and finally all the elements constituting him, may cross to the *sifat*, the best can cross from *sifat* to *zat*. At that stage a person can see God directly. But still the curtains are there. There are 70,000 curtains between human beings and God. Only the prophets can see God directly. The saints stay at the prophets' feet. They cannot see as the prophets do.

'The Prophet Muhammad (P.B.U.H.) is closest to God. The five greatest prophets, *ul ul azam peambar*, were, in descending order of rank, Muhammad, Jesus, Moses, Abraham and Noah. Then comes Adam. There are 313 *murselin* who reached different stages within the sphere of the *zat*. There are thousands of curtains in the *zat*. Some 124,000 prophets reached different stages within it.

'In moving from the *haqiqat* of Moses, it is found that the *haqiqat* of Jesus is empty. This is because Jesus is still alive. The *haqiqat* of Muhammad (P.B.U.H.) is divided into two: Muhammad was created by God—*Ahad*—one, unity; he is really one with God. But to disguise this a *mim* (the letter "M") was introduced as a curtain, thus his name was given as AHMAD. But when the Prophet came to earth his light was far too dazzling so a second *mim* was substituted for the *alif* ("A") as a second curtain, thus giving the name MUHAMMAD. Reaching each *haqiqat* exposes one of these curtains. After the death of Jesus, which will occur just before the Day of Judgement, his *haqiqat* will occupy the lower of the two in the *haqiqat* of Muhammad. This was revealed by Shaikh Ahmed Faruqi Sirhindi (1564–1624), the *Mujaddid-i Alf-i Thani*, Renewer of the Second Millennium, *imam-i rabbani*, the Divinely Inspired Leader' [see also Schimmel 1975: 367; ter Haar 1992].

'When a great *pir* dies his soul goes to the stage it reached during his life-time, even further. It can see the *zat*, God's being, although there are different stages, many curtains, within this dominion. In our *tariqa* one of the highest ranked saints is the *ghaus*, the sustainer, but the most elevated rank [*mansab*] is that of *qayummiyid*—the *qayyum* is a supreme saint in the hierarchy of saints. Our saint celebrates the day he achieved his rank [in the *'urs*]. No one really knows what rank he has reached. Hence, beyond the *ghaus*, we believe, are other ranks—the highest ranking is the *qayyum*, then the *iman*, then the *khalifa*. Following these are the *qutb-e-afrad*, the *qutb-e-arshad*, the *qutb-e-madar*, and then the *qutb-ul iktab* in descending order. This is according to Naqshbandi sources. Saints are not allowed to claim that they have secret powers. Yet the miracles are seen by all. People "in practical" [practising Sufis] know and understand. The Naqshbandi are the only *tariqa* members who can reach right to the perfections and realities [*haqiqat*] of the prophets.

'The *Shari'at* is divided into an open, public part and a part which is secret. Within the Qur'an *sharif*, one part, is open, *muhakmat*, the law, the verses are clear. One part is ambiguous, *mutashabihat*, the verses have several mean-ings. The third part, *mukatiat*, are the words, the letters at the beginning of chapters. These are the secret of the Book. The prophets know their meaning as do the highest saints. Their meaning is revealed and passed from "chest to chest", from saint to saint in the *silsila*. *Muhakmat* is the open law for every-one; *mutashabihat* splits the people [into those who understand and those who don't].

'The *ruh* of a human being that goes back to *'alam-e-arwah* crosses the Attributes of God and at that point the meaning of the letters is revealed. These constitute the secret powers of God and these souls then have access to these powers, but they are not allowed to tell anyone. Ordinary souls, after death, have no powers to interfere or come back in other bodies. They see what is happening but cannot intervene. But the souls of saints and prophets have these powers, just as when they were alive they could see *'alam-e-arwah*, the World of Souls. The souls of saints are empowered: the *shaikh* in Birmingham's soul can link to the soul of the *shaikh* in Pakistan. The *shaikh*'s soul reaches out to the soul of his followers. The Prophet (P.B.U.H.) has a link with God and with human beings. Since the Prophet's death, 1,400 years ago, there has been the need for people to link to him and via him to God.

'In the final stage of the journey of the soul, *baqa bi'l-lah*, the soul lives forever. The *nafs* is finally transformed as the soul of a human being is taken out of the shadow to reach the attributes. It comes back to earth linked both to God and to people, to human beings. This is *nafs mutma'inna*. At this point the saint has a new body, he lives forever. Sufis are alive in the grave and their bodies are left untouched in the earth. Their souls are active, they can hear and see what is happening, they can help people after their death. They do not die. Instead of dying they are transferred from one world to another, they have "gone behind the curtain"—*wasal kar gae* [met with God], *parda kar gae* [gone behind the curtain]. They reach out to heaven even while still alive so they cannot die. Their souls can leave their bodies at will. But according to the *Shari'at*, they are not allowed to reveal that they have these powers. Only the prophets are allowed to reveal their powers. Yet all the prophets and saints are able to help people after their death. This is a secret thing.

'While *fana fi'l-la* is the outcome of the journey towards God, *baqa bi'l-lah* is the journey within God, within the sphere of God's attributes. The return journey also has two phases. The first of these, *anil'lah bi'l-lah*, is the coming back within God's attributes; the second, *seyr fil ishia*, is the return to earth in order to teach others [*seyr* = walk, ramble, journey]. In the first two phases the soul goes up, *'uruj*; in the second two phases it goes down, *nazul*. Those who never descend are the *auliya 'ujalat*, saints who reach God but remain isolated, who isolate themselves and cannot teach (this refers to the Naqshbandi theory of *wahdat-el shuhud*, the idea that the mystic reaches God and 'witnesses' his being/attributes before returning to earth, rather than 'merging' in them, *wahdat-el wujud*, as proposed by Ibn 'Arabi). God is one and no one can merge with Him. After the death of a saint he gets very close to God [*qurb*], but still without merging with Him. Those who return to earth return with a *mansab*, a post, a rank. Each *mansab* has a spiritual domain.

'The congregation of ranked saints is known as *ahl-e munasab*. The saints, both living and dead, meet each other regularly. There are 4,000 saints in the "management", but not all of them know each other. There are 300 *akhyyars* who do know each other. There are forty *abdal* [who guarantee the fertility of the earth], seven *abrar* [pious], four *autad* [pillars] 3 *naqib* [substitutes] and above them the *qutb*, (pole, axis, of the earth). This is according to Data Ganj Bakhsh. The *qutb-el madar* of the world is also called *ghaus*. In our *tariqa* the *ghaus* is above the *qutb*. The *qutb-el madar* is the conduit of food and protection from God. The *qutb* only reaches the shadows. In our *tariqa* the highest ranks go well beyond this. It is said that the whole Qur'an is concentrated in the first word, *bismillah*, in the name of God; in the letter "B" of *bismillah*, and finally, in the dot of the *beit*. To reach ultimate knowledge of truth, reality, essence in a dot is the final stage.

'There are two types of ranks: the "managers" of the earth, but above them are those who have the divine lights, *hidayat*, in their chests. They are known as *iman hidayat* (*nur-i iman*). From these *ahl-e hidayat* comes the *qutb-e arshad* (who missionises) and *qutb-e afrad*. The latter is the source of the hidden, *batin*, knowledge.

'The Naqshbandi *tariqa* is very safe, very hard [*pukhta*, reliable], very true. It is very high [*hundia*], very respected [*buzurgi*], very complete [*qamr*]. It takes you fast, it is very close to the Qur'an and the *sunna*. We reject *bid'at* [unlawful innovation]. The end of the other *tariqas* is the beginning of this *tariqa*. In this *tariqa* the curtain [screening God's realities from man] goes forever. The other three *tariqa* start with the four elements and the *nafs*. That is why the followers of these *tariqas* must leave their homes and go into the jungles to practise, where they eat leaves and that kind of thing. These are very hard *tariqas*.[14] In our order we start with the *qalb*—the *nafs* and the four elements follow automatically, *zimni*, of their own accord. When the soul reaches *akhfa*, the top *latifa*, the two *lata'if* of *'alam-e-khalq* (*nafs* and *qalbia*) are automatically complete, the body and vital desiring soul are utterly purified. This is called *jazba*, which means attraction, desire, feeling [*jazb* = sucking, hence he who is sucked in by God's love is *majzub*, a person who forgets himself and the world]. It means being totally enveloped in the love, the *mahabbat* of God.

'We follow the *silk*, the thread, path, series, the *suluk-e-sufiya*—the path of the Sufis. The path has ten *maqamat*, stations, on it in the journey towards God. These are: (1) *tauba* [forgiveness]; (2) *taqwa* [fear of God, reverence]; (3) *sabr* [patience]; (4) *shukr* [gratitude]; (5) *tawakkul* [trust in God]; (6) *ummed* [hope]; (7) *mushahida* [witnessing]; (8) *faqr* [poverty, asceticism]; (9) *zuhd* [renunciation]; and (10) *raza* [happiness, contentment].

'There are four different ways to reach *fana fi'l-lah*: (1) via *jazba* [attraction, love only, *mahabbat*]; (2) via *saluk*, without *jazba*, through practice and self-denial. The *salik* is the devotee, ascetic, hermit, recluse. There are ten stages to *saluk*: going out in the jungle [wilderness], practising [praying, doing *zikr*], fasting, keeping away from people, working hard, following the *sunna* of the Prophet (P.B.U.H.). This is a very hard way. (3) going via *saluk* in order to find *jazba*; (4) *mehbub*: going via *jazba* and *saluk* comes of itself [*zimni*]. This is the best way to reach Allah, the only way to reach all the way to him.

'Those Sufis who use the first method, that of love only, have the love of God but they cannot reach *fana fi'l-lah*, they cannot go beyond the Sphere of Possibilities [of *'alam-e-amr*] into the sphere of the Shadows of the Attributes, the Small Dominion. So too travelers [*salik*] who merely follow the path

---

[14] These are obviously stereotypes which do not conform with what members of other *tariqa* say of themselves.

of practice cannot cross into the Shadows since they have no love. Such a person knows what will happen tomorrow (he can predict the future), his *nafs* is clean and he can see everything up to the *'arsh-e-mu'allah*. He knows more than the *majzub* who knows nothing. The third [the traveller-lover] follows the path of practice in all its detail and he reaches *fana fi'l-lah*, but the fourth [the lover-traveller] is not compelled to do so. He does not have to follow all the ten stages of the path in detail to reach *raza*, God's assent, approval of the soul.

'Travelling via *mahabbat* allows the *salik* to achieve *majmu'a* [totality, from "crowd, assembly"], an encompassment of total knowledge. *Jazba* encompasses practice [*jazba havi saluk*]. Hence, while the *salik majzub* [the traveller-lover] can cross into the sphere of realities, achieve *fana fi'l-lah* and possibly *baqa bi'l-lah*, this will take him a very long time, perhaps a lifetime, and he can never reach the final stage. This can only be achieved by the fourth method, that of the lover-traveler, the way of Naqshbandi. This *tariqa* runs with the hidden powers of the *pir*. That is why it is called the *tariqa* of the Prophet. Here you don't need to leave your home, your wife, and so on. There are only two things you have to do:

1. follow the *sunna* of the Prophet (P.B.U.H.);
2. love/respect your *shaikh*.

This means that you cannot ever object to the *shaikh*, whatever he does or says. You have to believe that what he does is right, even if you see it [it appears to you to be] wrong, but what is behind it you cannot understand. It is easier to go into the jungle. This respect [*adab*] means you cannot even talk loudly, shout, speak to others in his presence; you must keep your attention on him, you cannot sit in company and turn your face away from him, you cannot eat in front of him (unless it is a commensal meal), or disagree with him, or use any of his objects, and there are many other things. Even those living in his lodge must be respected—his family, dogs and cats, everyone. The *shaikh* is the person who guides you and you cannot do anything alone. No one else can show you the path. Only the *shaikh* can take your soul out of your body and put it into *'alam-e-amr*.

'The respect and love for the Sufi saint is the first stage of Sufism. It has four internal stages: (1) *rabta shaikh*: the stage of falling in love with one's *pir*. The weakest sign of the love is when you see the *shaikh* in a dream; (2) the stage of seeing the *shaikh* when performing *zikr*, in practice [*'amal*], with your eyes closed; (3) the stage of seeing the *shaikh* with your eyes open; (4) the stage of imagining yourself as the *shaikh*, placing his picture [*tasawwur-e-shaikh*] on yourself. In this first stage, *fana fi'l-shaikh*, the *shaikh* tells you: "Keep me before your eyes, try to remember me, how I look, what I wear, how I speak, what I do. If you try hard and practise, a day will come when you close your eyes and see me. Then, when you look in the mirror you will see not yourself but your Pir Sahib." One day a man finds that he cannot tell the difference between himself and the *shaikh*. When that happens all the time, it opens the way to heaven. The human body is dirty. To clean your body you have to put yourself in a clean body [of the *pir*].

'To reach God is not just a matter of learning from books. The *pir* has secret knowledge, you must learn with his guidance. If you want to see God in your life you must kill yourself before your death [*marne se pele marjana*]. Killing oneself is part of *fana fi'l-shaikh*. This is the most difficult part. Once it is achieved a man can go on to the prophets' meeting. The prophets are not dead; they are alive, and they meet daily. Until a human being has changed from a dirty to a pure, clean body, he cannot go to their meetings. Then a divine light enters his chest, his body is cleansed and he can go to the prophets' meetings. We call this divine light *nur Allah*.

'The next stage, *fana fi'l-rasul* is one where you perform the same act as in *fana fi'l-shaikh*, this time evoking the Prophet's image in his absence. In the final phase of this stage, a man can exchange his body for the Prophet's body and then he can see God.

'The next stage is *fana fi'l-lah* which brings a change into God's body. Not literally, but it means that a man can see nothing but God. This sight belongs to the heart, not to the eyes or head. This is *batin*. A person sees with the chest lights, not the lights [eyes] in the head. With the light of the heart a man sees nothing but God. *Fana fi'l-lah* is the stage of Sufism when a person finishes himself, he kills himself inside God by the heart. The heart is given another life.

'The final stage is *baqa bi'l-lah*. At this point a person is sent back down to earth in a second life. He is linked to God and to people so he can spread God among the people. This is the stage when a man can receive God's *faiz* which he can transfer to people as blessings [*barkat, du'a*], heal them, solve their problems and bring them prosperity.

'The way to the annihilation/purification of the soul/heart is through *zikr*. There are several different types of *zikr*, some communal, some private, some loud and melodic, some silent [*khafi*, the silent *zikr* of the Naqshbandi]. The practice of *zikr* on the Sufi path is best at night, during the last third of the night, just two hours before dawn and the morning prayer. The night is the time of *Sufiya*. It is then that they should do *zikr* and *'amal*. In *zikr* you breathe in the name of God, "Allah", holding your breath as long as possible, then breath out, saying "hu". While holding the breath one can hear one's own heartbeat, and if one performs *zikr* correctly, eventually the heart will take on the chant, Allah, Allah, Allah, so that all the time the heart beats Allah, Allah. At this point the heart will burst through, open up the *'arsh-e-mu'allah*. The heart is on the left of the chest, the *ruh* is on the right. Having achieved the heartbeat of Allah the same move is repeated with the *ruh*. The *ruh* is made up of four *lata'if* so that altogether [including the *qalb*] there are five divine points of spiritual training and journey towards God. Each stage is more advanced than the one before it.

'On the Day of Judgement a terrible voice will come down from the sky. Everything on earth will be destroyed—mountains, the sky. The terrible voice is that of an angel. No one can imagine the chaos that will occur among the living. It will be like an earthquake. The sun will come very close. No one will know what to do. All the dead will rise from their graves. The sinners will be given their 'amal nama, their evil deeds, sins, in their left hands. The just will have their good deeds ['amal] placed in their right hands. They will go permanently to heaven, and so too will sinners whose punishment is completed. No one can be sure whether his or her soul will go to paradise directly. Sometimes Allah forgives a person's sins. When the soul re-enters the body it will be recreated. Without the soul there is no life. There are seven heavens, with the highest nearest to God, and seven hells with different degrees of punishment.

'On the Day of Judgement people will appear before God as a group, led by the prophets and *pirs, auliya*, who will speak for them and ask God to forgive them, and they will then be forgiven and sent to heaven [*jannat*, paradise]. They know that if they stood alone before God they would not go to heaven. In a country like Pakistan which is not truly an Islamic country it is very hard to be a good Muslim. It is the same everywhere. Only the saints will go to heaven automatically. The *jalal*—the full power of God—is so overwhelming that even prophets are afraid to come forward, they appeal to one another to represent them before God. Ultimately, they prevail on Muhammad (P.B.U.H.) who bows before God. In response God changes into a merciful, divinely beautiful God [*jamal*] and forgives all the believers and followers of the prophets and *pirs*. This is written in the Qur'an: "Who is he who intercedeth with Him save by His leave" (Holy Qur'an, *surah* II, Ayat 255). Before the power of God only those given permission from God will be able to recommend people [to go to heaven]. Tell this to the disbelievers, your idols will not be able to recommend you. Only the people whom God loves and truly accepts (i.e. the prophets and saints, and other good people) will be able to give *shafa'at* [recommendation]. First, the Prophet (P.B.U.H.) will recommend, and after him lesser prophets, then the *auliya* and finally the others. We believe that the only reason for the Day of Judgement is so God can prove to all the sceptics and disbelievers the real power of the prophets and saints; otherwise, God has no need for such a day since he knows about each person already, whether they are good or bad, sinners or innocent.'

METAPHYSICAL KNOWLEDGE: THE JOURNEY OF THE SOUL

There are probably as many versions of Sufi theosophy as there are Sufi mystics, poets, writers and interpreters of Sufi texts and sayings. The theosophy presented here was elaborated by Hajji Karim, the Naqshbandi

Manchester *khalifa* of Zindapir. As we have seen, the *khalifa* relied upon published sources in Urdu, including the letters of Shaikh Ahmed Sirhindi and the writings of other Naqshbandi mystics, as well as on his discussions with his fellow *khulafa* in Birmingham. Our conversations on Sufism took place during innumerable sessions at his home in Manchester and at the lodge in Pakistan.

Hajji Karim is a British Pakistani from Mirpur. When we first started our conversations he was approaching forty. He came to England in his early teens to join his labour migrant father. Leaving school at 16, he worked for many years in a foundry in Birmingham, where he first met Sufi Sahib, and through him became a disciple and then *khalifa* of the Zindapir. Despite his lack of formal education, what is remarkable about his account of Sufi philosophy is its total integration and sheer structural brilliance. Although Sufi Karim's mastery of texts has not enabled him to reach personally to the elusive realms of Sufi knowledge, it nevertheless supports his continued faith in Sufism.

The personal embodiment of Sufi cosmological theory in a Sufi dream is exemplified by a story told by Hajji Ibrahim. It happened to him directly, he said, while he was on Hajj in Mecca in 1983. After the final *namaz*, about 11 p.m., the *shaikh* went to the Haram Sharif for all-night vigil, at times praying, at times circumambulating the *ka'aba*. Hajji Ibrahim was acting as the *darban* of the *shaikh* at the time. After the *ishraq*, just before sunrise, the *shaikh* told his followers:

'Let only Ibrahim stay with me. So all the other *murids* went off to have their breakfast. Then, at about 6.30–6.45 a.m., a beautiful *shaikh*, I don't know which country he was from, came walking into the Haram Sharif. He was over six feet tall and very beautiful, wearing Arab dress, a white *jalabiya* and a white turban.'

To my question about his appearance, Hajji Ibrahim replied:

His face was red, like yours. He was about fifty-five years old, with very big eyes, and a black beard with a brush of grey in it. I saw my *shaikh* cover his face with his *chaddar*. I didn't understand why he was doing that. As the sun was rising, my *shaikh* gave me a signal not to tell the man who he was. The *Khana Ka'aba* was on the left, my *shaikh* on the right, and the stranger walked between the two. As he stood between them he paused and knelt. I gestured to him to walk by but he said: *"Sabr, intizar"* [Patience! Wait!]. By this time I saw that my *shaikh* had covered his whole face except for his eyes. Then the man asked me: "Who is this man?" I said, "This is my baba" [my grandfather]. "What is his name?" "We just call him Hajji." "Everyone here is a Hajji. Tell me what his name is." I could not tell him because my *shaikh* had signaled me, but he said, "God tells me that this is *haza nafr* [our man]. He is not just an ordinary man, he is *Shaikh Kabir*" [a great saint]. At this point the *shaikh* motioned to me that I could tell the stranger his name. So I said: "His name is Zindapir, from Darbar-e-Alia Ghamkol Sharif in Pakistan." Then the stranger stood up and gestured as if to touch the *shaikh*'s feet with his hands but Zindapir quickly unveiled himself and embraced him [preventing him from kneeling]. Then the stranger sat down in front of our *shaikh*. He told Zindapir: 'One night I asked God: I want to see which of our members is the *ghaus* of the world. For three or four years I have been waiting, and today, I am thankful to God because I met this man in our house, so I am very fortunate to have met the man who is *azim asti* [the *shaikh* popular with *jinns*, men and angels]. Zindapir asked, "What do you want?" The beautiful stranger replied "I only want you to pray for me." Zindapir said: "You pray for me." The stranger insisted "No, Zindapir, you pray for me." This happened three times and I saw that there were tears in the stranger's eyes. He said: "Pray for me because I have a very short time." So Zindapir opened his palms and prayed *du'a* for him: "Whatever you want, God protect you." Then Zindapir said to him: "Come with me to my house and have breakfast." The stranger *shaikh* said: "Thank you, I am full, just looking at your face. Please give me permission to take your leave. I want to go now." So Zindapir said: "*Ijazat hey* [you have permission], thank you" and then he gave an army salute. The stranger then walked backwards without turning [a sign of respect]. Eventually, he turned, gave a *salaam*, saluted and went.'

Who was the stranger? Hajji Ibrahim believed that the stranger was the Prophet himself. He, Ibrahim, was the only one who saw it. There were lots of people there, coming and going, but no one from Ghamkol Sharif. Did he ever discuss it with the *shaikh*? What was the point? He was there with him. No, he never mentioned it. He did tell Sufi Sahib and others later on. I commented that the *karamat* happened to him rather than the *shaikh* but this apparently had not occurred to him and he dismissed the suggestion. As he saw it, he had been privileged to witness a real encounter which had happened to his *shaikh*, and which proved that he was the highest of all the *shaikhs* in the world at present.

Both the intellectual work of Hajji Karim and the miracles tales of *murids* like Hajji Ibrahim demonstrate that the broader existence of a universal mystical ideology is a key feature of the legitimising apparatus of Sufi control. While on the surface, miracle and morality tales tell a local story, the universality of their plots is grounded in this broader religious episteme which explains the uniqueness, perfection and spiritual power of God's friends, the *auliya*, over nature and temporal power, and his direct access to the Prophet and God.

'AMAL: SECRET KNOWLEDGE AS SOCIAL CONTROL

During the course of my research I was repeatedly told that hidden knowledge in Sufism is arrived at through experience rather than through

intellectual scholarship; the way to gnosis is via the heart, through the
practice of *zikr* and the love of a *shaikh*. This Sufi privileging of knowledge as experience over knowledge gained from written sources is one
which may be subverted, since esoteric knowledge is paradoxically a more
public commodity than the mystical experience it supposedly reflects. This
has not, however, undermined the charismatic power of the saint, for the
'real' hidden knowledge believed by his disciples to lead to mystical revelation is of specific technical directives—practices of seclusion and meditation associated with the repetition of qur'anic verses and *wazifa*—which
only the saint knows, and which are thought to be the sole means of advan-
cing on the Sufi path. The saint's *ijazat* is essential before embarking on
any form of ritual practice. Without his knowledge and guidance, it is
believed, a person may go insane, be 'lost' forever in mystical ecstasy.

Hence it is Sufi written texts—rather than revelation through experience—that may open up for ambitious disciples the realms of gnosis and
the religious imagination. But these Sufi texts also serve to legitimise the
saint's absolute authority. This is because, although disciples may have
read widely in Sufi Naqshbandi texts, the key, they believe, to the realms
of Sufi secret knowledge-as-experience still lies ultimately with the saint,
and the saint in this case refuses to talk about these matters altogether.

Sitting in the lodge one day with a minor *pir*, Pir Maqsud, a close affine
of Zindapir and a grandson of Baba Qasim of Mohra Sharif, my saintly
companion confided in me that he would like to go 'into practice' (i.e.,
become a saint). I expressed my puzzlement: 'But you are a *pir*, the son of
a *pir*, the grandson of a *pir*—how is it that you are not in practice?' 'To go
into practice,' he told me, 'you need the permission of the *pir*.' 'But,' I
wondered, 'there are *martaba*, degrees, stages, on the path. Can you not
reach them by doing *zikr*, cleaning and purifying your heart and soul?'
'No', he explained, '*zikr* is not enough. Everyone knows how to do *zikr*.
To do *'amal* you need the permission of the *shaikh* because in *'amal* you
say an extra prayer a prescribed number of times without pause—which
means not sleeping, possibly for as long as thirty days. This is why people
stand in the water or hang upside down. The *shaikh* himself has not
slept for over forty years. The *shaikh* prescribes both the ordeal and the
wazifa.' 'Of course,' he added, 'the saint can transfer all his powers in an
instant with his eyes if he chooses to do so.'[15] To become the recipient of
this instantaneous transfer is, of course, a dream of all *khulafa*.

[15] This transfer of grace is known in the Sufi literature as *tawajjuh* (see Schimmel 1975:
237; ter Haar 1992: 64).

My companion went on to tell me that he would very much like to be a real *pir* because his father's disciples come to him and respect him, and he accepts their vows of initiation, but in his inner heart he knows he is not a real *pir*, even if they don't realise it.

Zindapir, it seems, is reluctant to open up before his disciples and *khulafa* the upper spheres of *'alam-e amr*. He does give *ijazat* to those close to him to perform *dam*. Each affliction has its *dam* and these he reveals to his close disciples one by one, as favours granted for good conduct.

My assistant in 1991, Hajji Ibrahim, had been a devoted disciple of the saint for over twenty years, and had worked in the lodge as an act of religious service for several years. Did he not wish for promotion on the Sufi path? I asked. He explained that he had, in fact, been promoted several times. The *shaikh* had given him the power to blow *dam* for snake bites, for pain, for several other things—five *dams* in all. Each *dam* was given separately. Now he can do all of them, any *dam*.

The authority of the saint over his disciples is immense. No one makes a move, however trivial, without his permission. The fear of his wrath is deep and anguished. Grown men have told me they feared that all their good works and devotion over twenty years would be 'wiped out' by the saint in his anger. Zindapir's power is never challenged. First, because his disciples love him deeply. Second, because they believe he knows their deeds and sees into their hearts wherever they are. Third, because he controls the powers of fertility, worldly success, exorcism and healing. Fourth, because on the Day of Judgement, they believe, he will mediate with God to grant them salvation, despite their sins. For those seeking his guidance, moreover, his power lies in his ability to show them the way to divine knowledge.

Yet in literalising Sufism in magical formula, these disciples deny the powerful message of Sufism, that of world renunciation, even when, as in the case of Hajji Karim, they know it in theory. One might be tempted to argue that the saint fosters and manipulates this faith in magical formulae and procedures. But this would be to misunderstand his dilemma. As a true mystic, he knows that the granting of litanies and procedures cannot lead a person to the realm of divine realities. Only an absolute act of self-denial, of world renunciation, can do so. Ultimately, then, each individual has to find his own path to divine knowledge—this is the paradox of Zindapir's secret and one he stresses openly: 'If you love God, the people will love you. If you believe in God, people (*makhluqat*) will start believing in you. If you remember yourself then you cannot remember Allah.'

The choice between tyranny and heteronomy is between two kinds of self-denial (abjection to the saint or denial of worldly pleasures), only one of which is real.

CONCLUSION: SACRED INTIMACY AND
THE MYTHOLOGICAL IMAGINATION

Sufi cosmology is, as Corbin (1969) has argued, a world of theophanic visions drawing on the power of the imagination. For Sufis, this world is

real and objective, as consistent and subsistent as the intelligible and sensible worlds; it is an intermediate universe 'where the spiritual takes body and the body becomes spiritual' (Corbin 1969: 4).

But while there may be some Sufi mystics who do actually experience wondrous theophanic visions, Sufi cosmology can also be approached as a highly elaborate and abstract intellectual and symbolic system; a structurally integrated system, validated, in theory, by experienced theophanies. To explore this intellectual universe requires an imagination which is not contemplative but rigorous and structuralist—the mythological imagination of the *bricoleur*. It is this imagination, which is beyond love or asceticism, which Hajji Karim possessed, and which moved him to delve into the sources of Naqshbandi thinking in order to construct his diagrams. But the fact that he did not experience theophanic visions in the manner suggested by the diagrams he had drawn, with such care and attention to detail, remained for him a source of deep frustration.

For Zindapir, the power of sainthood was beyond abstract concepts. In one of our nightly meetings, I asked the *shaikh* about the Day of Judgement. He smiled broadly and replied:

'Ah, that is when the *faqirs* will have all the power, not the kings and '*ulama*. The tombs of kings don't get *izzat*; only the *auliya*, the men of God, get respect in life, and in death their respect grows and grows. If you go to the Emperor Shah Jahan's tomb in Lahore there are no people there. But at Data Ganj Bakhsh there are thousands of people.'

This was a theme he liked to repeat on other occasions too.

Hajji Karim told me that there was once a *shaheed* (martyr) of *jihad* whose grave was uncovered by chance. They found him still alive; he had turned over on his side and was covering his face (*munh*). Another time the *ziyarat* of a famous *pir* was dug up—they found his body as perfect as on the day he died. 'How is this possible?' These are things 'above thought' (*khayal ke uppar*, beyond understanding). The saint has the capacity, at his will, to transfer all his powers in an instance to the next in succession.

The *pir* never talks, Hajji Karim lamented, about the mystical ideas of Sufism but, at most, he gives practical instructions. He keeps saying you should fulfil God's *raza*. But how can we do God's will when this is the tenth and final stage on the path which can only be fulfilled when one has achieved the contentment of the *nafs* (*nafs mutma'inna*)? The *pir* does not explain what God's *raza* is, except to tell us to follow the path of Islam.

10

SUKUN

DEMONIC MIGRATIONS, PERSONAL
AFFLICTION AND THE QUEST FOR HEALING

AFFLICTION, AND THE REDISTRIBUTIVE ECONOMY
OF THE LODGE

The healing powers of saints are often constructed as their dominant characteristic, a key attribute of their power and in the case of certain saintly pretenders, the source of their infamous notoriety. Zindapir's cult is no exception. Every day truckloads of supplicants arrive at Ghamkol Sharif to see the saint and seek redress and blessing for a wide variety of afflictions. On Fridays, holidays and *'urs* festivals the stream turns into a veritable flood as minibuses ferry supplicants from Kohat, joined by others arriving in private cars, on motorbikes or in government vehicles. Healing is undoubtedly a central activity of Ghamkol Sharif as of most Sufi cult centres. The saint devotes hours every day, often well into the early hours of the morning, to meeting supplicants, whom he usually takes in groups of men or women, supervised by a male or female gatekeeper (*darban*).

Zindapir prides himself on never asking anyone's name or demanding payment for his healing. During his lifetime, no donation boxes were displayed anywhere in the lodge, despite the fact that such boxes are an almost universal feature of saintly shrines elsewhere in South Asia. Rather than giving money, supplicants were fed from the *langar* before they met the *shaikh*. Nevertheless the quest for healing is associated with a cultural imperative to make a gesture of sacrificial giving. There is no need to demand payment; supplicants insist on making their donations to the *langar* or in the form of *nazrana* (tribute) or *shukrana* (token of thanks) to insure the efficacy of the cure or blessing.

The fact that the income of Ghamkol Sharif derived largely from supplicants' petty donations was one of the most closely guarded secrets of the lodge, much more so than the esoterica of Sufi mysticism. Knowledge about the finances of the lodge was the secret preserve of the

213

shaikh's family, along with a very tiny circle of his closest *murids*, selected from among those living in the lodge. Constant attempts were made to prevent me, the anthropologist, from ever gauging the lodge income arising from the multitude of supplicants' daily donations. I was aware of this secretiveness, and therefore made little attempt to inquire into what was obviously a sensitive area. It seemed evident to me even without investigation that the lodge must derive at least part if its income from supplicants, and at the same time I accepted that whatever people gave, they gave voluntarily, without undue pressure.

One Friday there were vast crowds of both women and men waiting outside the *shaikh*'s door. I interviewed some of the devotees before attempting to join the women going in to meet the *shaikh*, But despite my efforts, I found myself being pushed back by the sheer crush of bodies in the waiting room. Left with little choice, I hung around outside, mingling with the crowds. I could see that Hajji Ibrahim, my appointed companion, was panicking: he knew that from where I stood, I was in a strategic position to view the giving of *nazrana/shukrana* as groups came out from their meetings with the *shaikh* and went to obtain their recommended *ta'wiz*.[1] realised in retrospect that this was why the helpers at the lodge were always trying to keep me from hanging around the courtyard outside the *shaikh*'s door.

It was then for the first time that I caught a glimpse of *nazrana* being given. It was handed over by one of the supplicants to a volunteer worker from Lahore, a middle-class woman who had come to donate her labour for the forthcoming *'urs*. She was given forty rupees in four ten-rupee notes by an elderly woman who asked her to pass it on as *nazrana*. This sum, then about one pound sterling, was, I guessed, a standard donation from the poor, especially from women. It seemed likely that most people gave a fifty-rupee note. I figured that even if the *shaikh* had an average of only thirty supplicants a day visiting him (a very conservative estimate), he must be earning £ 1,000 net per month in small change. I noted that after a large group had been to see him, and had in all likelihood donated hundreds of bank notes on their way out, the *ta'wiz* keepers covered their baskets with cloths, then transferred them elsewhere, so that once again there were no signs of money visible among the *ta'wiz*. Only once did I catch a glimpse of rupee notes mixed in with the *ta'wiz*. All signs of monetary transaction are strictly banned in the vicinity of the *shaikh* and are kept well-hidden from sight.

---

[1] Amulet (from the root 'to seek protection').

22. Disciples waiting to see Zindapir during the *'urs* at Ghamkol Sharif

It may seem that this subterfuge is a sign of the falsity and hypocrisy of the saint and his family. But this is to misunderstand the redistributive economy of the *darbar* which is ultimately sustained by individual supplicants' donations. Much of the income of the lodge, arising from such donations, is used to build up the lodge itself and support its vast regional and global organisation. In many respects the lodge is a public space, a place of God owned collectively by all the saint's disciples and open even to strangers who are given a place to sleep and food to eat. While it is true that the *shaikh*'s family derives material benefits from the lodge's income in the form of expensive consumer goods and superior education, most of the income from supplicants' petty donations is channelled back into the lodge itself, expanding the accommodation and facilities for pilgrims, decorating the mosque, sustaining the daily *langar* and supporting the large retinue of retainers that the saint's family has gathered over time, many of them because they were homeless or destitute. The *shaikh* is generous with needy disciples and supports his *khulafa* in their attempts to build up branches of the cult. He not only gives all disciples embroidered caps and shawls as tokens of his special connection, but he donates money for their daughters' dowries, or in cases of dire need.

There is thus a symbiotic relation between money raised through the individual traffic of supplicants coming to the lodge and the ability of a saint to build up his regional (or global) cult organisation. One cannot

23. Handing out amulets (*ta'wiz*) at the saint's lodge

exist without the other. Thus Richard Werbner argues in relation to the organisation of the Mwali High God regional cult in South Central Africa:

…[t]he individual supplicants' traffic, so crucial for a priest's accumulation of great wealth, is not and cannot be divorced from the congregational traffic: one sustains the other. A priest must manage both together, or risk a decline in both. This is so, in part, because the priest gets funds from the supplicants' traffic which he can use, as he sees fit, to subsidise transactions with messengers and their congregations. …[Moreover] This traffic comes from well beyond a priest's current region, and brings to it some of its future staff. Thus members of wards about to form a congregation or would-be-messengers may first come to an oracle as individual pilgrims… (R. Werbner 1977: 202).

As in the Mwali cult, the individual supplicant traffic is a source of recruitment into Zindapir's cult. Many *murids* and *khulafa* first come to visit the *pir* in order to seek cures for their afflictions or blessings for new ventures.

Beyond the miraculous curing powers of the saint, it is important to recognise the healing qualities of the lodge itself for supplicants. The presence of the saint has transformed the site of the lodge into a sacred landscape. Many experience it as a haven of peace and security in an otherwise cruel and greedy world. The *shaikh* and the lodge bring to supplicants *aram*, healing, through rest, ease, relief, quiet, comfort. This notion of Sufi healing was revealed to me by one of the *pir's* family.

Sukun

'Abda, the young, English-born wife of Chotta Pir, Zindapir's grandson, told me:

'When you live here, in the *darbar*, you become very aware of the enormous problems, different kinds of problems, faced by the people who come here from all over the country. For example, there is a very serious, unacknowledged problem of depression in Pakistan. Depression is not regarded as an illness and nothing is done about it. Women in *parda*; women living in extended families who need more privacy; women who never get out, or are picked on by their relatives—their only escape is to come to see the *pir*.'

But what does coming to the *darbar* give them?

'Coming to the *darbar* gives them peace of mind, someone to lean on, perhaps some hope or confidence.'

This notion, 'peace of mind', was one which I came to know as a basic Sufi conception, *sukun*. *Sukun*, from the root 'to inhabit', meaning calmness, tranquility, is a Sufi state of mind which emanates from the mystic and imbues all his surroundings.

Thus Zindapir repeatedly asked me:

'Tell me truthfully, is there anywhere in Europe where you could feel so safe and secure and peaceful as you do here? You see, this is the House of God. You know it is the House of God because of the peace that is here.'

According to Schimmel, *tawakkul*, the station on the Sufi path marking the achievement of hopeful trust in God's kindness (Schimmel 1975: 118),

…is one of the basic truths of Sufi psychology: as soon as every feeling and thought is directed in perfect sincerity toward God, without any secondary causes, neither humans nor animals can any longer harm the mystic. Thus *tawakkul* results in *perfect inner peace* (Schimmel 1975: 119, emphasis added).

Sukun also refers, so one of Zindapir's *murids* told me, to the resting of the soul in peace after death, in the next world (*akhirat*) after the Day of

Judgement. As we saw in the previous chapter, in Sirhindi's thought the
heart at peace is the entry point to the final stage of the Sufi journey (ter
Haar 1992: 49, 56, 139). *Nafs mutma'inna* is the achievement by the soul
of total peace.

Rab Nawaz, Zindapir's right hand man and poet, eulogises the peace of
Zindapir in one of his *qasidas*:

> The heart [*qalb*] is filled
> With this strange talk [*kya kya bat*] of tranquility [*sukun*],
> The heart at peace [*itminan*]
> Is the remembrance [*azkare*] of Zindapir.

Desirado Pinto who studied the shrine of Nizamuddin in Delhi reports
that initially, he had assumed that people visited the shrine to make specific petitions. Over time he found, however, that a majority of supplicants came regularly without a clear purpose. Thus one supplicant, a
businessman, told him:

> 'I do not ask for anything for the saint knows and sees to all my needs. When I
> come here, *I feel a sense of peace and quiet* and I forget the world with all its
> meanness and problems' (Pinto 1989: 118 emphasis added).

The same sentiment was echoed by another supplicant who said: 'I feel a
deep sense of happiness and peace whenever I am here, close to the saint.'
(ibid.: 123)

Sukun is a little analysed yet fundamental aspect of Sufi healing, one
which does not simply refer to saintly miracles or the exorcism of afflicting *jinns*. The saint heals through his achieved charismatic quality of
deep calm and inner peace and these infuse his lodge and its environment. Just by being in the lodge the anxieties and fears of supplicants
may be transformed into 'peace of mind'. To come within the ambience
of the saint, like eating from his *langar*, is in itself healing.

Women of the *pirzada*, the *pir's* household, have been depicted as
remote from the daily life of a saint's lodge (Jeffery 1979). There is no
doubt that they lead privileged lifestyles in apparent isolation from the
vast majority of supplicants, many of whom come from extremely
impoverished backgrounds. Theirs seems to be a charmed existence, hidden behind the high walls of the saint's home. But this isolation, I discovered, was an illusion. The women of the *pir's* family at Ghamkol Sharif
take seriously their duties towards female supplicants. They visit them
regularly and allow themselves to be touched and embraced physically, as
supplicants try to reach out bodily to the presumed charismatic qualities
the women have inherited from saintly ancestors.

As I watched a group of clearly impoverished women supplicants crowding around the two young, beautiful wives of the *pir's* grandsons, I had to admire the way the two women, apparently unafraid, smiled sweetly and patiently down at the crowd, taking lightly the danger of being mobbed by the press of bodies reaching out to touch and kiss them. They listened attentively to the women's tales of woe, stories amplified later, in daily stock-taking sessions, by male members of the saint's family, and by female servants, many of whom were themselves adopted into service in the *pir's* family because they had been abandoned or left destitute.

When I asked 'Abda how she came to know about the supplicants' troubles, she explained that sometimes the women don't want to confide even in Pir Sahib, they want to talk to another woman. She said that in Pakistan people thought that going to a psychiatrist was a sign of madness. So instead, the women come to the *darbar*. It is the only place open to them.

JINN STORIES

Often depression takes the form of affliction by *jinns* or other unspecified spirits. There is a whole lore about *jinns*, who are mentioned in the Qur'an and are said to live, as Boddy puts it, in a 'parallel world' (Boddy 1989). In Ghamkol Sharif the methods used to exorcise *jinns* are gentle and verbal rather than violently physical, and rely on special anti-*jinn* amulets to smoke out afflicting demons. There are no sticks used to beat possessed women, as is common at most shrines. The power of Zindapir is such that *jinns* are said to leave women because of their desire to remain in the saint's presence. *Jinns*, I was told, were *murids* of the *shaikh* and they get instruction from him in the path of Allah.

People may acquire personal *jinns*. One close *murid* of the *shaikh* told me that he had a friend who was a *jinn*. He had been his friend for ten years, he said. The *jinn* was a good Muslim and had accompanied this *murid* to Mecca on Hajj. Whenever he comes, the *jinn* always knocks first on the door and asks if he can enter. 'You can have a conversation with him, he sits in a chair, he eats when I eat.'

'Is he powerful?'

'Yes, very. He can strangle a man. He travels through the air. He visits my friend who lives 400 miles from here, otherwise you could meet him yourself. Every Thursday he goes to visit my friend over there. He [the *jinn*] will remove my watch [without my being able to see him]. He has a

name. He will talk while being invisible. Next time you come I will introduce you to him.'

This *murid* is an accountant and manager of a large factory, a modern
man in many ways with a fluent command of English.

A somewhat similar tale was told to me by an army colonel about his
father who was a well known *pir.*

> 'My father had a *jinn* as a servant. His name was Jumaa Khan. He could do any
> task, even ripen the fruit out of season, anything. It was a four-hour walk to
> Abbotabad but he could do it in half an hour, go and bring back the fruit
> requested. My father found out that he was a *jinn* once, when he was traveling
> on horseback and came to a place where there was usually a stream. Because
> of the rain the stream had turned into a river and was impassable. When my
> father got there it was raining. The *jinn* said, "I will take you across." My father
> answered, "No, you cannot." Then the *jinn* almost ran across the water. So my
> father knew he was a *jinn.* When he told the *jinn* that he'd been exposed the
> *jinn* vanished. I heard this from my father. He recently told the story.'

The colonel, a daughter's son of Baba Qasim of Mohra Sharif, continued:

> 'At Mohra Sharif there are spirits around the place. There is a room with a
> wooden prayer bench [over] a stone where Baba Qasim used to sit and pray.
> Recently they wanted to clean the place and lay new tiles on the floor. They
> had to pick up the bench cover cloth [*takht-posh*, implying that the stone bench
> was a throne]. They picked it up and repaired it, and uncle [the *gaddi nishin*]
> had to shift to another room. In the night they heard strange sounds of knock-
> ing on doors and teasing, and they felt sure a lot of harm had been done—there
> were doors slamming, sounds of the floor being swept. But when they opened
> the door there was no one there. Mother suggested that maybe someone had
> got in. They opened the window but there was no one to be seen. There were
> some people working and some other ladies who had heard the sounds of win-
> dows slamming but when they opened the door there was nothing. My uncle
> then said, "Put the bench back." This happened only ten days ago. My mother's
> sister felt as though a big load sat on her during her sleep. She felt something
> jumped backwards. It had sparkling eyes like a cat's eyes, but there was noth-
> ing there. There were things moving like flames.'

Such named and protective *jinns* are both rare and closer to spiritual
agents, *mu'akkal* or *muwakkal*, appointed guardians to whom power is
delegated, who are said to help the *pir* in his healing and protective activities. Thus the colonel continued:

> 'My uncle said that as a child he used to have a small girl who worked in the
> house. One day he saw her lying with her mouth down on the *takht-posh*. He
> asked: "What are you doing? You are insulting the place!" He tried to pick her

up and take her out. But she weighed a ton. He got scared and left her alone. When he looked back there was no one there.'

I was told that the *shaikh* has, as his *murids*, good spirits, undefined beings whose substance was described ambiguously as something between angels and *jinns*, who he sends along with the *ta'wiz* he hands out. These *mu'akkals* have their identifying signs, much like the magic square on the amulet that the saint had given me. This is why, once a *ta'wiz* is folded and refolded into a tiny square it is not supposed to be opened. If it is opened it loses all its power, as the *mu'akkal* leaves it.

Unlike such named *jinns*, however, most Pakistani *jinns* are unnamed, anonymous and malignant spirits, at best capricious and amoral, at worst intentionally afflicting demons, members of *Shaitan's* 'group', as one *murid* put it to me. When possessed people speak with the voice of the possessing *jinn* and they are addressed as though they were the *jinn*. I never witnessed an exorcism but it seems clear from the stories I was told that the *pir* may hold quite a lengthy conversation with the *jinn*, persuading him to depart.[2]

A typical example is that told by a *khalifa* about his mother-in-law who was once possessed by a *jinn*. The *jinn* spoke through her (i.e., with her voice) to a *pir* but once it agreed to leave, she recovered, although she felt pains in her head and body, he said.

Some illnesses, the *khalifa* explained, are named—such as heart attacks. These are not regarded as having been caused by a supernatural agent, either intentionally or accidentally. They are illnesses from God, and all the *pir* can do is postpone a person's fate. This is because a person's fate or destiny (*qaza*) is conceived of as in some measure *mu'allaq*, suspended, open to the intercession of a saint or spiritual person. No one, however, can intervene in a person's inevitable, divinely decreed predestination (*qaza-e-mubram*), the final, unchangeable decision by God about a person's fate.

Intentional afflictions are signaled by inexplicable events: accidents, catastrophes, unexpected illnesses (such as sudden blindness), or mental sickness. Such afflictions are known as *bala*, a general term used also for afflicting spirits, and their cause is often unclear. *Bala* may be caused by people sending harmful agents and performing *kala jadu*, black magic. Such cases of *jadu* involve sending either *jinns* or bad *ta'wiz* to harm a person. These are usually placed on the threshold, under the doorway or floor where they are likely to be stepped on.

[2] For a discussion of exorcism as a process of incorporation or materialisation in which the *pir* acts on both the physical and spiritual planes see Ewing [1984: 110–14].

The *pir* treats *bala* with *dam*. He first murmurs the verses under his breath and then blows them out in the direction of the person with a sudden, forceful, spitting motion, 'tfff'. This indicates the invisible but swift movement of the verses through space, imbued with the inner power of the saint, towards the afflicted person. Possession by *jinns*, is also cured (*shafa*) by the *pir*'s *du'a*, his supplicatory blessing over a person which is usually a communal event. At the saint's pronouncement, '*du'a!*', all the people present cup their hands in front of their chests and lower their eyes towards the cupped hands. The *pir* murmurs the blessing under his breath. When it is over the people pass both hands over their faces in a downward movement, thereby encompassing their whole body. Often, tears stream from their eyes as they do so. By cupping their hands they catch the *faiz*, spiritual grace, of the saint, and its healing effect.

The *pir* also distributes amulets, *ta'wiz*, imprinted with numerical magic squares or verses from the Qur'an. Most often, these are folded up into tiny squares which are placed in lockets around a person's neck and worn at all times. They may also be immersed in water and drunk, or burnt and smoked. At Ghamkol Sharif, there are special *khulafa* overlooking the production of *ta'wiz* which are imprinted with rubber stamps onto strips of paper and then cut up into squares. Part of the esoteric knowledge of a saint is his knowledge of composing *ta'wiz*, although minor *pirs* may also acquire such knowledge. Nevertheless, the *ta'wiz* of a powerful saint are regarded as superior and more powerful than those of a minor one.

Sometimes the *pir* taps a painful, disabled or afflicted part of the body with his stick, murmuring a prayer. Another, more general form of Islamic protection is *sadaqat*, donation to charity or, in extreme cases as we have seen, a sacrifice given away in its entirety. *Sadaqat*, like *dam*, protects a person from evil influences, but the appeal in this case is directly to God's protection (see P. Werbner 1990a: ch. 4).

Hajji Karim told me that after his father died, his *biradari* in Birmingham hired people to go after him and harm him. But they failed, and he didn't even realise at the time that he'd been attacked. This was because the *ta'wiz* given to him by Zindapir protected him.

Affliction by *jinns* can also be accidental and this is especially so in the case of children. The abode of *jinns* in Pakistan is said to be in wild, derelict or deserted places, the *jangal*. Children playing under trees, in wastelands or uninhabited spots, may accidentally step on a *jinn* who then possesses them. This is when they are taken to a *pir*, usually at quite a young age, and given an amulet to wear around their necks. They are rarely seriously harmed by the *jinn*, but they behave oddly, crying incessantly and without reason, bothering their mothers or moving around restlessly, a sure sign that they have been afflicted. *Jinns* who afflict children are conceived of as amoral beings, striking out haphazardly when they are disturbed. But *jadu* and *nazar*[3], black magic and the evil eye, are deliberate acts of envy and are, Hajji Karim said, very bad. Only some people, he added, have black tongues.

By contrast to *jadu, nazar*, the evil eye, though also arising from envy, is usually caused either by a complete stranger or a close relative. It is sometimes inadvertent, and is directed especially against children who appear particularly beautiful. The following case is typical.

Haq Nawaz, the *darban* of the *shaikh* at the time of my visit in 1989 and 1991, had suffered from blindness as a child. When he was young, he said, he had very beautiful eyes. One day his mother was darkening his eyelashes when a man told her—his eyes are so beautiful, they have no need for that. Then, when he was in the seventh grade at school, his eyesight began to fade. It got worse and worse until he had to be taken out of school. His parents were told to go to the doctor but they said they would go to their own doctor (i.e. the *pir*) first. Haq Nawaz did not remember much of the visit to the *shaikh*. He told me he thought that the *pir* just blew *dam* on him, nothing else, and gradually, his eyesight recovered. Now he sees better than most people. His father was a *khalifa* and the *darban* before him, and he took over the role after his father died. By 1999, Haq Nawaz had founded his own branch of the lodge, adjacent to his natal village.

Fear of *nazar* is all pervasive. I was told that the buffalo are milked when no one is around in order to protect the milk from *nazar*. So too, all food bought in the market is kept covered for fear of *nazar*.

Hajji Ibrahim showed me the *ta'wiz* for *jinns* being prepared by the *khalifa* who sits outside the entrance to the *shaikh*'s inner sanctum. The *ta'wiz* is a long, thin piece of paper which is rolled diagonally into an elongated, thin shape and wound around with a blue thread to look something like a cigarette. The end of the paper is then lit and the person afflicted by the *jinn* breathes in the smoke through his nostrils. The taste and smell of the inhaled smoke were, I found, acrid, sharp, and extremely nasty.

On the paper are written the names of five devils: Iblis, Shadad, Haman, Namrud and Firon.[4] Iblis is the lord of the devils.

---

[3] From the word 'to see'.

[4] Namrud and Firon are also the infamous biblical tyrants Nimrod and Pharaoh.

224

'How does it work?' I asked.

'You breathe in the names of the devil five times (three might sometimes be enough). The devil then commands the *jinn* to leave the person.
The devil is angry with the *jinn* and says to him: Why are you here, causing me to be burnt?'

'But,' I said, 'if *jinns* and devils are made of fire, why should the devil
bother about fire, or fear being burnt?'

My interlocutors fell silent. It was evident that for them it was sufficient that the devil feels attacked by the *ta'wiz* so he commands the *jinn* to
depart. As among the Azande, it seems that the cosmological coherence
of the healing process is not at stake here, and its logic is not fully pursued. Talking to people on other occasions, there was general unanimity
that *jinns* were made of fire while angels were made of light (*nur*). The
devil is a fallen angel who refused to bow before man. Perhaps, I suggested, he was made of light? After some discussion, however, the general conclusion was that he must be made of fire, a view summed up
decisively by one of the women present. This left unresolved the question
of why the devil feared burning.

MULAQAT: MEETINGS WITH THE *SHAIKH*

Despite the relatively elaborate cosmology of affliction Pakistanis recognise, the aetiology of most illnesses is left unexplained by the *pir*. The
meetings with the *shaikh* are necessarily short because there are often
large numbers of supplicants waiting outside to see him. This is particularly so during the *'urs* days when he meets people all day long, through
the night and into the early hours of the morning. Sessions are usually
packed.[5] Partly for this reason, communication between *pir* and supplicants is terse, and consists mainly of supplicants briefly describing the
reason for their visit. There is nothing like the intimate and elaborate
exposure of the micro-dynamics of social life to be found in Tswapong or
Kalanga divination (R. Werbner 1973, 1989: ch. 1), or the lengthy rhetorical questions posed by Azande to their oracles, and through which they
speculate on the possible social causes of affliction (Evans-Pritchard
1937). Nor do supplicants acquire status and long term sociality in a cult
of possession. It is left to the *pir* to decide on the method of healing or of

---

[5] Ewing (1984: 109) reports that in the sessions she observed, there could be as many as
forty or more followers seated at the feet of the *pir*.

resolving a supplicant's problem, and since he is believed to have direct insight into the cause of the affliction, communication with him is brief, laconic and factual. All encounters invariably end with *du'a* and a command by the *pir* to perform the five daily prayers and obtain a *ta'wiz* 'outside' his meeting room.

The brevity and standardisation of both complaints and saintly responses raise the question of how healing may be effected in Sufi cults. Crapanzano echoes Victor Turner in proposing that healing among the Hamadsha, rather than being a function of the patient-curer relationship, arises out of a 'sharing of illness' and the sociality of membership in a spirit possession cult (1973: 216–17). Against this view, Katherine Ewing suggests that saint healing in Pakistan is the result of an 'intense dyadic relationship' between saint and follower (1984: 114).

No doubt, Pakistani curing does not, on the whole, lead to the emergence of a community of suffering as healing does in many spirit possession cults. But it is important not to miss the emotional ecology of the lodge itself, its nurturing role and the social support offered there, all of which are experienced as contributing to the healing process. The healing powers of the *langar*, the ambience of *sukun*, the mutual love between disciples, go beyond a dyadic *piri-muridi* relationship even if ultimately, they are perceived to emanate from the *pir's* extraordinary persona. In this atmosphere of trust a 'sharing of illness' between supplicants does seem occur, even on a casual basis during brief encounters. The pilgrimage to the lodge in the company of relatives itself serves to make a patient the central focus of familial concern.

Some supplicants become fellow disciples but this usually occurs at a post-healing stage. Within any *mulaqat* there are some who have come to do *bai'at*, that is, to be initiated into the order through a pledge of allegiance to the saint. In the case of women initiates, the *pir* extends a white *chaddar* which the women hold at one end, while he holds the other end. An elaborate liturgy of prayers is then followed, with the women repeating the words of allegiance after the *shaikh* and listening carefully to his instructions. The first step on the Sufi path is always to ask forgiveness for prior deeds. Most *murids* are content to remain at this stage and never progress beyond it.

As has been widely reported from other shrines in South Asia, people visit the *pir* for anything from infertility, disability, depression and chronic illness to marital, financial and career problems (see, for example,

Pinto 1989: 114–15). In any *mulaqat*, participants will all hear each other's problems as these are aired before the *pir*. But a good deal of the healing process seems to take place outside the saint's inner sanctum, before or after meetings, in conversations among women supplicants or with residents of the lodge. It is in these confessional conversations that people expose their problems in detail.

For example, in 1991, while we were sitting in the room of Salima, the *pir's* female *darban* and his loyal confidant, a woman came in with an older woman and a very young child. The woman was distraught with grief. Her two daughters and daughter-in-law had been in a road accident and her daughter, the mother of the child, had been very badly injured in the face by glass and on her chest and body, and had been lying unconscious in Peshawar hospital for three days. Their car had crashed with a coach, whose driver had tried to escape but had been caught. She said her daughter was very unlucky because her husband drinks (but he was not the driver). She went in to see the *shaikh* of her own accord. Salima and her sister, along with the various other women who arrived as the news spread, commiserated with the mother and wiped away tears, although they returned to their cheerful conversation once she left the room. They knew the daughter and said she was *bahut acchi*, very nice. The mother, they told me, is a very good *murid* of the *shaikh* and comes from a very rich family.

The kinds of afflictions encountered by the *pir* in a single session reveal the variety of issues he deals with. In a session in 1991, for example:

1. One woman brought her daughter with problems of insanity. Her husband had left the daughter ten months before and since then she has been insane (*pagal, janun*).
2. One woman was suffering from headaches.
3. One old woman came because her daughter had three daughters and no son.
4. One woman had no children.
5. One woman said her son was taking exams and she wanted him to succeed.
6. One woman said her child was very careless and naughty.
7. One woman said she was always unhappy and always ill. [The *pir* was annoyed with this woman because she wanted to give him *shukrana* and he shouted at her angrily.]
8. One member of Pir Khel had come to see the *shaikh* to ask for a *ta'wiz* because she wanted to build a new house.

My notes of the session the following morning show a preponderance of women with chronic ailments:

1. The first patient had acute pains in her knees and thighs, and also a fever. And she could not stand. The pain started two years ago. She had been to the doctor but he could not do anything about it. She felt very weak. She came with her two daughters. One daughter also had a fever but she didn't want to visit the doctor. The other daughter had a pain. They came from Karian near Rawalpindi.
2. A second woman was from Jangal Khel and had a urinary problem which started a year ago. She had not been to the hospital but she had been to the *pir* before. In her house her daughter-in-law, she reported, is a doctor but she didn't want to tell her about it (no explanation given).
3. A third woman had pains in her hips which started two years ago. She came from Dir. They live in Saudi Arabia and she had been to see the doctor but he hadn't been able to help.
4. One old lady from Jhelum had problems with her eyes which were very weak.
5. Another old lady from Jangal Khel, mother-in-law of one of the other ladies, also had eyesight problems.
6. One lady had a pain in her leg. The doctor had examined her blood and told her the name of her disease. She was from Jangal Khel and had come here for the first time.
7. Another lady had kidney pains which started eleven years before. Her sister-in-law is a doctor and she examined her blood but hadn't been able to help. She was also from Jangal Khel (clearly, a whole group of women had arrived to see the saint. It was Friday and many people from Kohat had come for the Friday prayers at the mosque).
8. One of the women had come from Talagan in the Punjab. She was vomiting blood and the doctor had told her she had TB. He had given her medicine, and this had been going on for two-and-a-half years but she still hadn't recovered. When she used the medicine she got better, she said, but when she stopped it started again.
9. The final lady was from Peshawar. Her child had a fever. She had seen the doctor who gave the baby medicine but the baby had not recovered.

There were also instances of mental illness recorded by my assistant who had managed to brave the crowds of women pressing in to see the *shaikh* one Friday:

1. One woman told the *pir*: 'I have only one daughter. She is very sensitive. We are very poor and she is very unhappy, so she's gone mad [*pagal*].'

2. One lady brought her sister: 'My sister is very fond of studying but she says, my brain is very weak so I can't understand anything.'
3. A third woman told the *pir*: 'My daughter is very sensitive [*hassas*] and she doesn't pray regularly. Sometimes she laughs a lot, sometimes she weeps, she is insane.'
4. 'We have only one brother who is unmarried and he is always quarrelling with us, his sisters. We want a *ta'wiz* to protect us from him.'

According to my assistant, there were also a few cases of women with marital problems. One woman had come because her husband had taken a second wife and was no longer interested in her. Some women had daughters and they were looking for good husbands for them. The *pir* gave them *ta'wiz* so they would be lucky in their searches. Other cases I recorded were of infertility and miscarriage, unemployment, marital conflict ('my husband does not understand me'), heart problems, physical shaking and sick children.

Close female disciples often got special attention from the *pir*. Thus, the daughter of a woman *murid* from Bannu who had been working for the *'urs* came to see the *pir* from Bannu. Her baby son had just had tetanus, he was in hospital for ten days, and now he could not even hold his head up although he was about five months old. She came in after the other women supplicants had left and was treated as a special case. The *pir* blew *dam* on her four times, each time counting whatever prayer he uses on his knuckles, then blowing towards her suddenly. In addition, he gave her one folded *ta'wiz* and a whole bunch of unfolded ones.

Interviews conducted with men waiting to see the saint showed that many simply wanted to see him. Others had problems to resolve. As in the earlier cases cited above supplicants who were ill tended to consult both the *pir* and medical authorities:

1. One man came from Nusheira in the Frontier. He had brought his daughter to see the *pir*. Her husband, who works in PIA (Pakistan International Airlines), was troubling her but she did not want to separate from him. He had come for a *du'a* and *ta'wiz*. He himself is not a *murid* but his driver had been a *murid* for fifteen years.

'How did you become a *murid*?' I asked the driver. He was a tailor, he said, and fifteen years ago his business was making no money; he looked everywhere but could not find any work. A person he knew who was a *murid* of the *shaikh* suggested that he come here. He was given a *ta'wiz* and *du'a* and after that he became a very successful tailor.

2. One old man came from Kohat just to see Pir Sahib. He is a *murid* and became one in 1953. At that time this place was only a *jangal*. Pir Sahib used to sit alone and there was no one with him. The supplicant told me he was an advocate and member of the People's Party. All the party people had gone to 'Pindi for a grand convention but he didn't want to go so he thought he would pass the time with the *pir*.

3. One youngish man had come from Kohat. He works there in Semat Factory. He'd come about infertility. He has two wives but no children. He came here once before six years ago. He had now just started treatment with a gynaecologist in the hospital, and had taken pills for one out of a three-month course. So he had come to the *pir* for *ta'wiz* and *du'a*, alone, without his wives.

4. One man came from Mardan in the Frontier. He was ill and went to the doctor, but he had not recovered so he had come now, for the first time, to the *shaikh*. He had been a *murid* for five years.

5. One person came from Sohawa in the Punjab. He wanted to meet the *shaikh*. His brother is a *murid*. But he hadn't come to do *bai'at*. He'd just come to see him.

6. One person said he'd come here first in 1953. He was just passing by and he became a *murid*. He comes from Sialkot, to commemorate *gyarvi sharif*. He has an MA in English.

7. One young man was only 23 years old. He'd been to the *'urs* before. He is a law student in Islamabad, at the Muslim Law College. He came for an amulet, to help him pass his exams in November. He is a *murid* and his whole family are *murids*. He is from Kohat. His father is a government contractor and a very loyal *murid* with close ties to the *shaikh*.

8. One man had come with his son, about six years old, whose left leg is weak. He'd been to many doctors and to the hospital, but they had not managed to cure him so he'd come to see the *shaikh*.

It is in relation to this enormous variety of problems and afflictions that saintly miracle stories are told, of cripples who walked out of his room unaided, of the blind who recovered their sight. I never myself saw such a miracle but I was assured that they were a frequent occurrence. On that very day, Salima's sister told me, the girl who had come in to see the *shaikh*, the one who couldn't walk and whom he'd poked all over with his stick and shouted at, had managed to walk to the bus unaided.[6]

---

[6] It is conceivable that he was shouting at a *jinn* who then departed.

A miracle tale about the saint's ability to cure was told to me by the husband of a highly educated woman doctor from Kohat. A man bitten by a snake was in hospital being treated for shock and bleeding profusely from all his orifices. The family rushed to see Zindapir who gave them a *ta'wiz* and *dam* in water which one of them drank (on the spot). Later they checked the time when the man had recovered from the snake bite and it turned out to be exactly the same moment in which the drinker imbibed the blessed water.

It was noticeable that when the *shaikh* treated the women his face was almost expressionless, like the face of a professional doctor, very matter-of-fact. He dealt with each case quickly and efficiently, now and then asking a clarifying question. Clearly, he must have been a very hand-some, striking man in his youth—his eyes are deep set, he brows straight, he has a strong aquiline nose and a wide firm mouth. Although very old, he still looks distinguished. He gave the women *ta'wiz* or salt blessed by him and wrapped in a *ta'wiz*. He threw the *ta'wiz* over the wooden barrier and the woman in charge handed them to the supplicant. When people came just for *du'a* he gave them a single *ta'wiz* to keep for the future. If they were ill, he gave them several. The salt was even sent overseas. It was sent to the son of Ayub Khan in America, I was told. Hajji Karim told me he still had some left in Manchester which he gave out to people, and he would probably take fresh salt back with him. The power of the salt emanates, I was told, from the blessing blown over it, but salt was better than sugar (it travels, it's divisible, it endures, it is life-giving).

One of the *ta'wiz* the saint showed me was of a magic square in which all the numbers added up to fifteen in each direction: across, top to bot-tom, and diagonally. He said it had helped someone who'd been refused a visa to England at the British consulate in Lahore. The man went back there and got his visa. He gave me the *ta'wiz* and said it would help me, not only to get a visa, but also to make my enemies love me.

4 9 2
3 5 7
8 1 6

Unfortunately, I eventually lost the amulet.

Among the supplicants one woman had come to see the *shaikh* to tell him that eighteen years ago she had been childless and had been to see him then. He had blessed her and she had borne children and then, although her husband died, she was still happy.

MURIDS' STORIES OF INITIATION THROUGH AFFLICTION

Some of the women disciples working as volunteers at the lodge told me that there are women who come to see the *shaikh* just to get a *ta'wiz*, which he gives them and then tells them to be off. But other women are his *murids*, they love him (*mahabbat*) and desire (*shauq*) or yearn to see and hear him. He allows these women to sit with him longer. He prays a special *du'a* for them. Then, while they are sitting in his room they might ask him for a *ta'wiz* or seek advice about a personal problem. One woman from Kohat told me that she had been the *shaikh*'s *murid* for twenty years, since she was very young. It was evident that she knew the *pir* well. She chatted and smiled at him freely, and he responded with a ready smile and easy talk, whereas with stranger women he is stern and matter-of-fact, sometimes even abrupt. On such occasions one sees his potential capacity for anger, if not ruthlessness.

In the case of his closer *murids*, the *shaikh* listens with care to their tales of affliction and suffering. I was present when a female *murid* told him at length about her marital problems while he tried to comfort her, as she cried and laughed alternately.

Many of the *murids* were first initiated after an illness or some other form of affliction, as we saw was true of the Mwali cult reported by R. Werbner (1989). In such cases it is not clear sometimes whether the affliction was an excuse for initiation or its cause. It is nevertheless clear that the cult expands along with the traffic in individual supplicants.

A disciple from Lahore told the story of how he first became a *murid*: a palm reader had told him that he would have two babies, but both would die. Then, his first child died at birth, so when his wife was pregnant again, he went to see Sufi Bashir, Zindapir's *khalifa* in Lahore, who told him not to worry, your next son will be born a fine, healthy boy and I will give him the name of Mohammad Israeel Haq. His son was duly born and is now in nursery school. The *khalifa* had prayed for him and now the social security have allowed him free education, out of 1,100 applications only a few are granted. He has two children, a boy and a little girl. His wife is also a *murid*.

A second disciple, from Chakwal, had only recently become a *murid*. This year in August he was ill, he told me, and was given many medicines by the doctor, but they didn't help, so he came to the *shaikh* who gave him a *ta'wiz, dam* and *du'a*. He was mentally upset, very worried. His head was spinning around. A high school graduate, he is in army service. His illness occurred while he was in the army. He came here but the first time he did not do *bai'at*. The *pir* told him he first had to perform his daily prayers regularly. After the first visit he started praying regularly five times a day. He came back twenty-five days later and was initiated by the saint. He had requested the *shajara sharif* when he came here the first time, and he read it regularly five times a day. He felt very happy after taking *bai'at*. His older brother has been a *murid* since 1986.

Another *murid* first came to the lodge in about 1966. He had come to Kohat for a driving test as a heavy lorry driver in the army. So he came to see the *shaikh* for *du'a* and found that there were a lot of people working on the building of the mosque. The *shaikh* was supervising. He then visited the lodge a second time and this time he brought with him some sweets for the builders and asked the *shaikh* to distribute them. The *shaikh* said: 'I'll say a prayer for you and you distribute the sweets yourself.' He was very young and shy so he requested the *shaikh* again—'No, you do it.' So the *shaikh* distributed the sweets and also said a *du'a* and gave him a *ta'wiz*. He cleared his test with a Number 1 pass. Then, he was in the army, stationed in Lahore for eleven years and later in Hyderabad, and there he had some trouble—he was responsible for a helicopter which went astray and crossed the border into India. As punishment he was given a jail sentence and dismissed from the army without a pension, so he went to the *shaikh* and told him his problem. The *shaikh* comforted him and told him to go home and work. So he went home and worked a little as a farmer and as a house painter, and did nothing more about it, just as the *shaikh* had instructed him. Then, about eight years later, an army officer came to his house by car and said he'd been searching for him for eight years, because his pension had started eight years ago. At this point (miracle in hand) he became a *murid* (and a rich man). He returned to the *shaikh* and told him about the pension and thanked him. This was in 1986. He also asked the *shaikh* if he could help him find regular work by praying for him. Then, his application to become an agricultural security guard officer was successful and since then he has worked as a security guard in the tribal forest area. He had to pass a test in order to get the job. I asked if there were other *murids* in the organisation? Yes, the director general of agriculture, Peshawar zone, was already a *murid* of the *shaikh* when he got the job. There are also lots of *murids* in his village.

I spoke to one disciple who lives in Islamabad where he works as a plumber for the ministry of works. He became a *murid* eleven years ago. His four-year-old son was ill and he went to an old *murid* of the *shaikh* in

Islamabad who did *dam* and *du'a* and the boy recovered straight away, in the very room where they were sitting. So he became a *murid*. Another man's son who was born with a big bulge on his head was treated with *dam* by the same *murid* and the bulge healed after three days.

This *murid* commented that there is no one like Zindapir—not at Golra Sharif, not at Bari Imam. Whenever he feels sad or worried he comes here and his anxieties evaporate. He tried Golra Sharif two or three times but it didn't feel right. The first time he came here he felt very happy. When the *pir* said his *du'a* he felt cold (*thanda*) inside.

DEMONIC MIGRATIONS

So far my discussion has focused almost entirely on Zindapir's regional cult in Pakistan. But as migrants have traveled to the West so too have their afflictions and the harmful spirits associated with them. The global reach of Sufism is, it seems, also the global reach of *jinns, jadu* and other malevolent influences.

Unlike in Pakistan, *jinns* abound in England but instead of living in deserted or derelict places, in the wild, in England they live among the people. So I was told in 2000 by a minor healer and *ta'wiz* writer in Oldham, a declining industrial mill town in Greater Manchester. I pointed to the Pennines, the range of mountains circling Oldham to the north and east: 'Why don't they live in the Pennines?' He shook his head. Clearly the Pennines were far too English to attract the *jinns*. He told me that he had had a terrifying dream about a *jinn* who asked him to lead all the *jinns* in prayer. Even now, he said, *jinns* still visit him in his dreams twice a month. They can change their shape, you know, and while they look strange and can be identified (eventually), they can take on a human form. Some are good and some are in cahoots with the devil.

Jinn stories were prevalent in Manchester even among the younger, British born, generation of Pakistanis. Indeed, they seemed to hold a special fascination for them. Young Pakistanis associate *pirs* with protection from *jinns*. One young man I met told me that he knew people, not immediate friends but a friend of his sister, and friends of friends his own age, who had been afflicted by *jinns*. One person had seen a woman without a head, another a woman with her hands dripping blood. *Jinns* hung out in unoccupied places like parks. They pretended to be children and played with other children, afflicting them so that they came home crying tirelessly, with no reason. They could take on the shape of a human being. In one case, he said, *jinns* attended the mosque and ate a whole sheep, but they were still hungry. This was when the *pir* got suspicious and began to suspect that they were not really human. How do *pirs* resist *jinns*? There are good *jinns* who help the pirs. Some are good and some are bad.

I expressed surprise that there were *jinns* in England. He said they were everywhere, there were double the number of *jinns* than human beings. Because Muslims know about them, they can recognise them. He and his friends, he said, spend a lot of time telling each other scary stories about *jinns*. His younger brother said he couldn't bear even to listen to the stories—they were too frightening. Some *jinns* were quite grotesque. The older brother showed me the three *ta'wiz* he wore around his neck: one for health, one in a silver case that just contained a verse from the Qur'an, one that his father had brought him from Pakistan. He carried them all on a single chain. None came from a local *pir* in England, he said.

The world of *jinns* and *jinn* stories is clearly one that young British Pakistani teenagers inhabit as a matter of course. *Jinns* are all around them, mostly invisible but ready to pounce. The belief in them fits with the popularity of TV serials like *the X Files* and of gothic, horror and supernatural movies. Perhaps it is part of a more pervasive sense among young people in Britain that much is hidden, and that science cannot explain everything. Such beliefs in no way mitigate Islamic piety and observance. The two brothers were both very religious, attended the mosque and said their prayers regularly.

Jinns have migrated elsewhere beyond the Muslim world. I was told of exorcisms of *jinns* afflicting Christians in the United States and South Africa by two *khulafa* of Zindapir who attended the *'urs* in March 2000. *Pirs* are said to be able to see *jinns*, unlike most people. Baji Saeeda, the woman head of the British branch of the Azeemiya order who is based in Manchester, told me that most of the time people just see *jinns* in their imagination; they aren't really there. She could tell the difference between imaginary and real *jinns*, but the latter were relatively rare. Similarly, Hajji Karim dismissed *jinn* talk and said that out of a hundred people who claim to be afflicted by *jinns*, perhaps one is really so. There were many *pirs* who mislead people. He cited infamous cases of bogus *pirs* in England: Chishti in London, who took videos of himself seducing female supplicants (and was tried and found guilty); Jilani, who had attempted to kidnap his daughter's boyfriend among other alleged violent crimes; a *pir* from Oldham who had beaten a young girl to death with an iron bar, supposedly in an attempt to exorcise a *jinn* possessing her. According to

Karim, two of his assistants had jumped on her chest and broken her ribs. Each was sentenced to five years in prison.

A tragic instance of a man in Manchester who believed his *pir* when he told him that *jinns* were the source of his children's very serious disability is that of Saleem. I first met Saleem in 1989. At the time he was a keen follower of a well known pir living in Wedgewood, widely believed to be a great healer, especially effective in cases of *jadu* and *bala*. Despite the fact that doctors had told him that his children suffered from a congenital disability arising from the fact that he and his wife were related consanguineously, he preferred to believe that the disability was caused by *jinns* in the basement of his house in Manchester, who had been disturbed when he moved in. He even shifted to the adjoining semi-detached house to appease the *jinns*. I pick up Saleem's story as he told it to me in 1999, after he became disillusioned with *pirs* and their healing powers.

The Pir in me: When healing fails.

Saleem lives in a beautifully decorated house with a giant TV. He is an expert butcher and works in one of the premier 'Indian' (Pakistani) restaurants in Manchester. But his life and that of his wife have been completely overwhelmed by the tragedy of their disabled children.

'You know,' he began, eighty per cent of the time the doctors are right. They told me from the start that my wife and I had only a one-in-four chance of having a normal child. But I didn't believe them. Instead, I listened to *pirs*.'

'At Wedgewood you pay £ 40–50 for an appointment [to see the *pir*]. This is wrong. Such work should be done for the sake of God.'

Two of his children have died, one at the age of fifteen, and he has two very handicapped daughters born after the birth of his single son who is a fine, healthy boy, now studying at University. After the son was born the doctors called him for a private consultation and suggested to him, tactfully, that maybe he should stop having any more children? But at that time he still believed in *pirs*. The illness is congenital, the brain does not develop. The daughters cannot walk or feed themselves. Here in England, he told me, they get the best treatment, very expensive. The children have only survived because of the care they provide for them. But it is very hard and his wife gets very upset.

He said:

'We kept going to these people [the *pirs*]; they kept us in the dark. They kept saying, the next time will be better. But they knew nothing. They had no cure.

'I've come to the conclusion that if everything is okay these things [like *jinns*] don't affect you. The family who moved into our previous house next door have normal children. Mr C. (my assistant) kept telling us not to believe in *pirs*. Anyone who prays can become a *pir*. There is only one Allah, and you can pray to him directly. Even my wife—her belief [in *pirs*] has gone.

'Someone said to my wife: "I have never seen anyone who cares for such children as you do." Usually, they are just sent to institutions. People leave such children to die in hospital.

'I went to court and told the coroner: "I know that the doctor has killed my daughter because the *pir* told me that he gave her the wrong medicine." The coroner said: "I don't like to deceive [doubt] your faith—but I do believe in modern medicine." Two doctors said that her heart was abnormal. The *pir* was saying that "they" [the doctors] did that, but "we" [the *pir*] shall do it [save the child]. Did they even come [to the coroner's hearing]? Did he [the *pir*] save the child? My child was in a special care unit. Why didn't he repair her heart? We are suffering [with the daughters]. They don't sleep at night.

'You know, the people who go there—they are stupid. They kiss the steps. They shake the *pir*'s hands and then put their hands over their faces. You don't need all that. The Qur'an has everything… Allah has given everything.'

He was cautious about criticising the *pir* openly since other *murids* who had claimed he was a fraud had been dragged into fights. But he told a story of one of the *pir*'s close relatives who died because of neglect when he had a heart attack. The *pir* refused initially to send him to the hospital and when he was finally taken there, it was too late.

'Even then I still believed in the *pir*. But nine years ago, when my second daughter was born, I realised the truth: You [a person] are the biggest *pir* if you go in the right direction [are honest]. If you are fiddling [if you cheat] then you go to *pirs*. My father-in-law said: "If you pray five times a day and are a good man, you will be a *wali* of Allah."

'Maybe if I had been more educated I would have known from the start. I suffered from lack of knowledge. Educated people use their brains. [But his brother-in-law is educated and he still has 'blind faith' in the *pir*.] My problems kept me believing. I didn't have to pay. He [the *pir*] was always sympathetic. I didn't have to queue. In that way he helped me. But he misleads people. Dr B. called me for a consultation. He asked my wife to go off. My youngest daughter is a pretty girl but very handicapped. He suggested that we don't have any more children. They are very costly, we pay for people to come from Pakistan to help with them.

'I consulted a *pir* from Coventry. He was a nice person. But he cannot change your life. You must be your own *pir*. If I grow a beard, pray, become generous—I could become a *pir*, start a [religious] business. Then you turn your place into a mosque, live on charity. But they are all crooks. People give them money for Allah. They come collecting for mosques in Pakistan but then they pocket the money for themselves.

'Yes, I was a *pir-bhai*. I was very close to the other *murids*. We had very good relations. We used to do *zikr* and mainly *qawwali*. M. (my assistant) advised me: "Don't gossip about them behind their backs [after he abandoned the *pir*] and they will leave you alone."'

The Pir in me (2)

The idea that one can find the *pir* in oneself through personal prayer and reach directly to God is, of course, a modernist idea, one which Saleem's tragic experiences impelled him to discover. A similar discovery was made by Safiya, a middle-class, educated woman, divorced, who had worked throughout her life as a district nurse.

She first started going to *pirs* after her mother died. She was very depressed and her ankles and legs swelled up so much that they hurt very badly. The doctors could do nothing. She was persuaded by her neighbour who was (and still is) suffering from a bad depression to go to the *pir* of Wedgewood, Saleem's prior *murshid*. Like Saleem, she expressed real fear of repercussions if the *pir* ever heard that she had maligned him. She spoke to me confidentially.

You know, this fellow that I am going to talk about, he is a very strong person, so I don't want anybody coming back to me. Because he has got his *murids* and they come after you, He is very strong [powerful] in the sense that he has a lot of followers. You know, to get an appointment... people come to see him from all over [the country] and they can't even get an appointment.

'After my Mum passed away and I got very depressed, my feet swelled. I tried homeopathy first. The woman I went to was a GP...She treated me for a year but my feet just got worse and worse. The doctors have done all the tests but they're all normal. I work closely with the GPs at the health centres and they all know me. Even now, my GP has done all the tests again. In the summer my feet were bad again, but there is nothing [the tests showed nothing]...They burn and they go red and itchy. The warmer it is, the worse they are.

'...I recite a lot of qur'anic verses and I find that that has given me great relief. There are certain very important verses. Mohammad was very distressed because he had no son—the *surah* that was revealed to him at that time says: "You don't have to worry. You have got everything and your enemies are the ones that are going to suffer, not you."... It, the *surah*, just came to my head. No one gave it to me. You know what happened? Last *Ramzan* I did a lot of praying. Because of all these problems. In the night I would wake up and recite that particular *surah*. I thought: 'I have never recited this *surah*, why is it coming to me so much?' I didn't know how many times [to recite it], or when, so I asked a lot of people and they told me to just recite it as much as I liked. Just recently my friend went to Pakistan and met a very religious *'alim*. He told her to tell me to recite it 300 times and it would give me a lot of relief. So that's what I've been doing.

'My neighbour in Whalley Range asked me to go to the pir in Wedgewood. She really brainwashed me. She told me she had been very depressed but was feeling a lot better. You know, when you are very ill you are just prepared to try anything. At first I felt a little better but my feet never got better. I don't know if it was just psychological or what. Psychologically, I felt a little better. I kept saying to myself: Yes, I will feel better, I will feel better. I went to him for two years. Sometimes I went every two weeks. And he charges like anything! The normal payment for a session was £ 30. £ 50 in an emergency. He is a millionaire. You see his sister-in-law and his wife wearing golden bangles, huge. And the funny thing is, the people are just flocking to him. You sit there and you might be there 'till 5 o'clock until you see him. You have to wait four hours.

'...I stopped going to him three, four years ago. I met some English people there. Obviously, I wanted to talk to them. And they all said he had done things for them that helped them. Everybody. Obviously, if you are going to pay £ 30 you must be satisfied. But this friend is still depressed, and she is in a dreadful state. She has been diagnosed with ME [exhaustion following severe influenza]. But she still goes to him, almost every week. She is also taking anti-depressants.

'...He gives you 10–15 minutes and he gave me a *ta'wiz*. I never became a *murid*. I was just going for treatment. He didn't say I had been afflicted by *jinns*. He said I was affected by *kala 'ilm* but he didn't explain anything...I was [really just] depressed because I lost my mother. My mother was a good friend. She lived with me and we went out together so when I lost her, she was my mother, she was my friend. The GP wanted to give me anti-depressants. He was very good. He knew I was in the profession but he said to me: "You tell me what you want." I said: "Look here, I don't want anti-depressants. I'll try to fight it myself." He didn't push me.

'It's very, very hard. I used to feel very tired. I used to come home and collapse in the evening. The people at work were very, very good for me. My colleagues were excellent. Plus, I think, my work. I worked with the over sixties. There were a lot of depressed people among them and I had to cheer them up. I used to think that I'm better off than them. And that helped. I think it is very important to be allowed to mourn. That is very important...[I used to tell clients:] "Look here, you can cry with me, no problem."

'...Everybody around me in Wedgewood said they had got better. One of the boys who worked there said he was almost dying and had been to a lot of *pirs*, and this one saved his life. Since then he'd been working there as a volunteer. He had complete faith in him. Maybe I had no faith.'

After her disillusionment with the *pir* of Wedgewood, Safiya visited a series of other healers: another *pir* in Manchester who asked for a donation for a new hall he was building, a Chinese woman doctor who charged her half price but nearly poisoned her with her concoctions, a new-age Sufi woman masseur whose treatment ended when Safiya began to cough up blood, a homeopathic woman healer, and finally Sufi Sahib from Birmingham who gave her a *ta'wiz* and scriptures. Throughout all these treatments her feet got progressively worse.

Then she started to read her chosen *surahs*. She gets up at 3.30 a.m. to pray an optional prayer, recites her rosaries, choosing the prayers herself.

'It just got into my head that I must read this and I must read that [she listed various verses of the Qur'an].

'...People think I am mad but I tell you something, when I went to S. [one of the healers], she is a very religious lady but she said, don't quote me please, she said to me that you are reading too much and it is not good for you. She stopped me reading because she said that this is causing you all the trouble.

'Then all kinds of accidents and mishaps began happening to me. So I quickly started to read again.

'In summer it is very hard to do *namaz* at 11.30 p.m. and get up to pray at 3.30 a.m. ...I get up at 3.30 and by the time I finish it is 5 o'clock. They [her legs] are really a lot better now, they are really better. I have never had them this good... You know, my father was very against *pirs*—he told me never to go to *pirs*. But I was very vulnerable. Maybe I had no faith but I built up my own cure. Something [i.e. selected verses from the Qur'an] just came to me.

'...Sufi Sahib came to Manchester...There were women lining up to see him. But the pain I had after I saw him... I would never go to him again.'

She asked a woman why she kept going to see a *pir* despite the fact that he hadn't helped her? 'I keep hoping,' she said.

'...Why doesn't he [the Wedgewood *pir*] treat the poor free? This was a business, full of secrecy...He won't accept cheques, only cash...I met an English lady whose daughter had been to school with him [in the UK]. She said that even at school he was always curing people and fulfilling their wishes. Originally he was free.'

As a source of redistributive wealth, healing is at the heart of Sufi cult organisation. A great Sufi is expected to be a powerful healer and income from healing allows a saint to build up his lodge and support his *khulafa* and the geographical expansion of the cult. But because healing is the most visible aspect of Sufism, open to the public, it is also the most susceptible to manipulation and cheating. From being a redistributive mechanism within a Good Faith economy, healing can become a lucrative source of personal income. As such, it depends on persuading clients to rely exclusively on the services of a particular *pir* as miracle maker.

Zindapir and the *pir* from Wedgewood may be seen as two extremes on the continuum of healing. Zindapir provides an environment imbued with peace; a haven, a place of escape with an ambience of sacredness. He recommends praying and recruits supplicants as disciples. He also provides the usual amulets, blessed salt, water and food. But he demands no specific payment for his treatment and earnings from healing come in small sums and are mostly reinvested back into the cult and its infrastructure. His *khulafa* emphasise repeatedly that healing is not his main concern.

By contrast, the *pir* from Wedgewood charges very high, fixed fees and attempts to prevent his followers from seeking treatment elsewhere. He feels under siege, threatened by dissatisfied supplicants and ex-disciples, and he uses violence or the threat of violence to suppress gossip and dissent. Nevertheless, his reputation as a miraculous healer is widespread and supplicants of many different ethnic and religions backgrounds from all over Britain visit him. I myself interviewed Hindus, Sikhs, Jews and Christians all waiting to see him, and many of the participants in his *'urs* told me miracle stories about his healing powers.

The cosmological framework within which healing occurs includes a world of malignant spirits and intentional sorcery. These, as shown, have traveled to England and elsewhere in the West along with Pakistani migrants. Demonic migrations may be grasped as part of the settling down process; the reconstitution of extended families and neighbourhoods, and with them of the jealousies and anxieties such sociability often entails.

As depressions and other illnesses increase, or as children cry without reason, *jinn* stories begin to proliferate and take on an imaginative hyperbole among young people. Yet the influence of modern, individualistic forms of religious worship is also evident in Britain, as indeed it is throughout the Muslim world. Once they become disillusioned with *pirs* and other healers, supplicants begin to discover the saint in themselves and to develop their own personalised liturgies of prayer. They accept the imperfections and uncertainties of the world and no longer seek a saint as a crutch for pain and suffering. Instead, they seek inner peace and endurance through personal forms of worship which make sense to them.

For many, however, the quest for healing is ultimately a social quest, a quest for human support and sympathy. Female supplicants exchange suffering stories among themselves, as Grima has described is common among Pathan women (Grima 1992). They tell their sorrow stories to the women of the *pir*'s family who lend them a sympathetic ear and an encouraging smile, and sometimes offer a practical solution. Rather than being isolated with their problems or subjected to the mercy of cruel relatives, they find a sympathetic and supportive environment in the lodge, a 'place

of peace'. The *pir* is a healer through an act of transference: imaginatively both mother and father, he appears to absorb the anguish and pain
which supplicants bear as individuals. They feel certain that he under-
stands their problems through and through by virtue of his inner power
and insight, and that he has the ability to resolve these problems. He offers
them imaginative protection and the certain knowledge that they are cared
for by him wherever they might be.[7] For most supplicants, then, healing
is a social pragmatic as well as an imaginative process, in which the saint
and his lodge mediate a world of sympathy and emotional support.

[7] On this protective sense which empowers supplicants even when away from the *pir* see
the previous chapter. Also, Nanda and Talib (1989: 136–7), who argue that,

When uncertainty strips the self naked and the situation renders it defenceless the self
wraps itself in the armoury of spiritual certainty. Sitting on the carpet or in the khanaqah
or entombed in the venerated dargah, the saint repairs the soul that would otherwise be
scrapped in the world of the soulless…Thus the Sufi remains staunchly Stoic (ibid.: 143).

11

DU'A

POPULAR CULTURE AND POWERFUL BLESSING AT THE *'URS*

Much has been written about the Barelvi movement in South Asia, a movement that arose in the nineteenth century to defend popular Islam and the veneration of saints from Islamic reformist attacks (see Metcalf 1982). Yet there has been little appreciation of how the Barelvi movement is interpolated into the saintly shrine system in South Asia, or how the connection between saints and the *'ulama*, chief spokesmen of the movement, is sustained. The key to this relationship, I suggest here, is the *'urs*, seen as an open, inclusive popular festival. It is through the many thousands of annual *'urs* festivals held annually at shrines and lodges throughout the length and breadth of Pakistan that Sufi regional cults link into and sustain the wider Barelvi movement. With the global extension of Pakistani centres of migration the provenance of this symbiotic relationship has also extended. Yet while the *'urs* provides a platform for the *'ulama*, it is also an occasion which reinforces the supremacy and autonomy of saints and re-enacts the ambivalent relations of interpendency between saint and *maulvi*, shrine and mosque.

The *'urs* is both a ritual and a giant popular religious festival. It is also the hub of the organisational power of a Sufi regional cult, underpinning its reproduction and enabling its continued geographical extension. These three aspects of the *'urs*: ritual, popular cultural and organisational, are all essentially intertwined. In the first part of this chapter, I analyse the embeddedness of the *'urs* in the broader Barelvi movement and popular folk culture. The chapter then considers the *'urs* as a performative ritual moved by the power of blessing to its final dramatic moment. The different phases of the *'urs* analysed in earlier chapters are here shown to be part of a single structured ritual process. Finally, the chapter reviews the centrality of the *'urs* as the organisational nexus of Zindapir's translocal, regional and global cult.

POETS, SINGERS AND ORATORS

In some ways the 'urs is like a giant poetry reading session—an impromptu and improvised get together of poets, singers and orators. During the 'urs at Ghamkol Sharif the space of the lodge, usually so tranquil and pastoral, is filled with blaring and often discordant sounds transmitted through a powerful sound system, and reaching into every nook and cranny of the lodge. There is no escaping the sound which often continues until 4 a.m., only to start again about an hour later. This whole live show is moderated by a 'stage secretary' appointed especially for the 'urs. He is normally based at the *darbar* mosque next to a stage and microphone. The moderator in 1989 was himself a poet, living in Kohat. Although he had not slept a wink over the three days and nights of the festival, he told me, he still felt fresh. This he attributed to the power of the *pir*. At any hour of the day or night, festival participants may approach him, volunteering to sing *na'ts*, or *qasidas*. Learned scholars volunteered

24. Women pilgrims singing praise songs to the Prophet

to give religious lectures or sermons. Anyone may volunteer, even a non-*murid*, he said. He, the stage secretary, first tests the performers before allowing them to perform live.

On the first day of the *'urs* it is mainly *na'ts* that are sung. At this point there are rarely any *tazkiras* (commemorations) or *taqrirs* (sermons). This is because the *maulvis* do not arrive until later in the *'urs*. They usually arrive on the second day in the afternoon, I was told. Each of the performers is announced over the microphone, their names and the places they come from publicised throughout the *darbar*. The gaps between performances are filled with chantings of *zikr, khatams* (a reading of the whole Qur'an) or the various daily prayers.

'Urs 1989: I am given a typed programme declaring that this is the 42nd *'urs* at Ghamkol Sharif. At first glance the programme looks very formal and detailed. On closer inspection, however, I discover that it is extremely vague and contains no named performers. Rather, the generic forms of performance constituting the festival are simply repeated again and again. This generic repetition, I realise, underlines the spontaneous, improvised nature of the whole event. The empty vessels are yet to be filled. I reproduce the programme here, titled *42nd Annual Urs of Darbar-e-Alia Ghamkol Sharif, Kohat*:

1. 42nd Annual Urs of *Darbar*-e-Alia Ghamkol Sharif is being celebrated from 18th October, 1989, to 20th October, 1989 according to the following programme:

18.10.89

1st Congregation 0900 hrs. to 1300 hrs.
(a) Recitation from Holy Quran.
(b) Naats in Urdu, Pashto and Punjabi by the Prominent Naat Khawans of the country.
(c) Speeches in Urdu, Pashto and Punjabi by the famous religious speakers.

2nd Congregation 1430 hrs. to 1600 hrs.
(a) Recitation from Holy Quran.
(b) Naats in Urdu, Pashto and Punjabi by the Prominent Naat Khawans of the country.
(c) Speeches in Urdu, Pashto and Punjabi by the famous religious speakers.

3rd Congregation 2300 hrs. to 0400 hrs.
(a) Recitation from Holy Quran.
(b) Naats in Urdu, Pashto and Punjabi by the Prominent Naat Khawans of the country.
(c) Speeches in Urdu, Pashto and Punjabi by the famous religious speakers.

The programme thus continues to repeat itself until the afternoon of the very final meeting on the third day of the *'urs* which in 1989 took place on 20 October:

2nd and final Congregation of the Convention after Jumaa Prayer to
Azan-e-Asar (1430–1630)

(a) Recitation by prominent Qari of Pakistan.
(b) Khatam-e-Khawaj Gan, Zikarullah and Shajara Sharif.
(c) Naat by prominent Naat Khawan of Pakistan.
(d) Speech by the Learned Muslim Scholar.
(e) Salat-u-Wassalam.
(f) Dua by the Pir Sahib GHAMKOL SHARIF.

There is a postscript attached:

2. In addition to above, Zikar Jahar i e Zikarullah before each prayer except Maghrab Prayer has also been arranged throughout all the three days of the Urs Sharif. Secondly, Khatams of Holy Quran, Khatams of various *surahs* of Holy Quran, Khatams of Darood Sharif and Khatams Khwaj Gan will also be arranged after the Fajar Prayer.

The programme is the same every year, and most years the organisers do not even bother to produce a programme. The *'urs* is really a happening. No one knows, for example, who will be the last two distinguished sermon givers or Qur'an readers except perhaps the main organisers. The popular cultural success of the *'urs* depends largely on improvisation and public voluntary participation, and it is these that help make it into a successful cultural and intellectual performance, just as voluntary contributions, donations and labour enable it to be a giant feast or a logistically complex three-day meeting. Such voluntarism is crucial to the success of the festival. It is truly the product of communal effort and none, with the possible exception of the invited speakers in the final session, gets paid for performing. What performers get is publicity and an enhanced reputation. The *'urs* is a genuinely open meeting of amateurs and semi-professionals. Over time, amateur *na't* singers and *'ulama* on the *'urs* circuit may acquire a name and, as their fame grows, the *na't* singers may turn semi-professional while the *'ulama* may secure good posts in Barelvi mosques. Some performers, however, may just enjoy appearing at their favourite *'urs*. Hajji Ibrahim, for example, has a very melodious voice and is fond of a certain Punjabi poet. He sometimes sings his *na'ts* at Zindapir's *'urs* or at the *'urs* at Bohra Jangal. Twice he was invited to sing on Radio Pakistan, he told me, but on both occasions he declined.

During the 'urs in March 2000, I interviewed some of the prominent *maulvis* and *na't* singers who performed in the final prestigious session of the 'urs. Their careers highlight how the openness and inclusiveness of the Barelvi movement as a movement is sustained through a circuit of such public festivals. The movement has, of course, gained much strength since the founding of Pakistan, especially through its network of Islamic schools and colleges. Its thousands of mosques, located in towns and villages especially in the Punjab, have always been independent. Jamal Malik (1998b) traces the historical development of Barelvi schools in postcolonial Pakistan and shows how, united under a single umbrella organisation (*tanzim*), they have gradually been integrated into the broader educational curriculum and their degrees accredited and recognised. This has come along with increasing state financial support and control. The growth in the numbers of Islamic higher education graduates has, however, Malik argues, led to a surfeit of unemployed *'ulama*. Elsewhere Malik (1990; 1998b: 5) hints at the political strategies deployed by the leaders of the Barelvi political organisation, the JUP (*Jam'iyyat-e-'ulama* Pakistan) and its mystical association, the *Jam'iyyat-al Mashaikh* Pakistan. On the whole, these organisations' tendency has been to cooperate with Pakistan's successive regimes. Measured in electoral terms the political power of the movement has remained negligible, but it retains its cultural-cum-political influence among its large Barelvi constituency.[1]

Given the surplus of *'ulama*, a reputation as an acute and persuasive speaker is an important step on the ladder to a post as *imam* of a major mosque. The giant audience at an 'urs enables aspiring clerics to display their intellectual profundity and oratorical skills. *Na't* singers can gain a reputation leading to further invitations to perform on the 'urs and *na't mahfil* circuit and, if they are lucky, to a recorded cassette and a slot on a radio or TV show. The 'urs of Ghamkol Sharif is widely publicised in the press and through posters plastered on walls throughout the major cities and towns of Pakistan. In addition, personal invitations are sent out to *murids* and to *'ulama* or *na't* singers who have previously participated in it. A detailed register which includes names and addresses is updated from time to time and tens of thousands of invitations are sent out annually before each 'urs.

---

[1] In the Pakistani elections in 2002 some religious parties won more seats than usual, but this was due to unique circumstances (strong anti-American feelings; the leaders of both main parties banned).

The *'ulama* and *na't* singers are usually provided with rooms in one of the lodges. During the *'urs* in March 2000, several of them were staying in the same lodge with me. All three men interviewed had been invited especially to perform at the final and most prestigious session of the *'urs*. From the interviews it emerged that they had been selected in advance, but through chance encounters.

The *na't* singer is a large man with a trimmed beard. One of the *maulvis* is a roly-poly man, spilling out of his clothes. The other is well groomed and sports a small beard.

The *na't* singer's name translates, he said, as 'Pride of Performance'. He is well known, he told me, and has produced cassettes of his songs as well as being the recipient of many prizes. He is both a *na't* singer and a *qari Qur'an* (reciter of the Qur'an). He began by explaining that saints and *'ulama* are connected to one another. The *'ulama* are responsible for conveying religious knowledge; they help the *pirs* by propagating their messages, while the *pirs* lead by example, through their way of life, actions and preaching. He himself is a member of a family of *'ulama*. He is the only one in the family blessed with a melodious voice, bestowed upon him by Allah.

When I asked about his performances in the past three months he laughed and said there was not a night free. Could he give an example of where he had appeared in the past week? He had performed, he said, in Multan, at Fateh Jang, at Waqant and at a seminar in Islamabad. Apart from this last event, all the others were *mahfil na'ts*, meetings of *na't* singers. When I asked if he had been invited he laughed once again and said: 'There is a saying in Islam—don't go to God until He calls you.' For a living he works in a Pakistan Ordinance factory. He is thus a semi-professional singer.

How did he come to be invited here? He has been here twenty eight times before, he said. Also, he met Chotta Pir, the grandson of Zinda-pir, at a *mahfil* at the shrine of Bahauddin Zakoria, a Suhawardi saint. On 6 January he had attended an *'urs* at Idgah Sharif. The *pir* there is a Naqshbandi, as he is himself.

By contrast to the *na't* singer, this was the first time that Mufti Muhammad Iqbal Chishti had attended the *'urs* at Ghamkol Sharif. He began by saying that the *'ulama* role at the *'urs* was to teach people to respect the *auliya* and follow in their footsteps. Last month, he said, he had attended three *'urs* festivals. The first was for Hazrat Nur Muhammad Moharvi Chishtiya at Nawarnagar. The second at Sial Sharif, district Sarghoda.

This was for a Chishtiya *shaikh*, Khwaja Shams Uddin Siarwari Chishtiya. The third was for Khwaja Ghulam Kamal Uddin at Mianwala. He himself is the grandson of Nur Muhammad Moharvi in the *tariqa*, and he is also a *khalifa* in this Chishti order.

He is the *maulvi* of the Jami'a Masjad Rizviya in the centre of Lahore. He leads the prayers at this mosque and delivers *taqrirs* at three other mosques in Lahore every Friday. Being a Chishtiya, I asked, how did he come to know about Ghamkol Sharif? There are posters everywhere, he said. He met Chotta Pir in district Bahavalpur in the Jami'a mosque. He was giving a *khutba* (sermon) there. Chotta Pir had come there with a group of disciples. He invited him to speak at the *'urs*.
Why did he agree?

The *darbar* is famous everywhere. A lot of people had told him of the Pir Sahib, how he had done *chilla* and had a revelation in Medina telling him to come to this place. The Pir Sahib's *faiz* goes on in his life and after his death.

Does it matter that he is a Chishti while Zindapir was a Naqshbandi?

'All the *auliyas* are the same', he said, 'but they reach God through different paths.'

The final *maulvi* interviewed, Taher ul Qadiri, is a founder and leader of a new political party or movement. He told me that he had ceased giving sermons at *'urses* fifteen years ago, but because he knew Zindapir and had missed his funeral, he decided to respond to Chotta Pir's invitation. Zindapir loved him, he said, and supported his movement. Qadiri is a sophisticated scholar with a good command of English and a comparative perspective on Islamic mysticism. He repeated to me some of the basic tenets of Sufism in a lucid and coherent manner, stressing that anyone could become a saint through ethical and ascetic practice (and by implication, that this was not hereditary and reserved for Sayyids only). He gave a detailed account of the beliefs surrounding death in Islam and in Sufi eschatology. This was also the theme of his sermon at the *'urs*. Although his presentation was very clear, it nevertheless reflected standard Barelvi views on the soul after death.

Above all, the three interviews indicate that there are no strict separations between Sufi regional cults, saints or orders; they are not exclusive sects. On the contrary, the *'urs* shows and enacts the fact that they are embedded in a wider social and religious movement. This is true in Birmingham as well, where the *'urs* gathers *na't* singers and *'ulama* from many different parts of Britain.

POPULAR CULTURE

In many ways the *'urs* is just sheer fun: the colourful tents, the streams of people, the smell of wood burning and meat cooking in the large *langar* pots, the *qafilas* arriving with their banners, animals and sacks of grain; the noise, the feeling of being on holiday. There is a buzz in the air, an underlying current of excitement. Friends and acquaintances run into each other. *Khulafa* and old army mates embrace. In the *'urs* of 2000, I wandered around the market and camping grounds with a young British Pakistani, licking ice-cream while we bought small mementos and cas-settes of prior *'urses*, and watched men carry *chaddars* in procession to the saint's tomb. My companion had come from Derby to spend some months with his family in Kashmir.

There are many activities going on simultaneously. Women dye their hands with henna and hold *milad mahfil* recitations in honour of the Prophet. Some gather together to sing *na'ts* and *qasidas* from special books, printed or written out by hand. Plump ladies and middle-aged men climb up the steep hill to the saint's cave, showing surprising agility. From down below they look like ants as they follow each other single file up the hill. Once there, they pause a minute to gaze down in wonder and pride at the lodge below. Children get underfoot or climb the surrounding hills.

Even wealthy, middle-class women sleep on mattresses or quilts spread on the floor, squashed together like sardines. The Pakistani square tents which hold the men are cosy, but for those women sleeping on the veran-das of the women's quarters it can get very cold at night, while the sound at times is quite deafening. Sufi Sahib leads the all-night *zikr*, transmitted over the sound system in loud military staccato. One of his companions, a man at least ten years his junior, marvels at his amazing stamina: 'I don't know how he does it!' People eat together in large groups or wander as individuals into the *langar* area for a bowl of meat and *chapati*. It is all very casual and good humoured.

The spontaneity of the *'urs* at Ghamkol Sharif is a key to the enjoyment and attraction of the event. Although as I have proposed the *'urs* is a rit-ual, it is not a tightly organised affair. It also lacks some of the ritual elab-oration characterising *'urs* festivals at older shrines such as Ajmer, Bahraich or Nagor Sharif, which have developed over hundreds of years (see Moini 1989; Mahmood 1989: Saheb 1998). Even the laying of *chad-dars* on the saint's grave—a common custom at saints' shrines in South Asia—only began for the first time at the *'urs* after Zindapir's death, in

1998. In Birmingham there is no shrine and no laying of *chaddars*. But despite this apparent lack of structure, the *'urs* is nevertheless a structured ritual moved forward by the power of blessing.

THE SYMBOLIC COMPLEX OF BLESSING

The key to the *'urs* as ritual can be found in the fact that no one leaves before the final *du'a* of the *shaikh*. Once the *du'a* is over there is a mad rush to the buses and trucks. In less than an hour no trace is left of the city of tents which had covered the valley except the billowing dust raised by the departing vehicles' wheels. The dust takes several hours to settle. Then it is all over.

Throughout this book we have traced the progression of the *'urs* at Ghamkol Sharif from its first moment, *julus* or *qafila*, the movement through space which inscribes the earth with the name of Allah; second, *karamat*: once they reach their destination pilgrims retrace the mythology of the lodge by visiting its sacred sites; third, *langar*, sharing in the communal food through which the saint nurtures the congregation; fourth, *mulaqat*, the meeting of groups with the *shaikh* to take *bai'at*, receive *ta'wiz* or simply bask in his light. This is when he gives his special disciples or *khulafa* gifts of caps, scarves or gowns, the latter worn by them over the year and imbued with his charisma. Like a thread running through the whole *'urs*, from the moment pilgrims leave their home, is the fifth key ritual act of the *'urs, zikr*, recited throughout the three nights of the *'urs*. Along with *zikr* are *na'ts*, praise poems to the Prophet. Sixth is *shajara*, the reciting of the sacred genealogy of the order. This is read out in the final session of *'urs* after all the *khulafa*, dressed in black on white, approach the stage along with *pir* himself. Seventh is *taqrir*, the exegetic speech by a learned scholar. Finally, we reach the *du'a*.

In different ways all these ritual acts are ways of reaching out materially to the saint's grace. I use the word grace here deliberately because too much weight has, in my view, been put by scholars of Sufism, including anthropologists, on *barkat* or *baraka*, as though this one term could sum up the complex ideas about charisma and blessing held by Sufi followers. In reality, I found, there is a whole lexicon of terms referring to subtle differences in modes of saintly blessing. These terms together form a *symbolic complex of blessing*. The subtle variations between the terms are important, because they provide insight into the way Sufi cosmology is embodied and embedded in more usual ways of Islamic ritual blessing.

Perhaps the most central Sufi term for saintly blessing, at least in South Asia, is not *barkat* but *faiz*, a word I have translated as divine grace and which followers use to refer to the divine light flowing through the saint and from him to his disciples. It is a light which both illuminates and feeds or nurtures. It reaches into the hearts of men and women even over great distances, whenever they pray a prescribed liturgy or evoke the image of the saint in front of their inner eye. The saint literally glows with *faiz*. He can project it at will, transferring it at a glance to a trusted *khalifa*. It shines with his munificence and beneficence, an inner quality which his appearance and facial expression reveal.

On the day after the 1991 *'urs* I dropped by the women's quarters to meet the volunteers who were washing up the thousands of dishes left over from the *langar*. An educated woman from Lahore, a freelance writer in Urdu, told me: 'The *pir's* light is responsible for everything you see, it all comes from his light. He has a tenth sense to see into people's feelings and emotions.' She had been seeking someone (i.e. a *pir*) but all the *pirs* in Pakistan are frauds and thieves, she said. 'He [Zindapir] is the only one in the whole world. I will obey his orders whatever he tells me because he thinks only of the good of a person. He is concerned about all the people's good, even these poor people' (she pointed to some of the women washing up).

'What benefit does he give?' I asked.

'He gives spiritual satisfaction through the light emanating from him,' she replied. When she is in difficulty she brings his *tasawwur* in front of her eyes and she immediately gets help. Standing helplessly on the road, a vehicle appears to give her a lift. This has happened a thousand times.

In ethical terms, then, *faiz* is the light of generosity, kindness and concern emanating from the saint and communicated to his followers. Through *faiz* a *pir* creates the tie, *rabita*, binding him to his followers. *Faiz* is the embodiment of his spiritual power, *ruhaniyat*, another key term which is used to express the *pir's* spirituality as a powerful force. *Barkat* is the third term in this symbolic complex. In Islam *barkat* (*baraka* in Arabic) may come directly from God without the intercession of a *pir*. It may be mediated by the community or the poor. When people hold a sacrifice or give part of an offering to the poor, they regard the commensal food following their prayers as imbued with *barkat*. In this sense it is a generic Islamic term for divine blessing. *Barkat* imbues objects, such as the salt given out by the *pir*, or the *langar*, with the power of procreation, proliferation, fecundity, expansion, life, fertility and growth (of children, crops, wealth, job prospects, health and so forth). *Barkat* is magical and contagious. The very touch of a *pir* can imbue an object with *barkat*. This means that the *pir* himself is charged physically with *barkat*, which explains why he is constantly mobbed by devout followers, endangering his life in their attempts to touch him. Linked to all these terms is a further term, *ruhani khorakh*, spiritual food. The *pir* is said to nurture his followers spiritually.

Finally, there is *du'a* and the blessings, *fazl*, received through the *du'a* in accordance with God's own judgement of what is best for his followers.

Du'a means supplication, benediction and blessing. Any person can say *du'a* on behalf of a congregation. In this sense *du'a*, like *baraka*, is a general Islamic term. But the *du'a* of a *pir*, said in the final day of the *'urs* after all the *zikr* recitations and *langar* feedings of the masses, is enormously powerful. It is believed that at that moment the soul of the dead saint which the *'urs* commemorates, and the souls of all the *auliya* and the prophets, gather over the congregation. Their combined spirituality is directed towards the saint's appeal to God for blessing and healing. That is why no one goes home before the final *du'a*. It is the whole point of the *'urs* ritual.

The *'urs*, of course, is also a wedding. That is why the women dye the palms of their hands with *mehndi*. While Zindapir was alive this wedding motif was not expressed in the ritual itself. It merely existed at the

25. Zindapir's final *du'a* at the end of the *'urs* at Ghamkol Sharif

26. Disciples gathered for the *du'a* on the final day of the *'urs* at
Ghamkol Sharif

conceptual level. Since his death, however, the wedding theme has come
to be enacted in practice very clearly through the placing of *chaddars* on
the grave. The men approach the grave carrying the *chaddar* by its four
corners so that it is raised horizontally above the ground, much as the
chaddar is carried to be placed over the bride's head during the *mehndi*
ritual (P. Werbner 1990a, ch. 9). As they process through the *darbar*,
people throw rupee bank notes intended as *nazrana* or *sadaqat* on to the
horizontally held cloth, just as they do at *mehndis*. The procession arrives
at the grave, singing, before the men jointly cover the raised mound,
much as a bride would be covered. Rose petals and other garlands of
flowers or bank notes are also thrown on the grave, just as they are at
weddings. I watched a top manager of PIA and his companion who had
come especially from Karachi, throw two whole baskets of fragrant rose
petals on to the grave. Maulana Qadri, the *'alim* who gave the sermon at
the final day of the *'urs* in 2000 explained:

'Urs means the spiritual marriage of the *wali*. Every year when the night comes,
when he looks at the Prophet it is called *didar-i yar* [gazing at a friend]. Whenever a person gets married he has *mehndi* on the hands and beads on the neck and
a garland of leaves. The last thing [you do at the wedding] is, you throw on them
rose petals. Whenever the flowers go on the grave of the *wali*, that is his *shadi*
[marriage]. People …[ask if] someone is sleeping, what can he do? What are you
going there [to the grave] for? The explanation of the sleep [of a *pir*] is exactly the

27. *Du'a* following the *julus* on the steps of Birmingham's Central Mosque

same as when a woman gets married. The first night she sleeps, she is lying on the
bed and she is sleeping. She lies on the bed, she closes her eyes but she cannot
sleep. She is sleeping but she is not unconscious. Similarly the *wali* is sleeping
but he is still awake. When the *wali* is lying in the grave and the people go to visit
him and pay respects, he listens to them and replies to them and fulfils their
wishes. It is not the end of his life—the only thing is that he has transferred from
one place to another. This was due to his effort and hard work ['*amal*, referring to
his asceticism and piety], and now is the time to be rewarded. Whatever he sowed
here he will reap there. Whatever his work, his reward is not exactly as in this
world—he is looking at the Prophet's face, at the *rahmat* [mercy, blessing] of
God, and is [basking] in the full light. This is the reason why we say that the grave
of the *wali* is always alive. And then you are rewarded from his grave with *faiz*.'

THE '*URS* AS THE ORGANISATIONAL NEXUS OF SUFI REGIONAL CULTS

In the final session of the '*urs* at Ghamkol Sharif the master of ceremo-
nies always announces to the '*ijtima*, the congregation, the tally of accumulated prayers dedicated to Zindapir which have been performed by all
the different branches of his cult worldwide over the past year. In 2000
this tally was:

50,000 *kalam-e pak.*
7 *crore* and 30 *lakh darud sharif.*

Surat Yassin 12 *lakh* and 18,000.
The first *kalimah* 11 *crore* and 60 *lakh*.
The *pir-bhai* of Chakwal, for the sake of Pir 'Alam, performed a special *Umra*.
Kalimah taiba 150 *crore* and 7,000 (1.5 billion and seven thousand!).

The MC concluded by saying: 'We hand over all these to Qibla Badshah Sahib' [Zindapir's son and successor].

These fantastic numbers, adding up to millions and even billions of prayers dedicated to the saint, are performed daily, weekly or monthly in many different localities of his regional cult, and are endlessly repeated. The *khalifa* from Lahore, from example, was very proud of the number of prayers his branch had accumulated that year. He used one of the *murids*, an accountant, to add up the prayers, he told me. We may say that in a sense the prayers form a unity in their very multiplicity, just as the regional cult which Zindapir founded is based on moments of separateness and moments of togetherness.

Every organisation needs events that bring together its key administrative staff. The *'urs*, held annually, doubles up as such a moment, in which representatives of all the main branches and many minor ones come together, while it is also the pretext for mobilising voluntary labour needed for new building works at the central lodge. Virtually everything one sees at the lodge was built in the weeks leading up to one or another *'urs*. Clearly, the *'urs* presents difficult logistical challenges because of the vast numbers sleeping and eating at such a remote place for three days and nights. On most of my visits I was proudly shown the new toilets being built either for the women or for the men. Such mundane concerns are very important in making the *'urs* a success.

In chapter 5 I argued that voluntary giving is a key to understanding the lodge as a good faith economy. Both the voluntary labour and the *langar* embody this economy and are dialectically related. This is because the *langar* creates very real logistical challenges. Unlike many other shrines in South Asia, the *langar* at Ghamkol Sharif is entirely controlled by the saint or his family. Both the cooking and the distribution of the food are centrally organised whereas at other shrines like Bari Imam or Data Ganj Baksh the *langar*, as we have seen, is mediated by commercial cooking. Crucially at Ghamkol Sharif, the source of the *langar* is literally the *pir* himself. The question of whether or not he has used voluntary labour and contributions in cash or kind to sustain the *langar* is secondary. He personally controls the giving of the *langar* and it is thus he who directly nurtures the multitudes.

Clearly the logistics of such an operation are much more complex than those at shrines where the *langar* depends on a commercial transaction. Like the need to provide lodgings for all pilgrims to the *'urs*, feeding vast numbers requires complex planning, from the utensils which have to be cleaned, the wood that has to be gathered, the animals that have to be slaughtered, to the food that has to be cooked, all in large quantities. The voluntary labour mobilised for all these activities underlines the good faith economy and creates the connections, forged in action, between a saint and his close followers. The ethics of feeding and providing shelter, as well as the voluntary labour devoted to preparing the decorations and sound system for the cultural performance, consolidate the moral relations between saint and disciple, and between disciples among themselves. They are crucibles on the path to God which create and foster ties between men or women. The voluntary labour underpins the distributive and redistributive economies that maintain the lodge as an ongoing concern. It ensures that a remote place, away from major centres of population, can stage a large-scale, three-day event such as the *'urs*. The same system is replicated on a minor scale, as we have seen, in most of the major branches of the regional cult and its global extensions.

AMBIVALENCES OF AUTHORITY

The *'urs* is based on many different sorts of interdependencies between saint and follower. Zindapir's *khulafa* devote their spare time and work on holidays to help with the building of the lodge and the preparations for the *'urs*. They do so selflessly, for the sake of their *pir*. This obscures the dependence of the *pir* and his family upon them. There are *murids* who serve at the lodge as volunteers, and some who work the fields of the saint near Shekhupura. The *pir* from his side gives his followers the privilege and opportunity to participate in the Good Faith economy and draw religious merit and Sufi boons from it.

Unlike other Sufi followers, Barelvi *'ulama* occupy a far more ambivalent position within this good faith economy, and particularly so in the case of living saints like Zindapir. Despite their disclaimers, the *'ulama*'s religious expertise, their learning and the authority of the scriptures they command, are inevitably pitched against the charismatic authority of the *pir*. Whereas they may be consulted on matters of law and asked to officiate at weddings and funerals, the *pir* is deeply loved by his followers who come to him for advice and support, and for succour in times of need.

While the *maulvi* preaches, the *pir* blesses. Perhaps for this reason the *'ulama* may well prefer saints who are safely interred in their graves.

There is also a difference in tone and ideology between saint and *maulvi*. Whereas Barelvi *'ulama* are strident and militant, advocating Islamic radicalism and revolution, saints are soft spoken and peace promoting. I have argued at length elsewhere (P. Werbner 1994, 1996a, 2001) that this stridency of the Barelvi *'ulama* stems from the intercalary position they occupy in the Sufi cult system, placed in the middle between saints and followers. This is particularly true of the more educated *'ulama* who hold important positions in major mosques or educational institutions and political organisations. The *'ulama* compensate for the weakness of their authority through their strident tones. Their militancy is also for this reason, however, utopian and millenarian rather than practical. At the *'urs* it is almost impossible even for a native Urdu speaker to understand parts of the *'ulama*'s speeches, once they take off in flight. The thunder and passion of their sermons contrast sharply with the wavering voice of Zindapir, telling the same tale year after year, which is nonetheless listened to in hushed silence by the congregation.

Nevertheless, as we have seen, the *'ulama* do support strongly the continued veneration of saints in South Asia. They endow the ritual practices and Sufi beliefs associated with saints and shrines with wider political and public legitimacy. Unlike other parts of the Islamic world, the existence of Barelvi *'ulama* in South Asia has meant that the belief in saints and shrines and in Islamic mystical ideas more generally has continued to flourish. Followers have not been compelled to choose between saint and *'ulama*, shrine and mosque; the two exist in symbiotic relation within the same movement. This has been extremely important for the continued vitality of Islam as a mystical movement on the subcontinent.

It seems also, although I have no firm evidence for this, that the role of the *maulvi* is strengthened once the originary saint, the living ascetic exemplar, the founder and builder of a new cult, passes away. His descendants, unless they become saints in their own right, are likely to be far more deferential and dependent on the services of the *'ulama*. During his life, there was no resident *maulvi* at the mosque of Zindapir's lodge. Brought in to recite the Qur'an during the saint's illness, a *maulvi* and a whole staff around him have since become permanent fixtures at the lodge. Their role is subservient but they nevertheless represent a movement away from pure mysticism to a more conventional, mosque-based Islam.

The *'urs* festival is the organisational, religious and cultural nexus of Sufi cults. It is the dynamic core of cults of living Sufi saints as they expand the ambit of their organisations. This is because the *'urs* is not just a festival but a ritual. To grasp it as a structured ritual, however, we need first to disclose the symbolic complex of ideas about blessing held by Sufi followers in South Asia. In this symbolic complex the *du'a* is the most spiritually powerful ritual act. It is the final transformative moment which follows a series of other ritual acts. Together these make up the ritual process through which space and person are sacralised during the *'urs*. Reciprocally, the *'urs* is the moment in which the charisma of a living or dead saint, embodied in his lodge or grave, is actualised before the whole congregation.

12

ZIYARAT

WORDS AND DEEDS—THE DEATH AND REBIRTH OF A LIVING SAINT

SOURCES OF CHARISMA

The Farangi Mahall of Lucknow, Francis Robinson tells us, recognised the supremacy of inspirational as against scholarly knowledge (Robinson 1984, 1987). This accords with a belief in Islam that in exceptional cases, illiteracy may signal powerful knowledge. The Prophet of Islam is believed to have been illiterate. The Farangi Mahall were followers of an illiterate saint. Robinson reports that all the members of this learned family,

> ...regarded their association with 'Abd al-Razzaq as crucial to their spiritual well-being, while the *sajjadas* of his shrine at Bansa, some thirty miles from Lucknow, were careful to pay the scholars of Farangi Mahall especial respect (Robinson 1987: 7; also 1984).

This adoration of an illiterate saint has to be set against the family's remarkable scholarly achievements. Its members were authors of literally hundreds of books on Islamic jurisprudence, logic and philosophy, proprietors of a famous madrassa and pioneers of a new Islamic educational curriculum. Yet they continued to officiate at the annual *'urs* celebrations at the 'Abd al-Razak's tomb, as well as delivering sermons at the *'urs* of many other leading saints (Robinson 1987: 6, 15).

Thoughts about words and deeds, literacy versus tangible aesthetic structures, the 'hardware of sanctity' as Landell Mills (1998) calls these, emerged as a theoretical puzzle for me after the death of Zindapir. Until his death, the annual *'urs* which was held at the lodge every October, commemorated the death of Baba Qasim, the saint of Mohra Sharif in the Muree hills who died in 1942 or 1943, and who had been his spiritual guide in the *silsila* of Naqshbandi Sufi saints. Zindapir died, an old man close to ninety, in March 1999, and the first *'urs* to commemorate his own death took place at the lodge in March the following year.

259

During his life, as we saw in chapter 4, Zindapir was a storyteller, and endless stories were told about him. Never leaving his room except to visit the lodge mosque, and once a year on pilgrimage to Mecca, Zindapir nevertheless was the source of a constant stream of morality tales. This feature of his persona, his creative role as mythologiser and fabulator of his own life, became a puzzle after his death. There were no texts written by the *shaikh* to stand in place of the living man and remind the pilgrim of who he was, what kind of a man. His death seemed to leave a kind of silence, a void, an absence of words.

It was a silence accompanied by a frenzy of building activities. The man Zindapir, the yarn spinner, the heroic trickster who always got the better of politicians and *'ulama*, seemed lost in this frenzy. Whenever and whoever I asked about him and his death, I got the same response: he is alive; he is a hundred times more powerful now in the grave than during his lifetime. One *khalifa* of the saint told me: his power is multiplied like the difference between the area covered by his feet when he was alive and standing upright, and the area covered by his prostrate body now that he is in the grave. I was told as proof that he sometimes leaves the grave and goes to Medina, leaving his grave empty as proven by the fact that he was sighted elsewhere.

Zindapir left no written documents behind him. An old *khalifa* living at the lodge, one of the dispensers of *ta'wiz* sitting outside the room where the *pir* met the people, used to admonish me regularly in broken English whenever we met: 'No books, no books,' he would say. By this he was underlining the fact that the power of a saint does not derive from his ability to write books, or study complex mystical treaties. *'Amal*, doing, active worship, is a key Sufi concept and the only way to achieve gnosis and mystical enrapture is through *'amal*.

Zindapir was not illiterate. He was said to spend hours every day reading the Qur'an, but nevertheless, his creative imagination was that of the oral storyteller, not the poet or writer. He thus left no textual trace or image.

It was well known that he did not allow his picture to be taken or displayed during his lifetime. After his death, traveling around the Punjab to meet some of his *khulafa*, I discovered that portraits of the *pir* both as an old and young man existed, and had been given by the *shaikh* as privileged gifts to select disciples in secret. These pictures were still not being displayed publicly after his death even though his family also owned such a portrait, as did one of the *khulafa* at Manchester. As yet these reminders

of who the *pir* was, or what he looked like, were secretly held, and sur-
reptitiously shown to honoured guests like myself, the anthropologist.

After his death, then, of Zindapir the man there was only a private
memory or a body in the grave. Frembgen (1998a) has described evocatively how the death of a *majzub* affected his immediate disciples very
deeply. Even though they believed that the saint was still alive in the
grave, they nevertheless missed the intimacy they had shared with him
while alive, the immediate physical and emotional contact which came
from washing, feeding and caring for him, or from sitting around him as
they chatted and smoked. In the case of Zindapir, few were privileged
with such intimacy since for most people he was a distant, awesome figure. Yet this did not explain why his personal distinctiveness, his charisma as a living man with his own personality, seemed to be lost after his
death. Most people I met did not express any sense of loss, of missing the
man Zindapir. There were notable exceptions which I will come to below,
but most people simply stressed the fact that the *pir* was alive, and that
his powers had increased and multiplied after his death.

Picture posters of saints in Pakistan establish face-to-face, intimate
contact between disciple and *shaikh* (Frembgen 1998b: 188–9) and a
broader sense of solidarity among followers (ibid.: 190). In their study of
the 'manufacturing' of charisma of a Jewish saint in modern Israel. Ben
Ari and Bilu (1992: 680) highlight the use of modern mediatized technology in this process of sanctification. A plethora of printed texts, communal projects and a media blitz close to the annual festival commemorated
the saint. The authors underline the 'quite extraordinary' speed with which
the production of charisma was achieved as a result (ibid.: 673). Citing
Lowenthal (1975: 31) they note that by contrast,

Charismatization or 'mythologization' of such magnitude is usually a lengthy historical process that prefers a 'remote and malleable past to a recent one, perhaps
too painful or too well known' (Ben Ari and Bilu 1992: 673).

At the other extreme Werth (1998) has recently shown that it is possible
for a saint's shrine to be venerated without an extensive mythological corpus, and with even the name of the shrine occupier forgotten. In the case
of Baba Sali, the Israeli Moroccan saint, the stories propagated about the
saint by his son and other disciples were the central mythic corpus proving his extraordinary personality and powers. Although a scholar and
scion of a scholarly dynasty, it was not apparently the saint's written legacy, then, but his asceticism and miracles during his lifetime, which were
regarded as key to his charisma (Ben Ari and Bilu 1992: 675).

Leaving aside the technologically driven speed of sanctification none of this seems either extraordinary or exceptional to contemporary scholars of Sufi Islam. Stories about saints and their asceticism or miracles abound in South Asia. So too do media and other forms of advertising or press and TV coverage of annual *'urses*. The selling of audio and video tapes of speeches at the *'urs* and of other manufactured consumer goods (pictures, pamphlets, hagiographies, and so forth), are a familiar sight. Dispensing amulets in the name of the deceased saint and other forms of curing continues at his lodge after his death.

Arriving in Pakistan following Zindapir's death, I fully expected to see the production of such artefacts. What I did not expect was my own personal sense that Zindapir's death had rendered him invisible not only in the flesh but in spirit as well. In his life I had known him to be both entertaining and immensely authoritative, at times capable of fearful anger, at times mischievous, a trickster who liked to play with the emotions of his overly devout disciples or with the false pretensions of politicians and *maulvis*, often for his own personal amusement but also for the edification of his followers. All these qualities together, which had created his charismatic personality, his 'magnetism' (*magnatis* or *mignatis* in Persian) as one *khalifa* called it, seemed lost. The way in which the pir's memorialising was proceeding had somehow, it seemed to me, erased Zindapir the person from memory.

But perhaps it was I, the anthropologist, who, in my search for meaningful texts had exaggerated the importance of the legends the *pir* told me repeatedly about himself? I had taken for granted that these would be his chief legacy, an oral history perpetuated after his death with increased force by his family and disciples. Other anthropological and historical accounts lent support to such an expectation.

In analysing the founder saint of a new Shadhiliya order in Egypt, Gilsenan draws heavily on the saint's biography written by a disciple, as well as on memories of those who had known Salama personally or stories about the saint's *karamat* which happened after his death through dreams and visitations (Gilsenan 1973: 13 *passim*). But can we say that in a sense, by gathering these tales the anthropologist here participates in the systematic mythologising of a saint? This question was doubly pertinent in the case of Zindapir if it turned out that his stories about himself remained unremembered and unrecorded by followers.

Since he had left no pictures or written texts and had prevented his disciples from writing down his sayings during his lifetime, what remained of Zindapir at the moment of death were above all tangible landmarks:

the lodge itself, nestled in the little valley, the lovely mosque with its intricate colourful decorations, the hostels for pilgrims and guests, the orchard and gardens, the landmarks of his early arrival such as the cave on the hill where he was said to have enclosed himself for three days and nights, and—perhaps most importantly—the *langar*. I realised that to my Western way of thinking words, creatively written or spoken words, are the ultimate expression of human existence and, indeed, great Sufis are known to Western scholars above all by their written texts. Annemarie Schimmel reports of Khwaja Mir Dard, the first Sufi Urdu poet and a Naqshbandi like Zindapir, that

...he loved writing: the capacity of logical and clear speech was, for him, the divine trust offered to heaven and earth, but accepted only by man (*surah* 33: 72)... Dard thought that 'a gnostic without a book is like a man without children...' (IK 592). His books were, indeed, his beloved children... (Schimmel 1975: 381).

Zindapir was not a writer. He was clearly a doer; an ascetic, a world renouncer, a man who blessed the crowds and fed the multitudes. In the interregnum following his death, there seemed little point, I supposed, in telling me the familiar miracle stories and legends about him. I had, as most people knew, heard these before. Like them, I was not a newcomer to the lodge or the cult. This was a moment above all of tangible doing, of remembering through reconstruction. The expectation from me, the anthropologist, was that I should recognise the continued spiritual power of the saint as a man alive from the grave and observe the process of his sanctification in visible objects.

But for some, Zindapir was more than just a doer and thus I perceived an emergent division at the moment of his death between different sorts of remembrancers, between those who stressed his embodied spirituality through their actions and those who stressed in words his uniqueness as a person, someone who had left an emotional gap in their lives. The latter were willing to admit that they actually missed the *shaikh* for what he was, irrespective of what he had become at the moment of death. These 'lovers' were, however, a tiny select minority by comparison to less articulate remembrancers.

COMMEMORATION

I had last visited the *darbar* in 1991, nine years earlier. During this period the lodge had been extended, with new hostels, new winter sheds for the cattle, further removed from residential areas, new cultivated fields (the *pir* had in the meanwhile been granted title to the valley's lands), a second tube well and a water tower. The mosque's interior had been decorated with delicate, intricate mosaic patterns in coloured mirrors. A *murid* had spent eight months on this decoration, donating his labour free of charge. There were magnificent new chandeliers. I noted with regret that the wrought iron gates adorned with flowers which I had watched being painted with loving care, had been removed. The steep path where I had cut my foot (as someone reminded me) climbing up to the cave in which, according to the sacred mythology, the saint had secluded himself in prayer to God when he first arrived, had been cleared and concrete steps built for most of the way up. The cave itself had been whitewashed and swept clean and was open to pilgrims. The *langar* had a new enclosure and had been shifted. It now even had a chimney although smoke still seemed to billow as usual straight into the faces of the cooks (the chief cook had changed). Dozens of external toilets for the men and women attending the *'urs* had been constructed, properly laid with pipes, concrete bases and sumps. In the hostel where I was staying an upright toilet had been installed and in the adjacent newly built hostel to which I later moved there was a proper shower as well, an unheard of luxury. These new hostels lacked the grace and garden landscaping of earlier structures but they were functional and clearly fulfilled a need.

But the most radical transformation in the lodge was the shrine being built over the *pir's* grave. Planned by a disciple who is an architect in Islamabad, it is a square structure with eight gothic arches, two on each side of the rectangle, flanking four sets of wide steps leading up, through an inner arched passageway forming a second, internal, rectangle, to the grave of the *pir.* This whole structure has been located in the courtyard outside the *pir's* room, where, during his lifetime, groups of supplicants and disciples would sit waiting to see him. That room itself has been preserved but can now only be reached by an inner secret passage leading from the present saint's room where the *pir's* son, Badshah Sahib, receives supplicants. This second room is the one to which Zindapir moved when he was very ill, during the last eight months of his life. In its courtyard he could sit and sun himself, I was told, when he was very weak.

To create the shrine structure, a whole set of guest rooms had to be pulled down, enlarging the courtyard substantially. The courtyard had been elevated five feet so that the old entrance, a walled marble structure which I had watched being built on a previous visit, was now dwarfed by the shrine. The *pir's* grave is at the centre of the shrine and because of its elevation, the *pir* is now buried very deep in ground, about eleven feet. His burial place, I was told, was set in concrete.

When it is finished, my guide explained, the shrine is planned to have twenty small domes and a central grand dome which will tower above the three cupolas of the mosque. It will be clad in marble on the outside and its interior decorated with the same type of mirror mosaic which now adorns the mosque walls.

The grave's head faces west, towards Mecca. It is decorated with flowers and with intricately embroidered *chaddars*. At its foot are two containers of salt. People prostrate themselves at the foot of the grave or its sides, kissing its edge and tasting a pinch of the salt. The area around the grave is carpeted. Two *hafiz* recite the Qur'an day and night through a microphone. They arrived when the *pir* was very ill and now reside permanently in the *darbar*, disrupting the deep silence of the valley with their continuous praying.

The men working at the shrine are all volunteer *murids* and after a while, they begin to sing the melodious *zikr* which is the hallmark of the order, its sweet notes competing with the din of prayers broadcast over the loudspeaker. The *'urs* is imminent and the workers have begun to clad the building scaffolding and the poles holding up the tent above the shrine structure with decorated silver tinsel.

Clearly, without words, the sacred mythology of Zindapir is being extended through these building works. Every place the *pir* occupied is treated as sacred space, historically enshrined: the cave, his room, the courtyard. The centre of all this activity remains the *'urs* and the logistics of its gigantic *langar*. But the respect accorded to the saint is expressed not in words, or not simply in words, but in the careful and detailed planning of his commemoration in mortar and stone. The stone and the grave speak silently, as it were. Zindapir's grandson who now manages the organisation of the lodge, the building work and preparations for the *'urs*, told me that they were trying as best they could to follow the principles laid down by the *pir*, his grandfather.

There are new myths as well, and some willing to admit their prior closeness to the departed *shaikh*. The *pir's* son, the present *sajjada nishin*, told me, in answer to my question, that he misses his father 'until the Day of Judgement'. Even if the mountains surrounding the lodge were made of gold, he said, this would not compensate for the loss of his father. He cannot be replaced even though they, the family, are trying their best.

His father sacrificed his life for God, Badshah Sahib said. When the *shaikh* went to Mecca for the first time in 1952, he vowed to God that he would sacrifice his only son to Allah. Badshah Sahib had no mother (his mother, Zindapir's wife, had died when he was very young). Later my companions commented on the enormity of this act: to sacrifice (the *pir* used the term in English) a child of three. No one could be like Zindapir!

Badshah Sahib, the *pir's* only son, had told me on a previous visit that he had led a miserable, unhappy life as a child, ignored by his father, living in the wilderness of the lodge as it then was, surrounded entirely by male company, or with uncaring relatives in his natal village nearby. Later he found solace in his marriage and children and was, above all, a family man. Now his sense of neglect, of childhood loss, had been transmuted into a story of glorious sacrifice in which he was the centre, the ultimate symbol. He was the son of Abraham sacrificed to God in the valley of Mina. A modest, retiring man who had avoided the crowds throughout his father's life, Badshah Sahib had been forced into the limelight by his father's death. The loss of his father had thus become for him a felt daily reality.

When I first arrived, I felt a sense of great loss by the saint's graveside, of sadness at his death since he was such a colourful, vivid presence in the lodge. But the adoration of the grave, the sense of an immanent powerful presence that it clearly evoked for followers, remained emotionally alien to me, beyond my sentimental comprehension.

Many disciples spent hours just sitting by the graveside. Their silent veneration drove home the fact that in many respects, Zindapir was more accessible now for most people than he ever was during his life. Now they could develop that sense of closeness and intimacy with him which most of them never had while he was alive. I realised in retrospect that for most followers he was a distant, fearful figure, unsmiling and stern, sometimes capricious. He was physically beyond reach, and meetings with him always took place in the company of others and lasted for five or ten minutes at most. Now any man could spend hours if they liked alone by his grave, communing with him without interruption or interference. The *shaikh* was thus, for the vast majority, paradoxically closer in death than in life.

This was especially so in the quiet period before the crowds began arriving for the *'urs*. Landell Mills (1998) has commented on the stillness

28/29. *Above*, Zindapir's grave inside the shrine, and *below*, veneration
of the saint

and immobility of the *pir* of Atroshi while still alive, so that the transition to death, he predicted, would not be as radical as it might otherwise be for a more volatile person. Although more accessible to followers than Atroshi, Zindapir too remained during his lifetime remote, enigmatic and immobile for most.

Nevertheless, for any saint the transition from life to death is a testing moment. So too, the period leading up to the *'urs* was a period of great tension for the *pir's* family and for his closest *khulafa*, those helping with the preparations for the festival. The funeral had been an enormous affair, I was told; people had come from all over Pakistan by private and public transport, by 'plane and train. There had been eulogies and weeping.

But funerals are like that. This was the first *'urs* for Zindapir, the first to take place in March instead of October. It followed *'Id*, a public holiday; many *murids* of the order are soldiers who were kept in barracks this year for an Armed Forces Day parade; the festival did not fall on a weekend. Would people come? A small *'urs* would reflect on the stature of Zindapir.

The moment of death is the moment in which the reality of sainthood is publicly proven. No amount of fancy building work can substitute for the crowds at an *'urs*. A lakh rupees' worth of personal invitations had been sent out to tens of thousands of *murids*. Posters had been plastered on walls in towns and villages. Advertisements had appeared in the major dailies. But there was still a sense of nervousness. The family had come from England to express solidarity and lend their support. Sufi Sahib, the English *pir* from Birmingham, was expected with an English delegation.

As the convoys of buses and trucks began to arrive, at first slowly, then in greater numbers, there was a sense of enormous relief. Nothing had changed. The great *langar* pots had been taken out and cleaned. The wood was piled high, the meat was bubbling in the pots, the *chapatis* were baking on outdoor metal stoves. Colourful tents were being pitched throughout the valley. The loudspeakers blared off-key praise songs and sermons, the sound system crackling unbearably as usual. The market traders had set up their stalls as they always do. The shrine was now decorated with a green dome over the grave, and with masses of tinsel and moving lights, much like a wedding tent. It had been carpeted for the *'urs* with plastic Persian carpets (the most recent Pakistani vogue) to withstand the tread of thousands of feet.

The convoys from different places carried *chaddars* and garlands of rupees, moving in procession on the dusty lane at the edge of the lodge's walled enclosures, past the mosque towards the shrine, outstretched hands holding the *chaddar* horizontally while the men marched, singing the *zikr*. Some bystanders threw rupee notes into the *chaddar*. Carrying the *chaddar* is of course a new custom at the *darbar* but a common mode of veneration at saints' tombs throughout Pakistan, which was here adopted naturally, it seems, without central planning. The aroma of rose petals filled the air around the shrine. Petals and *chaddars* kept changing, now green and gold brocade, now black and gold, marigolds, red roses, white petals. The shrine was in constant transformation as new groups arrived.

30. Carrying a *chaddar* to Zindapir's shrine

The final *du'a* ceremony was as awesome as ever. The *maulvis* recited their learned sermons; the *na't* singers sang their praise songs for the Prophet; Sufi Sahib from England, the most senior *khalifa* present, read the *shajara* of the order; Badshah Sahib said the *du'a* in a loud clear voice, much to the relief of his family and the organisers; a light propeller piper plane circled around (a recent innovation) casting down clouds of tinsel paper over the large, silent congregation outside the mosque. There were no incidents, no conflicts, everyone had been fed. The *'urs* was a little smaller than usual but there were good reasons for this. Next year it will be held on the weekend, after a twelve-month gap, and everyone now knew that the date had been shifted from October to March. It had been a very bright, sunny warm day. The organisers relaxed, drinking cups of tea, no longer guarding entrances. There was an atmosphere of celebration. It had all been a great success.

ORGANISATIONAL CONTINUITIES AND DISCONTINUITIES

It may be argued that Zindapir, always a capable organiser, ensured during his lifetime that his death would cause very few ripples; that everything would continue as usual. Perhaps the silence I seemed to find about him, along with the frenzy of building, were simply a sign of this institutionalised continuity, where the only major innovation, one which he himself could not initiate, was the shrine itself.

Clearly, for Zindapir's family there is much at stake in assuring that his shrine (*qabr, mazar,* or *ziyarat*) becomes a place of pilgrimage and that its ascendency is secured. In addition to the status that his position has always conferred on the family, there are financial, organisational and sentimental investments and obligations which cannot easily be ignored or shed off. For years the lodge generated a substantial income, mainly through supplicants' donations, and the family has acquired houses in Islamabad and Abbotabad, as well as cars and other luxury items, all of which need to be maintained. There is an army of retinues, disciples donating their labour voluntarily, but among them some who have been virtually adopted by the *darbar,* abandoned by their families or lacking any other sources of support. All have to be fed and maintained. Although the family does own substantial land at Shekhupura as well as a herd of cattle, buffalo and goats along with land in the valley itself, there is the *langar* to maintain on a daily basis and during the *'urs,* which is attended by some 30,000 people on the last day. Zindapir always took full responsibility for supplying the *langar* and this responsibility has been inherited by his descendants. None of them is presently educated sufficiently to earn independent incomes beyond the lodge, and their lives are enmeshed deeply in its day-to-day affairs.

There is also a sentimental investment in fulfilling Zindapir's mission and propagating his vision of Islam. An attempt is being made, as the grandson put it, to follow his principles. His photograph is not displayed, for example. Although there is a donation box near the shrine, no money is demanded from supplicants. The *langar* continues to be very generous, to include meat and *chapati* as well as rice. A great deal of money and thought have been invested in the building of the shrine, much of it from donations, but nevertheless devoted to the literal beautification of the saint rather than more mundane purposes. The grandson attempts to keep track of all the *khulafa* initiated by Zindapir, some of whom he says no one knew about, and new books of *murids*, their names and addresses, are being copied and updated meticulously. The *'ulama* and *na't* singers invited to the final *du'a* need to be of very high status. In all these ways the memory of the saint is honoured by his family.

There have been changes as well, however. Some of Zindapir's most intimate companions have been marginalised or banished from the lodge. Among them is a woman of the local Pir Khel Sayyid lineage in the *pir's* natal village of Jangal Khel, who devoted her life to serving the saint and had a very special relationship with him. I was told that she had been pocketing all the donations the women gave the *pir* and had acquired a bank balance of some 60 *lakh* rupees (£ 100,000). Whether or not she had, in fact, taken the money with the *pir's* silent consent, Zindapir's son made sure she left the lodge ignominiously, never to return, immediately after he died. He did not even allow her to collect her belongings, I was told. Another trusted friend of the *shaikh*, manager of a local textile factory, a political meddler and manipulator, was cast out to the social margins after the saint's death and was no longer a nightly visitor at the lodge. He had caused me personally a good deal of trouble with his gossip and scandal, and his literal fall from grace made the research much easier. Finally, another trusted *khalifa* had died at a young age.

A faithful retainer at the lodge who had assisted me during an earlier visit in 1991, was gleeful at this triumvirate's downfall. All those people who had been 'jealous' of him, he said, and had caused me so much trouble (some, clearly without my knowledge) were gone now and the lodge was a much more peaceful place.

For Zindapir's family the challenge was not simply one of ensuring the continuity of the regional cult that the saint had built up, but of the lodge's ascendancy as the cult's sacred centre. In the absence of a truly charismatic figure in the family, there was always the danger that one of Zindapir's *khulafa* would inherit the saint's mantle, as Zindapir himself had done after Baba Qasim's death at Muree in 1942. After all, the vast majority of his followers were Punjabis, and for many the *'urs* at Ghamkol Sharif involved an arduous journey of several hundred miles. Most of the *khulafa*, by contrast, were based in the Punjab itself.

The young grandson, Chotta Pir, barely thirty, who had assumed all the responsibilities of running the lodge, told me as we parted that Zindapir had got his *faiz* from Mohra Sharif (the place of Baba Qasim) and had passed it on to Sufi Sahib, the *pir* in Birmingham. But only Zindapir was the founder of a new place and order, on his own, independently, without any help. Sufi Sahib had given the name Ghamkol Sharif to the magnificent mosque he had built in Birmingham (there was a good deal of pressure on him from the lodge in Pakistan to do so, apparently, which he resisted for some time before succumbing). Sufi Sahib had received a good deal of help from the *darbar* whereas Zindapir invented the name of his order, on his own, without any help. Sufi Sahib established his place with the help of Zindapir's *murids*. Hence there was no one like Zindapir, the grandson declared. All Zindapir's *khulafa* work for the sake of the *darbar's* name. They are all the same, they work for the *darbar*, not independently as Zindapir did. Sufi Sahib attracts people because of Zindapir's name.

I was told by my companion, a close friend of the family, that last year Badshah Sahib, Zindapir's son, had honoured Sufi Sahib by asking him to say the final *du'a*. This year, under pressure from his family, Badshah Sahib asked Sufi Sahib to read the sacred genealogy of the order whereas he himself pronounced the *du'a*. There was to be no ambiguity as to the sacred centrality of the lodge and its resident family when it came to reaching out to Allah in prayer on behalf of the congregation.

The institutionalisation of charisma, as Weber called it, which follows the death of a saint has been a major preoccupation of scholars of Sufism (Gilsenan 1973). In large measure Zindapir had attempted to institutionalise his own charisma during his lifetime. But as a strictly Naqshbandi saint he had also prevented any open signs of adulation and overt expressions of adoration toward him. As Sufi Karim, my companion from Manchester, a man who had spent his life seeking the higher mystical realms on the Sufi path, remarked somewhat despairingly, Zindapir saw his main project as feeding the people. He was not a mystic who dwelt explicitly on the realms of esoteric knowledge or on his love for his *murshid* (Baba Qasim was rarely mentioned). He met and fed the people, he fasted and prayed, he told stories, he mythologised his arrival at the lodge, but he was not a poet or a speculative philosopher. Yet the family, far more inarticulate than the *pir* himself, needed a storyteller, a poet, a chronicler, if Zindapir was to be lifted above the run-of-the-mill multitude of saints' shrines that dot the Pakistani and South Asian landscape. The silence of the grave had to be filled; the spiritual power of the dead saint ultimately needed explication in words.

IN SEARCH OF THE AESTHETIC

Of course, the distinctiveness of the lodge derived partly from its loveliness and the mythic tale its sacred landscape embodied. The visual aesthetics of the various architectural projects at the lodge had always been a major preoccupation of Zindapir and his followers. In the past the lodge was also marked by its profound silence, interrupted only by human voices singing the special *zikr* of the order melodiously and evocatively. This pastoral peace was now broken by recitations of the Qur'an which were blared constantly, day and night, over the microphone, a sound which one member of the family said was pleasant to her ears. Naqshbandis have little appreciation of the subtle aesthetics of musical production since the order forbids the use of instrumental music. The human voice on its own is an unpredictable instrument, easily losing its way with rather painful consequences for the sensitive listener.

But along with architectural grace, it is poetry which has been the hallmark of Sufism and Ghamkol Sharif did have its poet, a *khalifa* who had written over 250 *rubayats* and *qasidas*, praise songs in honour of Zindapir, but had been forbidden by the *shaikh* to publish them. Many of the poems he had written had never even been seen by the *shaikh*. Now the saint's family were willing to bear the costs of publishing his collected volume of poems in Urdu and Punjabi.

For the past two years Rab Nawaz, the poet, had also been writing a book about the saint, his life story and miracles (*karamat*), his sayings and inner visions (*kashf*), his divine revelations (*ilham*), and his power to influence others at a distance (*tasarruf*). A very long chapter of the book, over hundred pages, was devoted to Sufism, he told me. The *khalifa* had sat with Zindapir during his last years, meticulously noting down the details of the saint's early life. His book, which included a treatise on *adab*, the proper conduct towards a *pir*, was already 400 pages long. He had ceased writing only at the request of the family, who were keen to get the book in print. During the two years he spent writing his book, seated in a little alcove opposite his mosque, Rab Nawaz said he felt as though he was out of this world.

I visited Rab Nawaz at his own lodge, nestling among fields in the Punjab plains, 15 miles west of Sohawa. It is fertile countryside, green with ripening wheat and barley, and his mosque is an architectural gem, decorated with coloured tiles down to the last aesthetic detail. So too are the hostels for visitors to his *'urs* with their ornate balconies and plaster friezes. Rab Nawaz helped to design and build the mosque at Ghamkol Sharif and his own mosque is modeled upon it, but scaled down out of respect for Zindapir and his family. He was one of Zindapir's closest friends and intimates, a *khalifa* who every year selflessly headed the *intizami* committee for the *'urs*. A thin-faced smiling bearded man in his late sixties, he had been the saint's devoted follower for forty years.

Rab Nawaz did not hesitate to express his deep sorrow at the death of his saint. Every morning, he told me, he stood at the gateway to the mosque, remembered Zindapir and wept. Then he thought about the *pir's* family, his son and grandsons, and prayed for their health; finally, he felt his love (*mahabbat*) and trust (*tawakkul*) for Zindapir.

Zindapir is the transcendental inspiration for Rab Nawaz's poetic imagination. He denied that he ever read other Sufi poets, a doubtful claim given the imagery deployed in his poetry. Asked about the process of writing he explained that before he writes a poem he gets a deep sensation of burning running from his mouth down to his abdomen. This feeling may go on for four days, at the end of which time a screen appears in front of his eyes, a screen on which his poem is written. He then sits down with pen and paper and copies the poem from the screen without looking at the page. He makes no changes to the poem. He just copies it neatly later into his book.

A close friend and companion, who sings many of the *qasidas*, told me that that when he sings, Rab Nawaz weeps. That is why he is very close to him. Rab Nawaz's poems, of which select verses are included below, express his longing for his saint.[1]

The heart is at peace

> The heart at peace [*itminan*]
> Is the remembrance [*azkare*] of Zindapir.
>
> O my fate [*qismat*] take me
> To the *darbar* [*darbari*] of Zindapir,
> Appearance [*nazar karne*] is remembrance [*samar*],
> Your lordship [*sarkari*] Zindapir.

---

[1] As in chapter 8, rhymed words and play of words are underlined. Bracketed words indicate the original term used in Urdu.

My invitation to death will wait
Until I see you,
I live with unfulfilled desire [*hasr te*]
The vision [*didare*] of Zindapir.

O garden [*firdaus* = paradise] why are you
So proud of your flowers?
There are so many flowers
In the garden [*gulzare*] of Zindapir.

Sometimes the intoxicated is without sense [*behosh mastana*]
Sometimes possessed [*wajde khaish*]
There were new qualities [*kafiyat*]
In the appearance [*sarshade*] of Zindapir.

Conversing with the dead [*wopae*],
The dead, the dead [*murda murda*] have arisen,
The sign of the Messiah [*ta masihana*]
In the talk [*guftari*] of Zindapir.

The hidden [*batin*] light [*chamak*] shining
In your brilliance [*anwar*],
A glance [*jhalak*] at the light of oneness [*wahdat*]
In the face [*rukhsare*] of Zindapir.

A mere gesture [*garba*]
will halt the End of the Days [*qayamat*],
There was peace and rapture [*wajd*]
In the walk [*raftari*] of Zindapir.

O Nawaz, why should I not remember [*zikr*]
Every living moment?
The heart starts beating on its own
The remembrance [*azkare*] of Zindapir.

A similar longing for the *pir* is evident in other poems as well:

The image in my heart

The image [*tasawwur*] in my heart day and night is of Zindapir,
The remembrance of Zindapir is day and night [*sham*],
The name [*nam*] of Zindapir has become an incantation [*wazifa*].

The king [*badshah*] of religious evangelising [*tonsi hai din*], Mustafa in the wilderness [*dehr me*],
Zindapir is religion, Zindapir is *Islam*.

One gaze [*nazar*] from him made a person perfect [*kamal*],
Blessed and perfect [*mubarak aur mukammal*]
Was the work [<u>*kam*</u>] of Zindapir.

So what if separation has removed him out of sight!
He is imprinted [*naksh* = mapped] on my heart,
Servant [<u>*khaddam*</u>] of Zindapir.

O Nawaz restless [*bekarar*], throat cut [*bismil*] and trembling [*rehgya*]
We hope for a new and pleasant day [*subha gahi*] at
The end [<u>*anjam*</u>] of Zindapir.

Here the poet compares himself to a sacrificial victim, killed by the death of his beloved master. One of the more beautiful elegies his companion sang for us when we visited Rab Nawaz's lodge was the following *rubayat*.

This imprint, from my heart

This imprint [*naksh*], from my heart [*dil*] will never be erased [*mita*],
The place [*darobam*] of Ghamkol can never be forgotten [*bhulahi nahi jate*],
Why are we not called [*bulayi*] to the sacred place [*dar-e aqadas*]?
Why cannot the distance [*fasle* = separation] to the destination [*manzal*] be shortened [*ghataye*]?

There is no other to me [*meri nazron me*] as beautiful [*hussin*],
None other comparable [*jachta*],
Since my eyes have absorbed [*basa*]
The lovely light [*nur jamal*] of my *pir*.

To God Almighty [*haq ta Allah*]
The appeal [*iltejar*] of Nawaz is:
When my life ends [*jan bahaq*], at that moment [*is ghari*],
To see the loveliness of my *pir* [*jamal-e pir ema*].

I cannot myself appreciate the Urdu in this poem but my research assistant, translating it, was quite overcome by its beauty.

Some *qasidas* have catchy tunes and are widely sung during *milad* and impromptu gatherings at the *'urs*. One of Rab Nawaz's daughters is a very fine singer and the women often appeal to her to sing her father's poems. This is one of the favourite *qasidas* which I heard sung both in October 1991 and, more recently, in March 2000. We have already encountered some stanzas from this song in chapter 8. Different versions were sung by Rab Nawaz's daughter and by his friend the *na't* and *qasida* singer, but they are abbreviated and united here in a single poem.

Gali gali

Your grace [*faiz*] is recited [*charche* = also: spread, as scent spreads] in every lane [*gali gali*],
Master [*aka*] of Ghamkol,
Lord [*khwaja*] of Ghamkol,
Your grace is recited in every lane.

We receive something in the name of God [*Khudda keliye*],
We raise [*pelae*] our hands in supplication [*du'a keliye*],
I came to your door [*dar pe*], as a beggar's leftovers [*gadda bankar*],
Your grace is recited in every lane.

By sadness [*gam*] seized [*hatho*], neither world nor religion [*na din*],
Now very near its end [*lab phar ayi*] is my precious life [*jan-e-mazaiyan*],
Apart from you [*jus*] where, to whom [*kahan, kyse*] could I go [*jaker*]?
Your grace is recited in every lane.

Your light [*nur*] with the lamp [*shama*] of my heart [*dil ki*] burns [*jali*],
My damaged life [*bigri*] mend [*banane*] in your lane [*gali*].
You are the *ghaus*, and the saints' pole [qutb *wali*],
You are the *ghaus*, and the revealed pole [qutb *jali*],
Your grace is recited in every lane.

In your robe [*daman* = lit. skirt], my heart is held [*pakra hai*] [i.e. you protect me],
In your love [*ulfat*], my heart is trapped [*jakra hai*],
Give a shout [*sada*] in every lane,
Your grace is recited in every lane.

Being yours, why am I restless [*bechain rahu*]?
In sadness, in pain, why day and night do I remain [*din rain rahu*]?
You are my benefactor [*hami*], secret [*khafi* = silence] and open [*jali* = revealed],
Your grace is recited in every lane.

Needy [*mohta*] of your prayers (*du'a*) is Nawaz,
Apart from you [*jus*] where, to whom could I go [*jise kahun*]?
I fall [*girta*] at your door [*akar dar pare*],
Your grace is recited in every lane.

Your grace [*faiz*] is recited [*charche*] in every lane [*gali gali*],
Master [*aka*] of Ghamkol,
Lord [*khwaja*] of Ghamkol,
Your grace is recited in every lane.

In this poem, as in others, the fame of the saint, recited and spreading like scent or gossip in every lane is repeated, along with his image as feeder of

the poor. The next poem elaborates on this theme of the pir as protector
and feeder.

Murshid of the Highest Places

Murshid of the highest station ['al-i maqam = station on the Sufi path]
Where the poor [ajeza] knock on the door [dastagir],
Guardian [pushte bana] of the destitute [beqasam],
O Khwaja of Ghamkol.

Knower [waqife] of God's secret [sirr-e khudda]
For the lost [e-gumra], a guide [rahnama],
O murshid, master mine [maula ema],
O Lord of Ghamkol.

You raise [pushte panahe] the destitute [beqasam],
O Lord of Ghamkol.

Even the smallest [zera] your kindness [mehre] nurtures [parvari],
Beloved of the great Master [Rab],
Fit you are [zaiba] to be a king [sarwari]
O Lord of Ghamkol,

In the country of mendicants [faqr me = saints] you are king [Raj hai],
Your head bears proudly [fakhr] the crown [taj he],
You who the voiceless's [be navaun] honour protect [kilaj hai],
O Lord of Ghamkol,

Whoever to your lodge [astan] came [pejo a gya],
Unrewarded [namurad] ne'er returned [o na phira],
The sight [nazar] of you is like alchemy [kimiya = transforming to gold],
O Lord of Ghamkol,

From all my troubles [mushkilon] save me [chura-i yo],
My bad times [bigri bat] put right [banayo],
My sins for God's sake [la i'lla] cover up [chopa-i yo],
O Lord of Ghamkol.

As long as Nawaz lives [jan hai],
Your name chanted [wird] on my tongue [zoban rahai],
Until my last breath [dam-e naza] I think of you [dian rahai],
O Lord of Ghamkol.

O Murshid of the highest station
Where the poor knock on the door,
You raise the destitute,
O Lord of Ghamkol.

Contact with the *pir* is like alchemy, transforming dross to gold, a familiar trope in Sufi poetry. Above all, the longing for Ghamkol is a constant
theme of the poet:

See heart it appears, the country of Ghamkol

See heart [*dekhe-e-dil*], it appears [*nazar aya*], the country of Ghamkol [*diyar-e-Ghamkoli*],
Every little thing [*zare zare* = atoms] is dancing [*machalti*] in the spring of
Ghamkol [*bahar-e Ghamkoli*],
Instead [*sava*] a heart aching [*ghamzada*] and tearful eyes [*purnam*],
Nothing else besides Ghamkol's river [*bheren*] of sacrifice [*nisar-e
Ghamkoli*].

Standard themes such as madness, intoxication and dreams, and the use
of stock Sufi imagery, intoxicating wine, the seal of the heart, stars, nar-
cissi and overflowing rivers, all convey the poet's love and desolation:

Intoxicated forever
Whosoever took wine, drinking once
Of the glass [*jam*] of Zindapir.

So what if separation has removed him out of sight!
He is inscribed [*naksh* = mapped] on my heart,
Servant [*khaddam*] of Zindapir.

Or, in another poem:

The watchful eye [*niga hey dida*] of narcissus [half closed, like the intoxicated
lover]
Seeks also to gaze at you [*didar ke talib*]
Ghamkol's loveliest sights [*dilkash nazare*] remember you [*yad karte hey*],
Oh, think of me, for God's sake, the helpless who remembers you.

Let me see in a dream [*khuab*] the graceful face [*ruhi zeba*] of Ghamkol's *pir*,
Evermore [*har dam*] these madmen [*diwane*] remember you [*yad karte hey*],
Pir of Ghamkol, how sorrowfully I long for you.

Your great benevolence [*darian nawazi*] is known worldwide [*shore 'alam
me*],
The shores [*kinaret*] of the sea [*behre*] of generosity [*sakhawat*] remember you
[*yad karte hey*],
Oh, think of me, for God's sake, the helpless who remembers you.
Nawaz is not the only destitute one [*be niwan*],
Burning with passion for you [*saze me jalta*],

In the garden of Ghamkol [*shabe sake*] the stars [*sitare*] Remember you [*yad karte hey*]
Pir of Ghamkol, how sorrowfully I long for you [*yad karte hey*]
Oh, think of me, for God's sake, the helpless who remembers you [*yad karte hey*]

TELLING THE GENERIC

In his book on Urdu poetry Russell dismisses *qasida* poems in a sentence as a minor form of poetry, typified by 'intricate verbal conceits and complex flights of rhetoric, together with often absurdly exaggerated flattery of patrons' (Russell 1992: 24). This compares unfavourably in his view with the *ghazal*. It seems to me, however, that Sufi *qasidas* are a poetic tradition which is both deeply expressive and allows disciples to endow saints with uniqueness, a distinctiveness beyond the generic. The declaration that the saint is alive and powerful in the grave, whether told as an explanation to the anthropologist or as a didactic lecture by a *maulvi* to the congregation attending the *'urs*, is something that may be said of any Sufi saint, anywhere. It lacks the uniqueness of the here and now, of this particular saint at this moment in history. As I suggested in chapter 4 and argue in the conclusion, and as has been recognised by others, most miracle stories have a singular deep structure. But by the same token, they differ quite radically in the tangible details of landscape and people in which their moral plots are set. *Qasidas*, like all Sufi poetry, employ stock phrases and imagery. Yet at the same time they locate a named saint in a named place, eulogised by a named poet. Ultimately that particular saint comes to be associated with the poetic words of love that the poet uses to praise him.

Unlike architectural structures, words and books travel; they reach distant places; they tell a bigger tale. Like Zindapir's emissaries, scattered around Pakistan and globally, it may well be that Zindapir will be remembered in future through Rab Nawaz's *qasidas* and morality stories about him, as much as through his *langar* and magnificent shrine.

Myths of saints are created by individuals in the first instance. Hajji Ibrahim, one of the few mythologisers left at the lodge, told me that he had been very close to the *pir* in the last three or four months of the saint's life, caring for him during his illness. This was his great luck, he said, and his blessings had increased immensely. He was in the hospital in the hours before the *pir* died. Zindapir did not die, he said, like other people.

He was attached to a heart machine but even after it stopped, the *pir* still continued to pray, *la ilaha illa'l-lah*. His heart had stopped but he was still praying. The doctor had told him, 'We cannot care for you at the lodge; in the hospital we have medicines and equipment.' The *pir* answered 'When wild animals are ill in the jungle where is their medicine?' The doctor replied that Allah helps them. The *pir* said 'I have been living in the jungle with Allah for all these years and now I will put my trust in Him only.' This tale of his final hours echoes other myths told of Zindapir in which the safety of this world is rejected in favour of trust in God.

After his death his face remained red, Hajji Ibrahim said, he looked as though he was just sleeping. At the moment of death the whole valley of the *darbar* filled with the most wonderful scent. It was not a recognisable smell like roses or jasmine but a unique smell, the heavenly fragrance of paradise (*jannat*). Cars lined up for the funeral all the way to the Afghan refugee camp. A couple of weeks later when they dug down to the grave to lay it with concrete, this same scent was so powerful that it clung to the grave diggers' clothes. One of them carried it with him to the Afghan camp.

Hajji Ibrahim, a relatively uneducated man, continues a long oral tradition of storytelling. There may be others in the *darbar* whom I did not meet who shared this talent for narration and myth making. During the interregnum when the shock of the saint's death seemed to render most people mute, Hajji Ibrahim stood out for me as unique. We cannot know how Zindapir will be commemorated in the future, or whether the anthropologist's desire to record such stories will artificially fix the fluid uncertainty of the saint's memory.

I asked Rab Nawaz 'It is said the *pir* is not dead?' He said that after the *pir* died he spent the whole forty days mourning period in the *darbar*, weeping all the time. When the the forty days were over he set off home. At the entrance to the *darbar* he stopped, weeping, and, turning in the direction of the dead *pir*, he spoke the same parting words which he always used to say whenever he parted from the *shaikh*: '*Ye dil, ye jigr, ye ankh, ye sar* [this heart, this liver, these eyes, this head], *ye sab tumhara hey* [these are all yours], *jao, jao, is par jao* [you can walk over them].' At this point Zindapir appeared before him and said, as he always did, with his two hands lifted, palms facing towards the speaker in a good humoured, dismissive gesture of 'go'. 'Go Rab Nawaz.' If anything proves that the *pir* is still alive this surely must be it.

13

CONCLUSION

GEOGRAPHIES OF CHARISMA AND THE
LIMITS OF POSTMODERN ANTHROPOLOGY

LIVING CHARISMA

What endows a living, originary Sufi saint with his charisma? What motivates men and women to join Sufi orders in a postcolonial society and globalising world? In this book I have shown that processes of religious incorporation, saintly veneration and charismatic formation must be understood in all their cultural and historical complexity. No single factor produces the effect of charisma of a living Sufi saint. It is conditional upon a receptive cultural environment and conventional expectations, and supported by bodily practices, narratives of unique individuality and, in the case of Sufi saints, a theory of transcendental connection to a distant God. Above all charisma is embodied in ritual performance, sanctioned by a newly generated sacred geography, and underpinned by voluntary mobilisation on a vast, transregional and transnational scale.

Contemporary Pakistan, a postcolonial society characterised by uneven development and marked differences in status and wealth, recruits migrants to serve in its armed forces and government ministries, and exports labour to the Gulf and to Britain. It is in these settings that fraternities of contemporary Sufis create civil society: voluntary organisations that cut across traditional village and kin ties, ethnic and social divisions, regions and provinces. The relations of amity and networks of useful contacts between Sufi sister- or brother-disciples are embedded in modern settings—factories, work places, the army, the police, Pakistan International Airlines. So too in Britain and the Gulf, Sufi fraternities thrive in the companionship created on building sites, in factories and in immigrant neighbourhoods.

In a period when the North West Frontier Province of Pakistan has come to be better known as the recruiting ground for the Taliban, Zindapir's cult represents an important reminder of the existence of a peaceful, tolerant Islam in South Asia. The Frontier may be a place of fundamentalist *madrassas* whose sole purpose is to train young men for martyrdom, in a struggle against all things western. But it is also a place renown for its *pirs*, alive and dead. Among Zindapir's disciples are Afghani refugees, Pathans, Punjabis, Sindhis and Kashmiris, peasants and urbanites, rich and poor. Against the puritanical strictures of the Deobandis, Zindapir's reform Sufism espouses a spirit of openness and generosity, which encourages followers to aspire to worldly success and prosperity, while envisioning a utopian world of nurture, tranquility and selfless giving.

The rise of Zindapir's regional cult points to the fact that Sufism as a movement in South Asia is alive, vibrant and intensely fulfilling for its followers. Against a sceptical view of charisma as irrelevant to postcolonial or globalisation theory, one may argue that transnational communication has enhanced the status of religious charismatic figures and their organisational reach. Osama bin Laden, one such figure, constructed his persona in the classic image of a Sufi world renouncer; a man who had abandoned his wealth to live in the desert for the sake of Islam. By contrast, the present book discloses the processes leading to the emergence of a more classical charismatic figure, living oppositionally on the margins of the postcolonial world. Unlike Bin Laden, Zindapir was opposed to violence (and, indeed, to the Deobandis and *Tablighis*). The book shows the moral discourses he articulated while pragmatically negotiating his cult's expansion through the minefields of Pakistani bureaucracy and politics.

Zindapir's charisma was not out of place and time. On the contrary, it was deeply embedded both socially and culturally in present day Pakistani society and it global extensions. Yet he was perceived as a unique individual who had transcended time and place. This is a key feature of saintly charisma. It is understood as an individual enchantment, an embodied magic which makes a saint's persona, his very body, contagiously powerful, even from the grave. The charisma of a saint infects his surroundings and any object with which he comes into contact. Charisma is felt as an unreachable remoteness, an aura of mystery which makes a saint infinitely desirable—magnetic, in Sufi parlance. Charisma is a luminous quality which physically embodies a divine force for growth, fertility and multiplication. It is a projection of inner peace; an aura of absolute, unquestionable, infallible authority.

This aura of mystery, power and authority, although believed to be intrinsic to the person and thus preordained and given at birth, is in reality acquired by an originary saint gradually, through a process of constant personal testing, publicly allegorised in moral fables. As this book has shown, this process is both culturally predictable and yet extremely difficult to achieve. It differs from the inherited charisma of saintly descendents in being a creative force around which a new organisation springs up.

Despite the widespread cultural fantasy of charisma in South Asia, only some, very special, individuals are perceived to acquire charisma in their own right. Such people are believed to be true saints, authentic and pure representatives of an ideal type or figure; exemplary, perfect persons. If they build a regional cult during their lifetime, their shrine becomes its focus after their death. The organisational arrangements, the flow of nurture, goods and pilgrims, have all been put in place already. Even the stillness and immobility of the saint, as Landell-Mills (1998) has pointed out, presages his death as a mere transition, a non-event.

The saint as charismatic fulfils the highest ideals of a society while at the same time appearing unique and beyond society. This effect of power is so compelling for followers that they believe him to reach into their minds, souls and hearts wherever they are, transcending physical obstacles of space and geographical distance.

The crucibles on the path to acquiring this personal, embodied magic are recounted, in the case of a living saint, as life history. But for these ordeals of a living saint's life to be believable, this study has shown, they must be corroborated by live evidence in the form of saintly ascetic practices and saintly generosity; by spatial conquest, social distinction and constant mobilisation. It may be that in the case of some saints, the legends after their death focus exclusively on the miracles they are said to have performed, and not on their exemplary lives (Crapanzano 1973: 30). In the case of Zindapir, however, whom I knew as a living saint, tales of his miracles were subordinated to his depiction as a supreme ethical subject, supported by moral fables of his ordeals, self-denial, generosity, and encounters with temporal power in which he exposed the hubris of present-day Pakistani politicians and learned scholars.

The introduction reviewed some of the theoretical debates arising from Max Weber's definition of charisma as a source of revitalisation and freedom from routinised social constraints. Weber stressed the antithesis between temporal authority and charismatic power, of centre and periphery, a theme developed by Victor Turner in his work on pilgrimage. Such dichotomous distinctions were later criticised, however, by regional cult theory, which defined these opposing forms of social relations as coexisting in dialectical tension within the same cult (R. Werbner 1977).

This study has addressed this debate through a detailed examination of certain Sufi cultural institutions and symbolic complexes which are frequently missed, disregarded or trivialised in the literature on Sufism, glossed as mere background to Sufi *pir* or shrine veneration. One such major institution is the *langar*, shown to be a defining and central motor of Zindapir's cult. Another, is the ritual inscription on newly colonised spaces, achieved through processions or the performance of *zikr*, and the cultivation of spaces already colonised. Such an analysis gives insight into the rise of Sufi orders as embodied, all-embracing, expansive counter-movements, constantly renewed through the regional cults they found.

SOURCES OF CHARISMA

Most monographs on Sufi cults devote a chapter to the saint's *karamat* (Gilsenan 1973; Crapanzano 1973; Eickelman 1976). Chapters 4 and 5 considered two paradoxes inherent in such exemplary tales in order to probe the compelling nature of saintly charisma: first, the paradox of the unique individual who is yet an exemplification of a type; and second, the paradox of the local in the global.

For his followers and disciples, the charisma of a Sufi saint is an expression of his extraordinary uniqueness. This means that the saint is, by his very nature, an utterly localised individual. The legends about his life objectify this localised uniqueness and concretise it in a woven fabric of localised detail.

Like his individuality, so too the power of a Sufi saint appears to be an absolutely localised, focused power, residing in him rather than in his office (Weber 1948: 247, 249, 296). This is almost by definition what makes him charismatic as against merely authoritative. 'Pure charisma,' Weber argued, is 'contrary to all patriarchal domination…it is the very opposite of the institutionally permanent' (ibid.: 248). Through charismatic appeal, the saint gains absolute control over his followers.

As a focused rather than dispersed sort of power, Sufi charisma might seem also to be the very antithesis of the kind of power which Foucault has argued characterises the modernist episteme: a power which has no central locus but is dispersed, grounded in the overwhelming self-evidence of a discourse and its panopticon methods of control through surveillance (Foucault 1977). Against this compelling coerciveness, charismatic leaders promise in Weber's terms a new found freedom by challenging an established social order and its institutionalised modes of social control. Paradoxically, however, in Sufism this promise of freedom has itself been institutionalised as a permanent feature of cultic social organisation.

The result is a duality: on the one hand, the spiritual power of Sufi saints, like other resistances to power, exposes the nature of institutionalised temporal power (Foucault 1983: 211). On the other hand, Sufi charisma is grounded in its own recurrent routinisations, structures of authority and modes of control. Sufi freedom and individual autonomy are, in this sense, an imaginative project, obviated by the displacement of one heteronomy or tyranny by another (see Levinas 1987: 22–3, 37–8, 58).

In the light of these considerations this book has explored the allegorical structure of Sufi legends as legitimising discourses of power—fables which are global and structurally recurrent while being, simultaneously, local and unique. To explain this duality I draw on a critical distinction made by Aristotle in the *Poetics* between the 'fable', or plot, defined as a sequence of morally grounded actions, and the embodiment of the plot in a cast of characters and a tapestry of concrete images. Whereas plots are paradigmatic, their embodiment constitutes a specific, imaginatively conceived, localised appropriation (Ricoeur 1981, ch. 8; see also Becker 1979: 213). The Sufi legendary discourses discussed in this book are marked by a recurrent, 'global' plot and a localised 'here-and-now' narrative. If the plot is fixed, its embodiment is creative, contextual and relational (Becker 1979: 215).

At the same time the narratives—myths and legends about a living Sufi saint—cannot be regarded simply as charters of legitimation. They are also, as the book has shown, the basis for eliciting a host of practical activities through which the saint has built up a vast religious organisation, stretching throughout Pakistan, and beyond it to Britain, Southern Africa and the Middle East.

Hence the second strand of this book's argument has been that the powerful coerciveness of Sufi knowledge, its effect of certainty, stems from its location within a broader universal religious ideology or episteme, in Foucault's sense. The episteme promotes self-discipline through an experienced sense of globalised, panoptican surveillance. Sufi structures of control are not, from this perspective, merely the outcome of disciples' personal allegiance to a charismatic individual. Instead, they are grounded in a threefold appeal to:

(1) *a discourse of legitimation,* in Lyotard's sense (1979), constituted by paradigmatic fables inscribed concretely in narratives about an apparently

unique and extraordinary individual. These narratives, recounted in chapters 4 and 5, mythologise the saint's supreme spiritual power and ascetism as exceeding that of any worldly, temporal politician;

(2) *a globally shared episteme*: a secret theosophy revealed through mystical experience, and supposedly arrived at through practice. In reality, however, in the context of global migration and print capitalism, this esoteric knowledge is widely known, as we saw in chapter 9, through published Sufi texts;

(3) *a technology of knowledge* through which the saint controls access to this mystical experience and eternal salvation, on the one hand, and to a global means of panoptic surveillance, on the other hand. This technology of knowledge, we saw in chapter 9, enables Sufi saints to sustain hierarchy, centralised organisation and absolute authority over their followers, even beyond the grave.

The book has traced these three dimensions of Sufi charismatic power through a focus on the transnational Sufi regional cult founded by a living saint, Zindapir. My account has highlighted the embeddedness of narratives of legitimacy about this saint in the two other modes of knowledge: abstract, metaphysical speculation, and social control.

In recording and analysing these moral narratives I faced a common dilemma of postmodern anthropology: how to represent certain religious knowledge from a sceptical standpoint for a dual audience: of the saint and his followers who had entrusted me with the mission of representing them to the world as the true believers they are; and for an audience of sceptical anthropologists whose interest is not in the reality of belief but in the way that that 'thing' called certainty is sustained, imposed or manipulated in the face of opposition, contradiction, change, ambiguity and uncertainty. My resolution has been to let the narratives about the saint speak, in large measure, for themselves, while focusing on the moral message they contain and the actions they inspire. As I argue below, however, in the course of writing this book I came to the view that the politics of anthropological representation are, in fact, inherently contradictory; that there is no conceivable collage which would be acceptable to devout disciples of the saint and to a sceptical academic audience.

ON THE POETICS OF TRAVELLING THEORIES

My argument needs to be set in the context of a controversy regarding the relation between (global) 'text' and (local) 'context'. The question can also be phrased specifically in relation to Islam as the problem of Islam, the one or the many. In the context of South Asian Islam the debate arose between those scholars who argue that Islam needs always to be analysed in its localised form and their opponents who stress the historical spread of orthodox Islam.

The debate began with Barth (1960) and Dumont (1966), who both reflected on the historical significance of South Asian Islam's unique hybridity. Somewhat later, a controversy arose in response to the publication of three volumes of anthropological essays which documented the widely varying practices and beliefs of South Asian Muslims in different parts of the subcontinent (Ahmad 1976, 1978, 1981).

In a critical review, the historian Francis Robinson argued that local accommodations (such as between Hinduism and Islam) need to be set against an increasing worldwide Islamicisation trend. Robinson stressed the worldwide sharing by Muslims of a common archetypal role model— the Prophet, and the influence of elite Muslim holy men and legal experts, as well as of print capitalism and other modernist trends, in propagating the spread of a more orthodox, legally-based, Islamic knowledge (Robinson 1983, 1986).

In counter-response Gail Minault and Veena Das, evoking interpretive and discursive approaches respectively, stressed the centrality of local textual interpretations, discourses and power structures in the appropriation of sacred Islamic texts (Minault 1984; Das 1984). Lindholm, reviewing the debate, goes beyond this view, first, to argue that caste-like hierarchies are common throughout the Islamic world and are not unique to India (Lindholm 1995); and second, that Islamic knowledge and practice in South Asia need to be considered apart from sacred texts, in the context of 'oppositional relations', as (local) '...struggle[s] for identity within a framework of often opposing interests' (Lindoholm 1986: 72).

In a seminal essay, Geertz (1968), comparing Moroccan and Indonesian Islam, proposed that global religions are necessarily embedded in the taken-for-granteds of local cultural milieus. These arguments take on renewed significance in the light of contemporary deconstructive arguments about meaning and intertextuality. Thus, Edward Said has argued that theories which 'travel' may lose their original radicalism while gaining in critical consciousness (Said 1984). So too, I want to argue here, Islam as a travelling religion may change radically but in a way which seems almost opposite to that which both Said and Geertz suggest.

In theory, and often in practice, when a world religion encroaches into an already charged social field, both religious practice and scriptural

On the poetics of travelling theories 289

exegesis are likely to be politicised and to *lose* the taken-for-granted, doxic transparency that they once possessed. Instead, such religions become highly self-conscious, reflexive ideologies. Intertextuality, in other words, relativises all knowledge. Recognising the intertextual dimensions of locally appropriated global religious texts is a critical theoretical advance for an understanding of the global and local politics of religion and its thrust towards greater reflexivity.

Two related questions are implied by the argument that travelling theories gain in reflexivity: first, if global religious knowledge, locally contextualised, is produced within a charged political field, in what sense can it still be said to be commonsensical, taken-for-granted and embedded unreflectively in a local cultural ethos and world view, as Geertz proposed? Second, in what respect do travelling theories which change, *also stay the same*? In what respect is Sufi Islam one rather than many?

To address these questions, I have followed Geertz in the first instance by shifting the focus to locally told narratives and away from published sacred texts. Unlike Geertz, however, my aim has been also to explore the underlying structures—the moral fables—animating such narratives. This book reveals that the structural logic of these fables, being implicit, is rarely questioned or challenged, even in politicised contexts. It provides believers with their sense of naturalised, taken-for-granted certainty. So much so that such fables, rather than being modified in travel, once adopted are a symbolic force reshaping the cultural environments they invade. This is so because in most cultures,

...Knowledge of plot constraints is unstated background knowledge, like the knowledge of grammar and syntax. It is learned indirectly, first through fairy tales and nursery rhymes (and their equivalent in other cultures), and then from the various media that have access to children (Becker 1979: 217).

Hence, going against the anthropological tendency to stress the local, I propose that Sufi Islam, despite its apparent variety and concrete localism, embodies a global religious ideology within a social movement which everywhere fabulates the *possibility* (if not the actualisation) of human perfection. Its shared implicit logic is revealed in the structural similarities between Sufi legends and modes of organisation in widely dispersed localities, separated in time as well as in space.

Since most Sufi mythologies are collected in hagiographies by devoted disciples after their master's death, it is often difficult to show how the different strands of a saint's life, as lived *in practice*, are woven *during his lifetime* into a structured mythic corpus (but see Malik 1990). The present book, based on fieldwork at the saint's lodge in Pakistan and among his several thousand disciples in Britain, has considered the way the genera- tion of myths and legends has been an integral dimension of the emer- gence of the man Zindapir as a 'living saint' and his foundation of a new Sufi regional cult. Like other living saints, legendary figures in their life- time, he has revitalised Sufi traditions by appearing to embody in his very life, as observed by his followers, a familiar lore of Sufi tropes.

The tapestry of legends, myths and morality tales told by and about Zindapir objectify the saint's divine grace and power through concrete images and remembered encounters. At the same time, the powerful validity of the legends and morality tales springs dialectically from the observed ascetic practices of the saint, which embody for his followers fundamental notions about human existence and sources of spiritual authority.

This dual basis for legitimised truth—saintly practice and concrete image—makes the legendary corpus about the saint impervious to factual inconsistencies. The 'myths' and 'legends' are conceived of as histori- cally accurate, true, exemplary narratives about an extraordinary individ- ual. If the myths contain self-evident truths which transcend the mundane and are not amenable to quotidian commonsense evaluation, this is because the subject of these tales, the living saint, is perceived to be an extramundane individual, a man outside and above the world, rather than in it.

This returns us to the question raised at the outset: to what extent is Sufism as a world religion differentially embedded in the commonsense notions of specific cultural environments? I would argue, against Geertz's relativist position, that the religious rationality and commonsense values implicit in Sufism *transcend* cultural and geographical boundaries. The underlying logic of the fables constituting this religious imagination is the *same* logic, whether in Morocco, Iraq, Pakistan or Indonesia. It is based on a single and constant set of equations, starting from the ultimate value of self-denial:

World renunciation (asceticism) = divine love and intimacy with God = divine 'hidden' knowledge = the ability to transform the world = the hegemony of spiri- tual authority over temporal power and authority.

The legends about powerful Sufis from Indonesia and Morocco which Geertz reproduces in order to exemplify the contrastive localism of Islam tell, in essence, the *same* processual narrative: (1) initiation through a physical and mental ordeal overcome; (2) the achievement of innate and instantaneous divine knowledge; (3) the triumphant encounter with temporal authority. The same legends can be found in Attar's (1990) *Memorial of Saints*, which records the lives of the early saints of Baghdad. What differs are merely the ecological and historical details: a flowing river and exemplary centre in Indonesia, desert sands and a fortress town in Morocco, the Baluch Regiment, an anti-colonial brigand's valley and corrupt politicians in Pakistan. A single paradigmatic common sense upholds this legendary corpus, while its local concrete details—regiments, rivers and desert sands, embody this common sense and suffuse it with axiomatic authority. But the symbolic structure underlying this commonsense is as unitary as it is inexorable.

The very uniqueness of the saint, proved in practice by his extreme asceticism, demands that his choices and actions, as embodied symbolically in the primary mythic corpus, be seen as transparently selfless and sincere. Above all, disciples insist that the humdrum, human, familiar motivations and aspirations which dominate the lives of ordinary mortals are quite irrelevant to an understanding their saint's life. Usual yardsticks of judgement are suspended in favour of a world of teleologically inspired acts of supreme courage, selflessness and faith.

THE DILEMMAS OF POSTMODERN ANTHROPOLOGY

The *shaikh* is a classic directing *shaikh* (Buehler 1998). Once he founds his central lodge he never leaves it, except to go on Hajj. At the same time he outlaws all technological representations or reproductions of his persona: pictures, texts, books, poetry. Pakistan TV (and the anthropologist) are not allowed to film the *'urs* despite repeated requests. He forbids his most beloved disciple, the poet, to publish his praise poems. Disciples who want to share in the *shaikh's faiz*, a physical emanation of light, can only do so through travel to the lodge. To be in the presence of the *shaikh* is to be nurtured by his intimacy with God as embodied by his very presence and the flow of food at his lodge.

This absolute refusal of all packaged representations, which might mediate his charisma more indirectly, was one which some of the *shaikh's* closest disciples attempted to subvert. These disciples were involved in the promotion of the saint nationwide and the organisation of the *'urs* as a major national event. We saw in chapters 4 and 8 that some of them were engaged in researching the life of the saint and had even produced a typed version about the lodge in English. My own appearance on the scene as

an anthropologist intending to write a 'book' about the *shaikh* seemed to
fit initially with this project, especially as my endeavour had the full support of the saint himself. But if I was to write a book, the contents of that
book would need to be carefully monitored.

From the outset I had worked closely with one of Zindapir's disciples.
To the very end, this disciple continued to support and participate in the
research, and—virtually until the current, final phases of writing—to
read and comment on everything I wrote. In this sense several chapters of
this study are the product of a collaborative effort and the present book
might be regarded as multi-vocal. For much of the time, the research was
supported fully by the *pir* in Birmingham as well as the saint in Pakistan.
This was a period when the cult was extremely peaceful and relations
between the cult branches in Pakistan and Britain appeared to be very
harmonious.

Yet such moments of peace and unchallenged authority are rare. Almost
everywhere anthropologists find themselves inserted into tense political
fields in which key protagonists are locked in relations of jealousy, competition and rivalry with one another. Even beyond an anthropologist's
identity as a Westerner, and in my case a woman and a non-Muslim, the
fieldworker is compelled to negotiate a minefield of local micropolitics,
and walk a tightrope between different interests and points of view. Such
fields of conflict are there, it must be stressed, irrespective of the presence of the anthropologist.

I have already mentioned that several close disciples were keen to subvert the saint's refusal to have anything written about him. When I arrived
at the lodge in 1991 on my second visit, I was repeatedly bombarded with
questions about the 'book' I had promised. When would it be completed?
This was also the occasion in which I was told that the saint had withdrawn his cooperation with the local 'researchers', and had taken back
the genealogies he had given them. Indeed, they gratefully copied my
copy, obtained on the previous visit.

It became evident to me that it would take a very long time to produce
an academic book about the cult, and that that book might not fulfil local
expectations. Since the pressure was on me to produce something (or so I
thought) I decided to engage in a little desktop publishing. The small
'book' I produced consisted of simplified and censored versions of chapters 3, 4, 5 and part of 8, It was a kind of mini-hagiography although it
also contained the genealogies I had been given, maps of the regional cult
in Britain and Pakistan, and beautiful coloured pictures of the lodge and
of the *julus* in Birmingham, along with pictures of Sufi Sahib being

greeted by his disciples. It was my first venture into desktop publishing and I learnt a lot about fonts, margins and pagination. It also taught me, as it turned out, a good deal about the lodge and the saint.

Altogether I produced (at some cost, pain and sweat) five copies: one for the *shaikh*, one for his son, one for Sufi Sahib in Birmingham, one for Hajji Karim in Manchester, and one for myself. The text of the book had been carefully read and corrected by Hajji Karim. The reaction in Britain was ecstatic. I received a letter of appreciation from the head of the management committee of Sufi Sahib's Dar-ul-'Uloom.

Then came the news from Pakistan: Zindapir had instructed Sufi Sahib and Hajji Karim to burn their copies, and I was requested to do the same. Why? Hajji Karim, who carried the news, said he had no idea. The order had come, and had to be obeyed. This was in 1993, not long after the Rushdie affair and its book-burning drama. My personal book-burning experience was an ironic reminder of that troubling event. I knew that the *shaikh* was innocent of any thought about *The Satanic Verses* and its incendiary fate, but there was no question that the gesture was intended to be dramatic. It shattered the harmony of the research.

My first reaction was one of disgust. The 'book' had been meant as a token of appreciation, given in good faith, and as far as I was concerned, all the *shaikh* needed to do if he did not like it was to put it at the back of his bookshelf and forget about it. Burning the book was hurtful to a lot of people, not only to me: several of Sufi Sahib's pictures were in the book; Hajji Karim had made an enormous contribution to the text.

Sufi texts are full of reports of such trials, to which a saint submits his disciples. Abjection, one might say, is the name of the game. Unusually, perhaps, I, the anthropologist, had to undergo this trial of faith along with others—although it has to be admitted that I never burnt my copy (in fact, at the time I did not have a copy for reasons which now escape me. I only had the original proofs).

The whole event was both zany and sad. I tried to find out what was wrong with the 'book'. I visited the *shaikh*'s son who was on a trip to England, and he assured me that there was nothing wrong with the book. I wrote a letter in Urdu to the *shaikh* which was never answered (he may never have received it). In the absence of any hard facts, I—along with friends and colleagues among those who knew the *shaikh* and the cult—engaged in productive speculation. One thing we all agreed on: Zindapir had not read the text. This still allowed for a number of possibilities:

1. The very existence of the book was anathema to the *shaikh* as a directing *shaikh*. This was the most likely explanation, but it also highlighted

my paradoxical position as an anthropologist researching a cult, supposedly with the aim of writing a book that was, in principle, as it
turned out, unwanted. Why was I welcomed at the lodge and treated
by the saint as an honoured guest?

2. The *shaikh* feared that I would turn the publication of the book into a
commercial venture beyond the control of the lodge. He might even
have feared that Sufi Sahib would be tempted by its commercial potential, hence the burning of all the existing copies. This seemed a plausible explanation.

3. The *shaikh* did not like the inclusion of pictures of Sufi Sahib in the
book. His own picture was absent, of course (I never took a picture of
him), and thus Sufi Sahib's image dominated the book. He might even
have disapproved of one of the pictures, showing a disciple bowing to
kiss Sufi Sahib's hands. This also seemed quite a plausible explanation. If the family had influenced his decision there were additional
possibilities:

4. He might have disapproved of the inclusion of his familial genealogy
which, as I indicated, had been withdrawn. This seemed quite plausible,
although to be read, the genealogies required a measure of expertise.

5. He might have disliked my mention of personal tragedies in his life.
This would have meant someone in the family reading the book with
care, which was unlikely.

The saint might also have been influenced by malicious gossip coming
from one of his trusted circle of disciples. This seemed quite likely. One
disciple, a self-appointed enemy, could read English with ease. In that
case, there were further possibilities.

6. He might not have liked the inclusion of different versions of the same
miracle stories which (from a Eurocentric perspective) cast doubt on
the validity of any one narrative. In particular, the story of the trip to
the valley by car rather than on foot was unauthorised and somewhat
unmiraculous.

7. I was told a rumour that the book was burnt because it contained writing on women. In fact, it did not, but this would be the sort of malicious gossip that would influence the *shaikh* (in 1991, I promised the
women with whom I spent most of my time that I would not publish
their pictures).

8. In 2000 Hajji Karim told me that it didn't matter what I wrote, as long
as I focused exclusively on the *darbar* in Pakistan. This implied that
the book was burnt because it was a multi-sited study which did not

focus exclusively on the saint. It was not, despite my playful imita-
tion, a proper hagiography. I knew then that Hajji Karim and the family at the lodge would be disappointed by the final book—a book on
the globalisation of Sufism in the postcolonial era which could not
ignore the British branch of the order.

I was saddened by the whole episode since I was very fond of the old
man. He had been extremely generous to me, and I did not like the
thought that I had upset him. For a very long time I refused to do any
more research and devoted myself to teaching. In any case, I had vowed
in 1991 never to go back to Pakistan until there was peace in the Middle
East, an elusive reality. But in 1999, there was hope of peace. I had heard
that the *pir* was ill and I thought it was time to go back.

By the time I returned, he had died. I was welcomed with open arms at
the lodge. Doors that had been tightly shut before opened. Key actors were
keen to talk to me. I refused to get drawn into any conversation about
books, and when pressed, cited the difficulty of finding a publisher. It
was clear to me by then that I was incapable of writing a book for the
darbar: that particular politically correct anthropological dream had
proved to be as utopian as peace in the Middle East (a few months after I
returned from Pakistan, the Middle East went up in flames; I could never
have paid my final visit). In 2000, I came as a friend and promised nothing. Why was I welcomed?

Whatever else, the book episode highlighted the enormous importance
the *shaikh* attributed to retaining his unmediated access to disciples. It
also revealed how difficult it was for him to read my motives for doing
the research.

The *shaikh* was said to have the power to see into the hearts and minds
of his disciples and of all visitors to the lodge wherever they were. I
clearly reflected the limits of this power. Pure research for the sake of scientific knowledge, or even for the sake of a career in England, were
beyond the comprehension of the *shaikh* and his immediate followers. It
was thus assumed, I realised in retrospect, that I must have ulterior, more
immediate and probably selfish, motives.

Most charitably, it was probably hoped that I had a secret dream of con-
verting to Islam. Western converts are a big prize among Sufis. In the
saint's favour it has to be said that he and his family never attempted to
proselytise. But when all my other possible motives had been eliminated,
by the time of my visit in 2000, attempts to convert me—which had
always been there—took on renewed force.

For the saint my presence as an Englishwoman and, after he found out my origins, a Jew, were grist to the mill of his legendary corpus. They proved conclusively his unique tolerance and the universality of his spiritual dominion. But others in the lodge sought more mundane reasons for my presence: I was a Jewish spy, I had formed a liaison with one of the disciples. These were the kinds of human motives that seemed to explain my stated desire to do 'research'. Malicious gossip about me reached my ears just before I left for Pakistan in 1991, and I had to decide how to deal with it.

To understand the reasons for the gossip, one needs to appreciate the nature of the lodge community. For most of the year, there are fewer than thirty residents at the lodge. In such a tiny community, with each person allocated a clear role, jealousy and resentment are inevitable if the daily order is disrupted. I was an outsider, a foreigner. There was a person at the lodge whose role it was to host foreigners. My visit undermined this role.

Ahmed Sahib, one of the saint's closest disciples, an educated man and an accountant by training, who was later promoted to become managing director of a major cotton factory in the adjacent town, acted as the *shaikh*'s interpreter, mediating his encounters with Pakistani VIPs and English-speaking visitors. Cultural brokers are familiar figures on the anthropological landscape, and experienced fieldworkers soon learn to shun them. As brokers, they are used to pronouncing official truths, often highly censored, while attempting to prevent the anthropologist from getting acquainted with the wide range of actors and opinions essential to any rounded understanding of socially embedded cultural practice.

Like in any research, the cult had closely guarded secrets. I thus had difficulty in obtaining certain types of information: genealogies, registers of disciples, maps, numbers attending the *'urs*. My request and quest for these modernist scientific 'facts' created unease and suspicion among close disciples and even the grandsons of the saint. My frequent and close meetings with the saint inspired jealousy and gossip among other disciples. I was a women and a non-Muslim in a cult dominated by Muslim men. My friendship with the *khalifa* from Manchester made me the unintended enemy of others.

There were constant attempts to limit the flow of information reaching me. These attempts came from disciples determined at all cost to preserve the magical aspects of the saint's charisma by concealing any facts that might reveal the limits of his dominion. It was important to these disciples that the saint's *wilayat* be defined by classic numerical tropes: a million followers, an annual *'urs* attended by 300,000. The fact that the lodge drew an income from supplicants was also a closely guarded secret. The supposed desolation of the lodge, far removed from civilisation, was another trope fostered. Ordinary empirical research threatened to expose the limits of the saint's *ruhaniyat*, his spiritual power. Or so it seemed to these disciples.

I arrived at the lodge for the first time with my Sufi guide from Manchester, Hajji Karim, the man who had introduced me to the order and had facilitated my research on the order's ritual celebrations in Britain. I did not require the services of Ahmed Sahib. My companion not only acted as translator during my nightly midnight meetings with the *shaikh*; as a regular visitor to the lodge over many years, he also introduced my to a range of other disciples and *khulafa*. He already knew where my research was going and shared my interest in its central themes. He was English enough, even though born in Pakistan (he had arrived in Britain at the age of sixteen) to appreciate the broader sociological as well as religious dimensions of the study.

Cultural brokers are there to filter information. His displacement made Ahmed Sahib an enemy, mainly of my companion but also in some measure of mine. He generated a flow of negative gossip about Hajji Karim in which I was partly implicated as well. When, on a subsequent visit, in 1991, having heard some of the more outlandish bits of this gossip, I accosted Ahmed Sahib (since my own honour and integrity were at stake) he did not deny (somewhat to my surprise) that he had spread the gossip or that it might conceivably be false. Instead, he departed in a huff to complain to the *shaikh*, and I only saw him again at the very end of my visit.

The *shaikh* resolved this crisis by entrusting me to his close women *murids* working at the lodge. This, and my lengthy conversations with an all-year-round resident and volunteer worker at the lodge, Hajji Ibrahim, who was appointed as my guardian, provided me with significant fresh insights into the lodge and the kinds of relations different disciples had with the *shaikh* and with each other. It also gave me the chance to visit Jangal Khel, the saint's village of origin, and to meet many members of the town's important lineage, Pir Khel. It positioned the saint in a broader social context. The visit, though productive, was nevertheless a difficult one. The *shaikh*'s son was away and his relative, who substituted as my immediate host, hostile. Ahmed's gossip refocused on my role as a likely spy and only the saint's trust and protection, along with my English passport, saved me, I believe, from a visit by the Pakistani police.

It seemed preposterous at first that I could be accused of spying, a middle-age woman with various ailments and a poor command of Urdu. But on reflection I realised that a convincing narrative might be constructed. After all, the saint was an army saint and the majority of his disciples were, or had been, soldiers. Kohat was still a garrison town. In the Middle East, the Israelis had kidnapped a Hizbullah holy man. The saint's dominion and power were regarded as transcendent and global. In the conspiracy theory infused atmosphere prevalent in Pakistan, a state virtually at war with India and a nascent nuclear power, the improbable might just seem possible. I nevertheless continued to interview disciples and gather facts, choosing to ignore the innuendos and implicit threats coming my way from Ahmed and his cronies. The saint remained as friendly as ever.

My fall from grace was probably precipitated by an incident that occurred during the *'urs* in 1989. On a visit to the women's quarters to take some photographs my purse was stolen. It contained a little money, my credit card and an American driving licence. The theft was a result of my own naïveté. In the weeks leading to the *'urs* the lodge had been so quiet and peaceful that, although I had been warned to guard my belongings, it was hard to imagine the danger of the crowd. In England, Pakistani women were, in my experience, well-groomed, placid and honest. I had never been robbed, even when my handbag was left in a corner during recordings of ritual and ceremonial events. Nothing had prepared me for the sheer poverty of the women attending the *'urs*.

The purse was stolen in the middle of the *'urs*, during a chaotic scramble at the gate of the women's quarters as some women tried to shove their way in and others to get out through a single narrow entrance, flanked by guards. The sum of money was trivial, the loss of the driving licence an irritation, but I could not be sure whether the thieves knew how to use the credit card. It seemed unlikely but I thought that just to be on the safe side, I should telephone a relative in England and ask her to cancel the card. My request to use the lodge telephone led to a predictable chain of events which I should have anticipated, knowing as I did by then that nothing happens in the lodge without the *shaikh's* permission: the *shaikh* was informed about the theft and he ordered a search of the women's quarters. His honour as host had been compromised, and although I was the victim, I was also to blame.

I was told by a host of people that the *pir* was upset, very upset. I kept protesting that I alone was to blame; that I could claim the money from the insurance company. First I was called to the saint's son's house. He informed me that I had not had a good day, I had had a bad day. I tried to explain that the day had been an excellent one and there was really no problem. Finally, to my embarrassment, I was summoned before the saint in the middle of the night, at the height of his most hectic involvement with the festival, and he insisted on giving me the money lost, a £ 10 note and 2,000 rupees in bank notes of 500 rupees each (at the time the exchange rate was 32 rupees to the pound sterling). Others had informed him that this was what had been stolen.

Later it emerged that seven members of a gang of thieves coming from Jhelum in the Punjab had been caught operating at the *'urs*. My purse was eventually found cast away on derelict ground and my licence and credit card posted to me. But my unblemished reputation as an honoured guest was henceforth associated with the lodge's failure to protect its guests.

The theft also drove home the extent of the saint's charisma. On my departure, the *shaikh* told me to keep the bank notes he had given me; they would grow and multiply and bring me great prosperity. When we reached Peshawar, I took out one of the 500-rupee notes in order to buy a Coke at a kiosk. It was a hot, dusty day and I had no other money. This simple act precipitated a major crisis among my companions. Ahmed, who was with us, sprang forward and exchanged my 500-rupee note for an identical one. Later, Hajji Karim exchanged pounds sterling for rupees. I gave him two of the bank notes and he tried desperately to persuade me to give him the remaining one. I refused, and later exchanged it for a 'normal' 500-rupee note with my hosts in Rawalpindi, middle-class people who professed to have no truck with *pirs*.

One other major conflict intervened in the research. For some time after 1991 I became involved with the affairs of the centre in Birmingham, helping one of the *khulafas* there to translate the poetic rendition of the spiritual genealogy into English, which appears in the opening pages of this book. I visited his home and was taken on a guided tour of the community centre. Later I attended the laying of the cornerstone to the new mosque. Around 1994, however, Sufi Sahib and Hajji Karim had a major falling apart over issues to do with the running of the branch in Manchester. A year later, there were reports in the press of Muslim organisational corruption in Birmingham, which seemed to implicate people close to the saint. There were unconfirmed rumours surrounding his management committee. Even earlier, in 1991, the saint had refused to allow one of his nephews to accompany me to Pakistan, perhaps because of the purse incident or the gossip about me. By this time my Jewish identity had become widely known.

I became *persona non grata* at the Birmingham cult centre. As I had never been in direct conflict with the saint, I tried to approach him via a friend's friend in Manchester, a close intimate of his, when I began a fresh round of research in 1999. I wanted his cooperation so I could interview his young, British-born disciples. The answer which came back was a definite no: I was a *kufr*, an infidel. I could not possibly write a book about Islam. It is possible that, more than anything else, it was the bitter quarrel with Karim that was the main cause of the saint's hostility, but his biases against non-Muslims were also given expression in this response, as they reportedly were in his dealings with the British state.

A few months later, when he met me at the lodge in Pakistan in 2000, he was clearly shocked. By the time he arrived, I had been at the lodge for a couple of weeks. I was welcomed with open arms by the *pir's* son, and was an intimate of the family. I was staying in the same lodge quarters as the party from England. On our first meeting, suppressing his surprise, the saint greeted me reasonably politely, while I covered my head modestly. Then, at the very next opportunity, he asked, a little casually, when I had arrived and had I come on my own? He didn't respond to my answer there and then, but later, returning from prayers at the mosque, he shouted from quite a distance: 'Are you studying Islam or something else?' I replied, perhaps foolishly (but we were conversing at a distance), that I was studying *tasawwuf*; to which he responded with intense anger: 'How can you study that without being a Muslim?' In my notes I comment that this was the end of a beautiful relationship.

This uncool behaviour was certainly not that of a saint. Unlike Zindapir's universal tolerance, this individual was clearly concerned to draw strict boundaries around orthodox Islam, and was highly suspicious of outsiders, the result, perhaps, of living in England for over forty years. But by then, I could afford to be magnanimous. Both he and I knew that he had been outflanked and outmanoeuvred. The rumours and gossip about me were—as far as the Pakistani order was concerned—a thing of the past, even though my identity as a non-Muslim and a woman were publicly known and had not changed.

By mourning the saint's death and returning to Pakistan for his very first *'urs*, I had passed the trial by fire of a true disciple. I was genuinely sad about the saint's death. I was very fond of his family and his *khulafa* in Pakistan. The final visit was one of sheer enjoyment. The atmosphere at the lodge was a lot easier and more relaxed and I was under far less supervision. There were no unexpected incidents marring the harmonious sense of peace and contentment. I made no attempt to gather facts and figures, although this might have been tolerated. The triumvirate who had maligned me had been marginalised, died or banished. To cap it all, the saint referred to me in his *du'a* on the final day, in front of the assembled multitude, a very great public honour.

THE LIMITS OF DIALOGICAL ANTHROPOLOGY

What can one learn from these incidents and encounters? Above all, I think, my account reveals that it is naive to believe that a truly collaborative anthropology is possible in the context of a broad-based, holistic ethnographic and sociological study. The dialogics of research are necessarily both positive and conflictual. As Jean Briggs (1970) shows so evocatively, one can learn a good deal about a social group and its most axiomatic values from misunderstandings and unintended breaches of etiquette. But such events are hurtful to all involved and depressing for the ethnographer.

Nevertheless, they are almost inevitable when the anthropologist cannot call all the shots, but still insists on doing that peculiar activity called 'research'. Ambivalences of power are commonplace in fieldwork encounters, despite the simplistic critical view that imputes clear superiority to the Western anthropologist. Ambivalence critically shapes the research. On the one hand, the anthropologist is a dependent. On the other, she makes difficult demands on the generosity, hospitality and tolerance of her hosts. At best, she can hope to be an honoured guest.

As an outsider, I was an unruly presence at the lodge, the subject of gossip, competition and rivalry. As a naive Westerner, I was liable to put myself unintentionally in mortal danger. My safety was an onerous responsibility for the saint. Yet it was at the moment of writing that the contradictory nature of my project became apparent in its most dramatic form. This conclusion has documented this drama in detail and spelt out its implications.

It is crucial to recognise that the anthropologist is always inserted into a tense political field of competition and honour. In a postcolonial world, her multiple identities are never ignored by her hosts, just as she cannot ignore or gloss over the internal politics and conflicts within the group she studies. It is the *social anthropological* analysis of local and transnational politics, rather than simply the *cultural* analysis of the plurality of cultural voices, that reveals the hidden, often painful truths of a social group. But these conflicts are also what compel the anthropologist to distance herself in the writing, and to aim ideally for the position of neutral observer.

Despite all the difficulties and hurdles of fieldwork, I experienced long periods of productive fieldwork. I enjoyed privileged access to the saint and his son, his grandsons and their families, as well as his most senior *khulafa*, key workers at the lodge, and my companion from Manchester. I enjoyed the company of many ordinary *murids*. I spent long days observing the preparations for the *'urs*. Since the research extended over more than twelve years, I gained some insight into the historical processes of charismatic formation. Some followers who, at one phase, kept their distance from me, became my friends later on. The great disappointment of cult members was that they failed to convert me to Islam, despite my evident admiration for the saint and fascination with Sufism as a ritual and religious system.

Postmodern anthropology advocates an interactive account of the research in order to overcome the anthropologist's stance of omniscient ethnographic authority. Deconstructing culture, it advocates the representation of plural voices. To this extent it has made an important advance in modes of anthropological writing. It has created a heightened consciousness of the inequalities of global power in which anthropologists write. But in the final analysis, I want to propose, a work can only be judged by the advances it makes in our capacity to make sociologically grounded cross-cultural comparisons, and to understand another cultural world in all its contemporary complexity, as an historically changing social formation.

The aim of this book has been to show how certain forms of social organisation and certain cultural logics may be widely shared across cultural and even civilisational boundaries. Such insight is necessarily gained through the slog of detailed empirical research. Although it demands cultural understanding and empathy—a transcendence of social and cultural difference—the product of the research can only ultimately be judged by, and is intended for, an audience of academic scholars.

If I have offended the sensibilities of members of Zindapir's order, or written the wrong book, this is not a sign of my ungratefulness for the hospitality and friendship they extended towards me. On the contrary, this book stands as a monument of my debt to them. It is, simply, that we follow different vocations, each with its own axiomatic truths.

REFERENCES

Ahmad, Aziz (1969), *An Intellectual History of Islam in India*, Edinburgh: Edinburgh University Press.

―― (1999 [1964]), *Studies in Islamic Culture in the Indian Environment*, 2nd edn, Delhi: Oxford University Press.

Ahmad, Imtiaz (ed.) (1976), *Family, Kinship and Marriage among Muslims in India*, Delhi: Manohar.

―― (1978), *Caste and Stratification among Muslims in India*, Delhi: Manohar.

―― (1981), *Ritual and Religion among Muslims in India*, Delhi: Manohar.

Ahmed, Akbar S. (1976), *Millennium and Charisma among the Pathans*, London: Routledge and Kegan Paul.

Ahmed, Akbar S. and Hastings Donnan (eds) (1994), *Islam, Globalization and Postmodernity*, London: Routledge.

Ajmal, Muhammad (1984), 'A Note on *Adab* in the *Murshid-Murid* Relationship' in Barbara Daly Metcalf (ed.), *Moral Conduct and Authority: the Place of Adab in South Asian Islam*, Berkeley: University of California Press: 241–4.

Ansari, Sarah F.D. (1992), *Sufi Saints and State Power: The Pirs of Sind, 1843–1947*, Cambridge: Cambridge University Press.

Appadurai, Arjun (1986), 'Theory in Anthropology: Centre and Periphery', *Comparative Studies in Society and History*, 28: 356–61.

Attar, Farid al-Din (1990 [1966]), *Muslim Saints and Mystics: Episodes from Tadhkirat al-Auliya'*, trans. A. J. Arberry, London: Arkana.

Barth, Frederick (1960), 'The System of Social Stratification in Swat, North Pakistan' in E. R. Leach (ed.), *Aspects of Caste in South India, Ceylon, and North-West Pakistan*, Cambridge: Cambridge University Press.

Basu, Helene (1998), 'Hierarchy and Emotion: Love, Joy and Sorrow in a Cult of Black Saints in Gujarat, India' in Pnina Werbner and Helene Basu (eds), *Embodying Charisma: Modernity, Locality and the Performance of Emotion in Sufi Cults*, London: Routledge: 117–39.

Bauman, Zygmunt (1998), 'Postmodern Religion?' in Paul Heelas (ed.), *Religion, Modernity and Postmodernity*. Oxford: Blackwell: 55–78.

Bayly, Susan (1989), *Saints, Goddesses and Kings: Muslims and Christians in South Indian Society, 1700–1900*, Cambridge: Cambridge University Press.

Becker, A.L. (1979), 'Text-building, epistemology, and aesthetics in Javanese shadow theatre' in A. L. Becker and Aram A. Yengoyen (eds), *The Imagination of Reality*, Norwood: Ablex Publishing.

Ben Ari, Eyal and Yoram Bilu (1992), 'The Making of Modern Saints: Manufactured Charisma and the Abu-Hatseiras of Israel', *American Ethnologist*, 19 (4): 672–87.

Blom Hansen, Thomas (1999), *The Saffron Wave: Democracy and Hindu Nationalism in Modern India*, Princeton NJ: Princeton University Press.

Boddy, Janice (1989), *Wombs and Alien Spirits: Women, Men and the Zar Cult in Northern Sudan*, Madison: University of Wisconsin Press.

Bonte, Pierre, Anne-Marie Brisbarre and Altan Gokalp (eds) (1999), *Sacrifices en islam: Espaces et temps d'un rituel*, CNRS Anthropologie, Paris: CNRS editions.

Bourdieu, Pierre (1977 [1972]), *Outline of a Theory of Practice*, Trans. Richard Nice, Cambridge: Cambridge University Press.

Briggs, Jean (1970), *Never in Anger: Portrait of an Eskimo Family*, Cambridge, MA: Harvard University Press.

Brisbarre, Anne-Marie (ed.) (1998), *La Fête du Mouton: Un Sacrifice Musulman dans L'espace Urbane*, Paris: CNRS editions.

Buehler, Arthur F. (1998), *Sufi Heirs of the Prophet: The Indian Naqshbandiyya and the Rise of the Mediating Shaykh*, Columbia, SC: University of South Carolina Press.

Clancy-Smith, Julia A. (1990), 'Between Cairo and the Algerian Kabylia: The Rahmaniyya *Tariqa*, 1715–1800' in Dale F. Eickelman and James Piscatori (eds), *Muslim Travellers: Pilgrimage, Migration and the Religious Imagination*, London and New York: Routledge: 200–17.

—— (1994), *Rebel and Saint: Muslim Notables, Populist Protest, Colonial Encounters (Algeria and Tunisia, 1800–1904)*, Berkeley: University of California Press.

Cohn, Bernard S. (1983), 'Representing Authority in Victorian India' in Eric Hobsbawm and Terence Ranger (eds), *The Invention of Tradition*, Cambridge: Cambridge University Press: 165–209.

Corbin, Henry (1969), *The Creative Imagination in the Sufism of Ibn 'Arabi*, trans. Ralph Manheim, Princeton NJ: Princeton University Press.

Crapanzano, Vincent (1973), *The Hamadsha: A Study in Moroccan Ethnopsychiatry*, Berkeley: University of California Press.

Das, Veena (1984), 'For a folk-theology and theological anthropology of Islam', *Contributions to Indian Sociology* (n.s.) 18 (2): 293–9.

De Heusch, Luc (1985), *Sacrifice in Africa: A Structuralist Approach*, Bloomington: Indiana University Press.

Delaney, Carol (1990), 'The Hajj: Sacred and Secular', *American Ethnologist*, 17 (3): 513–30.

Deleuze, Gilles and Felix Guattari (1984 [1972]), *Anti-Oedipus: Capitalism and Schizophrenia*, London: Athlone Press.

Diop, A. Moutapha and Laurence Michalak (1996), '"Refuge" and "Prison": Islamic Practices in the Foyers of the Ile-de-France' in Barbara Daly Metcalf (ed.), *Making Muslim Space in North America and Europe*. Berkeley: University of California Press: 74–91.

Draper, I.K.B. (1985), 'A Case Study of a Sufi Order in Britain'. M.A. thesis, Department of Theology, University of Birmingham.

Dumont, Louis (1957), 'World Renunciation in Indian Religions', *Contributions to Indian Sociology*, 1: 3–62.

Dumont, Louis (1972 [1966]), *Homo Hierarchicus*, London: Paladin.

Eade, John and Michael J. Sallnow (1991), 'Introduction'. *Contesting the Sacred: The Anthropology of Christian Pilgrimage*, London: Routlege.

Eaton, Richard M. (1978a), *Sufis of Bijapur, 1300–1700: Social Roles of Sufis in Medieval India*, Princeton NJ: Princeton University Press.

——— (1978b), 'The Profile of Popular Islam in Pakistan', *Journal of South Asian and Middle Eastern Studies*, II (1): 74–92.

——— (1984), 'The Political and Religious Authority of the Shrine of Baba Farid' in Barbara Daly Metcalf (ed.), *Moral Conduct and Authority: the Place of Adab in South Asian Islam*, Berkeley: University of California Press: 333–56.

——— (1993), *The Rise of Islam on the Bengal Frontier, 1204–1760*, Berkeley: University of California Press.

Ebin, Victoria (1996), 'Murid Traders on the Road: The Cultural Autonomy of a Senegalese Brotherhood as Agriculturalists and International Traders' in Barbara Daly Metcalf (ed.), *Making Muslim Space in North America and Europe*, Berkeley: University of California Press: 92–109.

Eickelman, Dale F. (1976), *Moroccan Islam*, Austin: University of Texas Press.

——— (1977), 'Ideological Change and Regional Cults: Maraboutism and Ties of "Closeness" in Western Morocco' in Richard P. Werbner (ed.), *Regional Cults*, ASA Monographs no. 16, London and New York: Academic Press: 3–28.

Eickelman, Dale F. and James Piscatori (eds) (1990), *Muslim Travellers: Pilgrimage, Migration and the Religious Imagination*, London and New York: Routledge.

Eisenstadt, S.N. (1968), *Max Weber and Institution Building: Selected Papers*, Chicago: University of Chicago Press.

Evans-Pritchard, E.E. (1937), *Witchcraft, Oracles and Magic among the Azande*, Oxford: Clarendon Press.

——— (1949), *The Sanusi of Cyrenaica*, Oxford: Clarendon Press.

Ewing, Katherine P. (1984), 'The Sufi as Saint, Curer, and Exorcist in Modern Pakistan', *Contributions to Asian Studies*, XVIII: 106–14.

——— (1990a), 'The Illusion of Wholeness: Culture, Self and the Experience of Inconsistency', *Ethos* 18: 251–78.

——— (1990b), 'The Dream of Spiritual Initiation and the Organisation of Self Representations among Pakistani Sufis', *American Ethnologist*, 17 (1): 56–74.

——— (1991), 'Can Psychoanalytic Theories Explain the Pakistani Woman?', *Ethos* 19: 131–160.

——— (1993), 'The Modern Businessman and the Pakistani Saint: The Interpenetration of Worlds' in Grace Martin Smith and Carl W. Ernst (eds), *Manifestations of Sainthood in Islam*, Istanbul: ISIS Press, pp. 69–84.

——— (1997), *Arguing Sainthood: Modernity, Psychoanalysis and Islam*, Durham, NC: Duke University Press.

Fabian, Johannes (1983), *Time and the Other: How Anthropology Makes its Object*, New York: Columbia University Press.

Foucault, Michel (1977 [1975]), *Discipline and Punish: the Birth of the Prison*, trans. Alan Sheridan, London: Penguin.

—— (1983), 'The Subject of Power' in H. Dreyfus and Paul Rabinow (eds), *Beyond Structuralism and Hermeneutics*, Chicago: University of Chicago Press: 208–26.

—— (1992 [1984]), *The Uses of Pleasure: The History of Sexuality*, vol. 2, London: Penguin.

Freitag, Sandria B. (1989), *Collective Action and Community: Public Arenas and the Emergence of Communalism in North India*, Berkeley: University of California Press.

Frembgen, Jürgen Wasim (1998a), 'The *Majzub* Mama Ji Sarkar: "A Friend of God Moves from One House to Another"' in Pnina Werbner and Helene Basu (eds), *Embodying Charisma: Modernity, Locality and the Performance of Emotion in Sufi Cults*, London: Routledge: 140–59.

—— (1998b), 'Saints in Modern Devotional Poster-Portraits,' *Anthropology and Aesthetics* RES, 34: 184–91.

Friedmann, Yohannan (1971), *Shaykh Ahmad Sirhindi: An Outline of His Thought and a Study of His Image in the Eyes of Posterity*, Montreal: McGill-Queen's University Press.

Fuller, C.J. (1980), 'The Divine Couple's Relationship in a South Indian Temple: Minaksi and Sundaresvara at Madurai', *History of Religions*: 321–48.

—— (1993), *The Camphor Flame: Popular Hinduism and Society in India*, Princeton NJ: Princeton University Press.

Gaborieau, Marc (1983), 'The Cult of Saints among the Muslims of Nepal and Northern India' in Stephen Wilson (ed.), *Saints and their Cults: Studies in Religious Sociology, Folklore and History*, Cambridge: Cambridge University Press: 291–308.

—— (1989), 'A Nineteenth-Century Indian "Wahhabi" Tract Against the Cult of Muslim Saints: *Al-Balagh al-Mubin*' in Christian W. Troll (ed.), *Muslim Shrines in India: Their Character, History and Significance*, Delhi: Oxford University Press: 198–239.

Gardner, Katy (1993), 'Desh-bidesh: Sylheti Images of Home and Away', *Man* (N.S.), 28 (1): 1–16.

—— (1995), 'Mullahs, Migrants, Miracles: Travel and Transformation in Sylhet' in T. N. Madan (ed.), *Muslim Communities of South Asia: Culture, Society, Power*, Delhi: Manohar: 145–76.

Geaves, Ron (2000), *The Sufis of Britain: An Exploration of Muslim Identity*, Cardiff Academic Press.

Geertz, Clifford (1968), *Islam Observed*, New Haven: Yale University Press.

—— (1973), *The Interpretation of Cultures*, London: Hutchinson.

—— (1983), *Local Knowledge*, New York: Basic Books.

Gellner, Ernest (1972), 'Post-Traditional Forms in Islam: the Turf and the Trade, and Votes and Peanuts' in S. N. Eisenstadt (ed.), *Post-traditional Societies*. New York: Norton: 191–206.

——— (1981), *Muslim Society*, Cambridge: Cambridge University Press.

Gilmartin, David (1979), 'Religious Leadership and the Pakistan Movement in the Punjab', *Modern Asian Studies*, 13 (3): 485–517.

——— (1984), 'Shrines, Succession, and Sources of Moral Authority' in Barbara Daly Metcalf (ed.), *Moral Conduct and Authority: The Place of Adab in South Asian Islam*, Berkeley: University of California Press: 221–40.

——— (1988), *Empire and Islam*, Berkeley: University of California Press.

Gilsenan, Michael (1973), *Saint and Sufi in Modern Egypt*, Oxford: Clarendon Press.

——— (1982), *Recognising Islam: Religion and Society in the Modern Arab World*, New York: Pantheon.

Gold, Ann G. (1988), *Fruitful Journeys: The Ways of Rajasthani Pilgrims*, Berkeley: University of California Press.

Goldziher, Ignaz (1971 [orig. 1889–90]), in S. M. Stern (ed.), *Muslim Studies*, vol. II, London: George Allen & Unwin Ltd.

Grima, Benedicte (1992), *The Performance of Emotion among Paxtun Women*, Austin: University of Texas Press.

Gupta, Akhil and James Ferguson (1992), 'Beyond "culture": Space, Identity, and the Politics of Difference', Theme Issue on 'Space, Identity, and the Politics of Difference', *Cultural Anthropology*, 7 (1): 6–23.

Habermas, Jürgen (1987), *The Theory of Communicative Action*, vol. 2, Oxford: Blackwell.

Hallencreutz, Carl F. and David Westerlund (1996), 'Introduction: Anti-Secularist Policies of Religion' in David Westerlund (ed.), *Questioning the Secular State: the Worldwide Resurgence of Religion in Politics*, London: Hurst: 1–23.

ter Haar, J.G.J. (1992), *Follower and Heir of the Prophet: Shaykh Ahmad Sirhindi (1564–1624) as Mystic*, Leiden: Oriental Institute.

Horton, Robin (1970 [1967]), 'African Traditional Thought and Western Science' in B. R. Wilson (ed.), *Rationality*, Oxford: Blackwell.

Hubert, Henri and Marcel Mauss (1964 [1898]), *Sacrifice*, London: Cohen and West.

Jaffrelot, Christophe (1996), *The Hindu Nationalist Movement and Indian Politics, 1925 to the 1990s*. London: Hurst.

Jeffery, Patricia (1979), *Frogs in a Well*, London: Zed Books.

——— (1981), 'Creating a Scene: The Disruption of Ceremonial in a Sufi Shrine' in Imtiaz Ahmed (ed.), *Ritual and Religion among Muslims in India*, Delhi: Manohar: 162–194.

Kakar, Sudhir (1982), *Shamans, Mystics and Doctors*, Chicago: University of Chicago Press.

Kepel, Gilles (1994), *The Revenge of God: The Resurgence of Islam, Christianity and Judaism in the Modern World*, trans. Alan Braley, Philadelphia, PA: Pennsylvania State University Press.

Kuhn, T.S. (1962), *The Structure of Scientific Revolution*, Chicago: University of Chicago Press.

Kurin, Richard (1984), 'Morality, Personhood, and the Exemplary Life: Popular Conceptions of Muslims in Paradise' in Barbara Daly Metcalf (ed.), *Moral Conduct and Authority*, Berkeley: University of California Press: 196–220.

—— (1990), 'Turbans, Skirts and Spirit: Folk Models of a Punabi Muslim Brotherhood' in Pnina Werbner (ed.), Special Issue on 'Person, Myth and Society in South Asian Islam', *Social Analysis*, 28: 38–50.

Lambek, Michael (1990), 'Certain Knowledge, Contestable Authority: Power and Practice on the Islamic Periphery', *American Ethnologist* 17 (1): 23–40.

Landell Mills, Samuel (1998), 'The Hardware of Sanctity: Anthropomorphic Objects in Bangladesh Sufism' in Pnina Werbner and Helene Basu (eds), *Embodying Charisma: Modernity, Locality and the Performance of Emotion in Sufi Cults*, London: Routledge: 31–55.

Lapidus, Ira M. (1984), 'Knowledge, Virtue, and Action: The Classical Muslim Conception of *Adab* and the Nature of Religious Fulfillment in Islam' in Barbara Daly Metcalf (ed.), *Moral Conduct and Authority: The Place of Adab in South Asian Islam*, Berkeley: University of California Press: 38–61.

—— (1988), *A History of Islamic Societies*, Cambridge: Cambridge University Press.

Levinas, Emmanuel (1987), *Collected Philosophical Papers*, trans. A. Lingis, Dordrecht: Martinus Nijhoff.

Lévi-Strauss, Claude (1966 [1962]), *The Savage Mind*, London: Weidenfeld and Nicolson.

Lewis, Bernard and Dominique Schnapper (eds) (1994 [1990]), *Muslims in Europe*, London: Pinter.

Lewis, Philip (1984), 'Pirs, Shrines and Pakistani Islam', *Al-Mushir* XXVI: 1–22.

—— (1994), *Islamic Britain: Religion, Politics and Identity among British Muslims*, London: I. B. Tauris.

Liebeskind, Claudia (1998), *Piety on Its Knees: Three Sufi Traditions in South Asia in Modern Times*, Delhi: Oxford University Press.

Lindholm, Charles (1986), 'Caste and Islam and the Problem of Deviant Systems: A Critique of Recent Theory', *Contributions to Indian Sociology* (n.s.) 20 (1): 61–73.

—— (1990), 'Validating Domination among Egalitarian Individuals: Swat, Northern Pakistan and the USA' in Pnina Werbner (ed.), 'Person, Myth and Society in South Asian Islam' Special Issue of *Social Analysis*, no. 28, University of Adelaide: 26–37.

—— (1995), 'The New Middle Eastern Ethnography (Review Article)', *JRAI (incorporating Man)*, 1 (4): 805–20.

—— (1998), 'Prophets and *Pirs*: Charismatic Islam in the Middle East and South Asia' in Pnina Werbner and Helene Basu (eds), *Embodying Charisma*. London: Routledge: 209–33.

Lings, Martin (1971), *A Sufi Saint of the Twentieth Century*, London: George Allen & Unwin.

Lowenthal, David (1975), 'Past Time, Present Place: Landscape and Memory', *Geographical Review*, 65 (1): 1–36.

Lyotard, Jean-Francois (1984 [1979]), *The Postmodern Condition: A Report on Knowledge*, trans. G. Bennington and B. Massumi, Manchester: Manchester University Press.

Mahmood, Tahir (1989), 'The Dargah of Sayyid Salar Mas'ud Ghazi in Bahraich: Legend, Tradition and Reality' in Christian W. Troll (ed.), *Muslim Shrines in India: Their Character, History and Significance*, Delhi: Oxford University Press: 24–47.

Malik, Jamal (1990), 'The Luminous Nurani: Charisma and Political Mobilisation among the Barelwis of Pakistan' in Pnina Werbner (ed.), *Social Analysis*, 28: 37–50.

——— (1998a), 'The Literary Critique of Islamic Popular Religion in the Guise of Traditional Mysticism, or the Abused Woman' in Pnina Werbner and Helene Basu (eds), *Embodying Charisma: Modernity, Locality and the Performance of Emotion in Sufi Cults*, London: Routledge: 187–208.

——— (1998b), *Colonisation of Islam: Dissolution of Traditional Institutions in Pakistan*, Delhi: Manohar.

Mandel, Ruth (1996), 'A Place of Their Own: Contesting Spaces and Defining Places in Berlin's Migrant Community' in Barbara Daly Metcalf (ed.), *Making Muslim Space in North America and Europe*, Berkeley: University of California Press: 147–66.

Mann, Elizabeth A. (1989), 'Religion, Money and Status: Competition for Resources at the Shrine of Shah Jamal, Aligarh' in Christian W. Troll (ed.), *Muslim Shrines in India: Their Character, History and Significance*, Delhi: Oxford University Press: 145–71.

Martin, Bernice (1998), 'From Pre- to Postmodernity in Latin America: The Case of Pentecostalism' in Paul Heelas (ed.), *Religion, Modernity and Postmodernity*, Oxford: Blackwell: 102–46.

Mayer, A.C. (1967), 'Pir and Murshid: An Aspect of Religious Leadership in West Pakistan', *Middle Eastern Studies*, 3: 160–9.

Meeker, Michael E. (1979), *Literature and Violence in North Arabia*, Cambridge: Cambridge University Press.

Melucci, Alberto (1989), *Nomads of the Present: Social Movements and Individual Needs in Contemporary Society*, London: Hutchinson Radius.

——— (1996), *Challenging Codes: Collective Action in the Information Age*. Cambridge: Cambridge University Press.

Metcalf, Barbara Daly (1982), *Islamic Revival in British India: Deoband, 1860–1900*, Princeton NJ: Princeton University Press.

——— (ed.) (1996), *Making Muslim Space in North America and Europe*, Berkeley: University of California Press.

Meyerhoff, Barbara (1974), *Peyote Hunt: the Sacred Journey of the Huichol Indians*, Ithaca, NY: Cornell University Press.

Minault, Gail (1984), 'Some Reflections on Islamic Revivalism v. Assimilation among Muslims in India', *Contributions to Indian Sociology* (N.S.), 18 (2): 299–303.

Moini, Syed Liyaqat Hussain (1989), 'Rituals and Customary Practices at the Dargah of Ajmer' in Christian W. Troll (ed.), *Muslim Shrines in India: Their Character, History and Significance*, Delhi: Oxford University Press: 60–75.

Nanda, Bikram N. and Mohammad Talib (1989), 'Soul of the Soulless: An Analysis of Pir-Murid Relationships in Sufi Discourse' in Christian W. Troll (ed.), *Muslim Shrines in India: Their Character, History and Significance*, Delhi: Oxford University Press: 125–44.

Nicholson, R.A. (1963 [1914]), *The Mystics of Islam*, London: Arkana.

———— (1967 [1921]), *Studies in Islamic Mysticism*, Cambridge: Cambridge University Press.

Nizami, K. Ahmad (1955), *The Life and Times of Shaikh Farid-Ud-Din Ganj-i-Shakar*, Aligarh: Muslim University History Department.

Özdalga, Elizabeth (1999), *Naqshbandis in Western and Central Asia: Change and Continuity*, Istanbul, Swedish Research Institute Transactions, vol. 9.

Parry, Jonathan (1989), 'On the Moral Perils of Exchange' in Jonathan Parry and Maurice Bloch (eds), *Money and the Morality of Exchange*, Cambridge: Cambridge University Press: 64–93.

Pinto, Desiderio (1989), 'The Mystery of the Nizamuddin Dargah: The Accounts of Pilgrims' in Christian W. Troll (ed.), *Muslim Shrines in India: Their Character, History and Significance*, Delhi: Oxford University Press: 112–24.

———— (1995), *Piri-Muridi Relationship: A Study of the Nizamuddin Dargah*, Delhi: Manohar.

Rahman, Fazlur (1968), *Selected Letters of Shaikh Ahmad Sirhindi*, Karachi: Iqbal Academy.

Rao, Aparna (1990), 'Reflections on Self and Person in a Pastoral Community in Kashmir' in Pnina Werbner (ed.), *Social Analysis*, 28: 11–25.

———— (1998), *Autonomy: Life Cycle, Gender and Status among Himalayan Pastoralists*, New York and Oxford: Berghahn.

ur-Rehman, Hafeez (1979), 'The Shrine and Langar of Golra Sharif', M.Sc. thesis, Quaid-i-Azam University, Islamabad.

Ricoeur, Paul (1981), *Hermeneutics and the Human Sciences*, Cambridge: Cambridge University Press.

Robinson, Francis (1983), 'Islam and Muslim Society in South Asia', *Contributions to Indian Sociology* (N.S.), 17: 185–203.

———— (1984), 'The "'ulama" of the Farangi Mahall and their *Adab*' in Barbara Daly Metcalf (ed.), *Moral Conduct and Authority*, Berkeley: University of California Press: 152–83.

———— (1986), 'Islam and Muslim Society in South Asia: A Reply to Das and Minault', *Contributions to Indian Sociology* (n.s.), 20 (1): 97–104.

———— (1987), 'Problems in the History of the Farangi Mahall Family of Learned Men' in *Oxford University Papers on India*, 1: 2, Delhi: Oxford University Press.

Russell, Ralph (1992), *The Pursuit of Urdu Literature: A Select History*, London: Zed Books.

Saheb, S.A.A. (1998), 'A "Festival of Flags": Hindu-Muslim Devotion and the Sacralising of Localism at the Shrine of Nagore-e-Sharif' in Pnina Werbner and Helene Basu (eds), *Embodying Charisma: Modernity, Locality and the Performance of Emotion in Sufi Cults*, London: Routledge: 55–76.

Said, Edward W. (1984), 'Travelling Theory' in *The World, the Text and the Critic*, London: Vintage.

Sallnow, Michael J. (1987), *Pilgrims of the Andes: Regional Cults in Cusco*, Washington, DC: Smithsonian Institution Press.

Saiyed, A.R. (1989), 'Saints and Dargahs in the Indian Subcontinent: A Review' in Christian W. Troll (ed.), *Muslim Shrines in India: Their Character, History and Significance*, Delhi: Oxford University Press: 240–56.

Schacht, J. and C. E. Bosworth (1974), *The Legacy of Islam*, Oxford University Press.

Schimmel, Annemarie (1963), *Gabriel's Wing: A Study into the Religious Ideas of Sir Muhammad Iqbal*, Lahore: Iqbal Academy.

—— (1975), *Mystical Dimensions of Islam*, Chapel Hill: University of North Carolina Press.

—— (1994), *Deciphering the Signs of God: A Phenomenological Approach to Islam*, Edinburgh: Edinburgh University Press.

Sherani, Saifar Rahman (1991), 'Ulema and Pir in the Politics of Pakistan' in Hastings Donnan and Pnina Werbner (eds), *Economy and Culture in Pakistan: Migrants and Cities in a Muslim Society*, London: Macmillan: 216–46.

Shils, Edward A. (1965), 'Charisma, Order and Status', *American Sociological Review*, 30: 199–230.

Strathern, Marilyn (1988), 'Commentary: Concrete Topographies', Theme issue on 'Place and Voice in Anthropological Theory' in Arjun Appadurai (ed.), *Cultural Anthropology*, 3 (1): 88–96.

Subhan, John A. (1960), *Sufism: Its Saints and Shrines*, Lucknow: Lucknow Publishing House.

Talbot, Ian (1998), *Pakistan: A Modern History*. London: Hurst.

Thompson, E.P. (1971), 'The Moral Economy of the English Crowd in the Eighteenth Century', *Past and Present*, 50: 76–136.

Trimingham, J.S. (1971), *The Sufi Orders in Islam*, Oxford: Clarendon Press.

Troll, Christian W. (ed.) (1989), *Muslim Shrines in India: Their Character, History and Significance*, Delhi: Oxford University Press.

Turner, Victor (1974), *Dramas, Fields, and Metaphors*, ch. 5: 'Pilgrimage as Social Process', Ithaca, NY: Cornell University Press.

van der Veer, Peter (1994a), *Religious Nationalism: Hindus and Muslims in India*, Berkeley: University of California Press.

—— (1994b), 'Syncretism, Multiculturalism and the Discourse of Tolerance' in Charles Stewart and Rosalind Shaw (eds), *Syncretism/Anti-Syncretism*, London: Routledge: 196–211.

Weber, Max (1948), *From Max Weber: Essays in Sociology*, London: Routledge and Kegan Paul.

Weingrod, Alex (1990), *The Saint of Beersheba*, Albany: State University of New York Press.

Werbner, Pnina (1990a/2002), *The Migration Process: Capital, Gifts and Offerings among British Pakistanis*, Oxford: Berg Publishers.

―――― (1990b), 'Introduction' in Pnina Werbner (ed.), special issue on 'Person, Myth and Society in South Asian Islam', *Social Analysis*, 28: 3–10.

―――― (1990c), 'Economic Rationality and Hierarchical Gift Economies: Value and Ranking among British Pakistanis', *Man* (N.S.), 25: 266–85.

―――― (1994), 'Diaspora and Millennium: British Pakistani Local-Global Fabulations of the Gulf War' in Akbar S. Ahmed and Hastings Donnan (eds), *Islam, Globalization and Postmodernity*, London: Routledge: 213–36.

―――― (1995), 'Powerful Knowledge in a Global Sufi Cult: Reflections on the Poetics of Travelling Theories' in *The Pursuit of Certainty: Religious and Cultural Formulations* in Wendy James (ed.), ASA Dicennial Conference Series on 'The Uses of Knowledge: Global and Local Relations', London: Routledge: 134–60.

―――― (1996a), 'The Making of Muslim Dissent: Hybridized Discourse, Lay Preachers and Radical Rhetoric among British Pakistanis', *American Ethnologist*, 23 (1): 102–22.

―――― (1996b), 'The Enigma of Christmas: Symbolic Violence, Compliant Subjects and the Flow of English Kinship' in Stephen Edgell, Alan Warde and Kevin Hetherington (eds), *Consumption Matters*, Sociological Review Monograph, Blackwell: 135–62.

―――― (1996c), 'Stamping the Earth with the Name of Allah: *Zikr* and the Sacralising of Space among British Muslims', *Cultural Anthropology*, 11 (3), London: 309–38.

―――― (1997), '"The Lion of Lahore": Anthropology, Cultural Performance and Imran Khan' in Stephen Nugent and Cris Shore (eds), *Anthropology and Cultural Studies: Questions of Method*, London: Pluto Press: 34–67.

―――― (1998), '*Langar*: Pilgrimage, Sacred Exchange and Perpetual Sacrifice in a Sufi Saint's Lodge' in Pnina Werbner and Helene Basu (eds), *Embodying Charisma: Modernity, Locality and the Performance of Emotion in Sufi Cults*, London: Routledge: 95–116.

―――― (2001), 'Murids of the Saints: Occupational Guilds and Redemptive Sociality' in Armando Salvatore (ed.), *Muslim Traditions and Modern Techniques of Power Yearbook of the Sociology of Islam*, vol. 3, New Brunswick and London: Lit Verlag and Transaction: 265–89.

―――― (2002), *Imagined Diasporas among Manchester Muslims: The Public Performance of Pakistani Transnational Identity Politics*, World Anthropology Series, Oxford: James Currey Publishers and Santa Fe: School of American Research Press.

—— and Helene Basu (eds) (1998a), *Embodying Charisma: Modernity, Locality and the Performance of Emotion in Sufi Cults*, London: Routledge

—— (1998b) 'Introduction: The Embodiment of Charisma' in Pnina Werbner and Helene Basu (eds), *Embodying Charisma: Modernity, Locality and the Performance of Emotion in Sufi Cults*, London: Routledge: 3–27.

Werbner, Richard (1973), 'The Superabundance of Understanding: Kalanga Rhetoric and Domestic Divination', *American Anthropologist* 75: 1414–40.

—— (1977), 'Introduction' in Richard Werbner (ed.), *Regional Cults*, London and New York: Academic Press.

—— (1989), *Ritual Passage, Sacred Journey: The Process and Organisation of Religious Movement*, Washington, DC: Smithsonian Institution Press.

Werth, Lukas (1998), '"The Saint who Disappeared": Saints of the Wilderness in Pakistani Village Shrines' in Pnina Werbner and Helene Basu (eds), *Embodying Charisma: Modernity Charisma: Modernity, Locality and the Performance of Emotion in Sufi Cults*, London: Routledge: 77–93.

Williams, Raymond B. (1984), *A New Face of Hinduism: The Swaminarayan Religion*, Cambridge: Cambridge University Press.

GLOSSARY

'abd	slave (of God), state of complete dependence on God and conformity to His will
'abad	cultivated
Abdal	'substitutes', mystical rank of Sufi saints who ensure the fertility of the world. According to one view at any one time there are forty living *abdals* in the world
'adam	non-existence, nonentity, annihilation
abrar	'the pious', mystical saintly rank, there are said to be seven *abrars* in the world
adab	proper conduct (as towards a *pir*), respectful, polite, etiquette
'adat	respect, etiquette, especially in behaviour towards a superior or Muslim saint
afrad	see *qutb-e-afrad*
afzal-u-zikr	virtuous, gracious *zikr*
ahl-e	people of, family
ahl-e munasab	the congregation of ranked saints
Ahmad	esoteric name of the Prophet Muhammad
akbar	greater, greatest, very great
akhfa	the 'most secret' *latifa*
akhirat	the end of the days, the Day of Judgement
'alam-e-amr	the world of divine command
'alam-e-arwah	the world of the souls/spirits created at the beginning of time, mystical stage on the Sufi path
'alam-e-bahut	the hidden world
'alam-e-hahut	the most hidden
'alam-e-jabrut	the world of divine decrees and spiritual powers
'alam-e-kabir	the great universe, the macrocosm
'alam-e-khalq	the world of creation, of becoming

'alam-e-lahut	the divine nature revealing itself
'alam-e-malakut	the angelic world
'alam-e-nasut	the world of the senses
'alam-e-saghir	the small universe, the microcosm
alif	first letter of the Arabic alphabet
'alim	a man learned in Islamic law and sciences
'amal	Sufi practice, especially mystical observances of an advanced kind, good deeds
'amal nama	evil deeds, record of deeds kept by the record-keeping angels
ambiya	prophets
ammara	sinfulness
ana	I, self, the ego
anjuman	voluntary organisation or association
'anqa	phoenix
aqidat	faith
'aqiqa	a custom observed at the birth of a child which involves shaving of the infant's hair and animal sacrifice (especially in the case of a son)
'aql	reason, rational faculty
'ara	a loose woollen cloak, usually black with stripes, worn by dervishes
aram	healing, cure, relief, rest, ease, quiet, comfort
'arsh-e-mu'allah	the throne of God between the world of creation and command
arshad	see *qutb-e-arshad*
arwah	plural of *ruh*
asar	third of the five canonical daily prayers
ashraf	noble descent, a category of higher caste
astan	lodge, abode
auliya	favourites, friends of God, saints
autads	'pillars', mystical saintly rank, the four saints supporting the four corners of the world
Ayat	verse from the Qur'an
'ayn	eye, essence, the letter *'ayn*

azim asti	the saint popular with jinns, saints and angels
baba	grandfather, honorific
bala	afflicting, evil spirits
bai'at	a vow of allegiance to a Muslim saint
banda	man, servant (of God), the person who performs *bandagi*, prayer
Barelvi	name of the religious movement in South Asia originated from the city of Bareilly in Uttar Pradesh, India, whose members venerate Sufi saints and shrines
baqa'bi'l-lah	eternal subsistence in God, a very high stage on the Sufi path
baraka/barkat	blessing, especially of growth, fertility and multiplication: saintly charisma
barsh	rain
barzakh	literally bridge or intermediary, limbo, an intervening state between death and the Day of Judgement. Upon death, a person enters *al-barzakh*
basharat	specific call or message, as from the Prophet Muhammad
batin/batni/batun	esoteric, hidden, a curtain, the inner eye
bhai	brother
bhain	sister
bid'a(t)	unlawful innovation in religious matters, said to be against Islamic principles
biradari	local agnatic lineage, in-marrying affinal group, Muslim caste, brotherhood
buzurgi	venerable, old, respected
chabi	*chapati* basket (Pashtu)
chaddar	very large square scarf, usually white, that covers the head and upper part of the body, sheet
chapati	flat bread
charsa	cannabis, hashish
chilla	forty days retreat of religious seclusion and meditation
chirriya	sparrow(s)

Chishtiyya	Sufi order originating in India
chogha	initiatory gown given by a saint to his *khulafa*, also known as *juba*
chul	desert
crore	100 *lakhs* or 100,000 × 100 (i.e. 10 million)
daftar	office, position
da'ira	circle
da'ira mumkinat	the circle of possibilities of creation
da'ira wilayat-e-sugra	circle of the small dominion
daku	dacoits, highway robbers
dalil	God's intimate, exemplar or proof of God's friendship
dam	the blowing by a saint or healer of Qur'anic verses over an afflicted person
daman	robe, cloak, skirt, metaphor for the being or body of the *pir*
dar	dwelling, habitation, house
dar-ul-'uloom	institution of religious learning (spelling follows local British usage)
darban	gatekeeper
darbar/dargah	royal court, Muslim saint's shrine, tomb, or, by extension, lodge
Darqawi	North African order
darwesh	a religious mendicant, a beggar, a Muslim saint, darvesh
daulat	wealth
didar	vision
din	religion
du'a	supplication, blessing, made by an individual addressed to God
dunya	the present world, world of creations
durud	'small' prayer imploring mercey and blessing for the Prophet said by Barelvi followers at the end of the main service or in *zikr* meetings
faiz (Arabic *fayd*)	divine grace and blessing with which a saint is endowed

fana	annihilation, extinction (*fi'l shaikh, f'il-la*) in one's *shaikh*, in God, one of the last stages on the Sufi journey
faqir	an ascetic on the Sufi path, mendicant, saint who practises asceticism needy of God's mercy
Faqr	poverty, asceticism, ethical stage on the Sufi path
Farq	difference, separateness, hence *farq badd-al-jamma*, difference following union
fatiha(h)	opening chapter of the Qur'an, used as a blessing, especially at funerals and saints' tombs
fazl	blessing of kindness
Firon	name of a devil, Pharoah, a man in the sway of his own power who forgets God
fuqara	plural of faqir, ascetic followers of God
gaddi nishins	successors, those who sit on the seat of a departed *shaikh* or saint
galib	empowered (by love)
garib	poor man or woman, humble, alien
Ghamkol Sharif	name of a Sufi lodge
ghaus	the sustainer, mediator, one of the highest ranked saints (some regard it as second in rank to *qutb*)
ghaus-e-zaman	the highest ranking saint of his time in some Sufi reckonings
ghazal	a love lyric, usually a relatively short poem knit together by a unity of metre and a strict rhyme scheme (AA, BA, CA, DA and so on)
ghee	clarified butter
girdah-e-bala	whirlpool of evil spirits
guna	sin
gurur, takabbur	vanity, arrogance (of the soul)
gyarvi sharif	communal meal held on the 11th of the month, commemorating the birth/death of Abdul Qadr Jilani
Hadith	traditions, sayings of the Prophet, validated by a chain of authorities
hafiz	A person who has memorised the whole Qur'an

Hajara	Hagar of the Old Testament, the slave wife of Abraham, mother of Ismail
hal	state of spiritual ecstacy or intoxication, considered a gift from God, condition, being
halal	lawful, meat of an animal slaughtered in a ritually appropriate way
Haman	name of a Devil, the prime minister of Firon, considered a sinner and arrogant
haq(q)	truth, justice
haq-ul-yaqin	true belief (in the oneness of God), real certitude
haqai'q-i-ilahia	the reality of God
haqai'q-i-ambiya	the reality of the prophets
haqiqa/haqiqat	truth, ontological reality
haqiqat-i-Ahmadi	the reality of Ahmad, stage on the Sufi path
haqiqat-i-ka'aba	the reality of the *ka'aba*, stage on the Sufi path
haqiqat-i-Muhammadiya	the reality of Muhammad, stage on the Sufi path
haqiqat-i-Muswi	the reality of Moses, stage on the Sufi path
haqiqat-i-namaz	the reality of prayer, stage on the Sufi path
haram	forbidden, taboo, sacred and protected
hasti	life
hava	air, spirit
hazrat	presence, dignity, a title applied to a great person
hidayat	divine lights
hijab	Muslim woman's traditional outer clothing hiding her hair, body contours and sometimes her face; a term used by Sufi mystics for that which obscures the light of God in man's soul
hijra	migration
hu	is, is existent
hundia	very high
Hujwiri	name of one of the first Sufi saints to arrive in the Subcontinent, buried in Lahore where his shrine is known as Data Ganj Baksh
Hurr	followers of Pir Pagara in Sindh
huzur	presence before God

'ibadat	religious ritual worship
Iblis	lord of the devils
idrak	beyond comprehension
'Id	Islamic festival. *'Id zoha* marks the last day of the Hajj, *'Id-el fitr*, celebrates the end of Ramadan.
'Id-milad-un-nabi	the Prophet's birthday
ihram	the two sheets the *Hajji* wears
ijaz	miracle
ijazat	permission, an authorisation given a person to transmit a given body of knowledge
'ijtima	congregation
Ilham	divine revelation
'ilm	knowledge, scholastic religious knowledge
imam	leader of prayers in the mosque, founder of Sunni legal school
insan	human being, person
intizam/intizami	arrangements, organisation; organiser/s
irfan	holy
ihram	the two sheets the Hajj wears
ishq	passion, love
ishraq	the morning canonical prayer, just before sunrise
Isma'il	Ishmael, son of Abraham and Hagar
ism-e-Allah	the name of God
isma-o-sifat	names and attributes
isnad	pedigree, an impeccable line of authorities in the transmission of *Hadith*
istakhara	indirect signs (a form of divination)
istiqamat	utter steadfastness, rank on the Sufi path
istiqraq	absorption (of the soul), stage on the Sufi path
itminan	at peace, tranquillity, the condition of the heart that has crossed the universe and achieved ultimate knowledge
izzat	honour, respect
jabal	mount

jadu, kala jadu	sorcery, black magic
jaga	place, awake
jalabiya	Arab cotton gown worn by men
jalal	full power of God, divine majesty
jalwa	lustre
jama'at	congregation, community, fellowship
jamal	divine beauty
jami'a	central mosque
jangal	jungle, areas outside human habitation
jannat	paradise
jazb/jazba	literally 'sucking', attraction, being sucked in, ful absorption in God's divine light
jhut	lies
Ji	honorific term of address, 'sir'
Jibreel	the angel Gabriel
jihad	struggle with the inner, base soul; holy war
Jilani, Abdul Qadr	Baghdadi saint of the eleventh century, founder of the Qadiriyya order and venerated as a founder saint in South Asia
jinn(s)	fiery spirit(s) or demon(s), often amoral, mentioned in the Qur'an, who may afflict or help humans and are said to live in a parallel world
juba	gown, often that worn by a saint and passed on as a gift to his *khalifa* or disciple
julus	procession, religious progress
jum'a/juma'a	Friday, Friday prayer
ka'aba/ka'ba	the black stone in Mecca, believed to be the centre of the universe, also known as *Haram Sharif*, where it is forbidden to enter to kill
kafir	unbeliever, an infidel, a non-Muslim
kala	Black (as in black magic)
kalimat/kalma	'There is no God but God and Muhammad is His Prophet'—the Muslim profession of faith
kamal/kamil	perfect, divine perfection
kamalat-e-nabuwat	the circle of the perfections of the prophets

kamalat-e-risalat	the perfection of the messengers
kamalat-e-ul ul azm	the perfection of great intentions
karam	kindness, blessing, generosity
karamat	miracle performed by a Muslim saint
Karbala	Place where the famous battle between the Prophet's grandsons and an evil ruler took place, the foundational myth of Shi'ism
kashf/kashfi	'unveiling', inner revelation or vision of God
kashf-ul-qabr	knowledge of graves
kashf-ul-qalb	knowledge of what is in people's hearts
kashti	Boat
khabar	News, knowledge
khafi	silence, 'more secret', the penultimate *latifa* (chest light)
khak	clay, of which Man is said to be made
khalifa	Caliph; deputy, envoy, emissary or vicegerent of a saint, often given permission to found a new branch of the order and/or initiate new disciples
khals	perfect
khanaqah	Sufi hospice, the place of teaching of a Sufi saint
khatam/khatam-e-qur'an	a reading of the whole Qur'an which is 'sealed' in one sitting, often distributed as chapters among several readers
khatib	orator, preacher, public speaker
khawaja	honorific term of address
khel	town or lineage in the North West Frontier Province
khidmat	charitable giving and especially service for the common good
khilafat	succession, deputy-ship, mantle, office and dignity of the *khalifa*, permission granted by a Sufi saint to a disciple to found a branch and/or initiate disciples
khirqa	Sufi gown, often passed on by a saint to his *khalifa*; patched frock, the sign of a dervish
khuab	dream
khud ba khud	of its own accord

khuda	God
khulafa	collective plural for *khalifa*
khushi	happy
khutba	sermon given during Friday prayers at the mosque
khwajah	'Sir', an honorific title
kufr	infidelity
kufristan	the land of the infidels, used to refer to the secular West
kun	'be' (the command given by God in the creation of the world)
lakh	100,000
la-maqam	beyond place, an epithet for Allah who is beyond place
la ihaha illa'l-lah	there is no God but God
langar	food cooked and distributed freely at a Sufi lodge in South Asia
lata'if/latifa	'lights' or openings on the chest through which God's grace enters and purifies a person, subtle centre or body
latif	very fine or subtle
loh	*chapati* stoves
ma'(a)rifa	mystical, secret knowledge
ma'(a)rifa-e-ladunya	secret knowledge of the world
madar	see *qutb-e-madar*
Madina	Medina, city to which the Prophet migrated and where his burial is on the Arabian peninsula
mahabbat	love
mahbub/mahbubiyat	beloved/loveliness
Mahdi	a saviour, expected to come just before the Day of Judgement and establish Islam over all unrighteous forces
mahfil	gathering, circle (as of musicians, or performers of *zikr*)
majid	holy
majmu'a	assembly, totality, aggregate, total knowledge

majzub	A person absorbed in, intoxicated by God
makhluqat	all creation, the people
maktubat	Letters, the letters of Ahmed Sirhindi
malfuzat	sayings of the saint, often collected after his death by his disciples
mamba'faiz	fountain or source of divine love
mansab	rank
maqam	place, station on the Sufi path, hence *'ali maqam*, the highest station
maqam-e-qalb	the place of the heart
maqam-e-takmil	the place of completeness
maqamat	a person of high rank
maqsud	final destination, desire, goal
marne se pahle marjana	dying before death, as when the *nafs* is 'killed'
martaba	degree, stage on the Sufi path
masjid	mosque
masruf	busy
mast, mastan	spiritual intoxication, intoxicated lover
ma'sum	pure, like a baby, protected, innocent
maulana	'Our Lord', a title given to a person of religious learning
maulvi	a Muslim religious expert on legal matters, cleric
mazar	shrine, burial site, mausoleum
mehfuz	inviolable, protected, safe from external temptation
mehndi	henna, plant that is used to make a red dye with a marked fragrance, used at weddings
milad-un-nabi	the birthday of the Prophet
mithai	traditional South Asian sweets, distributed on ritual occasions
mo'af/maf	forgive, pardon
mu'akkal/muwakkal	invisible guardians to whom power is delegated to help the *pir* in his healing and protective activities; invisible assistants of a Muslim saint
mu'allaq	suspended, open to intercession (said about human fate)

muhakmat	the law, the part of the Qur'an which is open and clear
muhibiyyat	divine love
mujaddid	renewer
Mujaddid-i Alaf-i Thani	the Renewer of the Second Millennium, reference to Ahmed Sirhindi, a Sufi reformer and key historical figure in the Naqshbandi order in India
mujaddid-e-waqt	renewer of the era
mujahid/mujaheddin	those who engage in *jihad*
Mu'inuddin Chishti	founder of the Chishti order, buried in Ajmer
mukammal	perfect and complete
mulaki/mala'ika	angel(s)
mulaqat	meeting, as with a Sufi saint
mullah	derogatory term for a religious prayer leader or dignitary
mumkinat	see *dai'ra mumkinat*
munasab	ranked, see *ahl-e-munasab*, the congregation of ranked saints
munh/muh	face, mouth
muqatta'at	isolated words or letters at the beginning of qur'anic chapters, the meanings of which are hidden
murad	beloved and desired (by God)
muraqaba	mystical vision during meditation, contemplation
muraqaba-e-mahabbat	mystical vision of love
murid	lover and desirer (of God), disciple of a Sufi saint
murid-bhai	fellow (lit. brother) disciple
musala	prayer mat
murselin	lesser prophets who reached different stages within the sphere of *zat*
murshid	Sufi teacher or spiritual preceptor, guide on the Sufi path
mushahida	witnessing, beholding, contemplating, ethical stage on the Sufi path
Mustafa	secret name of the Prophet, often used by Sufi followers

Musvi	Moses
mutashabihat	the verses of the Qur'an that are ambiguous, having several meanings
mutma'inna	total satisfaction, total peace
muwakkal	see *mu'akkal*
nabi	prophet
nabuwat	prophecy
nafl	a voluntary prayer, in addition to the mandatory ones, or a devotional act not enjoined by the *Shari'at*
nafs	carnal, vital soul or spirit, seat of desires
nafs-e-mutma'inna	the soul at peace
naksh	mapped, imprinted
namaz	canonical prayer, performed five times daily (*salat*)
Namrud	name of a devil
naan	flat bread, usually made of white flour, cooked in a tandoor, and regarded as a luxury
Naqshbandi	a Sufi order originating in Central Asia in the fourteenth century
na't	Sufi praise song for the Prophet
nazar	evil eye, often cast on young and particularly beautiful children
nazrana	tribute given freely to a saint or ruler
nazul	the second phase of the soul's journey, downwards
nisbat	connection (to God)
nishani	a sign (from God)
nishin	(see *gaddi nishin*)
niyat	vow, intention
nizam	order, as of the state
Nizamuddin Auliya	famous Chishti saint whose shrine is in Delhi
nur	light, in Sufi theosophy God's light or grace
pagal	mad
parda(h)/parde	veil, curtain, female seclusion
peambar	messenger

pinjara	cage
pir	saint, spiritual guide, Sufi mystic, founder or head of a religious order
pir-bhai	fellow initiate or spiritual brother of the same saint
piri-muridi	refers to the complex of saintly veneration between saint and disciple, often derogatory
pirzada	the *pir*'s establishment, family or descendants
qabr	grave
Qadiri	Sufi order said to be founded by Abdul Qadr Jilani in the eleventh century, Baghdad
qafila	convoy, caravan (of vehicles, camels, etc.)
qal(a)b	heart in a mystical sense, one of the *lat'aif*
qalandar	wandering ascetic, usually unkempt, who has abandoned family, friends and worldly possessions
qalbiyya/qalbia	*latifa qalbia*, is composed of the four elements: air, water, fire and clay
qari	reciter/reader of the Qur'an
qarib	Close
qasa	fate or destiny
qasida	Sufi praise poem eulogising a saint
qaum	people, nation, tribe
qawwali	mystical devotional singing, often inducing ecstasy
qayyum	existent, the highest ranking saint in some Sufi reckonings
qaza-e-mubram	directly decreed predestination
qibla	direction of prayer, towards Mecca
qosi	Bow
qurb	very close (to God), proximity
qurbani	animal sacrifice on 'Id
qutb	axis, cosmic pivot, the North pole, a title often given to one regarded as the highest living Muslim saint of his time, or to the highest of all the saints, alive and dead
qutb-e-afrad	a rank of the *qutb*, the cosmic pivot or axis
qutb-e-arshad	a rank of the *qutb*, the cosmic pivot or axis

qutb-e-madar	axis mundi
rab(b)	God, master
rabbani	Divine
rabita	connection, bond, between disciple and Sufi saint, or between the latter and God
rahmat	mercy, compassion, divine blessing
rak'at	genuflection during canonical prayers
Ramadan/Ramzan	the Muslim month of fasting
rasul	the Prophet Muhammad, a prophet or messenger
raza	contentment; God's willingness, pleasure; final stage on the Sufi ethical journey
riazat	intense worship of God
risalat	Prophecy
rishta	social connection, affinal relationship, marriage
roti	bread, usually flat bread
roza-e-mubarak	blessed fasting
ruh	eternal soul or spirit, survives beyond the life of the individual
ruhaniyat	spirituality, spiritual power
sabab	reason, cause
sabr	patience, steadfastness, an ethical stage on the Sufi path
sadqa/sadaqat	alms, sometimes in the form of animal sacrifice, given to avert misfortune in times of crisis or extreme danger
saf	pure, purification, stage on the Sufi path
sa'i	the running back and forth between the two hills of Saf and Marwa at Mecca, part of the Hajj ritual, which recalls Hajara's agonised running in search of water for her baby boy after their banishment
sajjada(h) nishin	'sitter on the carpet', successor of a Sufi saint
sakhi	generous
salb-i-yya	God's non-attributes
salik	wayfarer, 'traveller' on the Sufi path
saluk	the Sufi path

sawab	merit
saya	shadow, reflection
Sayyid	descendant of the Prophet Muhammad through his daughter, Fatima
shadi	marriage
shafa	cure
shafa'at	recommendation, intercession
shaheed/shahid	martyr
shahnat-e-zatia/zatiyya	essential splendour, stage on the Sufi path
shahud	omnipresence
shaikh	Sufi saint, master or *pir*, honorific title
shaikh-e-kamal	The perfect guide
Shaitan	The Devil
shajara	genealogy, family tree
sha'n	splendour and dignity
sharab	alcohol, wine
shari'a/shari'at	body of Muslim jurisprudential law, including the Qur'an and Hadith, along with later interpretations
sharif	noble, of noble descent
sharik	partner (with God), see *shirk*
shauq	desire, as for the presence of one's saint, longing
Shi'a(h)	major Muslim religious stream, centred on Iran, which starts from a belief in the leadership rights of 'Ali, the Prophet's son-in-law
shirk	polytheism, infidelity
shuhud	witnessing, vision, contemplation
shukr	gratitude, ethical stage on the Sufi path
shukrana	tribute to a ruler or Sufi saint
sifat	attributes
sifat-e-bashriyat	human attributes, stage on the Sufi path
sifat-e-shahnat	attributes of splendour and dignity, stage on the Sufi path
sifat-e-taraqi	attributes of progress, stage on the Sufi path
sifat-e-zaida	attributes of procreation, stage on the Sufi path

sifat ka saya	the shadows of God's attributes, stage on the Sufi path
silsila(h)	'chain' of succession of Sufi masters and their saintly disciples, spiritual genealogy
simurg	legendary bird
sirr	secret, stage on the Sufi path
subedar	JCO, junior-commissioned officer in the army
Suhawardiyya	major Sufi order whose founder first formulated the theory of divine light
suhbat	sitting in the company of a Sufi saint (in order to absorb his grace)
sukun	tranquillity, peace
sukr	intoxication
sultan-ul-azkar	the King of Prayers, a name of the ultimate *latifa*
suluk/silk	thread, path, series, journey, way on the Sufi path
suluk-e-sufiyya	Sufi journey
sunna(h)/sunnat	obligations and rules of customary behaviour based on the example of the Prophet's life as given in the Hadith
Sunni	major Islamic religious stream, the majority of Muslims worldwide, which accepts the authority of the Prophet's historical successors
surah	chapter of the Qur'an
tabar(r)uk	blessed, food that has been blessed, not to be thrown away
tabligh	proselytising, bringing the word of God to non-believers or lapsed Muslims
tahsil	an administrative district in a province
ta'ifa	Middle East term to describe the cult of a particular Sufi saint, organised fraction of an order
takbir	greatest, an epithet of God
takht-posh	bench, throne
talib	seeker; also student, *talib-i-ilm* religious student
talib-e-haq	seeker of God
tabliban	Seekers

tandoor	clay oven
tanzim	Organization
taqlid	blind conformity to established law or leader
taqrir	Sermon
taqat	power, hence *ruhani taqat*, spiritual power
taqwa	awe, piety, fear of God, which compels obedience to Him
tariqa(t)	Sufi way, Sufi order or brotherhood, Sufi cult
tasawwur	image, (usually of the saint) which a disciple invokes in his imagination
tasarruf	dramatic projection by a saint of his grace onto a disciple
tasawwur-e-shaikh	a disciple's visualisation of the *shaikh* during *zikr*
tasawwuf	Sufism, Sufi mystical theosophy
tauba	Repentance, ethical stage on the Sufi path
tauhid	a belief in the unity of God
tawaf	circumambulation, as around the *ka'aba* in Macca
tawajjuh	gaze, powerful concentration of a Sufi saint on his disciple
tawakkul	trust in God, absolute faith, a stage on the Sufi path
ta'wil	the 'carrying back' of the thing to its principle, of a symbol to what it symbolises
ta'wiz	protective amulet, usually given by a saint
tazkira	collection of biographical accounts based on both written and oral sources
tez	strong, powerful
thanda	cold, cool
Tijaniyya	name of a North and West African Sufi order
Tur	Mount Sinai
'ulama	learned scholars and religious leaders, especially in matters of Islamic jurisprudence, plural of *'alim*
'umma	the Muslim community or nation
ummed/umid	hope, ethical stage on the Sufi path
Umra	the performance of the Hajj rituals at times other than the prescribed Hajj ritual dates

uppar	above, beyond
'unsar arba'	the four elements
'urs	'marriage', religious festival held annually to commemorate the death/unification with God of a Muslim saint
'uruj	to ascend, ascent, ascension, rising exaltation, zenith, the first phase of the soul's journey
utarna	bring down, lower, depress, abase, cause to alight, remove, ferry
wahdat-ul-shuhud	'unity of witnessing', testimonial unity; the idea, associated with Ahmed Sirhindi, of a separation between God and the phenomenological world, according to which the mystic reaches God and 'witnesses' his being/attributes, rather than permanently 'merging' with Him
wahdat-ul-wujud	unity of being, existential unity; the metaphysical doctrine of phenomenological monism, associated with the theosophy of Ibn 'Arabi, according to which nothing exists outside God and all is of God's essence
wajd(an)	ecstasy, particularly that experienced in states of mystical intoxication, rapture, frenzy
wali	friend of God, Muslim saint, intimate of God
waqf	pious endowment for the upkeep of Muslim institutions
warta	whirlpool, in which the intoxicated Sufi gets caught
wasta	intermediaries
wazifa	incantation or liturgy of short prayers associated with a Sufi order and stage on the Sufi path and usually prescribed by a Muslim saint, which is repeated a prescribed number of times during the day
wazu	ritual ablution before prayer
wilayat ambiya	the dominion of the Prophets
wilayat-e-kubra	the great dominion, greater intimacy with God
wilayat-e-sughra	the small dominion, lesser intimacy with God

wilayat	the spiritual dominion of a saint, intimacy with God, friendship; also (secular) sovereignty over a region, guardianship, a foreign land
yahudi	Jew
yar	lover, friend
zabh/zibah	sacrifice, as at a saint's lodge
zahir/zahur	outer, visible, external knowledge or revelation
zakat	annual tithe or tax to charity prescribed by the Qur'an
zamin	land, the earth
zamindar	landowner, class of Muslim castes of a certain rank
Zamzam	name of the spring at Mecca
zat	essence, ontological being beyond attributes, the highest stage on the Sufi path; also species, caste, lineage,
zawiy(y)a	lodge in North Africa
zikr (Arab. *dhikr*)	'remembrance' of God's name through the repetition of a set liturgy of relatively short prayers, performed either alone or in company, and said to purify the heart
zikr khafi	the 'silent' *zikr* of the Naqshbandi order, spoken mentally without voice
zil	shadow, reflection
zimni	simultaneously, in tandem, by itself
zinda	living
zindabad	live forever
Zindapir	living saint, name of a Muslim saint
Zi(y)arat	visitation or pilgrimage to a saint's tomb; a saint's shrine
zohar	midday prayers
zuhd	renunciation, ethical stage on the Sufi path

AUTHOR INDEX

SUBJECT INDEX

Abbotabad 68–9, 71–3, 80, 130, 133, 163
Abdal mystical rank 47; *see* Sufi rank
Abdul Qadr Jilani 43, 97, 116, 142; *see also gyarvi sharif*, Iraq
abjection/subjction, in Sufism 136, 293
Abraham *see* Ibrahim
adab (etiquette) 204
aesthetics—20, 273
affliction(s) 225–31; as leading to initiation 231; by *jinns* 221; by God 221; intentional 221; accidental 222; congenital disability 235–7; depression 217, 225–31, 237–9; infertility 225–6, 229–30; left unexplained 224; marital problems 228; saint's insight into 225; in Britain 235–9; *see also* supplicants, *jinns, bala, kala jadu, nazar, ta'wiz,* healing
Afghanistan 62–3, 90; refugees from–93–4, 98
Ahl-i Hadith 55
Ahmad (Prophet's name) 197, 199
Ajmer Sharif shrine—3, 132
Alam Din 178–182
'alim 237, 253; *see 'ulama*
Anjuman (voluntary associations) 21
annihilation, of the soul 41–2, 169, 192–193, 201–205; *see also* soul, *fana*
anthropologist, as mythologiser 262; subject of amusement 124; recipient of gifts 94, 97, 120–121; Zindapir's picture revealed to 261; search for meaning 262; 'book' episode 292–3; research misunderstood 296; purse theft episode 298–9; gossip about 297, 300; harmonious relations 302; mentioned in *du'a*-301
anthropology, deconstructive discourses of-56, 302; fieldwork dilemmas 13–15, 136–137, 296, 300–2; postmodern 14, 291 *passim*, 302; dialogical 14, 292,

301–2; stress on local 289; cultural brokers 296–7; as science 296, 301
Arafat (Mt) *see* Hajj
army, centrality in Zindapir's cult 132–133, 154–155, 298; *see also* Pakistan, occupational guilds, disciples
asceticism, of saints 85, 254; of Zindapir 80, 85, 98–100, 147, 284; as validating myths about saint 290–1; of disciples 153; *see also* world renouncer
Azande oracles 224

Baba Qasim 66–8, 11, 160, 168, 220, 259, 271–2
Babaji Gyahrvinwala 157–158, 160–161
bai'at (vow of allegiance) 66–7, 69, 96, 133, 153, 225, 232, 250; *see also* initiation
Bakkarwal 47
bala (afflicting spirits) 221–2, 235; *see also* sorcery, *bhut*, affliction
Baluch regiment 68, 70, 72, 291
baqa (subsistence in God) 174, 194, 202–4, 205; *see also fana*, soul, Sufi path, station
Baqi Billah 4
baraka/barkat (blessing)—22, 102, 117, 170, 250–2; *see also* blessing, complex of blessing
Barelvi movement 10, 28–9, 242; development of 246; Sufi cults embedded in 248; *'ulama* 246–8; ambivalent authority of *'ulama* 256–7; strident tone 257; *see also 'ulama*
Bari 'Imam shrine 112, 233, 255
barzakh (limbo) 185; *see also* death
batin (esoteric) 199, 203, 205, 275; *see also* Sufi mysticism
Benares 27, 102
Bhutto, Benazir 96
bid'a(t) (unlawful innovation) 203

336